Palgrave Studies in American Economic History

Series Editor
Barbara Alexander, Department of Economics, Babson College, Babson Park, MA, USA

Since the social upheavals of the 1960s and 1970s and the free-market resurgence of the 1980s, American society has been enmeshed in a continuing process of profound change. Economic change has been oriented around the regulation of business, the information and telecommunication revolutions, and widening roles played by women and minority groups. Authors in the innovation area will assess how America arrived at its current position of technological dominance that is nonetheless under pressure from institutions that arguably are not well-configured for the future. Regulatory and legal historians will evaluate the reasons for concurrent regulatory breakdown and overreach in industries ranging from finance and health care to energy and land use. Finally, researchers working at the intersection of society and economic history will explore continuing struggles around issues of gender, ethnicity, and family structure, and the distribution of income, wealth, and political power. The series will address topics of interest to scholars, undergraduate and graduate students, and general readers drawn to the interplay of economics and cultural issues. Series contributors will be economics and business historians, or economists working with historians.

More information about this series at
http://www.palgrave.com/gp/series/14650

Lawrence H. Officer

A New Balance of Payments for the United States, 1790–1919

International Movement of Free and Enslaved People, Funds, Goods and Services

palgrave
macmillan

Lawrence H. Officer
Department of Economics
University of Illinois at Chicago
Chicago, IL, USA

ISSN 2662-3900 ISSN 2662-3919 (electronic)
Palgrave Studies in American Economic History
ISBN 978-3-030-66098-7 ISBN 978-3-030-66099-4 (eBook)
https://doi.org/10.1007/978-3-030-66099-4

This Palgrave Macmillan imprint is published by the registered company Springer Nature Switzerland AG
The registered company address is: Gewerbestrasse 11, 6330 Cham, Switzerland

To the Pioneers
Douglass C. North
Matthew Simon

"The estimation of the balance of payments by separate calculation of the payments and receipts on account of merchandise trade, freight, immigrants' funds, remittances, tourists, and other items, and the assumption that the net residual indicates capital flows are the basis of the study."

(North, 1960, pp. 573–574)

"Scientific procedure requires that each of the many components be properly identified and distinguished from other parts of the balance of payments."

(Simon, 1960, p. 630)

Preface

This book is largely a reaction to the four editions of *Historical Statistics of the United States*. Advances of scholarly research can be readily discerned in the changing content of *Historical Statistics*. Impressive in particular are the historical national income and product accounts, in particular GNP or GDP series, which expanded from the work of Simon Kuznets alone in the 1949 *Historical Statistics* to Kuznets, John Kendrick, and Robert E. Gallman in the 1960 and Bicentennial editions, and to these three authors *plus* Nathan S. Balke and Robert J. Gordon, Thomas Senior Berry, Louis D. Johnston and Samuel H. Williamson, Roger Ransom and Richard Sutch, Christine D. Romer, and Richard Sutch, in the Millennial Edition.

Yet this increasing progression of research has not been duplicated in the balance of payments. Indeed (except for formatting), the 1960, Bicentennial, and Millennial editions of *Historical Statistics* have *identical* balance-of-payments tables. This is not the fault of the *Historical Statistics* editors. Rather, it reflects the fact that scholars have not produced a new historical balance-of-payments table since 1960! This book corrects that omission.

I am grateful to Raymond L. Cohn, Drew Keeling, John Killick, Imran Rasul, and Thomas Weiss for granting me access to unpublished data of their research. I have benefitted from communication with John Killick, Matthias Morys, and Mira Wilkins. I learned much from the writings of Michael Edelstein and Douglas A. Irwin, with whom I worked on the

"International Trade and Exchange Rates" chapter of *Historical Statistics* Millennial Edition.

I acknowledge with immeasurable gratitude the input of Drew Keeling and Samuel H. Williamson. Drew exhibited immense intellectual generosity in sharing not only his data but also his knowledge—and in particular providing much insight into several components of the balance of payments. Sam provided constructive critique in the early years of the research and graciously co-authored a paper on the slave trade that constitutes an integral part of this book.

Sandra Diane Officer, my spouse, provided her customary understanding and advice regarding human behavior. Keith Olson, my mac consultant, helped beyond technical support.

Finally, I thank Barbara Alexander for a thorough reading of the manuscript. Her insightful comments improved the work substantially.

This book reflects a labor of love that spanned a decade of intense work. The intellectual excitement of developing the historical balance of payments surpasses that of all my previous research. Enhancing that excitement is my enormous admiration of the scholarly accomplishment of my predecessors, in particular: Paul B. Dickens, Raymond Goldsmith, Douglass C. North, and Matthew Simon: the foundation-authors of the *Historical Statistics* balance-of-payments table. Compared to my advantages, these scholars made do with limited data, with only a small number of complementary studies, and with no computer. Yet they brought the U.S. historical balance-of-payments table forward to a generally accepted standard. Of the aforementioned authors, the last two truly reached the level of intellectual greatness.

Therefore this book is dedicated to Nobel Laureate Douglass North and Matthew Simon. They are the most-accomplished pioneers in the U.S. historical balance of payments. Parts of this book update the work of North and Simon—and that of Dickens and Goldsmith. Other parts upgrade their work. But without North and Simon on which to build—there would be no book.

Glencoe, IL, USA Lawrence H. Officer
January 2021

Previous Books of Lawrence H. Officer

An Econometric Model of Canada Under the Fluctuating Exchange Rate, Harvard University Press, 1968.

The International Monetary System: Problems and Proposals (co-editor), Prentice-Hall, 1969.

Canadian Economic Problems and Policies (co-editor), McGraw-Hill, 1970.

Supply Relationships in the Canadian Economy: An Industry Comparison, International Business, and Economic Studies, Michigan State University, 1972.

Issues in Canadian Economics (co-editor), McGraw-Hill Ryerson, 1974.

The Monetary Approach to the Balance of Payments: A Survey (co-author), International Finance Section, Princeton University, 1978.

So You Have to Write an Economics Term Paper... (co-author), Michigan State University Press, 1981.

Purchasing Power Parity: Theory, Evidence and Relevance, JAI, 1982.

International Economics (editor), Kluwer-Nijhoff, 1987.

Between the Dollar-Sterling Gold Points: Exchange Rates, Parities, and Market Behavior, Cambridge University Press, 1996.

Monetary Standards and Exchange Rates (co-editor), Routledge, 1997.

Pricing Theory, Financing of International Organizations and Monetary History, Routledge, 2007.

Two Centuries of Compensation for U.S. Production Workers in Manufacturing, Palgrave Macmillan, 2009.

Everyday Economics: Honest Answers to Tough Questions, Palgrave Macmillan, 2009.

Translated into Chinese (traditional characters), Wealth, 2009.

Translated into Chinese (simplified characters), CITIC, 2010.

Translated into German, Börsenbuchverlag, 2013.

Contents

Part II Movement of People

Abbreviations

ARCC	*Annual Report of the Chamber of Commerce of the State of New York*
ARCENY	*Annual Report of the Commissioners of Emigration of the State of New York*
ARCGI	*Annual Report of the Commissioner-General of Immigration*
ARDM	*Annual Report of the Director of the Mint*
ARSTR	*Annual Report of the Secretary of the Treasury*
ASPCN	*American State Papers: Commerce and Navigation*
BGH	Bezanson, Anne, Robert D. Gray, and Miriam Hussey
BIPUS	*The Balance of International Payments of the United States*
BNA	British North America
BRV	Bandiera, Oriana, Imran Rasul, and Martina Viarengo
BWT	Bullock, Charles J., John H. Williams, and Rufus S. Tucker
CN	*Commerce and Navigation*
DGW	Dupont, Brandon, Alka Gandhi, and Thomas Weiss
DKW	Dupont, Brandon, Drew Keeling, and Thomas Weiss
FCN	*Foreign Commerce and Navigation*
Historical Statistics	*Historical Statistics of the United States*
MSCF	*Monthly Summary of Commerce and Finance*
NYAR	*New York Annual Register*
NYSR	*New York State Register*
OBE	Office of Business Economics
QRCBS	*Quarterly Reports of the Chief of the Bureau of Statistics*
SAUS	*Statistical Abstract of the United States*
TT	Terms of Trade

List of Figures

Chapter 6

Chapter 7

Chapter 9

Chapter 10

Chapter 12

Chapter 13

Chapter 14

Chapter 15

Chapter 16

Chapter 17

Chapter 18

Chapter 19

Chapter 20

List of Tables

Chapter 15

Chapter 16

Chapter 18

Chapter 19

Chapter 20

PART I

Why a New Balance of Payments

CHAPTER 1

Existing Historical Balance of Payments: A Survey

1 Primer on Balance of Payments

A country's balance-of-payments table is a recording of its international economic transactions denominated in a given currency over a specified time period. In this study the country is the United States, the currency is the U.S. dollar, and the time period annual. The transactions, also called "balance-of-payments items," can be arranged in an $n \times 2$ array. The n rows identify the items by type; presumably the greater the disaggregation of international flows, the higher is n. The two columns divide the amount of a given item into credits *versus* debits (items provided *versus* items received, earnings *versus* disbursements, receipts *versus* payments, inpayments *versus* outpayments). The terms "credits" and "debits" are preferred in generality, because of their neutrality and emanation from standard double-entry bookkeeping: decrease in assets or increase in liabilities is credited, increase in assets or decrease in liabilities debited. However, the alternative dichotomies have descriptive superiority for particular items. A simple balance-of-payments table is as follows.

L. H. Officer, *A New Balance of Payments for the United States, 1790–1919*, Palgrave Studies in American Economic History,
https://doi.org/10.1007/978-3-030-66099-4_1

Item	*Credits*	*Debits*
Goods	Exports	Imports
Services	Provided	Received
Income	Receipts	Payments
Unilateral Transfers	Received	Paid
Capital	Inflow	Outflow
Statistical Discrepancy	Excess of recorded debits over recorded credits	Excess of recorded credits over recorded debits

It is often stated that "the balance of payments always balances," that is, total credits equal total debits (so that only one of the credits and debits entries in Statistical Discrepancy would be applicable). The reason is that, in theory, the table is kept according to the principles of double-entry bookkeeping. Thus, in ideal record-keeping: every time a credit entry is made, simultaneously a counterpart entry is made (either an equal-amount debit entry or an equal-magnitude but opposite-sign credit entry). In practice, original and counterpart entries typically are recorded independently. So, while total credits and total debits are logically equal, empirically they diverge—and a "statistical discrepancy" or "residual entry" equalizes the totals. The old terminology "errors and omissions" (or, better, "net errors and omissions") has the property of full disclosure.

2 Official Balance-of-Payments Tables: 1919–1939

The official U.S. balance of payments began in 1923 with an annual volume *The Balance of International Payments of the United States* [BIPUS]. The initial issue presented a table for the year 1922, taken back annually to 1919 via work of John H. Williams of Harvard University.[1] Annual publications continued until 1940, for the year 1939. The 1924 document also extended the table back to 1919, thus showing the balance of payments for 1919–1923.[2] Subsequent issues episodically carried the latest table annually back to 1919, the last to do so being the 1938 publication, for 1919–1937.[3] It is a fair statement that coverage improved over time, albeit in jumps.[4] Hal B. Lary (1943, Table 1, facing p. 216) is the first author to exhibit a consistent table for the entire 1919–1939 period. His table is reproduced, with rearrangement of items, in a variety of publications.[5]

Thus there remained scope for non-official tables covering years prior to 1919—and there have been a surprisingly large number of these, published over a 189-year period (1818–2006). Given the number—I found 30 studies (of 25 authors, Tables 1 and 2)—it is surprising that there has been no systematic compilation or review of these tables. In fact, there have been only two surveys, and they are of a partial nature. Max J. Wasserman and Ray M. Ware (1965, pp. 50–59, 87–101) of University of Kentucky and Transylvania College, outline nine of the tables; they provide discussion more than appraisal. In contrast, Matthew Simon (1960, pp. 629–630, 708, 710), Professor at Pace College, has a critical eye, but examines only three predecessor tables.

3 Non-Official Balance-of-Payments Tables: 1790–1918

3.1 Methodology

Table 1 lists "contemporary" balance-of-payments tables, Table 2 "historical" tables. The difference is that "contemporary" has only one year (or one multiple-year time period) to which the table pertains, and the year (or latest year of the period) is close to the time of writing. There is one exception: Ezra C. Seaman (1846, 1857), who has 11 periods in two studies. The nature of his procedure is that the earlier periods are a leading-up to his current-year table.

Regarding Tables 1 and 2, a balance-of-payments "table" need not be tabular; it can be partially or entirely text. To be included in the tables, there must be an entry for at least one item beyond "Merchandise, Gold, Silver, [Ships]." "Undervaluation" or "overvaluation" of exports or imports refers to the author's adjustment to the official merchandise series. "Interest" incorporates dividends. "Capital" is long-term, except where otherwise stated. The tables distinguish between directly estimated items and the residual, the latter's nature of which is as stated or implied by the original author. Ideally, a table should explicitly show either the residual figure or total credits and total debits (the residual computable as the difference). The tables exclude "counterbalancing items," meaning flows that, rather than estimated, are assumed to offset one another.

Table 1 Contemporary balance-of-payments tables

Author	*Directly estimated items*[a]						*Residual*
	Time Span, Periods	*Merchandise, Gold, Silver*	*Services*	*Income*	*Unilateral transfers*	*Capital*	
Seybert (1818, pp. 281–283)	about 1818, one	merchandise	Freight[b]				Repayment of debt
Gallatin (1832, p. 21)	1821–1830, one	All, undervaluation of imports	Freight[b]				Repayment of debt[c]
Seaman (1846, pp. 266–272)	1820–1845, eight	All	Freight[b,d]	Interest[e]	Purchase of Florida	Debt default	Change in debt
Seaman (1857, p. 664)	1847–1857, three	All, undervaluation of imports, overvaluation of exports	Freight[b]	Interest[e]			Change in debt
Wells (1869, pp. 29–31)	1869	All	Freight[f], travel[f]	Interest[e]			Increase in debt
Young (1874, pp. 351–352)	1863–1873, one	All, undervaluation of imports	Freight[g]	Interest[e]			Increase in debt
Warner (1879, pp. 526–527)	1876–1878, one	All		Interest[e]		Debt default	Decrease in foreign debt
Heidelbach (1895a, pp. 648–649)	1894	All	Freight[e], travel[e]	Interest[e], profits[e]			Increase in debt
Commercial Year Book (1896, pp. 225–229)	1887–1893, one	All, undervaluation of imports	Freight[g], port costs[b,h], travel[e], fare[e]	Interest[e]	Immigrant funds		Increase in foreign debt

Author	*Directly estimated items*[a]						*Residual*
	Time Span, Periods	*Merchandise, Gold, Silver*	*Services*	*Income*	*Unilateral transfers*	*Capital*	
Bacon (1900, pp. 283–284)	1898–1900, one	All	Travel[e]	Interest[e]	Emigrant funds		Decrease in foreign debt
Bacon (1902, p. 7)	1899–1901, one	All	Travel[c,i], military	Interest[f]	Gifts[c]	Investment abroad[j], repurchase of securities	Net decrease in foreign debt
Paish (1910, pp. 172–192, 196–197)	1909	All	Freight[f], travel[f]	Interest[f]	Immigrant remittances		Increase in foreign debt

[a]Excludes offsetting items
[b]Receipts
[c]Also, unrecorded specie imports
[d]Includes profits on exports
[e]Payments
[f]Net
[g]Receipts and payments separately listed
[h]Passenger steamships separately listed
[i]Includes emigrant funds
[j]Direct and portfolio separately considered

Table 2 Historical balance-of-payments tables

Author	*Directly estimated items*[a]						*Residual*
	Time Span, Periods	*Merchandise, Gold, Silver, Ships*	*Services*	*Income*	*Unilateral transfers*	*Capital*	
Sterns (1898, p. 200)	1790–1820, one	All	Freight[b], port costs[c]	Interest[c]	Government[c]	Debt default	Decrease in foreign debt
Sterns (1899, pp. 52–54)	1821–1830, one	All, undervaluation of imports	Freight[d], carrying trade				Approximate balance
Bullock (1901)	1790–1901, eight	Ships excluded	Freight[c], travel[c], military[c]	Interest[c]		Foreign inflow	Balance with inclusion of other items
Laughlin (1918, p. 341)	1914–1917, one	Ships excluded	Freight[c,e]	Interest[f]	Immigrant remittances, relief	Securities returned, private loans, govt loans	Portfolio investment abroad
Bullock, Williams, Tucker (1919a)	1790–1914, six	All, undervaluation of imports	Freight[d], carrying trade, port costs[f], travel[c], insurance[c,g]	Interest[d]	Immigrant funds, immigrant remittances, govt[c,h]	Portfolio investment[i]	Errors and omissions

Author	*Directly estimated items*[a]						*Residual*
	Time Span, Periods	*Merchandise, Gold, Silver, Ships*	*Services*	*Income*	*Unilateral transfers*	*Capital*	
Bullock, Williams, Tucker (1919b, pp. 248–252)	1914–1918, one	Ships excluded	Freight[d], charter[c], insurance[c]	Interest[d]	Immigrant remittances	Securities returned, private loans, govt loans	Foreign-bank deposits in United States, unused credit lines, other items
Williams (1921, p. 201)	1914–1918, one	Ships excluded	Freight[d], charter[c]	Interest[j]	Immigrant remittances, Red Cross remittances	Securities returned, private loans, paper-currency outflow, govt capital	Foreign deposits in U.S. banks
Graham (1922, p. 231)	1860–1878, annual	All	Freight[d]	Interest[f]		Repayment of loans, loans floated	Omitted items
Taussig (1928, p. 296)	1869, 1894, 1901, 1909, 1912	Ships excluded	Freight[c], travel[c]	Interest[d]	Immigrant remittances	New loans (borrowing)	Errors in measurement
Dickens (1933, pp. 91, 131, 146, 271–285)	1897–1914, annual	Ships excluded	Freight[d], port costs[f], travel[d,k]	Interest[d]	Immigrant funds, emigrant funds,[k] immigrant remittances	Foreign investment in United States[l], investment abroad[l]	Short-term capital
Taylor (1951, pp. 201–205, 453–454)	1815–1860, four	All	Freight[d], travel[c]	Interest[c]	Immigrant funds,immigrant remittances	New loans, debt default	Errors in measurement

(continued)

Table 2 (continued)

Author	*Directly estimated items*[a]						*Residual*
	Time Span, Periods	*Merchandise, Gold, Silver, Ships*	*Services*	*Income*	*Unilateral transfers*	*Capital*	
Smith (1953, pp. 84–88)	1821–1841, annual	All, undervaluation of imports	Freight,[d] carrying trade, immigrant fares		Immigrant funds, govt[d,h]		Errors in measurement
Goldsmith (1955, pp. 1078–1085)	1897–1918, annual	Ships excluded, monetary gold separately listed	Freight and shipping[f], travel[f]	Interest[f]	Immigrant funds and remittances[f]	Foreign investment in United States[m], investment abroad,[l] govt loans, foreign short-term capital[n]	Foreign short-term capital (1914–1918 only)
North (1960, pp. 587–601)	1790–1819, annual	All	Freight[b], carrying trade, port costs[c], marine insurance[f,o]	Interest[f]	Government[c]	Debt default	Change in net liabilities to foreigners
North (1960, pp. 601–622)	1820–1860, annual	All, undervaluation of imports	Freight[d], carrying trade, port costs[d], travel[d,p], military	Interest[f]	Government[c], immigrant funds[p], immigrant remittances	Debt default	Change in net liabilities to foreigners
Simon (1960)	1861–1900, annual	All, undervaluation of exports (including gold), undervaluation of imports	Freight[d], carrying trade, port costs[d,q], marine insurance[d], travel[d,r], bankers' commissions	Interest[f]	Immigrant funds, emigrant funds, immigrant remittances[s]		Change in net liabilities to foreigners
Historical Statistics (1960, pp. 557–565; 1975, pp. 858–868)	1790–1900, annual	All, monetary gold separately listed	Transportation[d], travel[d,p,t], marine insurance[d,u], military	Interest[f]	Private[f], government[f]		Change in net liabilities to foreigners

Author	*Directly estimated items*[a]						*Residual*
	Time Span, Periods	*Merchandise, Gold, Silver, Ships*	*Services*	*Income*	*Unilateral transfers*	*Capital*	
Historical Statistics (1960, pp. 557–565; 1975, pp. 858–868)	1900–1918, annual	Ships excluded, monetary gold separately listed	Transportation[d], travel[d,p,t], military	Interest[d]	Private,[f] government[f]	Foreign investment in United States[v], investment abroad[w], govt loans	Errors and omissions

[a]Excludes offsetting items
[b]Receipts
[c]Payments
[d]Receipts and payments separately computed
[e]Includes insurance
[f]Net
[g]Includes commissions and miscellaneous
[h]Includes military
[i]Borrowing and lending separately listed
[j]Private receipts, government receipts, and payments separately listed
[k]Canada and overseas separately listed
[l]Direct investment and portfolio investment (with components) separately listed
[m]Bonds, preferred stock, and common stock separately listed
[n]Paper currency, deposits in Federal Reserve Banks, foreign-bank deposits in commercial banks, and "other" separately listed
[o]Includes brokers' commissions
[p]Includes fare receipts
[q]Passenger receipts separately listed
[r]Receipts: oceanic, transmigration to Canada and West Indies, and overland separately listed. Payments: oceanic (includes fare) and overland separately listed
[s]Via financial intermediaries and via prepaid tickets separately listed
[t]Includes fare payments
[u]Includes commissions
[v]Long-term and short-term separately listed
[w]Direct investment and portfolio investment separately listed

3.2 *Contemporary Tables*

Table 1 shows 12 studies, with two authors having double documents. There are three commonalities for the contemporary tables: the year-definition is fiscal rather than calendar, the residual is the change in net liabilities to foreigners, and there is no reference to the tables of predecessors. Also notable are the almost uniform inclusion of freight and interest, the incorporation of travel in postbellum work, the relative neglect of other services and unilateral transfers, and the only-sometime direct estimation of capital.

Walter B. Smith (1953, p. 281, note 4), of Claremont Men's College, references contemporary comments in *Niles' Register* over 1819–1823 that pointed out the need for merchandise and specie data to be supplemented with information on services and unilateral transfers. Not mentioned by Smith, Adam Seybert (1818), politician and scholar, had already begun that process with an estimate of U.S. freight income. Wasserman and Ware (1965, p. 51) observe that "Seybert saw the relationship between various service transactions, the balance of trade and foreign indebtedness." For Seybert, the residual of merchandise (recorded), freight (estimated), "commissions and charges" earned (not known), and specie inflow (not known) constitutes repayment of British-owned debt.

Albert Gallatin's (1832) study was written as a private citizen, having done with his public life as a politician, Secretary of the Treasury, and diplomat. Freight receipts are based on "the average rates according to the nature of the merchandise, and to the ports of destination" (Gallatin 1832, p. 21), and are stipulated for re-exports as well as domestic exports. He acknowledges existence of "items which cannot be ascertained" on both export side and import side, specifically mentioning freight on the carrying trade.

Seaman (1846), lawyer and writer, presents a running total of the stock of foreign debt, but a balance-of-payments table changing over time is readily discerned. Freight receipts include merchandise profits, the rate changed from 15 to 12½% in 1839. Seaman (1857) accounts for under-valuation of dutiable imports due to underinvoicing, whereas Gallatin's undervaluation of such imports is due to official undervaluation of the British pound. Wasserman and Ware (1965, pp. 52–54) praise Seaman for his understanding of the balance of credit and debit items in the table and for adjusting specie flow for domestic production and consumption (anticipating official balance-of-payments practice three-fourths of a century in the future), his only flaw being not integrating these two contributions.[6]

David A. Wells (1869) was an engineer and author; and, as Special Commissioner of the Revenue appointed by President Andrew Johnson, he provides the first official document containing a balance-of-payments table. He assumes smuggling and import undervaluation balance export undervaluation. He carefully determines net freight, and also estimates the amount of forgone trade credits from "almost complete annihilation of the large carrying trade" and "non-participation in the emigrant and other passenger-carrying trade" (Wells 1869, pp. 30–31). The residual figure is stated explicitly—the first contemporary table to do so. I agree with Wasserman and Ware (1965, p. 58) that "the methodology used by Wells in estimating the accounts appearing in his balance of payments was advanced for his time."

Another official report is Edward Young (1874), Chief of Bureau of Statistics. There is discussion and estimation of import undervaluation and smuggling. Again the residual figure is shown. Adoniram J. Warner (1879), Ohio Congressman, references Wells and Young. He retrogresses in not taking account of services, but does show the residual figure. Alfred S. Heidelbach (1895a), a banker, has clear reasoning that the deficit on services and income dominates the merchandise (including silver) surplus. His work is criticized by William B. Dana (1895a, b), and as a consequence Heidelbach (1895b) modifies his figures—but insufficiently for Dana.[7]

Commercial Year Book (1896), unfortunately of unknown authorship, a reprint of an article published in the previous year, is judged by Simon (1960, p. 630) as "probably the best balance of payment estimates by a contemporary." The document is impressive for the breadth of the services account and for estimates that are data-based. Also, the first estimate of a private unilateral transfer is provided. Immigrant remittances and non-first-cabin-passenger unrecorded travel expenditures (omitted debits) are assumed offset by foreign tourist receipts and funds brought in by unclassified immigrants (omitted credits). Totals of credits and debits are shown along with the residual ("debtor balance"). The study is nicely summarized in Wasserman and Ware (1965, pp. 88–90).

Nathaniel T. Bacon (1900, 1902)—entrepreneur-industrialist, philanthropist, and gentleman-scholar (per Richard Vangermeersch 2013,

p. 5)—assumes that immigrant remittances (debit) are offset by immigrant funds (credit), and that underestimated freight of imports to port (debit) is compensated by unmeasured port-cost and freight revenue (credit). In effect, the return on foreign investments in the United States is selected to cover any statistical discrepancy. The 1902 study provides the first estimate of military expenditures abroad. In general, Bacon provides an impressive table, notable for the attention given to capital flow in both directions, and the residual is shown.

George Paish (1910), an economist and prolific writer, who was later knighted, produced a comprehensive balance-of-payments investigation for the National Monetary Commission. The study is both theoretical and empirical, the latter constituting arguably the most famous contemporary work on the U.S. balance of payments. Paish assumes that immigrant funds (credit) equal the sum of emigrant funds and noncabin-passenger travel expenditures (debit). Freight includes consideration of port charges. Insurance is omitted, because the balance is considered close to zero. The residual figure is shown. Wasserman and Ware (1965, pp. 92–95) summarize both parts of the study.

3.3 *Historical Tables*

3.3.1 *Private Authors*

One might think that every historical study of the balance of payments, listed in Table 2, would provide a continuous annual table for successive years, but the seven studies preceding Frank D. Graham (1922) do not do so. Further, two of the three studies that follow Graham also violate this logical characteristic. Indeed, it was not until 11 historical tables had been published and over a half-century had passed from the first historical table that continuous annual tables became the uniform norm. Still, most of the private historical studies are generally superior to the contemporary works—in part because the former are typically authored by academic economists, in part because most of the studies occurred later than contemporary tables.[8]

The University of Chicago's Worthy P. Sterns (1898) developed the first historical table, for the three decades 1790–1820. The work is distinguished with scholarly care regarding concepts and data, and with systematic presentation. Stern discusses the f.o.b. versus c.i.f. valuation of official imports. He provides the first estimates of specie flow and sale of ships for the early period, and uses the "tonnage method" of estimating freight earnings. He assumes that U.S. travel payments are "relatively small," and that several flow pairs are offsetting: (1) Apart from payments to Barbary pirates and for Louisiana, government unilateral receipts and payments cancel out. (2) Port-cost receipts (credit) counterbalance undervaluation of imports (debit). (3) Net travel (presumably including fares, though unmentioned) *plus* immigrant funds (credits) equal "debits omitted." He shows total credits, total debits, and the balance (residual).

The next year, Sterns (1899) provided a table for the subsequent decade. Allowance for undervaluation of the British pound increases imports. Again, offsetting flows are assumed:

(1) Import underinvoicing (debit) counterbalances U.S. freight income on imports counted as payment (debit). (2) Travel expenditures abroad (debit) counterbalance immigrant funds (credit). Total credits, total debits, and the balance are shown.

Charles J. Bullock (1901), Professor of Economics at Williams College, provides the first study to cover over a full century. His work is analytical rather than data-oriented. The University of Chicago's J. Laurence Laughlin (1918) divides long-term capital into three components and shows total credits and total debits, with his figures forcing the residual to be zero. Overestimate of immigrant remittances (should be debit) are compensated by underestimate of relief funds (again should be debit). Incredibly, Laughlin places these items in the credit rather than debit column, resulting in a phony zero-balance.

For 1790–1914, Charles J. Bullock, John H. Williams, and Rufus S. Tucker [BWT] (1919a) was the "state of the art" prior to the works of Douglass C. North, Matthew Simon, and Paul B. Dickens.[9] Simon (1960, pp. 630, 707–710) views this study as his principal predecessor and critiques its shortcomings without mercy. Some counterpoising praise is appropriate. Together with BWT (1919b), almost 130 years are covered, and the breadth of items in the balance of payments is impressive. There is care in estimation and sharpness in analysis. Intellectual honesty is present, with acknowledgment of the "decidedly conjectural character" of the estimates of many items (BWT 1919a, p. 215) and the drawing on, or references to, earlier works (Sterns, Wells, *Commercial Year Book*, Bacon, Paish). Total credits and total debits are shown, and residual consisting of errors and omissions is implied. The later (1919b) table includes data on three components of long-term capital, the same breakdown as Laughlin. The residual (shown, along with total credits and total debits) is given a capital-account interpretation. Wasserman and Ware praise the 1919b study for its originality.[10] They also observe that this work "led directly" to the official balance-of-payments. The 1919b table was revised in Williams (1921), who shows total credits, total debits, and the residual ("net unfunded balance").[11]

Graham (1922), of Princeton University, is another predecessor table heavily criticized by Simon (1960, pp. 629–630). On the other side, Graham is the first author to present an annual table, albeit it is confined to the greenback period. He states that figures are in gold value, to which currency statistics are converted, and his denomination is followed by Simon. Graham computes total credits and total debits. Frank W. Taussig (1928), of Harvard University, compiles two sets of tables based on five earlier studies, including Wells, Paish, and *Commercial Year Book*. For the first set, total credits and total debits are shown.

Paul B. Dickens (1933) presents his Ph.D. dissertation from George Washington University.[12] The work is notable for the first post-greenback-period balance-of-payments presentation in calendar rather than fiscal years. His carefully developed series for credits and debits on long-term capital remain the standard and are unlikely ever to be superseded. Rates of return on investment are his own figures; but, for other current-account items, he makes use of predecessors, including Paish and BWT. The residual is shown and described as "balance uncalculated and unaccounted for" (Dickens 1933, p. 146). Movement of short-term capital is suggested as the principal explanation.

George Rogers Taylor (1951), of Amherst College, utilizes Stern and BWT for his table. He makes no adjustment for undervaluation of imports, though states that ten percent undervaluation is "a not impossible assumption" (p. 205). He sees foreign loans as small relative to merchandise exports in enabling growth in merchandise imports. For 1821–1837, immigrant funds (credit) are assumed to balance travel expenditures abroad (debit). Total credits and total debits are shown, as also done by Smith (1953). Smith is the third historical study to have an annual table. He pays unusual (and praiseworthy) attention to government unilateral transfers. He incorporates undervaluation of the pound in valuation of imports, and in general his sources are clearly stated.

Raymond W. Goldsmith (1955), Professor at New York University, presents a table based heavily on Dickens, also utilizing BWT (1919b) and Williams (1921). Current-account items are in net form. Government unilateral transfers are ignored. Goldsmith does not show the residual but uses it to estimate foreign short-term capital 1914–1918 (and beyond).

Nobel Laureate Douglass C. North (1960), University of Washington, boasts the first annual balance-of-payments table of substantial length—70 continuous years. Why does North divide his study into 1790–1819 and 1820–1860 periods? First, official data are inferior in 1790–1819 compared to the later period. Second, different techniques are used to estimate shipping earnings in the two periods, for reason both of substance (importance of carrying trade) and data availability. Third, the early period omits items that have importance only in the later periods: freight payments, private unilateral transfers, and tourist expenditures. For 1790–1819, there is an excellent discussion and consequent correction of official trade data, including delineation of f.o.b. versus c.i.f. valuation of imports. The 1820–1860 period is notable for the first U.S. freight-rate series for exports and imports, and the development of series for immigrant funds and remittances. The residual ("net balance") is shown. Reference is made to predecessors Sterns and Taylor.

Assumed offsetting flows: For 1790–1819: Port costs of foreign ships in U.S. ports (omitted credit) equal overvaluation of shipping earnings (overestimated credit). Excessive debt default 1816–1819 (overestimated credit) equals omission of immigrant funds (omitted credit) *plus* overpricing of manufactured imports from England (overestimated debit). For 1820–1832: The 10 and 20% additions to ad-valorem imports (overestimated debit) equal undervaluation of ad-valorem imports (underestimated debit) *plus* deviation of exchange rate from official valuation of British pound (underestimated debit).

Unquestionably, Simon (1960) set *the* standard for the historical balance-of-payments table. For any item that Simon covers, I either have to adopt Simon's technique or improve on it. His opposition to the technique of "offsetting flows" is telling: "This does not permit…assuming that one or more items on the credit side can exactly offset specific items on the debit side for one or for forty years" (Simon 1960, p. 630). The only counterbalancing assumed is the impact of higher fares for first-class cabin equaling the impact of lower rates for lower class cabins. For the greenback period, Simon follows Graham in stipulating uniform gold denomination and converting currency to gold dollars.

Simon (1960, pp. 630–631) argues for a disaggregate balance of payments: "the largest possible number of distinct items in the balance of payments on current account." Inconsistently, and following North, the capital account is treated in the opposite matter, with the residual representing the entire (net) flow of capital—and the residual is shown. Again in the North tradition, he adjusts official merchandise series, including estimating overland exports for years prior to official counting. There is innovative work on marine insurance and tourist expenditures, creative generation of oceanic passenger series, and detailed development of migrant funds and immigrant remittances.

3.3.2 Historical Statistics

There are four editions of *Historical Statistics of the United States* [*Historical Statistics*] (1949, 1960, 1975, 2006). Only 1960 (repeated in 1975) is relevant for the balance-of-payments table 1790–1918.[13] Under the auspices of the Office of Business Economics (OBE—predecessor of the Bureau of Economic Analysis), these volumes assemble—"integrate" is too strong a word—predecessor historical series along with other information, to construct an annual table for the full 1790–1918 period (and beyond). Actually, two tables are presented: for 1790–1900, a fiscal-year table emanating from North and Simon; for 1900–1918, a calendar-year table based on Dickens and Goldsmith. The OBE table makes only a few substantive additions to these authors: The gold entry for 1874–1900 is the change in the monetary gold stock (as it is for Goldsmith, beginning 1897), different from the strict trade criterion of North and Simon. Government unilateral transfers and capital are extended to incorporate entries for the Panama Canal and the Virgin Islands.

The 1790–1900 table combines entries; so, for our purpose, it is generally preferable to consult North and Simon directly. With the exception of monetary gold from 1874; ship sales, gold, and silver are included in merchandise. All "transportation" items are combined into aggregate credits or debits, similarly "travel" and "other transactions." Private unilateral transfers constitute one net entry. The 1900–1918 table improves on Goldsmith in presenting gross, rather than net, entries for the current account.

In essence, the OBE table consists of four periods with sources as follows: North for 1790–1819, North again for 1820–1860, Simon for 1861–1900, Dickens-Goldsmith for 1900–1918. The four sources generally differ in the methodology of generating any given item—resulting in inconsistent treatment over time. Yet OBE makes no attempt to link or smooth the divergent periods, resulting in abrupt breaks in the switching years (1820, 1861, 1900). And the assumed zero flows and offsetting items in the sources are retained. The abrupt change in the nature of the residual in 1900 is especially galling.

4 State of the Art

The discontinuities, supposed zero flows, and assumed offsetting items of the 1960 OBE table are sufficient reason to develop a new balance-of-payments table without these deficiencies. Yet, surprisingly, there is no table subsequent to OBE that has been published, not in *Historical Statistics* (2006) or elsewhere. This stagnant situation is sharply different from the experience with gross product (GNP or GDP). *Historical Statistics* (1960, pp. 132–143 various) contains only three gross-product series antedating the 1929 beginning of the official national accounts—two John W. Kendrick and one Simon Kuznets series. And the data prior to 1919 are for multiple-year periods rather than annual.[14] In contrast, *Historical Statistics* (2006, pp. 3–23 to 3–28, 3–59 to 3–69) boasts 12 gross-product series antedating 1929 (and 1919)—and all are uniformly annual.[15] The giant improvement in historical gross-product since 1960 suggests emulation for the balance of payments!

5 Plan of the Book

Part I of this book justifies construction of a new balance-of-payments table, and the (current) Chapter 1 surveys existing tables from that standpoint. Chapter 2 previews how this book overcomes the limitations of OBE and its North-Simon-Goldsmith foundation. Specific features are highlighted, including measurement decisions, improvement of OBE series, development of new series, and derived implications for the structure of the U.S. economy and for the importance of individual sectors that loom large at various times: slave trade, shipping, manufacturing, and travel.

Something should be stated immediately regarding the term "slave trade," as well as the associated words "slave" and "slavery." Language changes along with cultural norms. There has been a shift in wording, with the term "enslaved persons" often replacing "slaves," in recognition of the full humanity of the people exploited by slavery in general and by the slave trade in particular. Though the book largely retains the old usage, this is by reason of the book having its foundation in the existing literature and data sources, and a function of the book of facilitating future research on the topic. While data continuity is essential for such research and while this study deals only with aggregates, I acknowledge with humility that there were individual people—White and Black—behind the numbers. Whether they were victims, perpetrators, passive participants, or abolitionists, these people should be remembered.

The ordering of the balance of payments in this book is different from predecessors. In particular, OBE has the sequence: merchandise (including ship sales), principal services (transportation, travel—separate entries), income, other services (insurance, commissions, military expenditures—all one entry), unilateral transfers, capital, monetary gold. The time series of components of the new table is shown in three parts of the book. Part III, "Movement of Goods," consists of merchandise, gold, silver, ships, and slaves. Part IV, "Movement of Funds," is comprised of unilateral transfers, capital, and income. Part V, "Provision of Services," presents transportation, travel, fares, financial items, military expenditures, and the slave trade.

Prior to the three-parts balance-of-payments table, there is Part II, "Movement of People." The series in this part are inputs into items in Parts III, IV, V. I deliberately provide the "people-movement" series entirely in advance rather than piecemeal on an ad hoc basis–the practice of previous authors. The reason is threefold. First, each of the chapters in Part II generates series that are connected to each other, either statistically or conceptually. Second, the people-movement series are constructed via lengthy procedures, which would detract from the flow of presentation of the balance-of-payments series if addressed in Parts III, IV, V. Third, international movement of people could give rise to a "balance of people," analogous to the balance of payments but of independent interest. I do not provide this "balance," but the data series to do so are presented in an integrated manner in Part II.

Part VI puts time series of the new balance-of-payments table to use in several ways: aggregates and balances within the table, structure of the U.S. economy, and specific sectors of the economy (slave trade, shipping, manufacturing, travel). Finally, Part VII provides concluding comments.

Notes

1. *BIPUS in 1922*, pp. 20–21.
2. *BIPUS in 1923*, p. 17.
3. *BIPUS in 1937*, pp. 112–113.

4. An excellent summary of BIPUS publications is Wasserman and Ware (1965, pp. 104–110, 116–128).
5. *International Transactions of the United States During the War, 1940–45*, pp. 221–222; *The Balance of Payments of the United States, 1919–1953*, pp. 4–5; *Balance of Payments Statistical Supplement* (1958, pp. 10–12), Goldsmith (1955, pp. 1079—1080, 1084–1085), *Historical Statistics* (1949, pp. 242–243; 1960, pp. 562, 564; 1975, pp. 864, 867; 2006, pp. 5-455, 459-460).
6. On the latter contribution, see Chapter 8, Sect. 3.1.
7. See also the discussion in Wasserman and Ware (1965, pp. 85–88).
8. Not included in Table 2 are the private tables for 1919: Frank A. Vanderlip and John H. Williams (1920), the former a banker who played a role in developing the Federal Reserve Act, and Williams alone (1921). These are impressive works, but are superseded by the official figures, which begin for the year 1919.
9. Williams was a distinguished Harvard Professor. Tucker was also at Harvard University at the time. He later became an economist at General Motors, a position he held for over a quarter-century.
10. "Their greatest contribution, perhaps, was in the development of sources of data and techniques of estimating international transactions for which little information was available." (Wasserman and Ware 1965, p. 98).
11. The BWT and Williams tables are reprinted, in part, in *Historical Statistics* (1949, p. 242), *Balance of Payments Statistical Supplement* (1958, p. 10), and *The Balance of Payments of the United States 1919–1953* (1954, p. 4).
12. Dickens became an official in the Treasury Department.
13. The 1949 volume simply reprints BWT 1850–1918. *Historical Statistics* (2006) condenses the 1960 table and rearranges items to fit the then-current official table. The 1975 volume differs from 1960 only in the description "transactions in U.S. official reserve assets" implicitly projected prior to 1947, in place of the (correct) 1960 designation "changes in monetary gold stock."
14. The Kuznets series is for five-year periods even after 1919. There is also the value-added series of Robert E. Gallman; but it is only for Census years and its scope is narrower than GNP or GDP.
15. Three of the series extend the Kendrick and Kuznets series to annual observations. Two others—the "standard series" and "Millennial Edition" series—are compilations of previous work, comparable to the OBE balance-of-payments table in this respect.

References

Bacon, Nathaniel T. 1900. American International Indebtedness. *Yale Review* 9 (November): 265–285.

———. 1902. Why the United States Is Not Yet a Creditor Nation. *New York Times*, January 5, p. 7.

Bullock, Charles J. 1901. The Theory of the Balance of Trade. *North American Review* 173 (July): 111–133.

———, John H. Williams, and Rufus S. Tucker [BWT]. 1919a. The History of Our Foreign Trade Balance from 1789 to 1914. *Review of Economics and Statistics* 1 (July): 215–233.

———, John H. Williams, and Rufus S. Tucker [BWT]. 1919b. The History of Our Foreign Trade Balance During the Great War. *Review of Economics and Statistics* 1 (July): 234–254.

Commercial Year Book. 1896. Our International Balance Sheet, 225–231.

Dana, William B. 1895a. Why Do We Export Gold? *Commercial and Financial Chronicle* 60 (March 30): 542–544.

———. 1895b.Why Do We Export Gold? *Commercial and Financial Chronicle* 60 (April 13): 630–633.

Dickens, Paul B. 1933. The Transition Period in American International Financing: 1897 to 1914. Ph.D., diss., George Washington University.

Gallatin, Albert. 1832. *Memorial of the Committee of the Free Trade Convention*. 22nd Cong., 1st sess.

Goldsmith, Raymond W. 1955. *A Study of Saving in the United States*, vol. 1. Princeton: Princeton University Press.

Graham, Frank D. 1922. International Trade Under Depreciated Paper: The United States, 1862–79. *Quarterly Journal of Economics* 36 (February): 220–273.

Heidelbach, Alfred S. 1895a. Why Gold Is Exported. *Forum* XVIII (February): 647–651.

———. 1895b. Why Do We Export Gold? *Commercial and Financial Chronicle* 60 (March 30): 585.

[*Historical Statistics*]. 1949. Bureau of the Census. *Historical Statistics of the United States, 1789–1945*. Washington: Government Printing Office.

———. 1960. Bureau of the Census. *Historical Statistics of the United States, Colonial Times to 1957*. Washington: Government Printing Office.

———. 1975. Bureau of the Census. *Historical Statistics of the United States, Colonial Times to 1970, Bicentennial Edition*. Washington: Government Printing Office.

———. 2006. *Historical Statistics of the United States, Millennial Edition*, ed. Susan B. Carter, Scott Sigmund Gartner, Michael R. Haines, Alan L. Olmstead, Richard Sutch, Gavin Wright. Cambridge: Cambridge University Press.

Lary, Hal B. 1943. *The United States in the World Economy*. Washington: Government Printing Office.

Laughlin, J.Laurence. 1918. *Credit of the Nations*. New York: Scribner's.

North, Douglass C. 1960. The United States Balance of Payments, 1790–1860. In *Trends in the American Economy in the Nineteenth Century*, ed. William N. Parker, 573–628. Princeton: Princeton University Press.

Paish, George. 1910. *The Trade Balance of the United States*. Washington: Government Printing Office.

Seaman, Ezra C. 1846. *Essays on the Progress of Nations*. New York: Baker & Scribner.

———. 1857. The Panic and Financial Crisis of 1857. *Hunt's Merchants' Magazine*, December: 661–668.

Seybert, Adam. 1818. *Statistical Annals*. Philadelphia: Thomas Dobson.

Simon, Matthew. 1960. The United States Balance of Payments, 1861–1900. In *Trends in the American Economy in the Nineteenth Century*, ed. William N. Parker, 629–716. Princeton: Princeton University Press.

Smith, Walter B. 1953. *Economic Aspects of the Second Bank of the United States*. Cambridge, MA: Harvard University Press.

Sterns, Worthy P. 1898. The Beginnings of American Financial Independence. *Journal of Political Economy* 6 (March): 187–208.

———. 1899. The Foreign Trade of the United States from 1820 to 1840. *Journal of Political Economy* 8 (December): 34–57.

Taussig, Frank W. 1928. *International Trade*. New York: Macmillan.

Taylor, George Rogers. 1951. *The Transportation Revolution*. New York: Holt, Rinehart, and Winston.

Vanderlip, Frank A., and John H. Williams. 1920. The Future of Our Foreign Trade: A Study of Our International Balance in 1919. *Review of Economics and Statistics* 2 (April): 5–28.

Vangermeersch, Richard. 2013. The Correspondence Between Irving Fisher and Nathaniel Terry Bacon at the James P. Adams Library Rhode Island College. *Faculty Publications* 323.

Warner, Adoniram J. 1879. Resumption and Regulation of Currency. *Bankers' Magazine and Statistical Register*, January: 522–527.

Wasserman, Max J., and Ray M. Ware. 1965. *The Balance of Payments*. New York: Simmons-Boardman.

Wells, David A. 1869. *Report of the Special Commissioner of the Revenue*, House of Representatives Ex. Doc., 41st Cong., 2d sess.

Williams, John H. 1921. The Balance of International Payments of the United States for the Year 1920. *Review of Economics and Statistics* 3 (June): 169–212.

Young, Edward. 1874. Foreign Indebtedness of the United States. *Monthly Report of the Chief of the Bureau of Statistics*, February: 351–352.

CHAPTER 2

New Balance of Payments: Features and Implications

1 Why a New Balance of Payments

1.1 Overcome Limitations of Existing Studies

Length of Period: The beginning year of this study is 1790, the first year of sufficient data (and in conformity with predecessor authors); the ending year is 1919, the first year of the official balance of payments. OBE extends its table to 1919 and beyond, via the official table; but that involves a year-1919 series break. My one-year overlap between new and official table conforms to nonofficial GDP series ending in 1929, when the official national accounts begin.

Year Definition: Virtually all existing tables ignore year-definition inconsistency, of which there are many instances, and simply accept the changing official year.[1] There are three problems. First, the official year is often a fiscal year rather than the calendar year. Second, definition of the fiscal year varies over time. Third, the official year is commingled with other data for which the year-definition differs. In sharp contrast, I take care to have a uniform year-definition, consistent over time, for all series in this study—and that common year is the *calendar year*. The calendar year is the customary annual period for historical data, and it behooves balance-of-payments series to follow that usage. In most cases, I convert fiscal year to calendar year by taking the appropriate weighted average of

L. H. Officer, *A New Balance of Payments for the United States, 1790–1919*, Palgrave Studies in American Economic History,
https://doi.org/10.1007/978-3-030-66099-4_2

adjacent years.[2] Some situations warrant an individual-specific conversion procedure.

Conceptual Continuity: For many series (items), the sharp discontinuities in the OBE Table (1820, 1861, 1900) are associated with a change in source or technique. In the extreme, there is no estimate—in effect, an assumed zero flow—for certain segments of a series: travel (1790–1819), port charges on foreign passenger steamships (1848–1860, 1900–1918), marine insurance and brokers' commissions (1820–1860, 1900–1918), immigrant funds and remittances (1790–1819). More generally, some series have techniques of estimation that differ across time segments. The new table does not have these deficiencies: there are no imposed time-segment-specific zero flows and the method of generating a series is uniform for the entire time period, with allowance made for varying institutions and varying data availability.

Moreover, in sharp contrast to the entire literature, I correct basic data so that important distinctions are uniform throughout 1790–1919. (1) Immigrants are inclusive of alien residents. (2) Immigrant aliens are distinct from nonimmigrant aliens. (3) Oceanic trade is exclusive of overland trade.

Gross Flows: Netting gross flows (credit and debit flows) of a given item detracts from the comprehensiveness of the table, as does combining gross (or gross and net) flows. I avoid these shortcuts like the plague; but OBE and Goldsmith—and, to a lesser extent, North and Simon—are replete with them.[3]

Offsetting Flows: Predecessor application of this assumption is discussed in Sects. 3.2 and 3.3 of Chapter 1. In the present study, the only case of assumed offsetting flows is receipts and payments per international mail. Modern balance-of-payments tables include this item, but it would be difficult to develop a reliable historical series even of the net flow.[4] The bilateral nature of mail communication suggests that a reasonably measured net flow would be close to the assumed zero net flow, although the role of mail subsidies might mitigate that conclusion.

Zero Flows: For 1820–1860, North acknowledges exclusion of flows emanating from consistent undervaluation of merchandise exports, omission of overland exports, and neglect of U.S.-tourist fare expenditures on foreign ships. For 1861–1900, Simon assumes that aliens do not travel on U.S. ships, which implies zero fare receipts. My only explicit zero flow is wage receipts and payments. Wages are a component of income beyond interest and dividends, but "compensation of employees" is included in the official balance of payments only from 1986.[5]

Statistical Discrepancy: Goldsmith uses the residual to estimate short-term capital flows 1914–1919. North and Simon take the residual to be the entire net capital flow 1790–1900. OBE follows North–Simon. Decidedly, I do not use the statistical discrepancy to generate any other item in the table. Thus the residual is treated as "net errors and omissions" pure and simple, and can be utilized to judge the accuracy of the table as a whole (Chapter 18, Sect. 2.7).

1.2 Take Advantage of Data

Neglected Available Data: A host of existing data or information pertinent to generating a balance-of-payments table was neglected by North, Simon, Goldsmith, and OBE, including: on citizen travel and immigration, August Maffry (1939); on tourist expenditure to/from Canada, Frank A. Knox (1939); on price of ships, John G. B. Hutchins (1941); on government unilateral transfers, John B. Moore (1898), William M. Malloy (1910), William A. Dunning (1912), Edward M. Douglas (1932), and Paul N. Garber (1959); on freight rates, National Foreign Trade Council (1917), E. A. V. Angier (1920), Emory R. Johnson and Grover G. Huebner (1920), Henry W. Van Pelt (1921); on marine insurance, Robert G. Albion (1939), Albion and Jennie B. Pope (1942); on oceanic passengers, Albion (1938). I utilize all these sources.

Newly Published Data: I have the advantage of access to a mass of data not published until after my predecessors did their work. Some sources are: on citizen travel, Farley Grubb (1990), Oriana Bandiera, Imran Rasul, and Martina Viarengo [BRV] (2013); on immigration, Peter D. McClelland and Richard J. Zeckhauser (1982), Farley Grubb (1990), Hans-Jürgen Grabbe (2001), BRV (2013, and also for emigration); on price of ships, Donald R. Adams (1980); on industrial production, Joseph H. Davis (2004); on prepaid oceanic tickets, Maldwyn A. Jones (1980), Drew Keeling (2007); on capital account, Desmond C. M. Platt (1984), Peter M. Garber (1986), Mira Wilkins (1989, 2004), Barry Eichengreen (2000); on oceanic passengers, Drew Keeling (2012); on oceanic fares, Rolf Engelsing (1961), Simone A. Wegge (1998), Grabbe (2001), John Killick (2014), Brandon Dupont et al. (2017); on marine insurance, Christopher Kingston (2011); on immigrant remittances, Gary B. Magee and Andrew S. Thompson (2006). Also, there are compilations of useful historical series in *Historical Statistics* (1975, 2006). Finally, Lawrence H. Officer and Samuel H. Williamson (2020) underlie the slave-trade sections of this work.

Unpublished Data: Several scholars generously provided me with unpublished data: Raymond L. Cohn, series of immigration deaths at sea; Drew Keeling, oceanic passenger volume and fares by steamship line; John Killick, many oceanic series for the Copes line; Imran Rasul, file underlying the BRV passenger-arrivals graph; Tom Weiss, file of fares.[6] These data greatly enhanced the richness of the resulting balance-of-payments table.

2 Measurement and Estimation Decisions

Paper-Dollar Denomination: Graham, Simon, and OBE express their tables in gold dollars during the greenback period (1862–1878). This denomination has the advantage of comparability with the balance of payments of other countries but the disadvantage of resulting series that are neither nominal nor real but presumably some compromise between them. My table is expressed in currency dollars (currency, paper dollars, greenbacks), which have two advantages over gold denomination. First, there is conformity with the exchange rate, which typically was a greenback-sterling rate. Second, there is consistency with domestic prices, which generally were in greenbacks.[7]

Interpolation: The best discussion of interpolation techniques from an operational standpoint remains Milton Friedman and Anna Jacobson Schwartz (1970, pp. 321–328). As they do, I prefer "interpolation via series" over linear interpolation, providing an interpolator series that relates analytically to the given series can be found. Unlike Friedman and Schwartz, I eschew statistical methods of "interpolation via series" in favor of a simple procedure that I use extensively elsewhere (Officer 2009, p. 104). Let the given series Y be known for year 0 and year n, with all intermediate years missing, and let X be the interpolator series known for all years 0 to n. The ratio Y/X is linearly interpolated between 0 and n, and the missing years of Y are estimated as the product of the interpolated ratio and the known X.

Extrapolation: For extension of a given series via an extrapolator series, I link multiplicatively ("ratio-link"), generally via the latest (for forward extrapolation) or earliest (for backward extrapolation) overlapping year—the simple term "link" means just that. Where an average of several adjacent years is taken for the overlap, I state that explicitly.

Disaggregation: To enhance robustness, estimation of series is replete with logical disaggregations, hardly any of which are in predecessors. (1) The distinction between oceanic and overland movement is made for both people and goods. (2) For the slave trade, via Officer and Williamson (2020), there is disaggregation of both imports of enslaved persons (African, Caribbean) and carrying trade (pre-U.S. Louisiana and Florida, Spanish America, Brazil, non-Spanish Caribbean). (3) For gold and silver, specie and merchandise are separated. (4) Specie has a freight rate different from merchandise. (5) Carrying trade is divided into merchandise, specie, slaves, and rail transit. (6) Port charges are divided into freight and passenger ships [done by Simon, for 1861–1900], and also slave ships. (7) Long-term capital and short-term capital are made separate items [done by Goldsmith and OBE, but only for 1914–1919], with U.S. long-term investment abroad divided into direct and portfolio [as do Goldsmith and OBE, but only from 1897 and 1900, respectively]. (8) Foreign short-term capital has components mercantile debt, paper currency, and deposits at Federal Reserve Banks. (9) Immigrant remittances are divided into financial intermediation and prepaid tickets [following Simon]. (10) Head taxes consist of individual state or city receipts and federal receipts. (11) Travel and fares are separate items.

A three-level disaggregation is applied to U.S.–Europe oceanic fares (price of passage). *First:* cabin westbound, steerage westbound, cabin eastbound, steerage eastbound. *Second*, for each of the first-level items: sailing ships, steamships. *Third*, for the second-level sailing ships: U.S. packets, Falmouth packets, traders.

Six levels of disaggregation are used to generate oceanic passenger revenue. *First*: U.S.-ship revenue from U.S. residents, U.S.-ship revenue from foreign residents, foreign-ship revenue from U.S. residents, foreign-ship revenue from foreign residents. *Second*, for each first-level item: Europe versus rest of world. *Third*, for each of the second-level components: sailing ships versus steamships. *Fourth*, for the third-level Europe sailing-ship component: U.S. packets, Falmouth packets, U.S. traders, foreign traders. *Fifth*, for all upper-level items: U.S. tourists, immigrants and "transmigrants to Canada and West Indies" combined, alien tourists and distant-land transmigrants combined, emigrants. *Sixth*, for

U.S. tourists: Europe, West Indies and Central America combined, South America and Far East combined.

Comparison with Predecessor Series: For a given item, for comparison of the new series with a predecessor series, I divide the 1790–1919 period into four subperiods: 1790–1819 (early North), 1820–1860 (later North), 1861–1899 (Simon), 1900–1918 (Goldsmith). For each subperiod, I compute the average percentage "*algebraic* deviation" of the predecessor series from the new series; but first, if expressed otherwise, the predecessor series is made consistent with the new series in year-definition via conversion to a calendar-year basis. Second, if the predecessor series is expressed in gold dollars during the greenback period (1862–1878), a correction factor of 8.34% is added to the computed average percentage deviation for the 1861–1899 subperiod to obtain a result based on comparable currency denomination.[8]

Taking averages of *algebraic* deviations has the advantage of determining whether the predecessor series *underestimates or overestimates* the item relative to the new series. It has the disadvantage that positive and negative divergences are permitted to cancel—whence a conservative comparison of differences between new and old series. In Chapter 18 (Sects. 1.1, 1.2, 2.7), where comparisons of broad aggregates of balance-of-payments items are performed, I also compute averages of *absolute* deviations—which provide more scope for old versus new series differences.

3 Features of Study

3.1 Summary Balance-of-Payments Table

The new balance-of-payments table consists of annual component series running 1790–1919, and its component items are scattered throughout the volume. The schema that follows arranges, in a logical way, all component series the figures for which are either tabulated (table number stated) or listed in text (chapter stated). A blank cell indicates no entry. The schema includes aggregate totals only where included in the aforementioned tables, and excludes balances, which are tabulated in Chapter 18. Note that disaggregation underlies many items in the schema (per Sect. 2).

GOODS	Credits	Debits
1. Merchandise		
Conventional (Table 1 in Chapter 6)	exports	imports
Non-Monetary Silver (Table 1 in Chapter 6)	exports	imports
2. Ships (Table 1 in Chapter 6)	sales	
3. Slaves		
African		
U.S. Ships (Table 1 in Chapter 9)		imports
Foreign Ships (Table 1 in Chapter 9)		imports
Caribbean: U.S. Ships (Table 1 in Chapter 9)		imports

For lack of data, there are no entries for ship purchases and slave exports.

SERVICES	Credits	Debits
1. Transportation	receipts	payments
Freight		
Direct Trade (Table 1 in Chapter 13)	receipts	payments
Carrying Trade (Table 1 in Chapter 13)	receipts	payments
Port Charges (Table 1 in Chapter 13)	receipts	payments
Charter (Chapter 13)		payments
2. Travel	receipts	payments
Oceanic (Table 1 in Chapter 14)	receipts	payments
Overland (Table 1 in Chapter 14)	receipts	payments
3. Fares		
Sailing Ships (Table 1 in Chapter 15)	receipts	payments
Steamships (Table 1 in Chapter 15)	receipts	payments
4. Financial		
Insurance (Table 1 in Chapter 16)	receipts	payments
Bankers' Commissions (Table 1 in Chapter 16)		payments
5. Military Expenditures (Table 1 in Chapter 16)		payments
6. Non-Imported Slaves (Table 1 in Chapter 9)		payments

Carrying-trade receipts include slaves. Carrying-trade payments are only rail transport. Port charges include outfitting and provisioning slave ships. Payments for "non-imported slaves" are purchases of slaves not imported into the United States.

INVESTMENT INCOME	Credits	Debits
1. Private		payments
Long-Term (Table 1 in Chapter 12)	receipts	payments
Short-Term (Table 1 in Chapter 12)		payments
2. Government (Chapter 12)	receipts	

UNILATERAL TRANSFERS	Credits	Debits
1. Private	receipts	payments
Money Transfers (Table 1 in Chapter 10)		payments
Prepaid Tickets (Table 1 in Chapter 10)		payments
Migrant Funds (Table 1 in Chapter 10)	receipts	payments
Red Cross Remittances (Chapter 10)		payments
Other Remittances (Chapter 10)		payments
Head Taxes (Table 1 in Chapter 10)	receipts	
2. Government (Table 1 in Chapter 10)	receipts	payments

Of course, immigrant funds are receipts, and emigrant funds payments.

CAPITAL	Credits	Debits
1. Long-Term		
Private (Table 2 in Chapter 11)	foreign capital	
Direct (Table 2 in Chapter 11)		U.S. capital
Portfolio (Table 2 in Chapter 11)		U.S. capital
Government (Table 2 in Chapter 11)		U.S. capital
2. Short-Term		
Private		
Mercantile Debt (Table 2 in Chapter 11)	foreign capital	
Paper Currency (Table 2 in Chapter 11)	foreign capital	
Government		
Federal Reserve (Table 2 in Chapter 11)	foreign capital	
U.S. Government (Table 2 in Chapter 11)		U.S. capital

Paper currency is dollars abroad; Federal Reserve is deposits at Federal Reserve Banks.

SPECIE	Credits	Debits
Movements (Table 1 in Chapter 6)	exports	imports
Earmarked (Chapter 18)	net	

Gold earmarked for official foreigners is net of U.S. gold held under earmark abroad—thus the net change in earmarked gold is a credit if positive and equivalent to gold export.

3.2 *New Series*

The study generates many new data series, both within and outside the balance of payments. Entries in the new balance-of-payments table that are absent from predecessor historical tables are rail transit, short-term income, head tax, short-term capital items, and earmarked gold. Entries that appear in predecessors only as components of other items are non-monetary silver and fares.

Especially salient is the absence of the slave trade from previous tables, with the important exception of the "slave-trade balance of payments" constructed by Officer and Williamson (2020). In particular, neither North nor OBE even mentions the slave trade. One can only speculate that, prior to Officer-Williamson, the slave trade was ignored either because it was deemed quantitatively unimportant or because of lack of data.[9] The blithe term "slave trade" is shorthand for "the purchase of Black human beings, their forced transportation across the Atlantic or from the Caribbean or within the Caribbean, and their subsequent sale."

Other new continuous annual series 1790–1919 generated and presented in this study are (1) seven component series of international assets and liabilities (Table 1 in Chapter 11), used to estimate capital-account items, and (2) gross domestic investment (Table 1 in Chapter 19), a national-accounts series used in the derivation of macroeconomic implications of the table. To the best of my knowledge, these series are the first-ever series of their type constructed and tabulated for the 130-year time span.

An adjustment that corrects the official population series for war deaths consequent upon all major wars of the nineteenth century is developed and shown annually (Table 2 in Chapter 5)—the first such series for the entire century. The resulting revised population series is used in the construction of domestic-transportation series—passengers and price: stagecoach (1790–1840); omnibus, railroad, street railroad (all 1790–1900). The passenger series are shown as decadal annual averages (Table 1 in Chapter 5) and are used to develop travel and transportation price indexes (Figs. 1 and 2 in Chapter 14). I am not aware of these series in any previous literature, balance-of-payments, or elsewhere.

Consistent annual series of the number of people moved internationally to and from the United States are an important contribution of the study. This group includes the oceanic travel of tourists, oceanic and overland travel of migrants (Table 1 in Chapter 3), and the oceanic slave trade: African embarkations, U.S. imports, carrying-trade disembarkations (Tables 1 and 2 in Chapter 4—heavily indebted to Officer-Williamson). Per above, there are also new series of the volume of domestic transportation, both intracity and intercity (Table 1 in Chapter 5).

Many new price series are assembled or developed; they are shown in graphs: exchange rates (Figs. 1 and 2—Appendix); merchandise price indexes (Fig. 1 in Chapter 7); freight rates, overland (Fig. 1 in Chapter 6) and oceanic (Fig. 1 in Chapter 13); price of ships (Fig. 1 in Chapter 9); oceanic fares (Figs. 7–10 in Chapter 15); marine insurance rates (Fig. 1 in Chapter 16); rates of return on international investment (Fig. 1 in Chapter 12); price indexes for international travelers (Fig. 1 in Chapter 14); and component consumer price indexes (Fig. 2 in Chapter 14). Also, prices of slaves—embarked or imported (Fig. 2 in Chapter 9), and carried in trade (Fig. 2 in Chapter 13 and Fig. 1 in Chapter 17)—again reliant on Officer and Williamson. Again I point

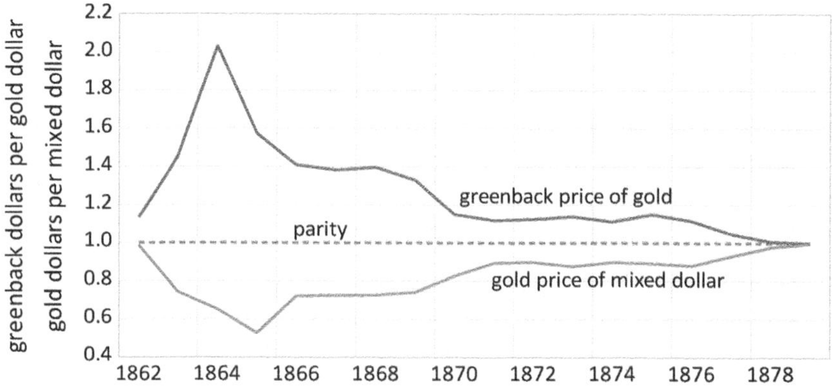

Fig. 1 Gold-dollar rates, 1862–1879. *Note* "Greenback price of gold" is the number of currency dollars (greenbacks) per gold dollar. "Gold price of mixed dollar" is the number of gold dollars per mixed (partly gold, partly currency) dollar. "Parity" is unity—the "normal" rate, were there no greenback period

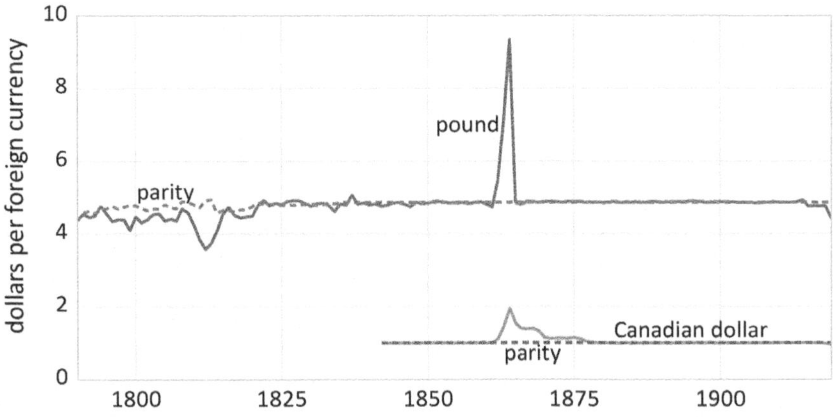

Fig. 2 Exchange rates, 1790–1919 and 1848–1919. *Note* "Pound" is the dollar/pound exchange rate, denominated as the number of currency dollars per pound. "Canadian dollar" is the U.S.-dollar/Canadian-dollar exchange rate, the number of currency dollars per Canadian dollar. "Parity" is "true mint parity" for the pound, unity for the Canadian dollar

out that "slaves" is the traditional term for the now-preferred "enslaved persons."

Finally, constant-dollar series are constructed for total goods and total services. These are aggregated from individual constant-dollar items and are exhibited in the form of an export–import ratio (Fig. 7 in Chapter 19). These series are absent from predecessor studies.

3.3 *Implications*

Regarding individual items in the balance-of-payments table, the study is primarily data-oriented. However, one cannot avoid discussion of determinants of items. Especially warranting recognition is the role of wars. In addition to a Civil War with enormous consequences, the United States fought four major wars during the 1790–1919 period: War of 1812, Mexican–American War, Spanish–American War, and Philippine–American War.

On the macro level, characteristics of the economy examined are openness, importance of goods versus services, and the terms of trade. On the sectoral level, attention is paid to four industries as they varied in importance over time: the slave trade and slave-produced commodities, shipping, manufacturing, and travel.

Appendix: Exchange Rates

A. Domestic

Greenbacks: In 1862–1878, known as the "greenback period," there was a dichotomy between the currency dollar and the gold dollar—and official merchandise import and re-export data, as well as *aggregate* domestic exports, are expressed in gold dollars.[10] These data, and other gold-dollar series that arise in the study, need to be converted to currency dollars. Fortunately, there was a free market in which irredeemable government paper currency (originally Treasury demand notes, later true greenbacks—but termed "greenbacks" throughout) exchanged for gold or gold dollars. From Wesley C. Mitchell (1908, pp. 4–13), I obtain the calendar-year annual average greenback price of gold directly and compute the fiscal-year (ending June 30) annual average price from his quarterly data. These conversion factors are denominated as the number of currency dollars per gold dollar.

Mixed Dollars: A second domestic exchange rate is applicable to the greenback period. Domestic exports for *individual countries and individual commodities* are recorded in "mixed values," partly gold dollars and partly currency dollars. Again, conversion to currency dollars is required. Charles H. Evans (1884, p. 194) provides fiscal-year annual series of domestic exports alternatively in gold dollars and mixed dollars. Taking the ratio of the series yields the gold-dollar price of the mixed dollar, the number of gold dollars per mixed dollar.

Presentation: Fig. 1 shows the calendar-year greenback price of gold and the fiscal-year gold price of the mixed dollar. For both domestic exchange rates, parity (the norm rate) is unity.[11] The calendar-year (fiscal-year) greenback price of gold is above unity 1862–1878 (1862–1879); the fiscal-year gold price of the mixed dollar below unity 1862–1879.

B. International

British Pound: International exchange rates are needed to convert foreign-currency-denominated series to dollars. During the greenback period, exchange rates continue to pertain to currency rather than gold;

so the depreciation of the currency (greenback) in terms of gold is incorporated. The dollar/pound was by far the most important exchange rate during the 1790–1919 period, and there are abundant data and of varying concept. For this study, the "dominant exchange-market instrument" is the concept criterion, leading to a series of the sixty-day exchange rate 1794–1865 (*Historical Statistics* 2006, series Ee615), sight exchange rate 1866–1912 (series Ee616), cable-transfer exchange rate 1913–1919 (series Ee636).[12] The sixty-day segment is extended to 1791–1793 via the series published in Secretary of the Treasury (1830, p. 78).[13] For 1790, absent known alternative, I link in 1791 via the Pennsylvania-pound/British-pound series (Markus A. Denzel 2010, p. 417). Figure 2 exhibits the full series ("pound," number of [currency] dollars per pound), along with dollar/sterling parity (*Historical Statistics* 2006, series Ee612—"true mint parity," per Officer 1996, pp. 56–57). One notes that the spike during the Civil War, associated with the greenback period, is not replicated in parity.

Canadian Dollar: Although no official Canadian dollar existed prior to the mid-1850s, it is reasonable to assume that implicitly there had been such a dollar since 1841, fixed at par with the U.S. dollar via legal valuation of the British pound and U.S. dollar (by virtue of Canadian-currency valuation of the sovereign and the eagle—James Powell 2005, pp. 21, 23). In fact, parity of unity is applicable throughout 1842–1919.[14] When there is no specific exchange-rate information, the U.S.-dollar/Canadian-dollar exchange rate is taken as parity.[15]

Of course, that default exchange rate would be disastrous for the greenback period. Fortunately, S. Turk (1962) compiled daily exchange-rate data (Canadian dollars per U.S. currency-dollar) from May 6, 1859 to December 30, 1879.[16] I eliminate observations for January 7–December 7, 1871, as they are very likely in error.[17] Then I average observations to obtain a monthly series, linearly interpolating missing observations that are prior to the greenback period.[18] Subsequently, using Mitchell's (1908, pp. 5, 9–10, 13) monthly gold price of the greenback as interpolator, I estimate the remaining missing observations.[19] Taking appropriate annual averages of monthly observations, I obtain the exchange rate 1859–1880 for calendar years and for fiscal years ending June 30. The calendar-year exchange rate ("Canadian dollar," number of U.S. [currency] dollars per Canadian dollar), together with the unity par, is plotted in Figure 2. As one would expect, the series is uniformly above par during the greenback period.[20]

Dollar exchange rates of other required currencies are not available; so are calculated indirectly via the dollar/pound and pound/currency exchange rates, as follows.

Spanish Peso: The British-pound/Spanish-peso exchange rate 1812–1865 is in Markus A. Denzel (2010, pp. 33–34). The old-peso rate 1812–1846 is converted to new pesos via the 1847 overlap.[21] The dollar/peso exchange rate (number of dollars per peso) is the product of the dollar/pound rate and the pound/peso rate.

Brazilian Milreis: From Denzel (2010, pp. 32–33, 455–456), the British-pound/Brazilian-milreis exchange rate 1808–1860 and the British-pound/Portuguese-milreis exchange rate 1790–1812 are obtained. The former series is estimated for 1790–1807 via the overlap ratio for 1808–1812, numerator and denominator averaged separately. Then the dollar/-milreis exchange rate (number of dollars per Brazilian milreis) is the product of the dollar/pound rate and the pound/Brazilian-milreis rate.

Austrian Crown: The crown/pound exchange rate for 1880–1907 is taken from Clemens Jobst and Thomas Scheiber (2014, p. 93).[22] The dollar/crown rate is the ratio of the dollar/pound to the crown/pound rate.

Notes

1. An egregious example is merchandise data, for which the official year is the 12 months ending September 30 for 1790–1842, the nine months ending June 30 for 1843, the 12 months ending June 30 for 1844–1915 (these three year-definitions termed "fiscal year"), and the calendar year for 1914–1919. Unlike North, Simon expresses his series in uniform annual period, namely, fiscal-year ending June 30. OBE (*Historical Statistics*) has a table discontinuity in 1900, switching from fiscal-year ending June 30 to calendar year.
2. A simple example: for a series (or series segment) with fiscal-year *t* ending September 30, the corresponding series (or segment) for calendar-year *t* is 0.75 of the fiscal-year series for year *t plus* 0.25 of the fiscal-year series for year $t + 1$. Some computations for intermediate series involve the reverse: conversion from calendar to fiscal year.
3. Goldsmith has five net flows: merchandise *plus* silver *plus* nonmonetary gold, income, freight (though shown gross 1916–1918), travel, private remittances. OBE, following North and Simon, nets income payments and receipts 1790–1900. OBE nets marine insurance *plus* brokers'

commissions 1790–1819 (per North) and 1861–1900; also private unilateral transactions and government unilateral transactions. Further, OBE combines the following items: ship sales, silver, and nonmonetary gold in merchandise; port charges and charter hire in transportation; fares in travel.

4. One could begin by consulting Frank Staff (1956) and Howard Robinson (1964), Post Office Department *Annual Reports*, various Congressional documents, and studies relating to the Universal Postal Union.
5. However, international "wage and salary receipts" and "wage and salary payments" are in the official *national accounts* beginning 1948. Of course, "compensation of employees" is in the national accounts from the first year, 1929.
6. Also, the Bank of Canada furnished an internal exchange-rate study.
7. The Far West is the most important exception.
8. For a given item, let R denote the gold-denominated predecessor series, N the currency-denominated new series, and DU the uncorrected percentage deviation of R from N. Then $DU = 100 \times \{(R-N)/N\}$. Let P denote the greenback price of gold (number of greenback dollars per gold dollar—per Appendix). For 1862–1878, P uniformly exceeds unity. For all other years, $P = 1$. If R and N are identical except for denomination, then, ideally and simply, $N = P \times R$ and $DU = 100 \times \{(R-(P \times R))/(P \times R)\} = 100 \times \{(1-P)/P\}$. DU is negative for 1862–1878, zero for 1861 and 1879–1899, and the average DU for 1861–1899 is -8.34. Therefore adding 8.34 percentage points to that average is in accordance with the $N = P \times R$ imposed condition. Note, however, that a refined procedure would recompute the predecessor series in currency from first principles and *then* compute percentage deviation. The simple technique here yields only an approximation but has the advantages of intuition and uniformity across balance-of-payments items.
9. Officer-Williamson note one predecessor of the slave trade entering the U.S. balance of payments. For five years of the colonial period, James F. Shepherd and Gary M. Walton (1972, pp. 141–144) present information on slave imports (but not the carrying trade), using data since superseded.
10. See *Historical Statistics* (1975, pp. 876–877; 2006, pp. 5-445–446).
11. On the concept of parity, see *Historical Statistics* (2006, pp. 5–562) and the references cited there.
12. On the dominant exchange-market instrument, see Officer (1996, pp. 62–63) and *Historical Statistics* (2006, pp. 5-565 to 566, 571). I begin the cable rate in 1913, although its true dominance likely occurred after World War I.
13. The series is of high quality—see Officer (1996, pp. 66–67).
14. On the issue of Canadian-dollar parity, see Alan B. McCullough (1984, p. 109), Powell (2005, pp. 21–39 various), and Denzel (2010, p. 435).

15. "Specific exchange-rate information" is as follows. Data for 1910–1912 are from Jürgen Schneider et al. (1991, p. 473), and for 1913–1919 are from Board of Governors of the Federal Reserve System (1943, p. 665).
16. Turk's contribution, located in the Bank of Canada Archives, was made known to posterity via footnote and reference in Powell (2005, pp. 36, 104). The number of observations varies monthly; and, via Powell, I add an observation for July 1864.
17. These observations are identical to those for the same time span in 1872. The evidence to drop these 1871 observations is twofold. First, the average of the absolute deviations of the 1871 figures from Mitchell's gold price of greenbacks is triple that of 1872—0.96 versus 0.32 cents. Second, among the dates of the repeat observations are six Sundays in 1871 but only one Sunday in 1872.
18. 1859: September, November; 1860: February–March, July–August, October–November; 1861: February–April, November.
19. 1862: April; 1863: April, September–October; 1871: January–December; 1879: January.
20. Also of use is the Canadian-dollar/gold-dollar fiscal-year exchange rate, computed as the product of the Canadian-dollar/U.S.-currency exchange rate and the greenback price of gold.
21. Not a true overlap, as it is the ratio for four months on the old unit, eight months on the new.
22. For 1880–1899, the crown/pound exchange rate is double the florin/pound rate.

References

Adams, Donald R., Jr. 1980. American Neutrality and Prosperity, 1793–1808: A Reconsideration. *Journal of Economic History* 40 (December): 713–737.

Albion, Robert G. 1938. *Square-Riggers on Schedule*. Princeton: Princeton University Press.

———. 1939. *The Rise of New York Port*. New York: Scribner's.

———, and Jennie B. Pope. 1942. *Sea Lanes in Wartime*. New York: Norton.

Angier, E.A.V. 1920. *Fifty Years' Freights*. London: Fairplay.

Bandiera, Oriana, Imran Rasul, and Martina Viarengo [BRV]. 2013. The Making of Modern America: Migratory Flows in the Age of Mass Migration. *Journal of Development Economics* 102 (May): 23–47.

Board of Governors of the Federal Reserve System. 1943. *Banking and Monetary Statistics, 1914–1941*. Washington.

Davis, Joseph H. 2004. An Annual Index of U.S. Industrial Production, 1790–1915. *Quarterly Journal of Economics* 119 (November): 1177–1215, data appendix http://www.nber.org/data/industrial-production-index/.

Denzel, Markus A. 2010. *Handbook of World Exchange Rates, 1590–1914*. Surrey: Ashgate.

Douglas, Edward M. 1932. *Boundaries, Areas, Geographic Centers and Altitudes*. Washington: Government Printing Office.

Dunning, William A. 1912. Paying for Alaska. *Political Science Quarterly* 27 (September): 385–398.

Dupont, Brandon, Drew Keeling, and Thomas Weiss [DKW]. 2017. First Cabin Fares from New York to the British Isles, 1826–1914. *Research in Economic History* 33: 19–63.

Eichengreen, Barry. 2000. U.S. Foreign Financial Relations in the Twentieth Century. In *The Cambridge Economic History of the United States*, vol. 3, ed. Stanley L. Engerman and Robert E. Gallman, 463–504. Cambridge: Cambridge University Press.

Engelsing, Rolf. 1961. *Veröffentlichungen aus dem Staatsarchiv der Freien Hansestadt Bremen*. Bremen: Schunemann.

Evans, Charles H. 1884. *Exports, Domestic, from the United States to All Countries*. Washington: Government Printing Office.

Friedman, Milton, and Anna Jacobson Schwartz. 1970. *Monetary Statistics of the United States*. New York: Columbia University Press.

Garber, Paul N. 1959. *The Gadsden Treaty*. Gloucester: Peter Smith.

Garber, Peter M. 1986. Interwar Movements of Dollars to Europe and the US Currency Supply. *Journal of International Money and Finance* 5 (March): 135–156.

Grabbe, Hans-Jürgen. 2001. *Vor der großen Flut*. Stuttgart: Franz Steiner.

Grubb, Farley. 1990. The Reliability of U.S. Immigration Statistics: The Case of Philadelphia, 1815–1830. *International Journal of Maritime History* 1 (June): 29–54.

[*Historical Statistics*]. 1975. Bureau of the Census. *Historical Statistics of the United States, Colonial Times to 1970, Bicentennial Edition*. Washington: Government Printing Office.

———. 2006. *Historical Statistics of the United States, Millennial Edition*, ed. Susan B. Carter, Scott Sigmund Gartner, Michael R. Haines, Alan L. Olmstead, Richard Sutch, and Gavin Wright. Cambridge: Cambridge University Press.

Hutchins, John G.B. 1941. *The American Maritime Industries and Public Policy, 1789–1914*. Cambridge, MA: Harvard University Press.

Jobst, Clemens, and Thomas Scheiber. 2014. In *South-Eastern European Monetary and Economic Statistics from the Nineteenth Century to World War II*, 55–100. Bank of Greece, Bulgarian National Bank, National Bank of Romania, Osterreichische Nationalbank.

Johnson, Emory R., and Grover G. Huebner. 1920. *Principles of Ocean Transportation*. New York: Appleton.

Jones, Maldwyn A. 1980. Scotch-Irish. In *Harvard Encyclopedia of American Ethnic Groups*, ed. Stephan Thernstrom, 895–908. Harvard: Harvard University Press.

Keeling, Drew. 2007. Costs, Risks and Migration Networks Between Europe and the United States, 1900–1914. In *Maritime Transport and Migration: The Connections Between Maritime and Migration Networks*, ed. Torsten Feys and others, 113–173. St. John's: International Maritime Economic History Association.

———. 2012. *The Business of Transatlantic Migration Between Europe and the United States, 1900–1914*. Zurich: Chronos.

Kingston, Christopher. 2011. Marine Insurance in Philadelphia During the Quasi-War with France, 1795–1801. *Journal of Economic History* 71 (March): 162–184.

Knox, Frank A. 1939. *Dominion Monetary Policy, 1929–1934*. Ottawa: Royal Commission on Dominion-Provincial Relations.

Maffry, August. 1939. *Overseas Travel and Travel Expenditures in the Balance of International Payments of the United States, 1919–1938*. Washington: Government Printing Office.

Magee, Gary B., and Andrew S. Thompson. 2006. 'Lines of Credit, Debts of Obligation': Migrant Remittances to Britain, c. 1875–1913. *Economic History Review* 59 (August): 539–577.

Malloy, William M. 1910. *Treaties, Conventions, International Acts, Protocols and Agreements*. Washington: Government Printing Office.

McClelland, Peter D., and Richard J. Zeckhauser. 1982. *Demographic Dimensions of the New Republic*. Cambridge: Cambridge University Press.

McCullough, Alan B. 1984. *Money and Exchange in Canada to 1900*. Toronto: Dundurn.

Mitchell, Wesley C. 1908. *Gold, Prices, and Wages Under the Greenback Standard*. Berkeley: Berkeley University Press.

Moore, John B. 1898. *History and Digest of the International Arbitrations*. Washington: Government Printing Office.

National Foreign Trade Council. 1917. *Ocean Shipping*. Washington.

Officer, Lawrence H. 1996. *Between the Dollar-Sterling Gold Points*. Cambridge: Cambridge University Press.

———. 2009. *Two Centuries of Compensation for U.S. Production Workers in Manufacturing*. New York: Palgrave Macmillan.

———, and Samuel H. Williamson. 2020. The Antebellum Slave Trade: Numbers and Impact on the Balance of Payments. *Research in Economic History* 36: 181–212.

Platt, Desmond C.M. 1984. *Foreign Finance in Continental Europe and the United States, 1815–1870*. London: Allen & Unwin.

Powell, James. 2005. *A History of the Canadian Dollar*. Ottawa: Bank of Canada.

Robinson, Howard. 1964. *Carrying British Mails Overseas*. London: Allen & Unwin.

Schneider, Jürgen, Oskar Schwarzer, and Friedrich Zellfelder. 1991. *Währungen der Welt I*, vol. 1. Stuttgart: Franz Steiner.

Secretary of the Treasury. 1830. *Report Respecting the Relative Value of Gold and Silver*.

Shepherd, James F., and Gary M. Walton. 1972. *Shipping, Maritime Trade, and the Economic Development of Colonial North America*. Cambridge: Cambridge University Press.

Simon, Matthew. 1960. The United States Balance of Payments, 1861–1900. In *Trends in the American Economy in the Nineteenth Century*, ed. William N. Parker, 629–716. Princeton: Princeton University Press.

Staff, Frank. 1956. *The Transatlantic Mail*. London: Adlard Coles.

Turk, S. 1962. *Some Notes on Foreign Exchange in Canada Before 1919*. Bank of Canada Memorandum, 27 June. Ottawa: Bank of Canada Archives 4B-200, vol. 5.

Van Pelt, Henry W. 1921. American Shipping Earnings and the Balance of Trade. *Federal Reserve Bulletin*, April, pp. 400–410.

Wegge, Simone A. 1998. Chain Migration and Information Networks: Evidence from Nineteenth-Century Hesse-Cassel. *Journal of Economic History* 58 (December): 957–986.

Wilkins, Mira. 1989. *The History of Foreign Investment in the United States to 1914*. Cambridge, MA: Harvard University Press.

———. 2004. *The History of Foreign Investment in the United States, 1914–1945*. Cambridge, MA: Harvard University Press.

PART II

Movement of People

CHAPTER 3

Free People: Oceanic and Overland

1 U.S.-Citizen Tourists: Oceanic

1.1 Arrivals

The number of U.S. tourists is required for travel and fare items (Chapters 14–15) in the balance-of-payments table. In the balance of payments, the word "tourists" is customarily used to describe all travelers temporarily abroad. So, at least statistically, the reasons for travel include not only recreation ("touring") but also business and visit (and possibly return) with family or friends. I accept all these reasons as within the rubric "tourists."[1]

1.1.1 Nationality Definition

The ***nationality coverage*** of official data on U.S.-traveler arrivals (return, inbound flow) is not so clear (Maffry 1939, pp. 3, 6, 10–11, 14–15, 85–88). The Act of March 2, 1819 specifies that passengers arriving by sea should be classified according to the "country to which they severally belong." The Act of March 3, 1855 uses a similar phrase. Maffry cites official documents to conclude that citizen-arrivals were solely ***native-born citizens*** until 1867 or 1870.[2] Thereafter "naturalized citizens were grouped with native-born citizens" (Maffry 1939, p. 10). However, Maffry also cites the Act of August 2, 1882, according to which naturalized Americans are "citizens" only if cabin passengers, and he states "some

L. H. Officer, *A New Balance of Payments for the United States, 1790–1919*, Palgrave Studies in American Economic History,
https://doi.org/10.1007/978-3-030-66099-4_3

evidence" that this rule was followed in the past. In all these Acts, "the treatment of naturalized citizens was nowhere specifically mentioned" (Maffry 1939, p. 87). Murkier and murkier. It may be that only in 1906—with "the fourfold classification of arriving passengers into (1) citizens, (2) alien residents, (3) alien visitors, and (4) immigrant aliens" (Maffry 1939, p. 14)—are naturalized Americans unambiguously grouped with U.S.-born citizens.

There is a logic in restricting U.S.-citizen tourists to native-born Americans, because our time period is encompassed by the pre-quota immigration era—and it is reasonable that in general the travel behavior of the naturalized foreign-born population was closer to that of alien residents than to U.S.-born citizens.

1.1.2 New York Port

BRV (2013, pp. 25, 31, Figure B) use original-source data ("passenger lists…prepared by the ship's captain before the ship departed") in lieu of the derived "official statistics" to generate an annual series of U.S.-born ("U.S.-citizen") *administrative-records* arrivals (equivalent to embarkations from abroad) in New York Port (Ellis Island) 1892–1924.[3] I derive a comparable New York *official-statistics* series, beginning with fiscal-year data on U.S.-citizen arrivals for 1856–1895 and 1898–1920.[4] For 1855–1862, overland arrivals via Oswego are included in New York Port (Customs District); they are removed via data in Edward P. Hutchinson (1958, pp. 998–999). For 1895–1898, I convert the administrative-records series to fiscal-year and use the resulting series to interpolate the missing, 1896–1897, years of the fiscal-year official-statistics series.

The next step is conversion of the 1892–1920 official-statistics fiscal-year series to 1892–1919 calendar-year series. Then the administrative-records/official-statistics ratio for New York Port constitutes a multiplier adjustment-factor series for official total (all U.S.-seaports) citizen arrivals 1892–1919.[5]

1.1.3 Total United States

Development of the official total-U.S. arrivals series requires some effort. From *Annual Report of the Commissioner-General of Immigration* [ARCGI] 1906–1920, I obtain fiscal-year U.S.-citizen oceanic admittances for all U.S. ports. Subtracting overland travel and travel through Canadian or Mexican ports, the result represents citizen arrivals from overseas.[6] For 1820–1895, 1898–1905, U.S.-citizen arrivals from foreign countries are taken from Maffry (1939, pp. 6, 11). Using the New York corrected official series as interpolator, I estimate the 1896–1897 figures.

For 1855–1862, I remove the New York (Oswego) overland arrivals and the only elsewhere recorded overland U.S.-citizen arrivals (Texas in 1855, a trivial amount, in Hutchinson 1958, p. 997). There are no reported inland arrivals 1863–1864, and I assume that all such arrivals 1865–1866 are immigrants.[7]

The resulting fiscal-year U.S.-citizen oceanic arrivals (inbound), all U.S.-seaports, 1820–1920 is converted to calendar-year 1820–1919.[8] Throughout this process I work in thousands. For 1892–1919, I apply the multiplier adjustment factor.

Then the series of U.S.-citizen arrivals (inbound) from overseas runs 1820–1919. To extrapolate the series to 1790–1819, I ratio-link it to total real merchandise exports and imports via the 1820 overlap. The assumption is that travel ("tourism") went along with trade.[9] Real rather than nominal trade is the extrapolator, because the number of travelers is "real" in denomination.[10] The series is not tabulated; instead the corresponding departures (outbound) series is column (1) of Table 1 (Sect. 1.2).

For comparison, I take the official U.S.-citizen arrivals series utilized by Brandon Dupont et al., [DGW] (2012, p. 147) and Dupont and Weiss (2013, p. 323): *Historical Statistics* (2006, series Dh321) for 1820–1890, 1908–1920; Department of Commerce (1956, pp. 44–45) for 1891–1895, 1898–1907. The series is converted to calendar year. The percentage deviation of the resulting "existing" series from the new series is shown as period averages in row (1) of Table 2. Not unexpectedly, the broad outlines of the BRV (2013, p. 31, Figure B) official versus administrative graph for New York are followed for 1892–1918, with similar systematic deviations of official from administrative figures. The averages are misleadingly high for 1861–1899 and 1900–1918, because of exceptionally large deviations for 1898–1902.[11] Eliminating 1898–1902, the 1861–1894, and 1903–1918 figures fall to 1.56 and 15.46%, with the 1820–1860 average remaining less than one percent. Nevertheless, the official series has years of noticeable divergence from the new series even prior to BRV, with three years exceeding five percent and another two years exceeding ten percent. In sum, the new citizen-arrivals series is substantially different from the accepted series.

DGW (2012, p. 146) do not extend the official series backward from 1820, but do state that the figure was "probably less than 2,000 in any year, and perhaps closer to 1,000." Their judgment is based entirely on

Table 1 Movement of free people (number of persons)

Year	*Oceanic Embarkations*			*Oceanic and overland*	
	U.S. tourists	*Foreign tourists and Transmigrants*	*Immigrants*	*Immigrant admittances*	*Emigrants*
	(1)	*(2)*	*(3)*	*(4)*	*(5)*
1790	893	247	11,340	10,996	122
1791	1019	348	15,949	15,418	169
1792	1070	424	19,431	18,777	206
1793	1178	452	20,733	19,949	214
1794	1391	336	15,421	14,890	162
1795	1777	316	14,506	14,011	153
1796	1844	324	14,834	14,306	155
1797	1653	216	9886	9627	109
1798	1646	100	4597	4441	49
1799	1871	98	4491	4329	47
1800	2539	201	9229	8916	98
1801	2807	740	33,926	32,646	350
1802	2309	516	23,665	22,798	246
1803	2081	161	7364	7092	76
1804	2511	196	8983	8669	94
1805	3031	191	8772	8466	92
1806	3512	155	7095	6898	77
1807	3194	109	4984	4814	52
1808	1464	79	3600	3485	37
1809	1982	138	6344	6155	66
1810	2143	129	5934	5769	62
1811	1658	218	10,003	9746	104
1812	1315	150	6895	6733	72
1813	507	27	1231	1205	13
1814	560	45	2040	2001	21
1815	1750	187	8584	9846	105
1816	2346	409	18,728	19,633	210
1817	2013	529	24,263	29,905	320
1818	2083	538	24,650	37,489	401
1819	2032	430	19,713	33,348	357
1820	2136	252	11,551	19,203	205
1821	2366	301	13,807	21,800	247
1822	1757	521	23,901	32,153	358

(continued)

Table 1 (continued)

	Oceanic Embarkations			*Oceanic and overland*	
Year	*U.S. tourists*	*Foreign tourists and Transmigrants*	*Immigrants*	*Immigrant admittances*	*Emigrants*
	(1)	*(2)*	*(3)*	*(4)*	*(5)*
1823	1918	528	24,213	32,265	357
1824	2010	290	13,273	21,775	247
1825	2845	350	16,048	24,840	286
1826	3120	322	14,744	23,546	267
1827	2963	469	21,500	34,265	380
1828	2678	643	29,497	39,748	447
1829	1930	850	38,978	52,449	586
1830	1491	895	41,034	64,454	703
1831	1265	1412	64,734	104,673	1133
1832	1157	1691	77,531	119,117	1299
1833	1324	1912	87,637	106,246	1197
1834	2660	2128	97,553	123,638	1375
1835	3442	1438	65,929	76,944	884
1836	4872	2406	110,300	135,272	1590
1837	5788	2550	116,876	135,476	1514
1838	6432	1218	55,843	59,510	711
1839	6795	2140	98,078	105,313	1224
1840	8385	2641	121,086	134,353	8995
1841	7741	2509	115,009	125,288	8386
1842	6607	3258	149,338	165,237	11,061
1843	5737	2205	101,059	109,889	7352
1844	6173	2661	121,972	131,480	8796
1845	5358	3775	173,054	184,638	12,355
1846	4432	5304	243,121	255,794	17,120
1847	4248	7055	323,396	345,954	23,158
1848	2968	7288	334,094	347,980	23,284
1849	3427	8924	409,067	420,405	28,134
1850	9879	8840	405,230	433,460	42,575
1851	30,243	12,116	555,394	568,529	70,267
1852	26,512	11,452	524,998	535,545	66,201
1853	33,307	10,891	499,242	507,010	62,682
1854	33,620	6890	573,761	589,398	72,867
1855	27,247	8260	255,725	262,453	32,307

(continued)

Table 1 (continued)

Year	*Oceanic Embarkations*			*Oceanic and overland*	
	U.S. tourists (1)	*Foreign tourists and Transmigrants* (2)	*Immigrants* (3)	*Immigrant admittances* (4)	*Emigrants* (5)
1856	23,037	5485	257,078	267,726	32,988
1857	21,018	5194	325,789	342,710	42,304
1858	21,942	4240	150,307	159,986	19,669
1859	35,182	3143	151,593	159,538	19,623
1860	26,665	4112	194,220	206,061	45,922
1861	21,059	2689	114,981	137,767	40,313
1862	22,404	3541	111,812	139,737	40,711
1863	24,235	2145	221,514	254,384	73,961
1864	28,958	280	244,728	282,738	82,040
1865	40,457	725	272,572	319,854	92,493
1866	38,822	6590	332,549	398,371	114,852
1867	40,777	5732	333,949	409,883	117,807
1868	34,421	9716	380,704	475,661	136,302
1869	31,230	14,824	421,532	523,371	149,374
1870	39,926	20,055	384,296	473,636	165,654
1871	47,750	21,300	392,259	475,495	188,941
1872	49,852	17,409	477,687	570,646	229,558
1873	49,169	15,292	423,032	509,118	204,636
1874	50,793	17,005	289,716	360,772	144,185
1875	50,932	19,540	209,129	243,664	96,420
1876	46,084	22,052	159,307	194,626	76,168
1877	42,825	20,976	138,457	170,074	65,615
1878	49,917	19,044	152,749	194,514	74,873
1879	54,345	21,711	292,948	381,064	145,106
1880	50,891	24,155	516,711	677,507	225,092
1881	52,232	25,398	698,728	879,955	266,434
1882	61,880	34,130	686,795	851,862	261,715
1883	80,449	41,328	552,770	690,569	212,595
1884	95,882	41,653	451,138	563,484	174,069
1885	94,570	34,199	377,274	441,593	136,459
1886	92,044	25,127	444,006	540,054	167,580
1887	96,756	23,260	553,853	695,108	216,481
1888	91,037	21,947	524,691	654,872	204,359

(continued)

Table 1 (continued)

Year	*Oceanic Embarkations*			*Oceanic and overland*	
	U.S. tourists	*Foreign tourists and Transmigrants*	*Immigrants*	*Immigrant admittances*	*Emigrants*
	(1)	*(2)*	*(3)*	*(4)*	*(5)*
1889	87,168	22,012	471,908	594,319	185,921
1890	91,277	20,698	527,898	671,549	339,522
1891	93,486	20,583	609,477	756,820	487,536
1892	96,173	31,653	574,691	684,677	441,506
1893	55,449	48,117	533,724	599,172	386,794
1894	83,459	23,928	262,707	309,937	197,581
1895	102,307	27,244	346,208	388,454	250,218
1896	96,418	28,022	336,531	376,056	242,245
1897	41,036	19,965	223,926	263,370	168,659
1898	24,046	19,368	238,427	281,657	180,681
1899	24,428	21,747	342,224	401,936	258,732
1900	36,312	26,778	451,961	520,376	364,930
1901	27,858	27,163	513,304	598,388	443,105
1902	33,238	28,238	730,446	853,962	634,984
1903	98,350	34,238	1,021,661	1,178,470	880,694
1904	147,891	32,520	870,261	1,043,169	775,275
1905	171,149	55,763	1,113,741	1,305,562	973,960
1906	180,028	119,283	1,301,193	1,566,319	1,170,494
1907	203,214	193,452	1,356,531	1,695,303	1,273,386
1908	208,929	94,283	432,857	605,550	441,331
1909	246,201	193,009	992,882	1,165,656	869,423
1910	261,987	173,821	1,084,071	1,358,315	1,156,590
1911	262,929	146,326	761,703	1,094,587	1,036,066
1912	261,151	206,470	1,031,830	1,413,382	1,347,901
1913	272,986	234,030	1,366,163	1,809,278	1,732,293
1914	216,975	132,286	699,673	908,291	841,474
1915	113,340	56,497	201,407	321,009	257,090
1916	82,778	63,070	276,801	411,625	338,484
1917	154,662	97,092	233,666	326,292	273,459
1918	211,956	237,461	303,265	380,795	337,078
1919	178,401	248,243	493,209	683,647	610,369

data for Americans arriving in France. My citizen-travel series for 1790–1819, averaging 1880 annually and with a maximum of 3512 (in 1806), is at a higher level than DGW indicate.

Table 2 Movement of free people: comparisons (percentage deviation of existing series from new series)

Group	*1790–1819*	*1820–1860*	*1861–1899*	*1900–1918*
(1) Citizen arrivals	–	0.94	19.78[a]	72.60
(2) Foreign tourists and transmigrants to distant lands	–	−10.46	−25.93	–
(3) Net immigration	6.42[b]	−21.26	9.82	269.78
(4) Net white immigration	3.22[c]	−27.31	–	–
(5) Immigration	–	–	−15.03[d]	−21.53

Note A negative (positive) sign means that the new series is larger (smaller) than the existing series. For discussion, see Sects. 1.1.3, 2.4, 5, 6

[a]1820–1894, 1898–1899

[b]1791–1819

[c]1800–1819

[d]1892–1899

1.2 *Departures*

Logically, the number of citizen departures is different from the number of arrivals. Some travelers may not return, due to sickness, accident, change in plans, or emigration. Therefore, except for timing issues, departures should exceed arrivals. Until 1910, official data are only arrivals. From ARCGI, for fiscal-years 1910–1920, I assemble a series of U.S.-citizen departures from U.S. ports, excluding recorded travel from Canadian or Mexican border stations (both seaports and landports). I convert to calendar years and the result is U.S.-citizen tourists for 1910–1919, as well as the numerator in an outbound/inbound (departure/arrival) series, 1910 figure. Following North (1960, p. 618) and Simon (1960, p. 664), I assume a ratio of 1.03 for 1790–1899; then I linearly interpolate the ratio for 1900–1909.[12] The product of the ratio and the arrivals series (Sect. 1.1.3) yields U.S.-citizen tourist departures (outbound) 1790–1909. The complete departures series, 1790–1919, is shown in column (1) of Table 1.

The influence of war in curbing overseas travel is obvious in low figures relative to neighborhood: 1812–1814 (War of 1812), 1861–1864 (Civil War), 1898–1899 (Spanish–American War), 1915–1917 (World War I). DGW, who perform excellent econometric work on the determinants of U.S overseas travel during our time period, take population as a trend variable—which is eminently reasonable, though real GDP might have served better. The influence of the business cycle is hard to see in the series, except for the crisis of 1893 (properly noted by Dupont and Weiss 2013, p. 324). The three authors see U.S.-citizen travel as mainly demand-determined, and deserve credit for utilizing a stock-market wealth variable geared to the upper-income traveler. It is arguable that such travelers (presumed to be the large majority of U.S.-citizen travelers) would be income and price (especially fare) inelastic or even nonsignificant, and the researchers' main results do not disappoint.

Yet the DGW analysis is subject to amendment. The upsurge of travel "in the late 1830s" is mentioned (DGW 2012, p. 146). The corresponding time segment is 1834–1840 in my series. Interestingly, fares may have played a role here. The U.S. packets were the epitome of first-class travel at the time, and their cabin fare, both eastbound and westbound is at its historical to-date minimum in 1834 (Chapter 15, Sects. 3.2.1, 3.2.2). Could there have been a "demonstration effect" or "shock effect" that resulted in higher travel? It may also be that relative price of travel would have shown greater significance had the authors used travel-specific price indexes rather than general consumer price indexes.[13] More fundamentally, the authors pay insufficient attention, at least econometrically, to the supply side of oceanic travel. Though they are very aware of technological innovation in oceanic shipping, selection of steamship share of all U.S. documented tonnage as a control for their demand equation is an extremely weak and much too-general a variable. Indeed, this variable is dropped in the later, Dupont and Weiss (2013), article. The jump in travel in the early 1850s surely is related to expanded steamship passenger service, and the increase in the mid-1880s probably is associated with enhanced amenities for first-class travel and expanded second-class opportunity.

1.3 Regional Breakdown

I follow Maffry (1939, pp. 18, 38) in disaggregating U.S.-citizen oceanic outbound travel into three destinations: Europe ("Europe and Mediterranean"), "South America and Far East," "West Indies and Central America." Maffry provides figures for 1919 (though no earlier), enabling construction of proportional shares for each area for that year. Though not actual counts, Maffry's data are the most reliable for any year of our time period. Simon (1960, p. 667) generates fiscal-year time series 1873–1894 for U.S.-citizen departures to the three destinations Europe,

Latin America, "Asia and Oceania." I assume that Europe versus non-Europe shares derived from his series are consistent with Maffry's Europe versus non-Europe shares.[14] It is also logical to assume that Simon's "Asia and Oceania" is comparable to Maffry's "Far East." Converting Simon's series to calendar year, I compute the Europe, Latin America, "Asia and Oceania" proportions for 1873–1893. Taking my cue from DGW (2008, pp. 12–14), I use official series of U.S.-citizen arrivals at various U.S. ports to obtain more data points—but I do so judiciously. The objective is to derive citizen destination-proportion series for Maffry's three regions for the entire 1790–1919 period. Underlining is used for component subperiods.

1.3.1 Europe

Thus far we have the Europe proportion of U.S.-citizen outbound travel for 1873–1893, 1919. The three main Eastern ports are New York, Boston, and Philadelphia. U.S.-citizen fiscal-year arrivals for Boston and Philadelphia are assembled for 1856–1874, 1893–1895, 1898–1905, 1906–1920.[15] The New York official series with interpolated values for 1896–1897 (Sect. 1.1.2) is used to interpolate these years for the Boston and Philadelphia series. Summing the three series, we have U.S.-citizen arrivals for the main Eastern ports for fiscal-years 1856–1874 and 1893–1920. For 1856–1874 and 1906–1920, I compile a sum series for other Eastern ports (Portland, Falmouth, New Bedford, Providence).[16] Using the main-ports series as extrapolator via the 1906 overlap, I extrapolate the other-ports series 1893–1905. I then add the main-ports and other-ports series to obtain an Eastern Ports fiscal-year series of U.S.-citizen arrivals 1856–1874, 1893–1920, which I convert to calendar year and express as a proportion of all-U.S.-ports official U.S.-citizen arrivals (Sect. 1.1.3). Using this series, I interpolate the Europe proportion of U.S.-citizen departures 1894–1918 between 1893 and 1919. Thus there is the Europe proportion 1873–1919. For 1856–1864, I set the Europe proportion of U.S.-citizen arrivals equal to the Eastern Ports proportion. Then I linearly interpolate the Europe proportion 1865–1872 between 1864 and 1873.[17] Thus we have the Europe proportion 1856–1919.

For 1790–1855, I extrapolate the Europe share of U.S.-citizen departures via the Europe share of U.S. oceanic trade, the latter share constructed for 1790–1856 via an involved process.[18] The series is a logical extrapolator—consistent with the 1790–1819 extrapolation of U.S.-citizen arrivals (Sect. 1.1.3), and bearing in mind that travelers are not only for tourism but also for business. The Europe proportion is projected back to 1790 via the 1856 overlap with the extrapolator series.

1.3.2 Oceanic Non-Europe

The U.S-citizen proportion for oceanic non-Europe equals unity less the Europe proportion, but the non-Europe share requires disaggregation.

Far East: I begin with the U.S.-citizen proportion for 1873–1893 via Simon above, and consider extrapolation via U.S.-citizen arrivals at Western ports.[19] While individual-port counts begin in 1856, only two Western ports recorded citizen arrivals prior to 1906: San Francisco 1868–1874, 1893–1920 (linearly interpolating 1896–1897), Puget Sound 1868–1874. Therefore citizen arrivals in all Western ports may be taken as zero 1790–1867 fiscal years, translating to 1790–1866 calendar years. And, by inference, the Far East proportion of citizen arrivals is also zero 1790–1866.

Seattle arrivals are recorded 1906–1920. I extrapolate to 1868–1874 and 1893–1905 via the 1906 overlap with San Francisco. San Diego and Portland are each positive only for a few years within 1906–1920; I assume their arrivals are zero for all other years. Summing the five ports, we have the fiscal-year arrivals series for Western Ports 1790–1867 (zero), 1868–1874, 1893–1920. Converting to calendar year and dividing by all-U.S.-ports official U.S.-citizen arrivals, we obtain the Western Port proportion of U.S.-citizen arrivals positive 1867–1873, 1893–1919. The series does not behave conducive to serve as interpolator—except that, over 1893–1919, it reaches a maximum in 1918. Therefore I set the Far East proportion equal to the Western Ports proportion 1918–1919, and linearly interpolate Far East 1867–1872 and 1894–1917. Thus we have the Far East proportion 1790–1919, with 1790–1866 zero.

Latin America: Note that, in terms of the citizen-arrivals data, Latin America is composed of South America, Central America, and West Indies. We have the Latin America proportion 1873–1893 from Simon. For 1919, using Maffry's figures, I compute the share of "South America and Far East" *plus* "West Indies and Central America," and subtract the Far East proportion per above. For 1856–1873, 1893–1919, I compute other-ports proportion of U.S.-citizen arrivals as one *minus* Eastern Ports and Western ports proportions. Using this computed series, I interpolate the Latin America proportion 1894–1918 and extrapolate it 1856–1872 via the 1873 overlap.

South America: For 1919, the South America proportion of oceanic citizen tourists is the Maffry "South America and Far East" proportion *minus* the Far East proportion. For 1856–1918, I extrapolate South America via the 1919 overlap with the Latin America proportion; and for 1790–1855 via the 1856 overlap with the South America share of U.S. oceanic trade, the last series not so easily obtained.[20] (Recall from above that, prior to 1867, the "Far East" proportion of "South America and Far East" is zero.)

South America and Far East: sum of "South America" and "Far East" proportions.

West Indies and Central America: one *minus* sum of Europe and "South America and Far East" proportions.

1.3.3 Comparisons and Allocation

The three component-series of U.S.-citizen departures are graphed as proportions in Fig. 1. The preponderant share of Europe as destination stands out, reaching a peak in 1864 (at 99%) and subject to a declining trend thereafter.[21] Though predecessor commentators lacked destination series, their intuition (Maffry 1939, pp. 8–9) or direct use of port series (DGW 2008, pp. 12–14; 2012, p. 145; Dupont and Weiss 2013, p. 322, note 7) permitted them to see the broad outlines of this behavior.[22]

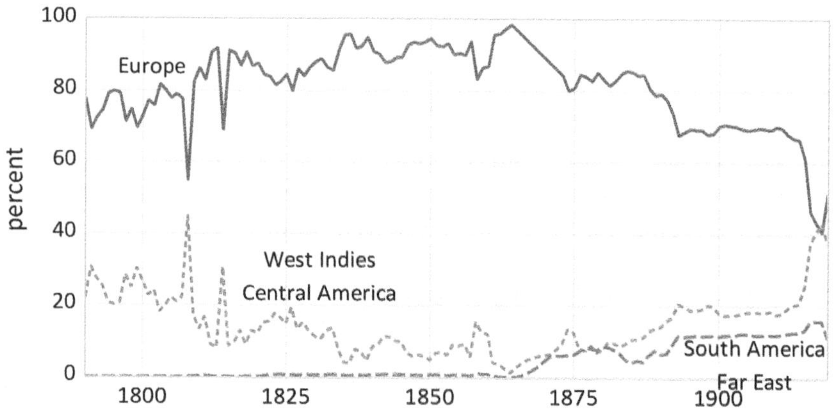

Fig. 1 Destination of U.S. Oceanic tourists, 1790–1919. *Note* Each series is the percentage of total U.S.-citizen oceanic departures. So the three series sum to 100%

They do not comment on the effect of war. In 1808, Europe's share falls to 55%, a reflection of U.S. policy that embargoed shipping—and thus oceanic travel as well as trade, though the former is not mentioned in the literature.[23] The deleterious effect of war on Europe's share is seen in the relatively low figures for 1814 (69%—War of 1812) and 1916–1918 (46, 43, 41%—World War I). Interestingly, a reduction in this share did not occur during the Civil War. It is noteworthy that the "West Indies and Central America" proportion exceeds that of "South America and Far East," with but three-years' exception (1877, 1879–1880). The proximity of the former region apparently outweighed the exotic appeal and profit opportunities of the latter.

The number of U.S.-tourist departures to Europe, South America and Far East, West Indies and Central America, is the product of the region's proportion and total U.S. tourist embarkations. Thus U.S.-tourist embarkations—listed in column (1) of Table 1—are allocated to the three regions.

2 Alien Travel: Oceanic Embarkations

Various alien-travel series are required for unilateral-transfer, travel, and fare items (Chapters 10, 14–15) in the balance of payments. Official historical statistics on alien oceanic arrivals at U.S. ports (often mistermed the, narrower, "immigration") have been subject to severe criticism, and the consensus is that these arrivals are underestimated.[24] Previous authors, including North and Simon, accept the official data; but, because of access to the impressive work of later researchers, there is no excuse to do so here. Making use of both of these researchers' results and what is beneficial in official data, I generate an alien-arrivals series that is conceptually consistent over time and has no directional bias—both in contrast to the official series.

The new-series end-segments data sources (BRV and Grubb) profoundly illustrate the underestimation of official statistics. For 1900–1920, BRV (2013, p. 32) data yield a 41% negative deviation of official statistics from the authors' preferred series. For 1820–1830, Grubb (1990, p. 36) computes a 37% undercount of official statistics.[25]

2.1 *Total Embarkations*

2.1.1 1892–1919

For the purpose of generating oceanic fares, the required immigration concept is embarkations, as distinct from arrivals or admittances. BRV (2013, p. 31, Figure A) develop an annual *administrative-records* series of total (foreign-born and U.S.-born) arrivals at New York seaport (Ellis Island) consistent with their series of U.S.-born citizens.[26] Subtracting U.S.-citizen from total arrivals, one obtains alien arrivals 1892–1919.[27] To obtain alien arrivals from embarkations, BRV exclude two percent of alien passengers recorded on ship manifests, due to death or debarment. I reverse the two percent—converting back to embarkations, in lieu of arrivals or admittances. The next step, as for U.S. citizens, is to obtain comparable official series for New York and total-U.S. seaports.

Two official data series on port arrivals exist for 1892–1920. SAUS uses Bureau of Statistics data to the maximum (1892–1895), then Bureau of Immigration data. ARCGI uses Bureau of Immigration data to the maximum (1892–1920). There are three reasons for selecting SAUS for our purpose. First, for reason of backward extension (Sect. 2.1.3): Bureau of Statistics figures exist back to 1867, whereas Bureau of Immigration begins in 1892. Second, SAUS has port data for nonimmigrant aliens 1892–1920 (except for 1896–1897), whereas ARCGI has them only from 1906.

Third involves the extent to which cabin-class aliens were recorded, and the issue is controversial.[28] It is clear that the Bureau of Immigration did not include cabin immigrants in its count until 1904. However, the Bureau of Statistics generally did include cabin immigrants in its arrivals count. In this judgment I follow August Maffry, a civil servant involved in the balance of payments, who was a meticulous examiner of immigration statistics. Maffry (1939, p. 11) implicitly sees Bureau of Statistics data to be inclusive of cabin immigrants.[29] He adopts the Bureau of Statistics data for 1892–1895 (the period of overlap with the Bureau of Immigration), and (of necessity) for all earlier years. His figures for 1892–1895 are decidedly higher than Bureau of Immigration figures (*Historical Statistics* 2006, series Ad1), and the explanation is primarily the inclusion of cabin aliens (*Historical Statistics* 1975, p. 98; 2006, pp. 1–543).

Maffry (1939, p. 11) documents his figures for 1900–1903 with the note "Alien cabin passengers numbering in the respective years 65,635, 74,950, 82,055, and 64,269 and an indeterminate number *in the years just preceding* are not included [italics added]." The "years just preceding" logically mean 1896–1899, as 1896 is the first year of his use of the Bureau of Immigration data. Therefore it is logical to conclude that the SAUS port data include alien cabin passengers for 1892–1895 and earlier. Matters not for 1892–1895, because both the New York and total official data embody the same treatment of cabin passengers for any given year—while BRV data include all passengers, cabin and noncabin (steerage). Thus the alien-cabin conundrum is either solved or averted, and we have the third justification for SAUS.

So, from SAUS, for fiscal years 1892–1920, I assemble alien arrivals/admittances for New York Port and total-U.S. as the sum of immigrant and nonimmigrant arrivals/admittances.[30] The concept is arrivals 1892–1904, admittances 1905–1920.[31] We require arrivals—but again no matter, as the New York and total-U.S. official data are consistent in concept for any year, and the BRV New York series is arrivals. I convert to calendar years 1892–1919. Then, comparable to the citizen ratio in Sect. 1.1.2 and for use below, I compute the New York Port administrative/official alien "embarkations"/"arrivals/admittances" series for 1892–1919, to serve as multiplier.

The desired multiplicand is total-U.S. alien arrivals less *recorded* non-oceanic (overland and coastal) alien arrivals. So we need to eliminate three items from total-U.S. arrivals.

(1) overland overseas-arrivals (via Canada or Mexico seaports), (2) overland Canada and Mexico resident arrivals, (3) coastal Canada and Mexico resident arrivals.[32] There are two sets of pertinent data: Canada and Mexico overland, composed of (1) + (2); Canada and Mexico country-of-residence, composed of (2) + (3).[33] Taking only overland data excludes (3), taking only country-of-residence data excludes (1); summing the data sets double-counts (2). The adopted solution is a compromise. For each year, for Canada and Mexico separately, for immigrant and alien-nonimmigrant arrivals separately, I estimate "overland and coastal arrivals" as the *maximum* overland or residence figure, in effect, the maximum of "(1) + (2)" or "(2) + (3)."[34] Then, for each year 1892–1920, I obtain recorded non-oceanic alien arrivals as the sum of the four "maximum" series (Canada immigrants, Canada nonimmigrants, Mexico immigrants, Mexico nonimmigrants), convert the summed series to calendar year, and subtract it from total-U.S. alien arrivals. Applying the multiplier to the result, we have alien oceanic embarkations 1892–1919.

2.1.2 1820–1830

For Philadelphia, for 1815–1830, Grubb (1990, pp. 32; 36, col. 3) assembles a fiscal-year (end September 30) series of passenger embarkations at foreign ports, derived from "the manuscripts of passenger manifests collected by the local customs officers for the port of Philadelphia." The series appears comparable to the BRV data, except that U.S.-born passengers cannot be separated out. Fortunately for our purpose, Grubb (1990, p. 33) argues convincingly that equating foreign-born with total passengers is a legitimate abstraction. I assemble the comparable official series for Philadelphia for 1820–1860.[35] The Grubb/official alien-embarkations ratio yields a multiplier series for fiscal years 1820–1830. The multiplier for calendar-year 1830 is the ratio of the Grubb (1990, p. 46) figure to the calendar-year-converted official series.

To develop the multiplicand, begin with total-U.S. official alien passenger embarkations (technically, arrivals) for fiscal years 1820–1831, found in Maffry (1939, p. 6) and many other sources. It is reasonable to assume British North America (BNA, future Canada) and Mexico alien arrivals are non-oceanic (coastal or overland); so they are subtracted.[36] Also, to the extent that transit overland arrivals are recorded, they must be excluded.[37] There are such arrivals via Canada for 1821–1823, and they are subtracted.[38] The constructed series, alien passenger embarkations for all U.S. ports, is the multiplicand for fiscal-years 1820–1830; its calendar-year conversion is the multiplicand for 1830. Converting the resulting (multiplier-*times*-multiplicand) fiscal-year series to calendar year, we have alien oceanic embarkations for 1820–1830.[39]

2.1.3 1831–1891

With alien oceanic embarkations constructed for 1820–1830 and 1892–1919, we require a series to interpolate the missing, intermediate, years. The 1831-to-1854 official arrivals/embarkations series in Maffry is extended to 1855–1905 by summing immigrants and nonimmigrant aliens (Maffry 1939, pp. 6, 11).[40]

Several corrections are required. First, the Maffry figure for 1831 excludes April, May, and August (Cohn 2009, p. 18). Using Grubb's (1990, p. 46) Philadelphia quarterly series, I compute the share of the missing months as 41%, implying a recorded proportion of 59%, increasing the Maffry figure from 22,633 to 38,672.[41] Second, the fourth quarter of 1832 incorporates data only for Boston/Charlestown and New York and does not distinguish citizens from aliens (William J. Bromwell

1856, p. 73; Maffry 1939, p. 6, note 4; Hutchinson 1958, p. 977). I use the average ratio of Boston/Charlestown and New York arrivals to all arrivals for fiscal-year (end September 30) 1832 and calendar year 1833 (Bromwell 1856, pp. 72, 77) to adjust Maffry's figure upward from 7303 to 11,341. Then I allocate that total to citizens and aliens according to their 1832–1833 average shares.

Cohn (2009, p. 22) considers the above to be the only important cases of lack of coverage whether by month or by port.[42] However, third, San Francisco arrivals are lacking for the fourth quarter of 1850 and the years 1851–1853. I adopt a simpler estimation technique than that of Donald Schaefer (1994, p. 65). For 1852–1853, making the assumption of no citizen arrivals and with all data pertaining to San Francisco, I estimate alien arrivals as the product of Chinese arrivals (per Shay) and year-1854 official/Chinese (per Bromwell/Shay) arrivals.[43] For 1851, I average the official 1850 (year-end September 30) and estimated 1852 (calendar year) figures. For fourth-quarter 1850, the San Francisco proportion of total-U.S. arrivals is taken as the average of the 1850 (year-end September 30) and 1851 (calendar year) proportions, and San Francisco arrivals are estimated accordingly. Then San Francisco is added to the official U.S. series for 1850 (fourth quarter) and 1851–1853. Finally, the series is converted to calendar year 1830–1892.

The next step is to omit recorded Canada (or BNA) and Mexico resident arrivals. These fiscal-year series 1820–1893 (assembled in Sect. 2.1.1, per note 33) are converted to calendar years 1820–1892 and subtracted.[44] Then recorded third-country (transit) arrivals from Canada (there are none from Mexico) need assembling and deduction. Hutchinson (1958, pp. 997–1003) identifies years of recorded inland arrivals over 1820–1893.[45] I use his compilation and Department of State Reports to restrict inland arrivals to third-country aliens.[46] This transit-arrivals series is converted to calendar year and subtracted.

The resulting series is what we want, provided the concept is embarkations. For years based on arrivals, deaths at sea need to be added. Hutchinson (1958, pp. 970–972, 993, 998–999) argues convincingly that the Bromwell (1820–1855) data are generally for embarkations and that this is uniformly true for the Department of State series (1820–1867), with exception years 1859–1860, 1864. The entire Bureau of Statistics series (1868–1895) is assumed arrivals, with no evidence to the contrary (Hutchinson 1958, pp. 979–980, 994). Arrivals are embarkations *times* the proportion of embarked aliens who survived the voyage;

so embarkations are arrivals *divided by* this proportion. The latter formula is used to convert arrivals to embarkations for 1859–1860, 1864, and 1868–1892. The survival proportion is one *minus* the proportion of embarked aliens who died at sea, series constructed in the Appendix (Sect. A).

Using the resulting series as interpolator, alien oceanic embarkations are estimated for 1831–1891 between 1830 and 1892. We now have these embarkations 1820–1919.

2.1.4 1787–1819

Grabbe (1989, p. 190) states: "There are countless relevant scholarly publications in which 1820 was selected as starting point based on the claim that no important immigration took place before then, but really chosen, it can be assumed, because the official American immigration statistics are only available starting from that year." True, scholars have long been frustrated with the lack of immigration data prior to 1820. So they presented and modified pre-1820 estimates, whether for individual years, as series, or for periods of a decade or longer.[47] However, "All estimates of immigration for the period before 1820 are purely conjectural...A term repeatedly used by writers on the subject" (McClelland and Zeckhauser 1982, pp. 32; 195, note 70). To their credit, McClelland and Zeckhauser (1982, pp. 38–42, 98, 100) construct a model that makes effective use of earlier writings on the subject, resulting in an annual series for 1800–1819. *Historical Statistics* (2006, pp. 1–546) comments that their estimates, though "crude...[and] very rough," "are considered the best available."

In fact, the McClelland–Zeckhauser series has been superseded by the 1783–1820 annual estimates of Grabbe (2001, pp. 85, 93–94), "the current authority on the 1783-1820 period" (Cohn 2009, p. 17, note 8).[48] Cohn selects Grabbe over McClelland-Zeckhauser for two reasons: its later development and its use of passenger lists. From my standpoint, there are three additional reasons to prefer the Grabbe series. First, Gabbe provides figures for a longer period. Second, in contrast to McClelland–Zeckhauser's orientation to arrivals and (worse) *net* immigration, Grabbe's concept is embarkations, as his series is based mainly on passenger lists (of Philadelphia port) and U.K. emigration data.[49] Third, Grabbe generates his total "from the bottom up," that is, via summing estimates by emigration region. In this he differs from all previous authors and enables adjustment of his figures to fit the concept of *all* alien embarkations (immigrants and nonimmigrants).

Using Grabbe's (2001, p. 93) regional series, for 1787–1920, I sum immigration from Great Britain, Ireland, Netherlands and Northern Germany, France (counted twice), Caribbean (counted twice), and all other regions. The reason that the France and Caribbean figures are doubled is that Grabbe (1989, pp. 193, 198; 2001, pp. 49–51) takes only half the arrivals from France and Caribbean, deeming the other half to be nonimmigrants.[50] In contrast, the concept here is *all* alien oceanic embarkations. Another adjustment is deletion of transit immigration via BNA, included in Great Britain and Ireland series for 1815–1820.[51] Finally, I use the adjusted Grabbe figures to extrapolate the existing 1820–1919 alien oceanic embarkations back to 1787, via the year-1820 overlap.

The series of alien oceanic embarkations for 1790–1919 is obtainable in Table 1 as the sum of columns (2) and (3), which are embarkations of nonimmigrants and immigrants.

2.2 *Immigrants Versus Nonimmigrants*

Nonimmigrants are variously described as "aliens not intending to remain in the country" (Maffry 1939, p. 10), "aliens who come to the United States for a temporary period" (*Historical Statistics* 2006, pp. 1–536), "alien visitors," "temporary visitors," "temporary arrivals," "transient aliens," "transients," and, most comprehensively, "foreign tourists, merchants, and others on business, and those in transit" (Cohn 2009, p. 21). I separate out nonimmigrants in alien oceanic embarkations by developing a series of the share of nonimmigrants in alien oceanic embarkations. For 1892–1919 the share is the ratio of nonimmigrant to total-U.S. arrivals/admittances, per SAUS (Sect. 2.1.1). From Maffry (1939, p. 11), nonimmigrant aliens and immigrant aliens for 1854–1892 are obtained for fiscal year, converted to calendar year, and the nonimmigrant/"nonimmigrant *plus* immigrant" ratio constitutes the nonimmigrant proportion for 1854–1891.[52]

Prior to 1854, there is no distinction of nonimmigrants from immigrants in official statistics. One can only guess at the nonimmigrant proportion, or extrapolate it into the past. All estimates are in the one-to-two percent range.[53] I calculate the average proportion for 1854–1858 as slightly outside that range, at 2.135 percent, and project it to 1787–1853. Then, for 1787–1919, nonimmigrant alien oceanic embarkations are computed annually as the product of the share and total embarkations, with immigrant embarkations the residual. Thus columns (2) and (3) in Table 1.

2.3 *Determinants*

The 1790–1914 time period was an era of "free migration," which came to an end only with World War I and the restrictive U.S. legislation that followed. There was a trend "pull" of immigration into the United States, emanating from long-term elements, such as a high land/population ratio, a growing economy, and enhanced supply of transatlantic transportation.

But what determined the ebbs and flows—or, as some write, the "timing"—of immigration? The works of John D. Gould (1979) and Timothy J. Hatton and Jeffrey G. Williamson (1998 2005) provide important insights and reviews of the literature, but these studies are not specific to the United States as destination. Looking at alien travel in general, "columns (2) and (3) combined" in Table 1, war played an important role—especially evident in the relatively low numbers in 1813–1814, 1861–1862, and 1915–1917. Also, Grabbe (1989, p. 198) demonstrates war as an explanatory variable of immigration 1783–1820.

For the antebellum period in general, Cohn (2009, chs. 2–4) provides insightful comments, especially concerning the jump in immigration "around 1830" (Cohn 2009, p. 47). He sees the higher immigration in 1815–1819 as a "push" from poor crops in Europe consequent to an Indonesian volcanic eruption. He cautions that not all factors are either "push" (reduced economic opportunities in Europe) or "pull" (expansionary phase of U.S. cycle), though the high levels 1846–1854 clearly result from a "push" (especially the Irish potato famine). In general, Cohn and other researchers note that attention must also be paid to U.S. and British laws ("Passenger Laws") setting limits on number of passengers per ship space tonnage (promulgated, then repealed or nonbinding), European policies discouraging emigration (imposed, then removed), immigration remittances (trend growth but with a cycle), internal U.S. attitudes/politics regarding immigration (rise of "nativism"—negative effect on immigration), and the cost of oceanic transportation (dominant-negative trend, thanks to innovations in supply, such as brokers arranging passage, the packet, and the steamship—but later subject to the counterforce of collusion among steamship lines).[54]

2.4 *Tourists and Distant-Land Transmigrants versus Canada and West Indies Transmigrants*

Following Simon, I separate out transmigrants (transits) to Canada and West Indies from the rest of oceanic nonimmigrant aliens (tourists and transmigrants to distant lands). Again I compute the pertinent share series: ratio of "arrivals in transit to Canada and West Indies" to "total oceanic tourists and transmigrants." For fiscal-years 1873–1895, the ratio is calculated from Simon (1960, pp. 662–663: column (7) divided by the sum of columns (2) and (4)). The ratio for 1906–1920 requires an involved computation. Marian R. Davis (1931, p. 656) provides series of (A) alien tourist arrivals and (B) alien transit arrivals. From ARCGI 1906–1920, table "Nonimmigrant Aliens Admitted," I assemble the series (C) oceanic alien transit arrivals to Canada, (D) oceanic alien transit arrivals to West Indies, (E) overland tourist arrivals, (F) overland transit arrivals.[55] For fiscal-years 1906–1920, the desired ratio is computed as [(C) + (D)]/[(A) + (B) - (E) - (F)]. I linearly interpolate 1896–1905, and convert to calendar years 1873–1919. For 1787–1872, I take the average ratio 1873–1875.

Transmigrants to Canada and West Indies are the product of the ratio and nonimmigrants, with oceanic foreign tourists and transmigrants to distant lands the residual. The share of foreign tourists and distant-land transmigrants ("complement" of the generated ratio—meaning "one *minus*" the ratio) is plotted for 1870–1919 in Fig. 2.[56] The decline from the 1893 peak to 1906 is noticeable, as is the cyclical behavior thereafter—but I have no obvious explanation.

Foreign tourists and transmigrants to distant lands are compared with the corresponding North–Simon series in row (2) of Table 2.[57] North–Simon is below the new series in averages, but at the end subperiods (pre-1840 and late 1890s) the divergence is in the other direction.

2.5 *Immigrants: Europe Versus Rest of World*

I develop the ratio of Europe to total immigration. For 1820–1920, I assemble the following immigration series from *Historical Statistics* (2006): total, Europe, other or unknown, Canada, Mexico.[58] I increase Europe immigration with the product of (Europe/total) and "other or unknown"[59]: Oceanic immigration is computed as total *minus* Canada and Mexico.[60] Europe and total are converted to calendar year.[61] Their

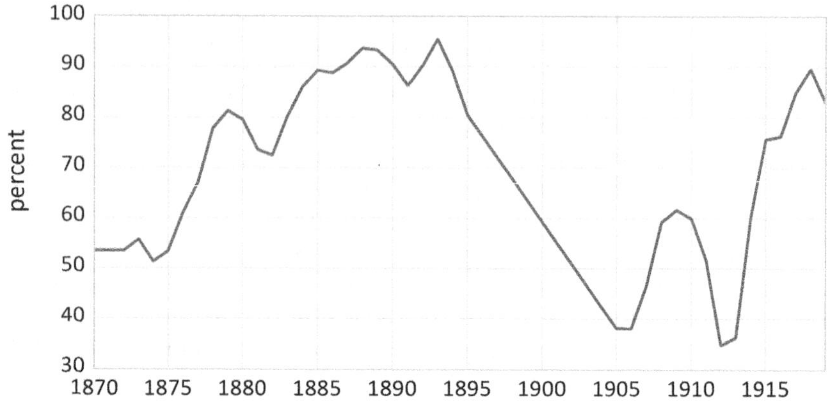

Fig. 2 Foreign tourists and distant-land transmigrants share, 1870–1919. *Note* The series is the "foreign-tourists and distant-land transmigrants" percent of "total oceanic tourists and transmigrants." The remainder is the percent share of "transmigrants to Canada and the West Indies"

ratio is the Europe share of oceanic immigration, 1820–1919. I use Grabbe's figures to compute the share for 1787–1819 (see Sect. 2.1.4).[62] Europe oceanic embarkations are the product of this share and total immigrant oceanic embarkations; rest-of-world oceanic embarkations are the residual.

The Europe oceanic immigration proportion is graphed in Fig. 3. Europe's share has a high level, averaging 87% over 1790–1919; but there are rare occurrences when the share falls precipitously—to 26% in 1798 and 12% in 1814. There are only five other years where the proportion is below 50%—four before 1814; the other, 1918. All these exceptions are related to war. Yet, surprisingly and again, there is no noticeable reduction in Europe's share during the Civil War.

3 Transit Immigration

The focus for transit immigrants is the Northern border; there was little transit through Mexico.[63] Both contemporary observers and later scholars considered transit immigration via BNA (or Canada) as a significant omission from official statistics.[64]

Fig. 3 Europe Oceanic Immigration Shares, 1790–1919. *Note* The series is the Europe percent of total oceanic immigration embarkations, with the rest-of-world share the residual

Per Grabbe, transit immigration is zero 1787–1814 and the sum of the British and Irish flow 1815–1820 (Sect. 2.1.4). From data in ARCGI (1894, p. 19), I calculate transit immigration for 1893 as a monthly average. The series in Imre Ferenczi (1929, pp. 362–363) is taken for 1853–1856, 1866–1891. Thus we have transit immigration via BNA for 1787–1820, 1853–1856, 1866–1891, 1893.

Beyond 1893, I adopt the BRV (2013, p. 44) approach: "throughout [1900-1920] we assume 40% of arrivals into Canada are *en route* to the US."[65] In my use, the assumption is weaker: a constant percentage, not necessarily at 40%. Total immigrant arrivals in Canada and arrivals from the United States for 1904–1919 are obtained from Malcolm C. Urquhart and Kenneth A. H. Buckley (1965, series A254 and A337). The difference constitutes oceanic arrivals. Summing immigrant arrivals from the United Kingdom and the other non-U.S. countries yields oceanic immigrant arrivals for 1891–1904 (*Canada Year Book* 1936, p. 186), which are transformed to calendar years 1891–1903. This gives us Canadian oceanic arrivals 1891–1919. I use this series as an interpolator for transit immigration 1892. Then transit immigration for 1894–1919 is estimated using Canadian oceanic immigrant arrivals as extrapolator via the 1893 overlap. So we now have transit immigration for 1787–1820, 1853–1856, 1866–1919.

Immigration to Canada through the ports of Quebec and Montreal (thus oceanic immigrant arrivals) for 1827–1866 are in Ferenczi (1929, p. 360). For 1820–1826, I adopt 11,000 as an annual figure.[66] For four subperiods of 1820–1861, McClelland and Zeckhauser (1982, p. 95) estimate the proportion of immigrants arriving at Montreal and Quebec City that re-emigrate to the United States. I annualize their numbers and extend the 1853–1860 figure to 1866. Then "proxy transit immigration" for 1820–1866 is the product of the McClelland–Zeckhauser proportion and Canadian oceanic immigrant arrivals. Using this proxy as interpolator, I estimate U.S. transit immigration 1821–1852 between 1820 and 1853, 1857–1865 between 1856 and 1866. Thus we have transit immigration for the full period 1787–1919.

4 Canada and Mexico Immigration

Even though land-border stations were complete in 1908, the jump in both Canadian and Mexican official immigrants 1908 to 1909 (*Historical Statistics* 2006, series Ad163, Ad164) suggests that this immigration was substantially undercounted even in fiscal-year 1908 (but not thereafter). I take the average ratio of Canada admittances to fiscal-year-converted oceanic immigrant embarkations for 1909–1911 and use it as a multiplicative factor to adjust official Canada admittances for 1892–1908.[67] The result (converted to calendar year) yields Canada admittances 1892–1919. For 1787–1820, I take Grabbe's (2001, p. 93, column C) BNA series.

My judgment is that the Bureau of Statistics (1903, p. 4350—slightly different from *Historical Statistics* 2006, series Ad163) recorded BNA-resident arrivals for fiscal-years 1870–1885 are reasonably complete, and their calendar-year equivalent gives us also 1870–1885.

Then I allocate Edward Jarvis' (1872, p. 456—noted by Hutchinson 1958, pp. 975–976) unrecorded "Provincials" (as distinct from "Europeans") immigration numbers annually 1821–1859 via the Bureau of Statistics (1903, p. 4346) series.[68] Finally, I use oceanic immigrant embarkations (Table 1, column (3)) to interpolate 1860–1869 and 1886–1891.

Mexican admittances 1909–1919 are from official data (*Historical Statistics* 2006, series Ad164). For earlier years, data on Mexican immigration are incomplete and unreliable.[69] Further, Mexican immigration is sui generis, not reliably extrapolated via official total immigration. So, for 1850–1908, I take a different tack. I obtain the inter-Census decadal change in Mexico-born U.S. population by first-differencing 1850–1920 Census data (*Historical Statistics* 2006, series Ad431) and multiplying the change by an estimated immigration/"population-change" ratio.[70] The result is inter-Census immigration. I convert the end-points (Census-year) figures to calendar year, and allocate intra-decadal immigration equally among years. I assume zero Mexican immigration prior to 1850, although undoubtedly there was some.

5 Immigrant Admittances

Immigrant admittances are the sum of three components. The first is oceanic immigration admittances, obtained by multiplying oceanic immigration embarkations (Table 1, column (3)) both by the proportion of embarkations who survived the voyage (one *minus* the proportion who died on the voyage), thus obtaining arrivals, and by the proportion of arrivals who were admitted (one *minus* the proportion who were debarred).[71] The second component is transit immigration (Sect. 3); the third, Canada and Mexico immigration (Sect. 4). Immigrant admittances are listed in column (4) of Table 1.

Naturally, the same forces that affect oceanic embarkations also affect admittances, though not to the same degree and with Mexico and Canada included in the "push." An additional influence is legislation. Beginning with the Chinese Exclusion Act of 1882, a series of laws gradually restricted immigration. None had a measurable effect on the aggregate; but the stage was set for the quota system instituted in the 1921 legislation.[72] It is also unlikely that alien head taxes, state and federal (Chapter 10, Sect. 1.6), affected aggregate immigration noticeably, though they might have influenced the place of landing.

A geographic division of immigration admittances is exhibited in Fig. 4. "Europe" is the European share per Sect. 2.5, "overland" the share of Canadian and Mexican residents, with oceanic non-Europe (not graphed) the residual. For the entire 1790–1919 period, the European proportion averages 83%, Canada and Mexico five percent, and oceanic non-Europe 12%. War plays an important role in replacing Europe's share by non-Europe, and also by overland in World War I. In earlier years, the Canada–Mexico proportion exceeds ten percent in only eight years and never reaches 20%. In contrast, the oceanic non-Europe share (approximately the complement of Europe) is above 25% in 20 years spanning 1790–1815.

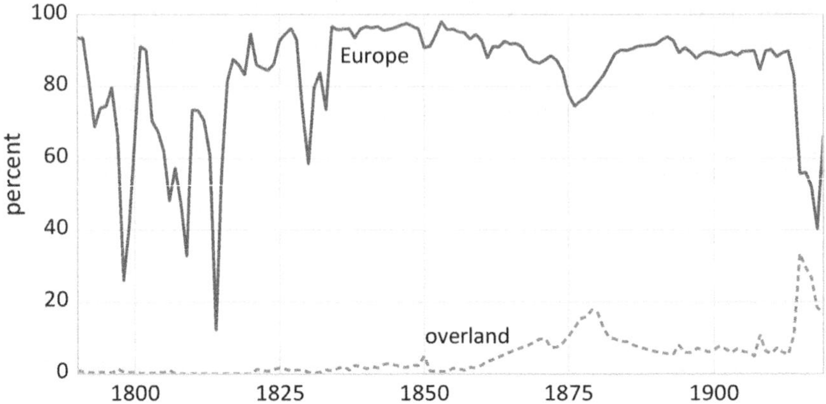

Fig. 4 Immigration-Admittance Shares, 1790–1919. *Note* "Europe" is the Europe percent of total immigration admittances, "overland" the "Canada and Mexico residents" percent. The residual (from 100 percent) is the oceanic non-Europe share

Using different assumptions from mine to make corrections to the official figures, Davis (1931, p. 657) presents a "consistent" immigration series for 1892–1919. I compare her calendar-year-converted series with my series. The percent deviation of Davis from the new immigration admittances is shown as period averages in row (5) of Table 2. Davis is substantially lower than the new series. Indeed, for only one year (1908) does Davis has the higher figure. This result is in line with the BRV (2013, p. 32) finding that immigration is underestimated officially.

6 Emigration

Official emigrant data do not begin until 1908. However, steamship data on all passenger departures (emigrants, citizen-tourists, alien visitors) exist from 1868.[73] These numbers have been criticized for incompleteness and inconsistencies.[74] Nevertheless, they—along with other series—have been used by scholars to derive alien departures/arrivals (emigration/immigration) ratios, also termed return-migration or outmigration rates. I do the opposite! I develop time-consistent ratio series from the work of previous authors and use the series to convert my immigration figures into emigration.

I begin with oceanic outmigration rates derived from the majestic research of BRV, who make creative use of Census data along with their immigration estimates. I recompute their outmigration rates for the 1900–1910 and 1910–1920 periods to exclude Canada (BRV 2013, p. 37). For 1870–1880, 1880–1890, 1890–1900, 1900–1910, I take the Simon Kuznets and Ernest Rubin (1954, p. 39) ratios; for 1850–1860 and 1860–1870, ratios that are extensions of Kuznets-Rubin (Walter D. Kamphoefner 1991, p. 295)—all adjusted to the BRV level via 1900–1910 overlap.[75]

Before the steamship, the oceanic voyage was long and generally arduous; so "few actual immigrants–as opposed to merchants or soldiers–anticipated returning to Europe, and the evidence shows that few did" (Cohn 2009, p. 125).[76] Based on expressions of this consensus view, I assign a return rate of 1.07% prior to 1840.[77] For the 1840s, the two adjacent decades are averaged. In general, I convert endpoints to calendar year (via weighted averaging of adjacent Census-period figures), but do not alter the stepwise nature of the numbers.[78]

The emigration/immigration ratio for Canadian residents is simpler constructed. BRV (2013, p. 37) figures are used for 1901–1919, with 1910 obtained by averaging the two Census-year figures. Linking to the oceanic ratio on the basis of the 1901 overlap yields 1851–1900. I project the 1851 figure to all earlier years, on the grounds that steamships replacing sailing ships was a minor issue for Canada.

Both the oceanic and Canadian emigration/immigration ratios have strong stepwise upward trends, ranging from 1.1 and 6.3% in 1787 to 98.6 and 43.2% in 1919. The 1900–1914 oceanic average (83%) is almost three times Keeling's (2012, p. 201) "migrant return rate" of 29%. BRV emphasize, and their results show, that both emigration and immigration have traditionally been underestimated. Applying the oceanic emigration/immigration ratio to Europe and to oceanic non-Europe immigration admittances (Sect. 5), the Canadian ratio to Canada–Mexico ("overland") immigration (Sect. 4), I obtain emigration to the three regions. Their sum is total emigrants, column (5) in Table 1. Figure 5 exhibits the emigration shares of Europe and overland (again with oceanic non-Europe, the residual, ungraphed). Except for scattered periods for overland, the graph is similar to admittances (Fig. 4).

Fig. 5 Emigration shares 1790–1919. *Note* "Europe" is the Europe percent of total emigration, "overland" the "Canada and Mexico" percent. The residual (from 100 percent) is the oceanic non-Europe share

7 Net Immigration

The conceptually most-comprehensive immigration measure in *Historical Statistics* (2006, series Aa13) is a composite series of *net* immigration inclusive of slave imports. My comparable series is total immigration admittances (Table 1, column (4)) *minus* total emigration (column (5)) *plus* slave imports, whether or not earning ship revenue (Officer and Williamson 2020, sum of columns (2) and (7) in Table A1.I, and column (1) in Table A1.II).[79] Expressing both series in years ending June 30, the percentage deviation of *Historical Statistics* from the new series is shown as period averages in row (3) of Table 2. The huge positive divergence of *Historical Statistics* in 1900–1918 (especially in 1911–1918) is due primarily to severe undercounting of emigrants, as BRV observe. On the other hand, *Historical Statistics* has a substantial shortfall for 1820–1860.

Removing slave imports, my net immigration is compared to McClelland–Zeckhauser (1982, p. 113) "white immigration," in row (4) of Table 2. The traditional-series underestimate for 1820–1860 is repeated (and even slightly greater). This is not surprising, as McClelland–Zeckhauser is the primary (though not the only) source of the *Historical Statistics* series for that period.

Appendix: Deaths on Voyage and Debarments

A. Deaths on Voyage

1875–1919: While deaths on voyage are conventionally ascribed to "immigrants," I express deaths as a percentage of all alien embarked passengers. The U.S. series begins 1875–1892, with deaths computed as the ratio of "deaths on voyage" to the sum of "immigrant arrivals," "nonimmigrant-alien arrivals," and "deaths on voyage" (data in *Quarterly Reports of the Chief of the Bureau of Statistics* [QRCBS]). The average for 1888–1892 is projected to 1893–1919.

1820–1860: Raymond L. Cohn kindly provided unpublished series of percentage deaths for New York and New Orleans arrivals.[80] I generate a corresponding series for Philadelphia by multiplying the New York series by the Philadelphia/New York 1820–1860 average death-rate ratio (Cohn 2003, p. 9). Using data in Bromwell (1856) and Bureau of Statistics (1893, p. 86), I derive the calendar-year shares of passenger embarkations for the three ports, and use these proportions as weights to derive the U.S. series for 1820–1860.

1787–1819: For 1787–1805, I adopt Grubb's (2011, pp. 73–74) figure of 3.83% for German immigrants to America, and obtain 1806–1819 via linear interpolation.

1861–1874: The New York death rate for 1864–1875 (except for 1874) is derived from data in Friedrich Kapp (1870, p. 241) and *Annual Report of the Commissioners of Emigration of the State of New York* [ARCENY].[81] Using New York as interpolator, I estimate the U.S. rate for 1864–1873 between 1860 and 1875, then linearly interpolate 1874. The Census data in Hutchinson (1958, p. 972) seem complete for 1860–1862, but definitely not for later years. So I use these data to extrapolate the U.S. rate to 1861–1862 via the 1860 overlap, then linearly interpolate 1863.

Results and Determinants: The series is plotted in Fig. 6. Call it a trend or not, but the death rate fell from over 3 3/4% in the 1790s to almost 1/20th of one percent in the 1890s. The low variation prior to 1820 is a consequence of lack of direct data. There are noticeable spikes over 1820–1874. The literature emphasizes contagious disease as the cause of deaths on arrival ships, though one should not exclude accidents, suicide, and even homicide. Outbreaks of disease and therefore deaths were episodic, but there is a clear declining trend beginning midcentury, and associated with steamships replacing sailing vessels. Interestingly, researchers believe

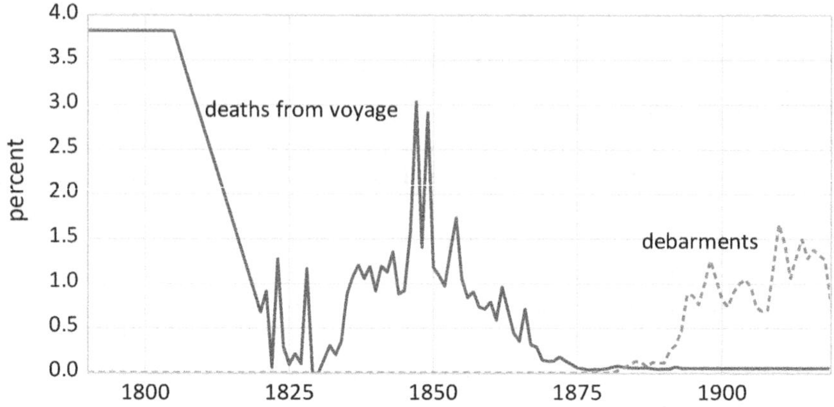

Fig. 6 Deaths from Voyage, and debarments, 1790–1919. *Note* "Deaths from voyage" and "debarments" are each expressed as the percent of alien arrivals at U.S. ports

that U.S. and British "Passenger Acts," legislation mandating shipboard health and safety practices, had little effect.[82]

B. Debarments

For 1892–1894, 1906–1920, the number of debarments at U.S. seaports is obtained directly from ARCGI.[83] For 1895–1905, the data include Canadian ports; debarments are obtained by applying the U.S. share of total alien arrivals (for 1905, admittances) at U.S. and Canadian ports. I convert to calendar year. For 1892–1894, using ARCGI data, I compute the average U.S./New York debarment ratio, which multiplies New York Port debarments 1882–1889 (ARCENY 1890, p. 11) to obtain U.S. debarments for these years. There is a series of immigrants "barred and returned" in QRCBS (1893, p. 411) for 1888–1891, and obtainable from ARCGI for 1892–1893. I express the series in calendar years 1889–1892 and use it to interpolate debarments 1890–1891.

From QRCBS (1893, p. 392) and ARCGI (1892–1920), I assemble a series of alien arrivals at U.S. seaports, consistent with debarments, and convert to calendar years 1882–1919. Finally, I express debarments as the percent of alien arrivals at U.S. ports, and graph the series in Fig. 6. Prior to 1882, there are no debarment data, and perforce zero debarments are assumed. Beginning 1884, the debarment rate exceeds the deaths-at-sea rate.

In an era of "free immigration," immigration admittances were restricted by debarments, and debarments were determined by policy.[84] There were two sets of legislation, each of which began to solidify in 1882: laws restricting Chinese immigration (beginning with the Chinese Exclusion Act of May 6), and laws specifying general grounds for exclusion (beginning with the Immigration Act of August 3).[85] The two sets conjoined in the Immigration Act of February 5, 1917, which banned immigration of Asians on geographic grounds. The Act of March 3, 1891 expanded classes of persons subject to debarment and the Act of 1917 even more so. It is no surprise that debarments jump in 1891; but the effect of the 1917 legislation is masked by wartime.

Notes

1. Cohn (1992, pp. 59–60) generates reasons for U.S. travel on sailing ships 1836–1853 as 40% tourism, 25% business, 24% business-tourism mix, nine percent family retrieval, and two percent government business. However, regarding steamship travel in the late 1840s and 1850s, he argues that most U.S. passengers were traveling on business.
2. There are two opinions in contrast to Maffry. Hutchinson (1958, pp. 970, 973–974) at first is in agreement with Maffry that birthplace was the country criterion but then argues that, at some point, the criterion might have become permanent residency; so, in effect, U.S. travelers would incorporate native-born citizens, naturalized citizens, and non-citizen permanent residents. Cohn (1992, pp. 47–51) suggests that "current citizenship" may have been the criterion as early as 1836–but his conclusion is "tentative," as based on analysis of a small sample of family travelers.
3. Imran Rasul kindly provided the Excel file containing the series. The authors correct the series for missing or incorrect data. As do BRV, I make the reasonable assumption that, for citizens, "embarkations," "arrivals," and "admittances" are all equal.
4. The source is *Statistical Abstract of the United States* [SAUS] (1890, pp. 210–211; 1908, p. 102; 1920, p. 106). The heading is "U.S. citizens returning."
5. I am adopting the technique that BRV utilize for immigrants: "We assume that the *ratio* of immigrants into Ellis Island relative to all sea ports as recorded in official statistics is correct, even though the number of immigrant inflows at each port is likely measured with error" (BRV 2013, p. 43).

6. The assumption is no U.S.-citizen coastal arrivals from Canada or Mexico.
7. In 1859 all overland arrivals via Detroit are immigrants; and Detroit constitutes the bulk of overland arrivals in 1865–1866, for which years Oswego does not have arrivals (Hutchinson 1958, pp. 999–1000).
8. Conversion to calendar year is an involved and careful process, because of the variety of fiscal years: 12 months ending September 30 (1820–1832, 1844–1850), nine months ending September 30 (1843), calendar year (1833–1842, 1851–1865), six months ending June 30 (1866), 12 months ending June 30 (1867–1920). Use is made of the official figure for the fourth quarter of 1850 (5.594 thousand) and an estimated figure for the fourth quarter of 1832 (0.244 thousand, calculated as total sea arrivals less alien arrivals—from Sect. 2.1.3, below). Though we will be confronted with even more-complex conversions in the remainder of this study, I will not further provide details of conversion processes.
9. Maffry (1939, p. 9) writes: "During the period 1820-54 the activity of trade was apparently a principal influence upon the volume of oversea travel by native-born citizens."
10. Merchandise exports and imports are columns (1) and (2) of Table 1 (Chapter 6). Merchandise price indexes are in the Appendix to Chapter 7. The indexes are normalized to 1820 = 1. Real exports are the ratio of exports to the normalized export price, and real imports similarly. The sum of real exports and real imports is the extrapolator series.
11. As expected, these outlier observations for the entire United States are also observable in the BRV graph for New York.
12. For 1870–1900, Kuznets and Rubin (1954, p. 57) assume that departures exceed arrivals by only 0.5%. The North–Simon three-percent figure, applicable for earlier time, is not inconsistent with the official (fiscal-year) 1910–1914 ratios of 1.25, 1.12, 1.16, 1.12, 1.25. In contrast, DGW (2012, p. 148) and Dupont and Weiss (2013, p. 321) argue for, and utilize, arrivals data alone.
13. Travel price indexes are constructed in Chapter 14 (Appendix).
14. Simon (1960, p. 666) does not reveal how he constructed his area series, describing them only as the result of "a complex process involving both many assumptions and detailed calculations." Simon was a careful and thorough researcher; so I accept his series.
15. Sources: for 1856–1874, SAUS (1890, p. 210); for 1893–1895 and 1898-1905, SAUS (1908, p. 102); for 1906–1920, ARCGI. Charlestown is included with Boston in the SAUS data.
16. Same sources as for Boston and Philadelphia. Figures for Portland and Falmouth are unavailable 1906–1920, New Bedford and Providence unavailable 1856–1874. Presumably, the ports are relatively unimportant during the missing time periods.

17. Over 1856–1873, the Eastern-Ports series is at a maximum in 1864 and then has a declining trend to 1871.
18. For fiscal-years 1790–1874, merchandise exports to Europe and to non-Europe are obtained from *Statistical Tables Exhibiting the Commerce of the United States with European Countries* (1893, pp. VIII–IX), supplemented with *Reports of the Secretary of the Treasury* (1837, vol. III, p. 658). Exports to British North America [BNA] and Mexico are constructed from data in Chapter 6 (Sects. 3.1.1 and 3.1.2). Subtracting exports to BNA and Mexico series from non-Europe yields merchandise exports to oceanic non-Europe for fiscal years 1790–1874.

    Statistical Tables also provides merchandise imports from Europe and non-Europe, and *Monthly Summary of Commerce and Finance* [MSCF] (August 1901, p. 612) imports from Canada and other BNA colonies, both 1821–1874. Imports from Mexico are derived from series in *Commerce and Navigation* [CN]. Merchandise imports from oceanic non-Europe are Europe less Canada and Mexico, for fiscal years 1821–1874.

    Merchandise trade with Europe is the sum of exports and imports 1821–1874 and extrapolated to 1790 via the 1821 overlap with exports. The same technique yields oceanic merchandise trade with non-European countries. Europe trade and non-Europe oceanic trade are converted to calendar year 1790–1873, and the Europe proportion of U.S. oceanic trade is computed as the ratio of Europe to Europe *plus* non-Europe oceanic trade 1790–1856.
19. Sources are SAUS (1890, pp. 212, 214; 1908, p. 103) and ARCGI (1906–1920).
20. Merchandise exports and imports to/from South America 1821–1857 are in MSCF (August 1901, pp. 643–644); they are summed to obtain trade with South America. From *American State Papers: Commerce and Navigation* [ASPCN], I assemble merchandise exports to Brazil 1790–1821 and use the series to extrapolate South America trade to 1790. Converting to calendar year, we have trade with South America 1790–1856. The ratio of South America trade to the sum of Europe and non-Europe oceanic trade (note 18) constitutes the South America proportion of U.S. oceanic trade.
21. The reasons for Europe (including Britain) as the primary destination are varied. First, there was the custom of the travelling elite to tour the Continent. ("Americans traveling abroad in the eighteenth and early nineteenth centuries had to have been the elite of society who joined British visitors on the Grand Tour of the Continent."—DGW 2008, p. 11) Second, the vast majority of native-born Americans (other than Native American indigenous peoples and descendants of Africans brought to the country as enslaved people) were descendants of European immigrants or settlers. Third, business travel was motivated by international trade

and investment, the bulk of which was with Europe. Fourth, innovations in shipping speed, safety, and comfort—from packets to steamships (see Chapter 15)—generally happened first in the North Atlantic.

22. Their comments differ in detail from my series. Thus Dupont and Weiss (2013, p. 322, note 7) estimate "perhaps as much as 90% of the overseas travelers before the Civil War went to Europe," whereas my average Europe share for 1790–1860 is 84%. Also, DGW (2008, p. 13) see the trend decline in Europe's share beginning after 1868 rather than my 1864.
23. The Embargo Act was in effect for only 14 months, but encompasses the entirety of 1808. Researchers believe that, in general, the Embargo was substantially effective. See Douglas A. Irwin (2005) and the references that he cites.
24. The literature is vast. For empirical investigation in line with the consensus, see George Tucker (1843), McClelland and Zeckhauser (1982), Grubb (1990), and BRV (2013). A view at variance with the consensus *in toto* (though consistent with it for individual countries) is that of Cohn (2009, ch. 2). A meticulous deconstruction of official historical statistics is provided in Hutchinson (1958).
25. I ignore Grubb's additional 13% discrepancy, because it is based on flimsy data. An earlier estimate of the official deficiency for 1820–1830 is, coincidentally, also 41%, that I calculate from the numbers in Tucker (1843, pp. 82, 84).
26. And the "total" series is included in the file that Imran Rasul kindly shared.
27. I use the term "alien" synonymous with "foreign-born." These arrivals are composed of "immigrants" and "nonimmigrant aliens" (Sect. 2.2).
28. Davis (1931, p. 650) writes: "[Regarding] aliens traveling first or second class. No point in the interpretation of the statistics is more baffling than the question whether these 'cabin aliens' were included in the totals."
29. For other discussions of the cabin-aliens conundrum, see ARCGI (1899, p. 3; 1903, p. 5), Davis (1931, pp. 650–651, 657), Hutchinson (1958, pp. 980, 982, 983–985, 989, 994, 1007, 1008). Hutchinson exhibits inconsistent views on the issue.
30. The source is SAUS (1908, pp. 102–103; 1920, p. 106). Nonimmigrant figures for 1896–1897 are interpolated via immigrant figures for 1895–1898.
31. Following ARCGI, Hutchinson (1958, pp. 1005–1012) states arrivals 1892–1903, admittances from 1905, and is ambiguous about 1904. However, in its initial table and in accompanying text, ARCGI (1904, pp. 4–6) clearly states arrivals for 1904.
32. It is a reasonable abstraction that coastal arrivals are exclusively from the two neighboring countries.

33. The data sources are ARCGI, its predecessor (*Annual Report of the Superintendent of Immigration*), and *Historical Statistics* (2006, series Ad163 and Ad164)—assembled 1820–1893 (also for use in Sect. 2.1.3). Useful information regarding inland border stations is in Hutchinson (1958, pp. 987, 1009).
34. For Canada, the maximum is overland, with exceptions: for immigrants 1892–1893 (zero) and 1916 (residence), for nonimmigrants 1892–1905 (zero). For Mexico immigrants, the maximum is residence except for 1892–1893 (zero) and 1906–1908 (overland). For Mexico nonimmigrants, the maximum is overland except for 1892–1905 (zero) and 1906–1907 (residence).
35. Sources are Bromwell (1856, pp. 21, 25, 29) and Bureau of Statistics (1903, p. 4366). The data for 1820–1831 are clearly embarkations (Hutchinson 1958, p. 970), thus comparable to the Grubb series.
36. Figures are obtained for 1820–1885 (for later use); the source is Bureau of Statistics (1903, pp. 4346, 4350–4351). After fiscal-year 1885, immigrants from Canada and Mexico stopped being recorded.
37. Inland arrivals of Canada or Mexico residents should not be deleted; for that would involve double-count exclusion.
38. The source is State Department Reports—see Hutchinson (1958, pp. 996, 1012).
39. Note that, while the numerator and denominator of the multiplier may include non-oceanic arrivals, the multiplicand makes that exclusion. Note also that, while data for April–May 1831 (hence for that fiscal-year) are missing in the official data for Philadelphia and the United States (see Sect. 2.1.3), they are included in the Grubb series. So these data anomalies are corrected.
40. Maffry is generally consistent with SAUS, except for 1904, for which his figure for nonimmigant aliens is greater than SAUS (1908, p. 103), ARCGI (1904, p. 6), and Hutchinson (1958, p. 1008). In general, the Maffry data are selected for two reasons. First, they are compatible with port (customs-district) data (which, incidentally, break from "calendar year" to "fiscal year end June 30" in 1866 rather than the 1868 of other series). Second, Maffry divides aliens into immigrants and nonimmigrants ("alien visitors") beginning 1854 rather than later.
41. Using another approach, Cohn (2009, p. 18, note 12) has 30,407 as a lower limit.
42. An adjustment not made, would be to estimate arrivals at Southern ports not under federal control during the Civil War. The numbers are likely to be small (Hutchinson 1958, p. 978).
43. The data sources are Bromwell (1856, pp. 145, 165) and Frank Shay (1876, p. 171).
44. These resident arrivals were not recorded in fiscal-years 1886–1893.

45. The years are 1855–1862, 1865–1867, 1886.
46. The computation is total inland arrivals less "belong in the United States" less BNA (or Canada) resident. For 1886, there is no country breakdown. I assume all are third-country, as there are no recorded Canada-resident arrivals for that year.
47. Reviews of the literature are in Hutchinson (1958, pp. 968–970), Ernest Rubin (1959, pp. 87–88), McClelland and Zeckhauser (1982, pp. 38, 96–97), Grabbe (1989, pp. 190–191), *Historical Statistics* (2006, pp. 1–545 to 546).
48. Grabbe (2001) is absent in *Historical Statistics*, perhaps because the work was published in German. However, some years earlier, Grabbe (1989, p. 194) had presented an English synopsis of his findings, including decadal estimates of immigration over 1783–1819.
49. For 1820, use is made of other data, including Bromwell (1856) and passenger lists of New York and New Orleans.
50. A similar view is Marcus Lee Hansen (1945, pp. 77–78). The years prior to 1790 are required for Chapter 10 (Sect. 1.1.4).
51. The data are in Grabbe (2001, p. 85, Table 11, rows 5 and 13).
52. North (1960, p. 618) states: "Before 1856 transient aliens were not separated from immigrants in our statistics of arrivals"—a statement echoed in Hutchinson (1958, p. 979). In fact, as mentioned in Sect. 2.1.3 (note 40), data exist for calendar years 1854–1855.
53. Young (1871, p. XIX) recommends deducting about 1 2/3% from alien arrivals to estimate nonimmigrant aliens. Subsequently, for 1820–1855, the figure was stated as two percent (ARCGI 1892, p. 17), construed as the "official figure" (North 1960, p. 618). Davis (1931, p. 648) notes the two-percent official estimate and computes the proportion for 1856–1866 as 1 1/2%. Therefore she suggests "a 1 1/2 per cent or 2 percent" reduction for 1820–1855. Hutchinson (1958, p. 971) states: "Estimates of the proportion of temporary arrivals before 1856 are from 1 2/3 per cent to 2 percent." McClelland and Zeckhauser (1982, p. 35) use Census data to compute "transient aliens" as two percent of total alien arrivals in 1855–1860. North (1960, p. 618) believes that alien visitors constituted two percent of alien arrivals prior to 1840, one percent 1840–1860.
54. Michael R. Haines (2000, pp. 351–352) is representative of authors who see the overwhelming importance of the "pull" for cyclical as well as trend immigration (with the late-1840s potato famine the important exception). For a contrary view of the impact of Passenger Laws, see the Appendix (Sect. A).
55. The table is an origin-destination (last-permanent-residence to final-destination) matrix. (C) is BNA-total destination *minus* origin BNA, Mexico, United States. (D) is West Indies-total destination *minus* origin

BNA, Mexico, United States, West Indies. (E) is BNA-origin to BNA-destination *plus* Mexico-origin to Mexico-destination, (F) is BNA-origin to Mexico-destination *plus* Mexico-origin to BNA-destination.

56. Recall that the share is constant 1787–1872.
57. Sources are *Historical Statistics* (2006, series Dh320) and Simon (1960, pp. 674–675, column (1)). The series is converted to calendar year.
58. Series Ad90, Ad91, Ad97, Ad163, Ad164.
59. Cohn (2009, pp. 25, 29) assigns the entirety of "other or unknown" to Europe.
60. For 1851–1853, estimated arrivals at San Francisco are included (see Sect. 2.1.3).
61. For the fourth quarter 1832, estimated alien arrivals are incorporated (again see Sect. 2.1.3).
62. Europe consists of Great Britain and Ireland (less transit via BNA), Netherlands and Northern Germany, and France (counted twice). The years prior to 1790 are required for Chapter 10 (Sect. 1.1.4).
63. The opinion of BRV (2013, p. 44) and, with moderation, that of Ernest Rubin (1959, pp. 88–89).
64. For reference to contemporary views, see Rubin (1959, p. 88). Among later scholars are Rubin and Terry Coleman (1972, p. 22).
65. I follow BRV rather than the easy route of adopting Canadian and U.S. official counts of transit immigrants entering the United States from Canada (see Hutchinson 1958, pp. 985–987). The latter approach has four deficiencies absent in BRV. First, the increase in border stations increases the recorded flow artificially over time. Inland border stations were not established until 1904 and not completed until 1908. Second, prior to the inland border stations, with reports only at Canadian seaports, there was exclusion of "migrants who originally intended to reside in Canada but later entered the United States and those migrants who did not declare their intention of proceeding to the United States" (Hutchinson 1958, p. 987). Third, the count at inland border stations does not separate Canadian residents from transits. Fourth, there remains overland transit immigration that evades all border stations: "a complete counting of immigration via the land borders has probably never been achieved" (Hutchinson 1958, p. 987—see also Davis 1931, pp. 652–653).
66. Midpoint of official estimated annual range (McClelland and Zeckhauser 1982, p. 92).
67. Canada and Mexico admittances from Sect. 2.5, oceanic embarkations from Table 1, column (3).
68. Hutchinson (1958, p. 975) is not sanguine about the series prior to the 1860s, but all required here are the *relative* annual figures.
69. "The information about Mexican citizens [immigrating] is scant and unsatisfactory…before 1908"—Davis (1931, p. 654). "Hence, given the

paucity of evidence on Mexican inflows, we…assume these are zero rather than potentially over estimate their number at least in some years"—BRV (2013, p. 44).

70. I project the total-U.S. population rate of natural increase (*Historical Statistics* 2006, series Aa19) to the Mexican-born. (For the Civil War decade, I average the rates of the adjacent decades.) For the six decades spanning 1850–1910, the estimated immigration/population-change ratio is the product of "one *minus* the rate of natural increase" and "the 1910-1919 ratio of the immigration/population-change ratio to one *minus* the rate of natural increase."
71. Deaths at sea and debarments are generated in the Appendix.
72. That is the judgment of Roger Daniels (2004, chs. 1–2). See also Hutchinson (1981).
73. See Maffry (1939, pp. 13, 15), *Historical Statistics* (2006, series Ad2).
74. See Kuznets and Rubin (1954, pp. 58–59), BRV (2013, p. 29).
75. For the 1850s, I adopt Kamphoefner's (1991, p. 295) directly estimated Kuznets-Rubin ratio; for the 1860s, that ratio is an outlier (possibly due to a misprint); so I replace it with the average of alternative interpolations between the 1850s and 1870s, these interpolations via Kamphoefner's German and British figures. Kuznets-Rubin were the conventional wisdom on return migration until BRV—see Susan B. Carter and Richard Sutch (1998, p. 304), *Historical Statistics* (2006, pp. 1-547 to 548), BRV (2013, pp. 29, 35–36).
76. See also Cohn (2009, pp. 10–11).
77. A figure of 1.64% for 1832 is calculated from data in Thomas W. Page (1913, p. 54). Kamphoefner (1991, p. 297) states that pre-1850 figures are "consistently under 1 percent," which I take as 0.5%. The average of the two numbers (1.07%) is applied to 1787–1839.
78. This is a case in which it is misleading to massage data to achieve smoothness.
79. For the balance of payments, only revenue-earning imports are counted (Chapter 4, Sect. 3.1).
80. The series underlie Cohn (1984; 2003; 2009, pp. 137–152). I arbitrarily double Cohn's (2009, p. 142) New York figure for 1847, to account for U.S. ships with disease onboard being diverted to BNA. I linearly interpolate five missing years of New Orleans.
81. Kapp's shown percentage of deaths of steerage passengers requires recomputation, to include deaths in the denominator of the ratio.
82. "Even the most elementary requirements of the [Passenger] Acts were not dependably enforced…it should never be assumed that they are more than statements of a government's well-meaning intentions" (Coleman 1972, pp. 287–288). See also Cohn (2009, pp. 151–152).
83. For 1906, debarments at landports are deducted.

84. For history, one may consult Hutchinson (1981), Daniels (2004, chs. 1–2), *Historical Statistics* (2006, pp. 1–526 to 527).
85. The Immigration Act of March 3, 1875 was the true beginning for both sets; but the restraints were relatively mild.

References

Annual Report of the Commissioner-General of Immigration [ARCGI]. 1894.

Annual Report of the Commissioners of Emigration of the State of New York [ARCENY]. 1890.

Bandiera, Oriana, Imran Rasul, and Martina Viarengo [BRV]. 2013. The Making of Modern America: Migratory Flows in the Age of Mass Migration. *Journal of Development Economics* 102 (May): 23–47.

Bromwell, William J. 1856. *History of Immigration to the United States*. New York: Redfield.

Bureau of Statistics. 1903. *Immigration into the United States... from 1820 to 1903.* [Reprinted from *Summary of Commerce and Finance* for June 1903.] Treasury Department. Washington: Government Printing Office.

Carter, Susan B., and Richard Sutch. 1998. Historical Background to Current Immigration Issues. In *The Immigration Debate*, ed. James P. Smith and Barry Edmonston, 289–366. Washington: National Academy Press.

Cohn, Raymond L. (1984). "Mortality on Immigrant Voyages to New York, 1836-1853." *Journal of Economic History* 44 (June), pp. 289-300.

———. 1992. Transatlantic U.S. Passenger Travel at the Dawn of the Steamship Era. *International Journal of Maritime History* 4 (June): 43–64.

———. 2003. Passenger Mortality on Antebellum Immigrant Ships: Further Evidence. *International Journal of Maritime History* 15 (December): 1–19.

———. 2009. *Mass Migration Under Sail*. Cambridge: Cambridge University Press.

Coleman, Terry (1972). *Passage to America*. London: Hutchinson.

Daniels, Roger. 2004. *Guarding the Golden Door*. New York: Hill & Wang.

Davis, Marian R. 1931. Critique of Official United States Immigration Statistics. In *International Migrations*, vol. 2, ed. Walter F. Wilcox, 645–658. New York: National Bureau of Economic Research.

Department of Commerce. 1956. *Survey of International Travel*. Washington: Government Printing Office.

Dupont, Brandon, Alka Gandhi, and Thomas Weiss [DGW]. 2008. The American Invasion of Europe: The Long Term Rise in Overseas Travel, 1820–2000. Working Paper 13977, National Bureau of Economic Research, Cambridge, MA.

———. 2012. The Long-Term Rise in Overseas Travel by Americans, 1820–2000. *Economic History Review* 65 (February): 144–167.

Dupont, Brandon, and Thomas Weiss. 2013. Variability in Overseas Travel by Americans, 1820–2000. *Cliometrica* 7 (September): 319–339.

Ferenczi, Imre. 1929. *International Migrations*, vol. 1. New York: National Bureau of Economic Research.

Gould, John D. 1979. European Inter-Continental Emigration 1815–1914: Patterns and Causes. *Journal of European Economic History* 8 (Winter): 593–679.

Grabbe, Hans-Jürgen. 1989. European Immigration to the United States in the Early National Period, 1783–1820. *Proceedings of the American Philosophical Society* 133 (June): 190–214.

———. 2001. *Vor der großen Flut*. Stuttgart: Franz Steiner.

Grubb, Farley. 1990. The Reliability of U.S. Immigration Statistics: The Case of Philadelphia, 1815–1830. *International Journal of Maritime History* 1 (June): 29–54.

———. 2011. *German Immigration and Servitude in America, 1709–1920*. London: Routledge.

Haines, Michael R. 2000. The White Population of the United States, 1790–1920. In *A Population History of North America*, ed. Michael R. Haines and Richard H. Steckel, 305–369. Cambridge: Cambridge University Press.

Hansen, Marcus Lee. (1945). *The Atlantic Migration, 1607-1860*. Cambridge, MA: Harvard University Press.

Hatton, Timothy J., and Jeffrey G. Williamson. 1998. *The Age of Mass Migration*. New York: Oxford University Press.

———. 2005. *Global Migration and the World Economy*. Cambridge, MA: MIT Press.

[*Historical Statistics*]. 1975. Bureau of the Census. *Historical Statistics of the United States, Colonial Times to 1970, Bicentennial Edition*. Washington: Government Printing Office.

———. 2006. *Historical Statistics of the United States, Millennial Edition*, ed. Susan B. Carter, Scott Sigmund Gartner, Michael R. Haines, Alan L. Olmstead, Richard Sutch, Gavin Wright. Cambridge: Cambridge University Press.

Hutchinson, Edward P. 1958. Notes on Immigration Statistics of the United States. *Journal of the American Statistical Association* 53 (December): 963–1025.

———. 1981. *Legislative History of American Immigration Policy, 1798–1965*. Philadelphia: University of Pennsylvania Press.

Jarvis, Edward. 1872. Immigration. *Atlantic Monthly* 29 (April): 454–468.

Kamphoefner, Walter D. 1991. The Volume and Composition of German-American Return Migration. In *A Century of European Migrations, 1830–1930*, ed. Rudolph J. Vecoli and Suzanne M. Sinke, 293–311. Urbana: University of Illinois Press.

Kapp, Friedrich (1870). *Immigration and the Commissioners of Emigration*. New York: Douglas Taylor.

Keeling, Drew. 2012. *The Business of Transatlantic Migration Between Europe and the United States, 1900–1914*. Zurich: Chronos.

Kuznets, Simon, and Ernest Rubin. 1954. *Immigration and the Foreign Born*. New York: National Bureau of Economic Research.

Maffry, August. 1939. *Overseas Travel and Travel Expenditures in the Balance of International Payments of the United States, 1919–1938*. Washington: Government Printing Office.

McClelland, Peter D., and Richard J. Zeckhauser. 1982. *Demographic Dimensions of the New Republic*. Cambridge: Cambridge University Press.

Monthly Summary of Commerce and Finance [MSCF]. 1901.

North, Douglass C. 1960. The United States Balance of Payments, 1790–1860. In *Trends in the American Economy in the Nineteenth Century*, ed. William N. Parker, 573–628. Princeton: Princeton University Press.

Officer, Lawrence H., and Samuel H. Williamson. 2020. The Antebellum Slave Trade: Numbers and Impact on the Balance of Payments. *Research in Economic History* 36: 181–212.

Page, Thomas W. (1913). Some Economic Aspects of Immigration Before 1870. *Journal of Political Economy* 21 (January): 34–55.

Quarterly Reports of the Chief of the Bureau of Statistics [QRCBS]. 1893.

Rubin, Ernest. 1959. Immigration and the Economic Growth of the U.S.: 1790–1914. *R.E.M.P. Bulletin* 7 (October/December): 87–95.

Schaefer, Donald. 1994. U.S. Migration, 1850–59. In *American Economic Development in Historical Perspective*, ed. Thomas Weiss and Donald Schaefer, 53–69. Stanford: Stanford University Press.

Shay, Frank. 1876. *Chinese Immigration*. Sacramento: State Printing.

Simon, Matthew. 1960. The United States Balance of Payments, 1861–1900. In *Trends in the American Economy in the Nineteenth Century*, ed. William N. Parker, 629–716. Princeton: Princeton University Press.

Statistical Abstract of the United States [SAUS]. 1890. Washington: Government Printing Office.

———. 1908. Washington: Government Printing Office.

Tucker, George. 1843. *Progress of the United States in Population and Wealth*. New York: Hunt's Merchants' Magazine.

Urquhart, Malcolm C., and Kenneth A.H. Buckley (eds.). 1965. *Historical Statistics of Canada*. Cambridge: Cambridge University Press.

Young, Edward. 1871. *Special Report on Immigration*. Washington: Government Printing Office.

CHAPTER 4

Slaves: Oceanic

1 Conceptual Framework

This chapter provides the slave-trade numbers (enslaved-persons physical movements) that underlie their incorporation into several balance-of-payments items—imports (Chapter 9), transportation services (Chapter 13), non-imported purchases (Chapter 17)—and examination of slavery as an economic sector (Chapter 20).[1] Slaves were imported into the United States but not exported therefrom—at least there are no data on the latter, though there was surely some overland export. And again the modern statement would be that "Blacks were purchased in Africa and the Caribbean, forcibly taken to the United States, and sold therein without their consent."

There are two ways to approach the slave trade. *First*, transported slaves were a type of good analogous to merchandise. And that is how I treat slavery in the balance of payments. Slaves were not exactly merchandise, because nearly all slave-ships were owner-operated rather than hired. The slave-ship was not simply a transport medium: it was the entire slave-trading enterprise! This characteristic means that slave trading did not involve the freight and insurance as normally defined in the balance of payments. *Second*, imported slaves were "involuntary immigrants" subject to ownership. In fact, that was the legal status of slave imports, and I adopt this approach in Chapter 20.

L. H. Officer, *A New Balance of Payments for the United States, 1790–1919*, Palgrave Studies in American Economic History,
https://doi.org/10.1007/978-3-030-66099-4_4

The analysis in the previous paragraph should not lead one into the trap of equating enslaved persons with "cargo" in any sense other than economic. In rejecting the personhood of enslaved people, the slave-trader was following an old practice that became a legal crime in some countries (Britain, Denmark, the United States) in the late eighteenth and early nineteenth century—but not in the other principal trading countries or in their colonies (France, Spain, Portugal, Brazil). Both a legal and moral crime by modern standards, slave-trading was criticized contemporaneously by some free people as ethically and religiously wrong.

2 African Embarkations on U.S. Ships

The number of African embarkations on U.S. ships is listed in column (1) of Table 1.[2]

This series is used in Chapter 17 to derive U.S. purchases of non-imported slaves. The series is the first of three components in Officer and Williamson (2020, Table A1.I, column (1)). Embarkations involved intent of controlled disembarkation, either in the United States (imports) or elsewhere in the Americas (carrying trade).

3 Slave Imports

3.1 Data

Columns (2) and (4) of Table 1 present U.S.-ship and foreign-ship African disembarkations in the United States that involve ship revenue and that therefore together constitute the physical component of U.S. imports from Africa. Column (3) lists U.S. imports from the Caribbean.[3] These series are used in Chapter 9 to construct slave-import debits. Excluded from columns (2)–(4) are disembarked slaves that do not earn revenue for the ship-owner, for example, landed after having been rescued from shipwreck or after having been taken by the action of navies, pirates, or privateers. I do not include these disembarkations in imports, because I define imports to be disembarkations for which payment is made.[4]

Table 1 Movement of Slaves: Africa and the United States

(Number of persons)				
Year	*U.S. ships embarkations*	*U.S. disembarkations earning ship revenue*		
		U.S. ships		*Foreign ships*
	African (1)	*African* (2)	*Caribbean* (3)	*African* (4)
1790	3101	169	55	0
1791	2982	371	0	0
1792	6259	1720	39	478
1793	5002	768	40	0
1794	3991	289	0	0
1795	5364	2061	463	0
1796	7595	4790	93	0
1797	6146	2019	179	0
1798	2187	183	279	436
1799	4913	0	0	3
1800	5903	254	0	0
1801	2708	368	0	171
1802	5604	46	0	738
1803	6723	535	97	533
1804	11,268	4272	1165	3804
1805	15,327	6137	319	4050
1806	20,874	9152	316	6768
1807	36,217	24,356	911	3002
1808	3150	780	95	0
1809	500	0	0	0
1810	1552	175	259	0
1811	776	0	0	0
1812	500	0	0	0
1813	500	410	0	0
1814	500	410	0	0
1815	500	410	0	0
1816	500	410	0	0
1817	500	410	0	0
1818	500	410	0	0
1819	500	410	0	0
1820	500	151	0	0

(continued)

Table 1 (continued)

(Number of persons)

Year	*U.S. ships embarkations*	*U.S. disembarkations earning ship revenue*		
		U.S. ships		*Foreign ships*
	African (1)	*African* (2)	*Caribbean* (3)	*African* (4)
1821	161	0	0	0
1824	186	0	0	0
1827	440	0	0	0
1829	1410	0	0	0
1830	0	0	0	0
1858	350	0	0	0
1860	126	0	0	0

3.2 *Behavior and Determinants*

There was a fundamental U.S. demand for slave imports, emanating from the production of plantation crops. Frustrating realization of this demand were state and federal laws restricting or prohibiting the slave trade or slavery itself; these laws were generally, but not always or totally, effective. In January 1798, Georgia became the last state to end legal imports. Not until December 1803 did a state (South Carolina) repeal its import ban. The *generally* relatively low figures (in both directions) for 1798–1803 in all columns of Table 1–*uniformly* low for columns (1) and (2)—indicate effectiveness of state slave-trade restriction. In December 1805 Congress began discussion of a law prohibiting slave imports from the beginning of 1808.[5] The law did not pass until March 1807; but an expectations effect led to enormous slave imports in 1806–1807. Table 1 shows that the federal law, strengthened by further legislation in 1818 and 1819, was effective from inception, extremely effective after 1810, and totally effective after 1820.[6]

The hypocrisy of Congress abolishing the slave trade but not slavery itself is striking. You could no longer be enslaved into the United States if born elsewhere, but would continue to be automatically enslaved if born of an enslaved person within the country.[7] A Civil War, an Emancipation Proclamation, and a Constitutional Amendment acted finally to abolish slavery in 1865.

4 Slave Carrying Trade

4.1 Data

U.S. ships carried enslaved persons between Africa and third countries and also between regions of the Caribbean. In this book (and, as usual, following Officer and Williamson) "carrying trade in slaves" implies buying the slaves at the origin, selling them at the destination, and transporting them in between—in contrast to "carrying trade in commodities," which involves only transportation. Destination regions are pre-U.S. Louisiana (1790–1803) and Florida (1790–1820), Spanish America, Non-Spanish Caribbean, and Brazil. U.S.-ship carrying-trade numbers of enslaved Africans are shown in columns (1)–(4) of Table 2, numbers of creole slaves (separated by gender, and transported intra-Caribbean) are in columns (5)–(6).[8] These series are used in Chapter 13 to compute carrying-slave credits.

And again I state that the treatment of enslaved persons as commodities in the carrying trade involved robbing human beings of their personhood, no less than for enslaved Africans bound to the United States.

4.2 Behavior and Determinants

The demand for slaves in the Americas outside the United States was strong throughout the antebellum period. Even prior to 1790, the main U.S. slave-trading states (all Northern!) had passed laws prohibiting the slave trade. In 1794 and 1800 Congress followed with legislation forbidding U.S. participation in the slave trade. These laws were ineffective until 1808. Further federal legislation in 1819 and 1820 helped restrict the carrying trade, but the trade did not end until 1829.[9]

Table 2 Movement of Slaves: Carrying Trade

(Number of persons)

	African				*Creole Male*	*Creole Female*
Year	*Louisiana and Florida*	*Spanish America*	*Non-Spanish Caribbean*	*Brazil*	*Havana*	*Havana*
	(1)	*(2)*	*(3)*	*(4)*	*(5)*	*(6)*
1790	0	1748	624	0	145	160
1791	0	1047	1120	0	269	285
1792	0	3000	533	0	481	522
1793	186	1359	1219	0	820	735
1794	0	1858	1074	0	911	387
1795	0	1389	1096	0	490	239
1796	0	1530	53	0	417	267
1797	0	2322	522	0	1388	829
1798	0	1541	120	0	735	274
1799	0	3935	0	0	1274	652
1800	92	3312	334	0	848	524
1801	0	1931	0	0	256	255
1802	340	3075	1247	0	1081	1118
1803	376	3334	1142	0	806	902
1804	192	2299	502	178	987	715
1805	0	5362	711	0	1058	599
1806	26	6695	636	0	699	527
1807	0	2016	137	196	1216	1209
1808	0	821	345	0	276	335
1809	0	404	0	0	0	0
1810	637	407	0	0	0	0
1811	0	0	51	0	0	0
1812	0	260	0	0	0	0
1821	–	141	0	0	0	0
1824	–	158	0	0	0	0
1827	–	0	0	406	0	0
1829	–	1256	0	0	0	0

Notes

1. The slave-trade content of this book is heavily grounded on Officer and Williamson (2020). Most data series are taken directly from Officer and Williamson; others are based on their work. Related text in the book mainly summarizes or paraphrases (and, in Chapter 20, extends) what is in Officer and Williamson. Until their paper there had been no incorporation

of slavery in any U.S. balance-of-payments table, although Shepherd and Walton (1972, pp. 141–144) provide partial balance-of-payments figures for the colonial period.

2. Missing years in the table involve zero values for all columns.
3. The sum of columns (2) and (3) is Officer and Williamson (2020, Table A1.I, column (2)). Column (4) is their Table A1.II, column (2).
4. A broader definition of imports would allow for non-revenue-earning disembarkations, perhaps by broadening the scope of unilateral transfers.
5. The earliest date at which the U.S. Constitution permitted Congressional prohibition of imports of people. See Officer and Williamson (2020, p. 182).
6. Columns (2)–(4) incorporate estimates of smuggling.
7. Typically, economic historians would interpret this duality not as hypocrisy or even inconsistency but rather as "rational behavior": Restricting slave imports enhanced the market value of existing slaves, hence the wealth of slave-owners. See Officer and Williamson (2020, pp. 197–198, note x) and Gavin Wright (2020, p. 370).
8. Columns (1)–(4) are from columns (5), [African component of] (3), (4), and (6) in Officer and Williamson (2020, Table A1.I). Columns (5) and (6) are the other components of their column (3). The intra-Caribbean trade (columns (5)–(6)) counts only Cuba as destination.
9. Missing years in Table 2 are years of no carrying trade. Note that the abolition of slavery in the British Empire was legislated in 1833, so could have had no impact on the U.S.-ship carrying trade (which ended in 1829). However, the British 1807 law outlawing the slave trade, along with enforcement activity of the British Navy, must have had some effect.

References

Officer, Lawrence H., and Samuel H. Williamson. 2020. The Antebellum Slave Trade: Numbers and Impact on the Balance of Payments. *Research in Economic History* 36: 181–212.

Shepherd, James F., and Gary M. Walton. 1972. *Shipping, Maritime Trade, and the Economic Development of Colonial North America*. Cambridge: Cambridge University Press.

Wright, Gavin. 2020. Slavery and Anglo-American Capitalism Revisited. *Economic History Review* 73 (May): 353–383.

CHAPTER 5

Passengers: Domestic

The volume of passengers in domestic transportation is used as weights in a price index of transportation for foreign travelers in the United States (Chapter 14, Appendix, Sect. B.3.d). Both local and intercity common carriers are incorporated. The local transport modes are the omnibus and street railway, and their volume is measured in number of passengers; the intercity modes are the stagecoach and railroad, volume expressed in passenger-miles.

1 Omnibus

The omnibus, powered by horses, was an extended stagecoach with fixed routes. It presaged the motorbus and was predated by what one may term the "early omnibus" or "pre-omnibus," perhaps the "hackney coach" (antecedent of the taxicab) with short routes. I generate a series of the number of omnibuses by considering New York City first and then the rest of the country. This is the only transport mode for which a series is developed for its entire history.

Based on data in *Manual of the Corporation of the City of New York* (annual) and George Rogers Taylor (1966a, p. 43), I develop the number of omnibuses in New York 1830–1869.[1] Taylor (1966a, p. 41) sees the origin of the omnibus as 1811, with service beginning slowly, "but by the

L. H. Officer, *A New Balance of Payments for the United States, 1790–1919*, Palgrave Studies in American Economic History,
https://doi.org/10.1007/978-3-030-66099-4_5

closing years of the 1820s numerous lines had begun operation." So I set the number of omnibuses at zero 1790–1810 and exponentially interpolate between 1810 and 1830.[2] Thus we have the number of omnibuses in New York 1790–1869.

According to *Historical Statistics* (2006, series Ba1366), there were 3200 bus drivers in the entire country in 1860. In that year, production workers in manufacturing worked an average of 10–11 hours daily (Officer 2009, p. 191). This suggests a ratio of about 1 1/2 bus drivers per omnibus, for continuous coverage averaging 12 hours daily and allowing for contingencies. So the number of omnibuses for the United States is estimated as 3200/1.5 = 2133. With New York having 536 (from above) in 1860, the rest of the country is left with 1597, extrapolated to 1861–1869 via the product of the New York number and the 1860 rest-of-country/New York ratio.

The literature shows that, from 1826 to 1857, cities beyond New York adopted the omnibus and existing cities increased service.[3] So I assume that there were zero omnibuses in the rest of the country 1790–1825 and estimate the number 1826–1859 via linear interpolation. I sum the number of omnibuses in New York City and in the rest of the country to obtain the U.S. figure 1790–1869.

New York omnibuses carried six million passengers in 1850 (Kenneth T. Jackson 1985, pp. 35; 335, Note 35), which works out to 14,118 passengers per omnibus. The first "genuine" omnibus appeared in New York in spring 1831 (John A. Miller 1941, p. 5; Brian J. Cuda 1990, p. 9). Pre-omnibuses were not as large or efficient; so I reduce the per-omnibus passenger figure by 50% in 1811–1830 and by 25% in 1831. For 1790–1869, the number of U.S. omnibus passengers is the product of the per-omnibus figure and the number of omnibuses.

I take the end of omnibus service to be 1890, midway between the *Historical Statistics* dates of 1880 (a positive figure for bus drivers) and 1900 (zero bus drivers). The omnibus was replaced by the street railway, but retained some activity until 1890 for three reasons: feeder service to other forms of transportation, government policy restricting railways in some parts of a city, and as a status symbol.[4] I linearly interpolate the number of omnibus passengers 1870–1889 between 1869 and 1900. There is no adjustment for government requisitioning of horses during the Civil War; because the effect is reflected in the New York numbers, and therefore in the rest-of-country figures. However, there needs to be an adjustment for the effects of the "Great Epizootic," an equine flu that occurred in November 1872 and spread virulently in the Northeast and mid-Atlantic cities. Many thousands of horses were too sick to work, and thousands died.[5] I assume that the equivalent of one-month of horse-drawn activity was lost nationwide due to this epidemic. Therefore the computed number of omnibus passengers is reduced by 1/12 in 1872. The omnibus series is positive 1811–1889.

2 Street Railway

Street railways ran on rails, just like intercity railroads; but were powered by horses, later by electricity. They are the reason for the demise of the omnibus: "iron rails allowed horses to pull twice the load at twice the speed of omnibuses" (Clay McShane and Joel A. Tarr 1997, p. 111). The passenger series is developed from the beginning to 1900. Just as for the omnibus, I separate New York from the rest of the country.

2.1 New York City

There are five components of New York's street railways. Revenue-passenger data, all for fiscal year, are incomplete for any one component; but estimation is accomplished interactively.[6] I begin with the (1) *street surface railways of Manhattan and the Bronx*, for which service began in August 1852.[7] There are figures for 1853–1875, 1880, 1890, 1900–1902.[8]

Turning to *elevated railways*, (2) *Manhattan* began passenger service in 1872 and (3) *Brooklyn* in 1880. The Manhattan series is assembled for 1872–1902.[9] Brooklyn is generated for 1880–1902, with Manhattan interpolating 1881–1889 and 1891—1899. The elevated-railways series are complete.

For 1875–1891, there are passenger data for Manhattan and the Bronx, street surface and elevated railways combined. Subtracting Manhattan elevated railways, the result is the interpolator used to estimate Manhattan and the Bronx street surface railways 1876–1879 and 1881–1889, and also to extrapolate 1891 via the 1890 overlap. There are figures for Manhattan surface railways alone for the year ending September 30. I convert to the standard fiscal year (ending June 30), and use it as interpolator for the (1) *street surface railways of Manhattan and the Bronx* 1892–1899, the series for which is now complete.

Turning to the (4) *street surface railways of Brooklyn and Queens*, service began with the Brooklyn City Railroad in 1853.[10] The series is assembled for 1860, 1870, 1880, 1890, 1900–1902. Linear interpolation yields 1853–1859 and interpolation via Manhattan and the Bronx street surface railways 1861–1869, 1871–1879, 1881–1889, 1891–1899. Brooklyn and Queens street surface is complete. Finally, for (5) *Richmond [Staten Island] street surface railways*, passenger data exist for 1869 (first year of service), 1880, 1888, 1900–1902. I linearly interpolate for the intervening years, thus completing the series.

Summing the five component series, I obtain fiscal-year total revenue passengers for New York City 1853–1902. On the basis of revenue information and the known five-cent fare, passengers are estimated for calendar year 1852. That figure enables calendar-year generation for 1853; simple conversion yields calendar year 1854–1902.

2.2 *Rest of Country*

1890–1900: For fiscal years 1890 and 1902: fare passengers in the rest of the country are computed as total U.S. fare passengers (Bureau of the Census 1920, p. 12) *minus* New York City passengers. Multiplying by the rest-of-country urban-population "June 30/December 31" ratio converts to calendar year (represented by June 30), and rest-of-country urban population serves as the interpolator for 1891–1900.[11]

1881–1889: Street-railways "length of line" (in miles) for the rest of the country at midyear is generated as total-U.S. *minus* New York City for 1880–1890.[12] This series extrapolates fare passengers 1881–1889 via the 1890 overlap.

1790–1860: Only "length of track" is available to estimate rest-of-country passengers in this early era, and only five cities in the 1860 Census have the data (deemed to pertain to the average for 1860, or, equivalently, to June 30).[13] For each city, date of initial service is obtained from various sources, and intervening years are interpolated.[14] The cities, with earliest year of service, are: Boston 1856, Cincinnati 1859, Hoboken 1860, St. Louis 1859, Philadelphia 1858. Summing the five cities, we have miles of track for the rest of the country. I calculate the passengers-per-mile ratio for Boston in 1860 (Taylor 1966b, pp. 39, 43), and project the ratio to all the cities for 1856–1860. Then I multiply miles of track by that ratio.

1861–1880: Using rest-of-country urban population, I interpolate number of passengers between 1860 and 1881. During the Civil War, many horses were requisitioned by the government for war purpose (Cuda 1990, p. 14).[15] While this effect is embodied in the number of New York passengers, the rest-of-the-country number requires adjustment. I arbitrarily reduce the figure by 25% in 1861 and 1865, 50% in 1862–1864.

2.3 *Entire Country*

The number of passengers is the sum of New York and the rest of the country. Just as for the omnibus, by reason of the Epizootic, I impose a 1/12th loss of activity in 1872. The series is zero 1790–1851 and not calculated 1901–1919.[16]

3 Stagecoach

I generate passenger-miles only for stagecoach activity in the East, and end the series in 1840, prior to significant stagecoach facilities for Western travel (for which data are lacking).

3.1 *Number of Passengers*

3.1.1 *Individual Cities*

Boston, 1800–1840: For 1800, 1820, 1825, 1829, 1832, and 1835, I have the number of stage lines serving the city. For the number of scheduled weekly-arrivals: of the six years, 1829 and 1832 are lacking—they are interpolated via the number of stage lines.[17] Weekly arrivals are linearly interpolated for the missing years between 1800 and 1835. For 1820 and 1835, there are estimates for the number of travelers arriving annually.[18] Interpolation via arrivals yields 1821–1834, and extrapolation via the 1820 overlap provides 1800–1819. I assume that after 1835 the number of arrivals and the number of passengers fell by five percent annually.[19] Thus Boston scheduled-arrivals and passenger series for 1800–1840.

Philadelphia, 1800–1840: The number of weekly arrivals is available for 1810 and 1819 (Oliver W. Holmes and Peter T. Rohrbach 1983, pp. 77–78). I use Boston weekly arrivals to interpolate 1811–1818 and to extrapolate 1800–1809 and 1820–1840, via 1810 and 1819 overlaps. The number of passenger arrivals 1800–1840 is estimated as the product of the Philadelphia/Boston weekly-arrivals ratio and the Boston number of passengers.

Albany and Baltimore, 1800–1840: In 1800–1820, these cities each had one-third the number of stage lines in Philadelphia or Boston (Holmes and Rohrbach 1983, p. 77). So, for 1800–1840, I estimate the number of travelers arriving in these two cities combined as one-third the Boston-Philadelphia total.

3.1.2 *Total United States*

1800–1840: I sum passenger arrivals for the four cities, and arbitrarily double the series to estimate stagecoach passengers for the entire country.[20]

1790–1799: The mileage ratio of "weekly transportation of mails in carriages furnished for the accommodation of travelers" to "length of the post roads" is obtained for March 3: 1793, 1797, 1801, with the 1793 figure projected to 1790–1792.[21] The ratio is linearly interpolated 1794–1796 and 1798–1800 and transformed to June 30 date (representing annual average). Annual miles of post road are obtained from Pliny Miles (1857, p. 363), and converted to calendar year. Then the product of the ratio and post-road miles extrapolates passenger arrivals to 1790–1799 on the basis of the 1800 overlap.

3.2 *Passenger-Miles*

Unknown is the average distance traveled on a stagecoach ride. To generate passenger-miles, one needs to make a guess. For 1790–1834, I arbitrarily take this distance as 100 miles.[22] With the coming of the railroad, average distance shortened. I assume, again arbitrarily, that the average distance fell by five-percent annually in 1835–1840. For 1790–1840, stagecoach passenger-miles are the product of average distance and number of passenger arrivals.

4 Railroad

1880–1901: For 1880, 1890, and 1891–1901, year ended June 30, the best passenger-miles data are in Albert Fishlow (1966, p. 585) and Harold Barger (1951, Table B-1). Census data are used to interpolate 1881–1889.[23]

1830–1879: I continue Fishlow, with 1839, 1849, 1859, 1870, for the fiscal year ended November 15.[24] Using end-of-year data on miles of road-operated 1829–1880, I construct corresponding annual-average

Table 1 Domestic passengers (millions–annual average over period)

Period	*Passenger-Miles*		*Passengers*	
	Stagecoach (1)	*Railroad* (2)	*Street Railroad* (3)	*Omnibus* (4)
1790–1800	17	0	0	0
1801–1810	32	0	0	0
1811–1820	53	0	0	0
1821–1830	122	0	0	1
1831–1840	224	49	0	8
1841–1850	–	328	0	17
1851–1860	–	1372	37	27
1861–1870	–	2930	228	16
1871–1880	–	5353	582	6
1881–1890	–	9773	1291	2
1891–1900	–	13,990	3174	0

road-mileage series for years ended June 30 and November 15.[25] Their "June 30/November 15" ratio multiplies the Fishlow figures to yield passenger-miles for the fiscal year ended June 30. Using road mileage for year ended June 30 as interpolator, I estimate passenger-miles, year ended June 30, for all missing years over 1839–1880. Using the same series as extrapolator, I estimate passenger-miles for 1830–1838 via 1839 overlap. The entire passenger-miles series is then converted to calendar year. The series is zero until 1830 and is not generated after 1900.

5 Presentation

All four domestic-passenger series are exhibited as decade annual averages in Table 1. The absence of stagecoach figures after 1840 is regrettable; but surely its intercity passenger-miles shortly thereafter were eclipsed—and then ever-more dominated—by the railroad.

Appendix: Population

A. Official U.S.-Population Series

Official U.S. resident population at July 1, 1790–1919, is from *Historical Statistics* (2006, series Aa7).[26] For 1790–1899, the source obtains intercensus-year figures mechanistically via interpolation (after accounting for net immigration).[27] The implication is that intercensus-year shocks do not affect the figures. The primary shocks are wars, especially the Civil War–but there are also other major conflicts: War of 1812, Mexican-American War, Spanish-American War, and Philippine-American War. The principal impact of wars is on deaths of the military-age male population groups. I develop a corrective series for this effect and thereupon adjust the official series. The richness of data enables a superior approach for the Civil War.

B. Initial Military-Age-Group Population

The Census years spanning wars are 1810, 1820; 1840, 1850; 1860, 1870; 1890, 1900. The military-age-group population for these years is considered final, obtained by summing figures for the relevant male age-race groups.[28] For 1811–1819, 1841–1849, 1861–1869, 1891–1899, exponential interpolation generates initial (estimated-official) military-age-group population.

C. War-Related Deaths

War of 1812: I accept Donald R. Hickey's (2006, p. 297) judgment of 15,000 deaths.[29] On June 18, 1812, the United States declared war. The U.S. victory at New Orleans happened on January 8, 1815. I allocate the deaths annually 1812–1815 roughly according to share of time of war.

Mexican-American War: I take the sum of Mark Crawford's (1999, p. 68) disaggregate figures, 13,780. On May 13, 1846, the United States declared war; the Treaty of Guadalupe was signed February 2, 1848. Again, deaths are distributed annually 1846–1848 via wartime proportion.

Spanish-American and Philippine-American Wars: Hugh Rockoff's (2012, pp. 83–84) numbers of 5462 and 7001 deaths are the most reliable. The Spanish-American War was entirely in 1898; the Philippine-American War occurred from May 1, 1898 to July 4, 1902 (Rockoff 2012, pp. 70–71). Deaths are allocated to 1898–1899 accordingly.

Civil War: Using the data in Darroch Greer (2005, Appendixes I and II), I generate four cumulative end-of-year series 1861–1865: "casualties" (killed in battle, wounded, taken prisoner) and "seasonal attrition" (died of disease), Union and Confederacy separately. Total Union casualties are converted to battle deaths by subtracting the highest figures for "prisoners and wounded" in other sources (Greer 2005, p. 5). Cumulative battle deaths are estimated annually according to casualties figures. Adding seasonal attrition yields end-of-year cumulative war-related deaths 1861–1865. For the Confederacy, the same computations are made, except that only the wounded (Robert W. Meinhard 1998) are subtracted—there are no data on prisoners.

Cumulative War-Related Deaths, End of Year: 1812, 1846, 1898—war-related deaths. 1813–1815, 1847–1848, 1899—previous-year figure *plus* war-related deaths. 1861–1865: sum of Union and Confederate end-of-year cumulative war-related deaths.[30]

Cumulative War-Related Deaths, Average During Year: 1812–1815, 1846–1848, 1861–1865, 1898–1899 obtained by appropriate averaging of beginning-of-year and end-of-year figures, allowing for months of zero cumulative deaths (prior to war) and of unvarying cumulative deaths (subsequent to end of war).

D. Final Military-Age-Group Population

Civil War Decade: Hypothetical no-war military-age-group population in 1870 is computed as the 1860-Census figure times the 1870/1860 official-population ratio, and is exponentially interpolated 1861–1869. The estimated peacetime survival rate of military-age-group males is the complement of the average death rate for male 15–39 age groups in 1900, the earliest available year, and legitimately applied to the Civil War decade.[31] The no-war military-age-group population corrected for normal deaths is the peacetime survival rate *times* the no-war military-age-group population. Final military-age-group population is no-war *minus* average cumulative war deaths for 1861–1865, exponentially interpolated for 1866–1869.

Other War Decades: For the remaining war decades, in which war-related deaths were relatively low, I adopt a simpler technique. For 1812–1815, 1846–1848, 1898–1899, final male military-age-group population is initial population less cumulative war-related deaths (average during year). For 1816–1819 and 1849, it is exponentially interpolated between (1815, 1820) and (1848, 1850). For 1820 (1850, 1900), reduction in final military-age-group population due to war is calculated as the 1820/1815 (1850/1848, 1900/1899) final-population ratio *times* 1815 (1848, 1899) end-of-year cumulative war deaths. For 1820, 1850, 1900,

Table 2 Correction to official population

(thousands of persons)

Year	*Correction*
1811	1
1812	−1
1813	−6
1814	−12
1815	−15
1816	−12
1817	−10
1818	−7
1819	−3
1841	1
1842	2
1843	3
1844	5
1845	6
1846	−2
1847	−9
1848	−14
1849	−7
1861	−32
1862	−160
1863	−342
1864	−515
1865	−644
1866	−530
1867	−409
1868	−280
1869	−144
1891	1
1892	1
1893	2
1894	3
1895	4
1896	5
1897	6
1898	−3
1899	−7

no-war military-age-group population is final population *plus* reduction due to war; for 1810, 1840, 1890, it remains final population. For 1811, 1841–1845, 1891–1897, no-war military-age-group population is exponentially interpolated between (1810, 1820), (1840, 1850), (1890, 1900), and set as final military-age-group population.

E. Revised U.S.-Population Series

For any year, the correction is "final *minus* initial" military-age-group population. The correction series (nonzero values) is exhibited in Table 2. Revised U.S. population is official population *plus* the correction.

F. Rest-of-Country Urban Population

For 1830, 1840…1910, the urban share of U.S. population is the ratio of urban to urban *plus* rural population; linear interpolation yields intervening years.[32] For 1830–1902, U.S. urban population is the product of the urban share and revised U.S. population. New York City population is also obtained 1830, 1840…1910, with intervening years exponentially interpolated.[33] For 1830–1902, rest-of-country urban population is U.S. urban population less New York population.

Notes

1. Linear interpolation is used for 1831–1832, 1835–1836, 1838–1844.
2. For the interpolation, I let the 1810 figure be one instead of zero.
3. See George Rogers Taylor (1966a, pp. 42–46), Frederick W. Speirs (1897, pp. 10–11), Charles R. Barker (1931, p. 250), Louis C. Hennick and E. Harper Charlton (1975, p. 9), Arthur J. Krim (1967, p. 38), Joel A. Tarr (1978, p. 4), Leland D. Baldwin (1937, p. 240), Walter B. Stevens (1909, p. 433), Glen E. Holt (1972, p. 325), John A. Miller (1941, p. 9), J. Thomas Scharf (1874, p. 512), and Nathaniel Dearborn (1848, p. 221).
4. See McShane and Tarr (1997, p. 111).
5. On the Great Epizootic, see Clay McShane (2001, pp. 274, 288; 2008), Frank Rowsome Jr. (1956, p. 28), McShane and Tarr (1997, pp. 105–106), Cuda (1990, p. 14), and Miller (1941, p. 32).
6. Data sources are *Report of the Public Service Commission*, vol. 2 (1907, pp. 25–26; 1913, p. 28), which is primary; *Record and Guide* (1892, p. 683); Harry J. Carman (1919, p. 145); *New York Times*, May 13, 1853, p. 4.
7. I do not include the, limited, pre-1852 streetcar service, because of lack of data. See Carman (1919, pp. 20–26), Krim (1967, pp. 59–60), and McShane and Tarr (1997, p. 111).

8. For 1855 and 1866, one road did not report; I increase the figures by the ratio of total to reported number of roads.
9. *Record and Guide* is used as interpolator to estimate 1881–1889. The year 1901 is obtained via linear interpolation.
10. William D. Middleton (1967, p. 15), and Cuda (1990, p. 13).
11. For population series see Sect. F of Appendix. With the typical streetcar fare fixed (at five cents—Chapter 14, Appendix, Sect. B.3.d), urban population is an appropriate converter and interpolator.
12. Data sources are Charles H. Cooley (1895, pp. 683, 692–693) and Edward D. Durand (1905, p. 6). "Length of line" is different from "length of track," the latter a larger number (Cooley 1895, p. 682). "Length of line" is the portion of track which is traversed for travel– the better measure for our purpose of extrapolating passengers carried. The series for New York City consists of Brooklyn and New York, and is linearly interpolated 1881–1888. Rest-of-country length of line is converted from December 31 to June 30.
13. The Census data are in Secretary of the Interior (1866, p. 332). The date for the track data is unstated; so I interpret the date as the average for the year 1860 or, equivalently, as at June 30. For Boston, Taylor's (1966b, p. 43) figure is selected as superior to the Census. "Length of line" would be a superior estimator; but data are not available.
14. Sources for initial service are Middleton (1967, p. 15), Miller (1941, p. 21), McShane (2001, p. 280), Rowsome (1956, p. 21), Cuda (1990, p. 13), Taylor (1966b, pp. 43, 46, 49), Stevens (1909, p. 433), and Speirs (1897, p. 11).
15. See also Miller (1941, p. 32), who writes: "Perhaps the horses welcomed this change from the monotony of their daily lives, but it was hard on the operating companies." A flippant remark, and impossible to test! However, one can state definitively that it was technological change in transportation—not war—that fundamentally changed the role of horses in the economy.
16. For lack of data, the series does not incorporate the earlier service of New York (1832–1851), New Orleans (1835–1860), Chicago (1859–1860), Baltimore (1859–1860), and Pittsburgh (1859–1860). See Taylor (1966b, p. 49), Krim (1967, pp. 59–61), Middleton (1967, pp. 15–16), Hennick and Charlton (1975, pp. 6–9), Bion J. Arnold (1910, pp. 35–37), Carman (1919, pp. 20–26), and McShane and Tarr (1997, p. 111).
17. Stage data for Boston are from Holmes and Rohrbach (1983, pp. 78, 179) and Louis Pelzer (1936, p. 3). I assume equality of the number of scheduled arrivals versus scheduled departures, and of the number of traveler arrivals versus traveler departures.
18. The figure "over 250,000" for 1835 is interpreted as 260,000.

19. "This [1835] was probably the high point, however, because in 1835 New England's first three railroads were being completed" (Holmes and Rohrbach 1983, p. 179). All three were completed by July 1835, and another in 1838 (Charles J. Kennedy 1962, p. 155).
20. "By 1820...the three southern states of New England and the middle states of the Atlantic seaboard...contained well over half the country's staging activity" (Holmes and Rohrbach 1983, p. 88). If one assumes that "well over half" means 60% and that the four cities account for 5/6th the stage activity in New England and the mid-Atlantic states, the four-cities' fifty-percent share of national stage activity is rationalized.
21. Source is *Number of Post Offices, and the Length of the Post Roads*, American State Papers, Post Office Department, vol. 1, p. 28. "Prior to 1800, few stages did not carry the mail; so, for those years the Post Office figures were a fairly accurate index of the growth in all staging facilities" (Holmes and Rohrbach 1983, pp. 74–75).
22. This is approximately the Boston-Hartford distance, about half the Boston-New York distance, and about one-third the Boston-Philadelphia distance.
23. Armin E. Shuman (1883, p. 11) and Henry C. Adams (1895, pp. 615–616).
24. The midpoint of the railroads' reporting dates (September 30, December 31) according to Fishlow.
25. Data sources are *Historical Statistics* (1975, series Q321) and, for 1829, John F. Stover (1987, p. 32). The Baltimore and Ohio Railroad, the first railroad in the United States, opened for business on January 7, 1830. I push the date back to December 31, 1829.
26. For 1789, I assume that the 1789/1790 and 1790/1791 population ratios are equal.
27. See *Historical Statistics* (2006, pp. 1–29, 34).
28. *Historical Statistics* (2006, series Aa293-299, Aa300-301, Aa373, Aa375, Aa377, Aa380-382, Aa385). The age range is 15–39, except 16–44 for War of 1812. For lack of data, Blacks are included only for 1890, 1900; and the "age 35-39" 1890 figure is estimated, using data for 1870.
29. For every war, the official casualties number (Anne Leland and Mari-Jana Oboroceanu 2010, p. 2) is lower than the figure developed by a private scholar which I accept and consider of greater reliability, for several reasons. First, government own-force casualties statistics tend toward downward bias for reasons of war morale, domestic politics, and the practice of excluding casualties based on weak information. Second, private scholars have a triple advantage. (1) They can utilize data sources that are addition to, and generally later than, official statistics. (2) They have the ability to apply statistical analysis to adjust official figures that are incomplete. (3) They can adopt a broader definition of "casualty" (examples:

death due to disease, or injury that results in death only after the war). In fairness to Leland and Oboroceanu, their title is "Information Research Specialist" in the Congressional Research Service. As such, their report "provides tables compiled by sources at the Department of Defense," and their protocol is the presentation of official figures without adjustment. To the credit of Leland and Oboroceanu, they provide useful descriptive notes on the data. If official casualties figures were used here, the revised U.S. population would be closer to the official resident-population series.

30. The Civil War final number is 816,927–higher than J. David Hacker's (2011, pp. 311, 348) "preferred estimate" of 750,000, itself higher than the "commonly accepted" figure of 620,000. Five earlier studies show figures ranging from 558,000 to 625,000 (Greer 2005, p. 5).
31. Source is *Historical* Statistics (2006, series Ab1013-1017). There is very little change in life expectancy for 20 and 40-year-old white males in 1860 versus 1900 (series Ab672, Ab675). Therefore one can apply the 1900 death rate, deemed the "normal" (peacetime) death rate, to the Civil War decade.
32. *Historical Statistics* (2006, series Aa699 and Aa712).
33. *Historical Statistics* (2006, series Aa832).

References

Adams, Henry C. 1895. Statistics of Steam Railroad Transportation. In *Report on Transportation Business in the United States at the Eleventh Census*, 591–620. Washington: Government Printing Office.

Arnold, Bion J. 1910. *Report on the Pittsburgh Transportation Problem*. City of Pittsburgh.

Baldwin, Leland D. 1937. *Pittsburgh: The Story of a City, 1750–1865*. Pittsburgh: University of Pittsburgh Press.

Barger, Harold. 1951. *The Transportation Industries, 1889–1946*. New York: National Bureau of Economic Research.

Barker, Charles R. 1931. *Philadelphia in the Late 'Forties*. Philadelphia: City History Society of Philadelphia.

Bureau of the Census. 1920. *Electric Railways*. Washington: Government Printing Office.

Carman, Harry J. 1919. The Street Surface Railway Franchises of New York City. Ph.D. diss., Columbia University.

Cooley, Charles H. 1895. Statistics of Street Railway Transportation. In *Report on Transportation Business in the United States at the Eleventh Census*, 681–839. Washington: Government Printing Office.

Crawford, Mark. 1999. *Encyclopedia of the Mexican-American War*. Santa Barbara: ABC-CLIO.

Cuda, Brian J. 1990. *Cash, Tokens, and Transfers*. New York: Fordham University Press.

Dearborn, Nathaniel. 1848. *Boston Notions*. Boston: Nathaniel Dearborn.

Durand, Edward D. 1905. Street and Electric Railways. In Bureau of the Census, *Street and Electric Railways 1902*, 3–235. Washington: Government Printing Office.

Fishlow, Albert. 1966. Productivity and Technological Change in the Railroad Sector, 1840–1910. In *Output, Employment, and Productivity in the United States*, ed. Dorothy S. Brady, 583–646. New York: Columbia University Press.

Greer, Darroch. 2005. *Counting Civil War Casualties Week-By-Week for the Abraham Lincoln Presidential Library and Museum*. BRC Imagination Arts.

Hacker, J.David. 2011. A Census-Based Count of the Civil War Dead. *Civil War History* 57 (December): 307–348.

Hennick, Louis C., and E. Harper Charlton. 1975. *The Streetcars of New Orleans*. Gretna: Pelican.

[*Historical Statistics*]. 1975. Bureau of the Census. *Historical Statistics of the United States, Colonial Times to 1970, Bicentennial Edition*. Washington: Government Printing Office.

———. 2006. *Historical Statistics of the United States, Millennial Edition*, ed. Susan B. Carter, Scott Sigmund Gartner, Michael R. Haines, Alan L. Olmstead, Richard Sutch, and Gavin Wright. Cambridge: Cambridge University Press.

Holmes, Oliver W., and Peter T. Rohrbach. 1983. *Stagecoach East*. Washington: Smithsonian Institution Press.

Holt, Glen E. 1972. The Changing Perception of Urban Pathology. In *Cities in American History*, ed. Kenneth T. Jackson and Stanley K. Schultz, 324–343. New York: Alfred A. Knopf.

Jackson, Kenneth T. 1985. *Crabgrass Frontier*. New York: Oxford University Press.

Kennedy, Charles J. 1962. Commuter Services in the Boston Area, 1835–1860. *Business History Review* 36 (summer): 153–170.

Krim, Arthur J. 1967. The Innovation and Diffusion of the Street Railway in North America. Ph.D. diss., University of Chicago.

Leland, Anne, and Mari-Jana Oboroceanu. 2010. *American War and Military Operations Casualties: Lists and Statistics*. Washington: Congressional Research Service.

McShane, Clay. 2001. Gelded Age Boston. *New England Quarterly* 74 (June): 274–302.

———. 2008. 1872: Great Epizootic. In *Disasters, Accidents, and Crises in American History*, ed. Ballard C. Campbell, 131–132. New York: Facts on File.

———, and Joel A. Tarr. 1997. The Centrality of the Horse in the Nineteenth-Century American City. In *The Making of Urban America*, ed. Raymond A. Mohl, 105–130. Wilmington: Scholarly Resources.

Meinhard, Robert W. 1998. War Statistics. In *The Civil War Battlefield Guide*, ed. Frances H. Kennedy, 465. Boston: Houghton Mifflin.

Middleton, William D. 1967. *The Time of the Trolley*. Milwaukee: Kalmbach.

Miles, Pliny. 1857. History of the Post Office. *Bankers' Magazine and Statistical Register* 7 (November): 337–365.

Miller, John A. 1941. *Fares, Please!*. New York: D. Appleton-Century.

Officer, Lawrence H. (2009). *Two Centuries of Compensation for U.S. Production Workers in Manufacturing*. New York: Palgrave Macmillan.

Pelzer, Lewis. 1936. Pioneer Stage-Coach Travel. *Mississippi Valley Historical Review* 23 (June): 3–26.

Record and Guide. 1892. November 26.

Report of the Public Service Commission. 1907. Vol. 2. New York City: Bureau of Statistics and Accounts.

———. 1913. Vol. 2. New York City: Bureau of Statistics and Accounts.

Rockoff, Hugh. 2012. *America's Economic Way of War*. Cambridge: Cambridge University Press.

Rowsome, Frank, Jr. 1956. *Trolley Car Treasury*. New York: McGraw-Hill.

Scharf, J. Thomas. 1874. *The Chronicles of Baltimore*. Baltimore: Turnbull.

Secretary of the Interior. 1866. *Statistics of the United States in 1860*. Washington: Government Printing Office.

Shuman, Armin E. 1883. *Statistical Report of the Railroads in the United States*. 1880 Census, vol. 4. Washington: Government Printing Office.

Speirs, Frederic W. 1897. *The Street Railway System of Philadelphia: Its History and Present Condition*. Baltimore: Johns Hopkins Press.

Stevens, Walter B. 1909. *St Louis: The Fourth City, 1764–1909*. St. Louis: S. J. Clarke.

Stover, John F. 1987. *History of the Baltimore and Ohio Railroad*. West Lafayette: Purdue University Press.

Tarr, Joel A. 1978. *Transportation Innovation and Changing Spatial Patterns in Pittsburgh, 1850–1934*. Chicago: Public Works Historical Society.

Taylor, George Rogers. 1966a. The Beginnings of Mass Transportation in Urban America: Part I. *Smithsonian Journal of History* 1 (summer): 35–50.

———. (1966b). The Beginnings of Mass Transportation in Urban America: Part II. *Smithsonian Journal of History* 1 (fall): 31–54.

PART III

Movement of Goods

CHAPTER 6

Merchandise Exports

Traded goods consist of conventional merchandise ("merchandise," "exports"), merchandise silver, ships, and slaves. In principle, both exports and imports can have all four components. In practice, exports exclude slaves and imports exclude ships. This chapter considers merchandise exports, which include both domestic exports and re-exports.

Merchandise import and export data as originally reported are collected in ASPCN, vols. 1–2. With the Act of February 10, 1820, official trade data greatly improved in quality and comprehensiveness. For 1790–1820, aggregate figures were revised in *Annual Report of the Secretary of the Treasury* [ARSTR] (1835, pp. 31–33). However, for detailed—albeit unrevised and incomplete—data in that period, resort must be had to ASPCN.

1 Basic Series

I begin with a basic series (initial value) of exports and then make adjustments to it. For 1790–1819, the foundation is North's (1960, p. 590) (fiscal year) series, which corrects official data for copying errors and recording deficiencies. I take the official series as the basis for 1820–1919: for fiscal years 1820–1915, *Foreign Commerce and Navigation* [FCN]

L. H. Officer, *A New Balance of Payments for the United States, 1790–1919*, Palgrave Studies in American Economic History,
https://doi.org/10.1007/978-3-030-66099-4_6

(1912, pp. 43–44; 1915, p. xi); for calendar years 1914–1919, FCN (1918, p. 11; 1919, p. 11).[1]

There is a controversy concerning whether pre-1821 official export and import data exclude gold and silver. I agree with Sterns (1898, p. 192) and North (1960, p. 599) that gold and silver are so excluded, as they are for the later years.[2] Hence the issue of the amount of their flow does not arise here; gold and silver are covered independently in Chapter 8.

2 Subtractions

2.1 *Ship Sales*

Ship sales are another matter. North, Simon, and other predecessors classify them separate from merchandise; but Simon neglects to exclude ships from the official export data. Ship sales, divided into steamers (metal vessels) and sailing ships (wood vessels), have entries in FCN 1868–1905, and I remove the figures from the basic series.[3]

2.2 *Overvaluation of Re-Exports of Ad Valorem Imports*

An informative balance-of-payments table has freight and insurance as separate items rather than embodied in merchandise or goods. Hence "free on board" (f.o.b.) rather than "cost, insurance and freight" (c.i.f.) valuation of exports and imports is warranted. That has always been the fundamental principle of U.S. official export statistics.[4] An exception is re-exports of ad-valorem imports, upon which imports—and therefore upon re-exports of same—the Act of July 31, 1789 mandated either a 10 or 20% addition to the foreign-port f.o.b. cost, depending on whether the import source is closer than the Cape of Good Hope or beyond (or at) the Cape. There is an interregnum (noticed only by BWT 1919, p. 218, note 9), running April 1, 1795–March 2, 1799 (Acts of January 29, 1795, and March 2, 1799), during which the overvaluation was not in effect. The overvaluation was terminated effective March 3, 1833 (Act of July 14, 1832). North (1960, p. 589) neglects to incorporate the impact of this overvaluation on exports, but I do so.

Re-exports of ad-valorem imports ("ad-valorem re-exports") are taken 1805–1814 from ASPCN vol. 1, 1815–1820 from ASPCN vol. 2, 1821–1833 from *Commerce and Navigation* [CN]. I assemble a series of total re-exports 1790–1825.[5] For 1790–1804, ad-valorem re-exports are total re-exports times the average "ad-valorem re-exports"/total re-exports" ratio 1805–1809. The next step is to divide ad-valorem re-exports into re-exports of imports from "Cape of Good Hope and beyond" and remaining ad-valorem re-exports.

I compile ad-valorem imports from "Cape of Good Hope and beyond" for 1790, 1795–1813 (ASPCN, vol. 1), 1814–1819 (ASPCN, vol. 2), and 1821–1833 (CN); total ad-valorem imports for the same ASPCN years and 1821–1861 (CN).[6] The ratio of "Cape of Good Hope and beyond" to total ad-valorem imports is computed for 1790, 1795–1819, 1821–1833 and linearly interpolated for the intervening years. For 1790–1833, re-exports of ad-valorem imports from the Cape and beyond are estimated as this ratio *times* ad-valorem re-exports.[7] Re-exports of "other" (meaning source closer than the Cape of Good Hope) ad-valorem imports are the residual.

For 1790–1794 and 1800–1832, overvaluation of ad-valorem re-exports is 20% of "re-exports of ad-valorem imports from the Cape and beyond" *plus* 10% of "re-exports of other ad-valorem imports." For 1795, 1799, and 1833: 1/2, 7/12, and 5/12 of the calculation applies, with computations for fiscal year ended September 30. For 1796–1798, the overvaluation is zero. The overvaluation 1790–1833 is subtracted from the fiscal-year basic series.

3 Additions

3.1 Overland Exports

Overland exports, whether to BNA/Canada or Mexico, were not included in official statistics until fiscal year 1871. While that year witnessed the beginning of recording of overland exports, reporting was voluntary, and therefore incomplete. North (1960, p. 602) argues that, for his time period (1790–1860), the unimportance of railroads means that the omission of overland exports does not require correction. Simon (1960, p. 632, Note 10) disagrees, quoting an official statement that, prior to the railroad, "a considerable portion of the foreign trade of the United States (across our land frontier) was even then [in 1820] transported, as some of it is still, on wagons, sleds and other land vehicles" (CN 1867, p. XXII). Only from April 1, 1893, per the Act of March 3, 1893, did the government require reporting of exports by railroad.[8] So, for 1790–1893, I develop an additive factor for the fiscal-year basic series.

Simon (1960, pp. 632–641) did the pioneering work here (for his time period, 1861–1900), and I follow him in considering exports to Canada and Mexico separately.

3.1.1 Canada

Simon Series: Simon's methodology for Canada involves obtaining comparable series of official Canadian imports of U.S. merchandise and official U.S. exports of merchandise to Canada, with the (presumed positive) difference estimating unrecorded overland exports. However, his application of the technique has five avoidable problems. First, Simon is taken in by the fact that, until Confederation (July 1, 1867), "Canada" consisted of Ontario and Quebec, with other BNA colonies joining later over time. For 1861–1867, his Canadian series is only Ontario and Quebec, whereas the U.S. series involves the entire Northern border. In contrast, I generate a Canada series for geographic region consistent over time and comparable to that of the U.S. series. Second, he unduly complicates the arithmetic by subtracting gold from total domestic exports rather than taking domestic merchandise exports directly, whereas I do the latter. Third, Simon (1960, pp. 635–636) makes a slew of arbitrary additions to the Canadian figures, which I reject. Fourth, Simon (1960, pp. 636; 637–638, cols. [8]–[9]) adds "inland freight charges" to the Canadian series; but the evidence is that both countries valued U.S. exports f.o.b. point of origin (BIPUS 1930, p. 13; Eliot G. Mears 1935, p. 506, Note 5). So I do not follow him here as well. Fifth, Simon computes the Canada-U.S. difference prior to adjustments to the Canada series; it is more logical to make the computation after the adjustments.

"U.S. Series" of Overland Merchandise Exports: A series of gold-dollar domestic merchandise exports to overland Canada or BNA (the latter *excluding Newfoundland and Labrador*–the desired, "exclusion," series) is collected 1802–1821, 1873–1893. A comparable "inclusion" series (*all* BNA) 1790–1802, 1821–1874 is also assembled.[9] The "exclusion" series is extrapolated to 1790–1801 via the 1802 overlap with the "inclusion" series and is obtained 1871–1872 via subtraction of exports to Newfoundland and Labrador (Bureau of Statistics 1896, p. 56). Thus we have the "exclusion" series 1790–1821, 1871–1893. Recall that official domestic exports below the aggregate level are in mixed dollars (Chapter 2, Appendix, Sect. A). So the "inclusion" and "exclusion" series are each multiplied by the gold-dollar price of the mixed dollar, to convert to gold dollars.

Re-exports to BNA are obtained "exclusion" 1790–1821 and 1871–1893, "inclusion" 1819–1874.[10] Overland merchandise exports 1790–1821, 1871–1893 are the sum of "exclusion" domestic exports and re-exports. The same sum for "inclusion" exports 1821–1871 interpolates "exclusion" 1822–1870, between 1821 and 1871. Thus we have the gold-dollar U.S. Northern overland export series for fiscal years 1790–1893.

"Canada Series" of Overland Merchandise Imports: Canada merchandise imports from the United States require considerable care for a series geographically and fiscal-year (end June 30, 1850–1893) comparable to U.S. exports. The years 1872–1893 are taken from Department of Trade and Commerce (1898 [*Special Report*], p. 257; 1908, p. 414), and include Ontario and Quebec (combined), Nova Scotia, New Brunswick, Manitoba, British Columbia, and Prince Edward Island. Earlier-year data on imports from the United States are generated for individual provinces 1850–1871.[11] The six provincial series are summed to yield Canada imports 1850–1871.

Simon (1960, pp. 636; 637–638, column [4]) has good reason to add five percent to the Canada series for underreporting prior to Confederation, increasing in steps to ten percent—and I copy him. Simon takes the Canadian-dollar/gold-dollar exchange rate at par; but I allow for a varying rate, albeit Canada was on the gold standard (Powell 2005, p. 33). Therefore I divide the Canada series by the Canadian-dollar/gold-dollar exchange rate (Appendix, Chapter 2, Note 20), thus effecting comparable (that is, gold-dollar) denomination of the "Canada series" and "U.S. series."

Adjustment: The addition to overland exports 1850–1893 is the "Canada series" *minus* the "U.S. series."[12] For 1790–1849, the adjustment is extrapolated via 1850 overlap with the "U.S. Series."

3.1.2 Mexico

Given poor Mexican data, Simon (1960, pp. 636, 639; 640–641, col. [2]) does the best he can do for 1861–1893, and I accept his adjustment series. For 1790–1861, I extrapolate the adjustment via merchandise exports to Mexico on the basis of the 1860 overlap. Exports to Mexico for 1825–1861 (extended to 1874, for later use) are in MSCF (August 1901, p. 618). Exports for 1790–1824 are extrapolated via exports to "Spanish South America."[13]

3.1.3 Total

The adjustments for overland exports to Canada and Mexico fiscal years 1790–1893 are summed and added to the series corrected for overvaluation (Sect. 2.2).

3.2 General Underreporting of Exports

The Act of 1893 was only partially enforced; regulations effective February 1, 1916, made the Act effective and more. "It is known that under the old order whole trainloads crossed the border without being recorded in the statistics and that statistics collected at seaboard ports were grossly inaccurate" (*Annual Report of the Chief of Bureau of Foreign and Domestic Commerce* 1916, p. 65). Based on numbers in this *Annual Report* (1916, pp. 64–65), I estimate underreporting of exports prior to February 1916 at about two percent.[14] So the above-corrected fiscal-year basic series 1790–1915 and the initial calendar-year basic series 1914–1915 are increased by two percent.[15] The fiscal-year component is then converted to calendar year. Neither Goldsmith nor OBE makes this adjustment.

3.3 Undervaluation of Overland Exports to Canada

Overland exports are supposed to be valued f.o.b. *at U.S. boundary* (port or frontier). However, BIPUS (1930, p. 13) reported that two Canadian economists had found that most U.S. rail exports to Canada were valued f.o.b. *point of origin*, that is, exclusive of freight to the Northern border. BIPUS counts the freight amount as a service credit (under freight-and-shipping), but it is more logical to treat it as an undervaluation of overland exports and therefore add it to merchandise exports. BIPUS estimated the undervaluation as $32 million in 1925 (the earliest estimated year). For estimation 1790–1919, I construct a synthetic undervaluation series composed as the product of the overland freight rate and overland exports to Canada.

Freight Rate: For 1925, the freight rate on overland exports to Canada is the midpoint of the range for 1925–1929 (BIPUS 1930, p. 13). For 1868–1892, it is the series in Simon (1960, pp. 637–638, col. [8]) converted to calendar year.[16] Then I turn to general railroad rates. Freight revenue per ton-mile (*Historical Statistics* 2006, series Df979), with 1892–1916 converted to calendar year, interpolates the overland freight rate 1893–1919 between 1892 and 1925. Freight revenue per ton-mile for Vermont railroads (Thurston M. Adams 1944, p. 49) extrapolates the overland freight rate for 1857–1867 via the 1868 overlap. North (1965, p. 245) provides rail freight-rate figures for various years over 1848–1858. I linearly interpolate missing years and use the resulting series to extrapolate the desired series to 1848–1856 via the 1857 overlap. That still leaves 1790–1847.

In the pre-railroad era, the primary land carrier of freight was the wagon, propelled by true horsepower. Both railway and wagon must have been carriers in the early days of railways. Unfortunately, the value and volume of non-rail land (that is, wagon) freight transportation services are a great unknown in U.S. transportation history. There are usable figures on price, but no data on volume So one cannot construct a combined rail-wagon price index. Therefore I extrapolate 1790–1847 via the wagon freight rate (cents per ton-mile) alone, overlap 1848.[17]The constructed freight rate ("exports to Canada") is graphed in Fig. 1.

Overland Exports: Overland domestic exports and re-exports to Canada 1871–1919, 1925 are summed and converted to calendar year as needed.[18] For 1790–1870 overland merchandise exports are extrapolated

Fig. 1 Overland Freight Rates, 1790–1919 and 1852–1919. *Note* "Exports to Canada" is the freight rate on overland exports to Canada, "imports from Canada" the freight rate on overland imports from Canada. In each case, the distance involved is from the domestic point-of-origin to the border. The series are expressed as percent of the value of exports or imports, respectively

via the U.S. Northern overland gold-dollar export series (Sect. 3.1.1), 1871 overlap. The addition to overland exports to Canada (from Sect. 3.1.1) is converted to calendar year and added to the desired overland-exports series.

Adjustment and Final Merchandise Exports: The product of the freight rate and overland exports is a synthetic undervaluation series that extrapolates the 1925 accepted value to 1790–1919. This series is added to calendar-year exports resulting from general underreporting of exports (Sect. 3.2). The result is merchandise exports expressed in gold dollars for the greenback period, whereas our methodology involves currency-dollar denomination throughout. Therefore, for 1862–1878, the series is multiplied by the greenback price of gold (Chapter 2, Appendix, Sect. A). Merchandise exports are listed in column (1) of Table 1.

4 Comparisons

Table 2 shows the magnitudes (in terms of percentages) of the five adjustments to the basic merchandise-exports series. For each item, the "Average" column shows the mean adjustment over the years (parenthesized) of non-zero adjustment, the "Maximum" column the largest-magnitude annual adjustment for each item. Not surprisingly, "addition to overland exports" is the largest correction by either measure. Recall that items (1)–(2) are subtractions, and (3)–(5) additions to the basic series. The averages suggest that, net, the new export series is higher than the North-official series, which is borne out in the next table.

The new series is compared with the "standard" merchandise-exports series in row (1) of Table 3. The standard series combines North (1960, pp. 590; 605, col. [1]), Simon (1960, pp. 640–641, column [9]), and FCN for later years. It is essentially embodied in the *Historical Statistics* (1975, series U2) balance-of-payments table. Recall (Chapter 2, Sect. 2) that period annual-average comparisons are made after conversion of the standard series to calendar year (in conformity with the new series) and after subtraction of the gold-dollar premium from the 1861–1899 result (to eliminate difference due to currency-dollar denomination of the new series). The outcome is that, while the standard series is low in general relative to the new series, the measured deviation is more pronounced in the antebellum periods.

Table 1 Merchandise, specie, and ships (millions of dollars)

	Merchandise		*Specie*		*Silver*		*Ships*
Year	*Exports* (1)	*Imports* (2)	*Exports* (3)	*Imports* (4)	*Exports* (5)	*Imports* (6)	*Exports* (7)
1790	21	23	0.17	0	0	0	0.36
1791	21	30	0	7.00	0	0	0.35
1792	23	31	0	2.00	0	0	0.40
1793	29	34	0.00	2.00	0	0	0.56
1794	38	48	0.00	1.50	0	0	0.83
1795	54	73	2.50	0	0	0	1.42
1796	67	78	2.50	0	0	0	1.89
1797	60	73	0.50	0	0	0	1.72
1798	68	69	2.00	0	0	0	1.43
1799	79	75	0	3.00	0	0	2.04
1800	79	92	0	0.50	0	0	2.93
1801	91	94	0.50	0	0	0	3.50
1802	70	71	0.50	0	0	0	2.69
1803	65	70	0.50	0	0	0	2.40
1804	85	94	0.00	1.50	0	0	3.05
1805	100	119	0.00	0.50	0	0	3.86
1806	107	130	0.00	0.50	0	0	3.65
1807	90	115	0.00	1.50	0	0	2.92
1808	31	59	0.00	3.50	0	0	0.91
1809	59	64	0.00	3.50	0	0	2.81
1810	70	67	0.00	3.50	0	0	3.92
1811	60	44	1.63	0.00	0	0	4.42
1812	38	52	1.63	0.00	0	0	2.65
1813	23	12	1.63	0.00	0	0	3.68
1814	20	31	1.63	0.00	0	0	1.09
1815	66	103	0.00	2.25	0	0	0.77
1816	93	134	0.39	0.00	0	0	1.70
1817	99	94	0.39	0.00	0	0	0.93
1818	95	102	0.39	0.00	0	0	0.93
1819	79	85	0.39	0.00	0	0	0.70
1820	73	69	0.39	0.00	0	0	0.36
1821	62	70	10.56	6.89	0	0	0.47
1822	69	91	9.70	3.80	0	0	0.32
1823	74	81	6.53	5.92	0	0	0.50
1824	81	86	7.46	7.82	0	0	0.68

(continued)

Table 1 (continued)

	Merchandise		*Specie*		*Silver*		*Ships*
Year	*Exports* (1)	*Imports* (2)	*Exports* (3)	*Imports* (4)	*Exports* (5)	*Imports* (6)	*Exports* (7)
1825	93	99	7.77	6.33	0	0	0.55
1826	79	88	5.53	7.20	0	0	0.79
1827	77	87	8.07	7.99	0	0	1.05
1828	70	90	7.41	7.47	0	0	0.81
1829	75	75	4.24	7.59	0	0	0.21
1830	80	81	3.89	7.94	0	0	0.50
1831	83	110	8.18	6.96	0	0	0.49
1832	92	107	4.90	6.20	0	0	0.30
1833	102	106	2.48	9.78	0	0	0.15
1834	116	115	3.18	16.72	0	0	0.25
1835	129	150	5.94	13.20	0	0	0.53
1836	132	169	4.74	12.68	0	0	0.54
1837	118	129	5.36	12.32	0	0	0.60
1838	115	114	4.83	14.71	0	0	0.37
1839	127	146	8.69	6.42	0	0	0.52
1840	136	106	8.82	7.91	0	0	0.84
1841	125	118	8.73	4.76	0	0	0.73
1842	116	86	4.12	10.51	0	0	0.51
1843	120	82	3.74	17.80	0	0	0.51
1844	120	113	7.03	4.95	0	0	0.42
1845	123	120	6.25	3.92	0	0	0.56
1846	151	120	2.91	13.95	0	0	0.81
1847	166	139	8.87	15.24	0	0	0.80
1848	155	152	10.62	6.51	0	0	0.68
1849	153	164	6.46	5.64	0	0	0.67
1850	174	204	18.49	5.04	0	0	0.76
1851	185	224	36.07	5.48	0	0	0.87
1852	195	250	35.08	4.85	0	0	0.77
1853	229	296	32.96	2.73	1.39	2.75	1.99
1854	236	292	47.79	2.06	0.93	3.15	3.70
1855	263	399	50.06	1.04	0.94	2.89	3.17
1856	304	443	55.12	3.82	2.32	4.51	2.79
1857	298	316	57.62	9.11	3.27	6.76	2.32

(continued)

Table 1 (continued)

Year	*Merchandise*		*Specie*		*Silver*		*Ships*
	Exports (1)	*Imports (2)*	*Exports (3)*	*Imports (4)*	*Exports (5)*	*Imports (6)*	*Exports (7)*
1858	292	310	55.56	6.85	2.70	6.51	1.54
1859	325	353	59.78	2.32	5.44	5.68	1.24
1860	291	325	43.16	22.40	5.23	5.04	1.15
1861	221	243	32.24	28.10	1.91	3.28	3.61
1862	243	255	55.96	11.01	1.95	3.72	9.15
1863	287	425	119.89	12.13	4.89	4.35	17.68
1864	362	591	165.70	17.97	14.23	5.34	18.73
1865	432	557	103.89	11.56	18.96	4.57	6.84
1866	478	617	80.39	17.77	25.85	5.32	1.46
1867	422	549	81.17	17.80	29.87	7.25	0.99
1868	422	572	80.15	15.97	29.70	7.77	1.35
1869	476	599	49.55	17.42	30.36	13.32	1.38
1870	500	578	58.51	10.88	32.33	16.52	1.06
1871	520	670	64.92	8.71	34.67	10.84	1.15
1872	576	740	53.06	9.78	39.39	10.02	1.80
1873	667	710	44.89	16.04	41.16	12.38	3.85
1874	647	629	56.21	18.46	32.10	8.98	3.51
1875	642	586	56.44	12.41	29.00	8.70	1.79
1876	671	522	32.47	19.04	30.61	12.53	1.65
1877	712	477	19.00	20.74	28.35	16.25	1.84
1878	740	457	7.12	9.55	22.65	15.71	2.11
1879	799	571	4.37	43.19	16.96	13.47	1.75
1880	889	672	3.19	90.39	15.17	11.41	1.51
1881	853	702	17.58	67.20	16.84	9.32	1.30
1882	821	743	22.09	26.06	18.52	9.43	1.64
1883	814	730	26.34	20.28	23.14	12.68	1.88
1884	770	670	25.28	24.72	29.90	15.57	1.54
1885	742	652	26.66	23.67	31.63	17.20	1.60
1886	731	714	26.93	31.83	27.90	17.56	1.50
1887	741	762	15.22	43.42	27.17	16.33	0.89
1888	756	790	40.44	27.11	32.36	17.04	0.56
1889	840	825	39.33	11.61	35.78	19.86	0.62
1890	915	855	53.03	15.59	28.73	19.53	0.63

(continued)

Table 1 (continued)

	Merchandise		*Specie*		*Silver*		*Ships*
Year	*Exports* (1)	*Imports* (2)	*Exports* (3)	*Imports* (4)	*Exports* (5)	*Imports* (6)	*Exports* (7)
1891	1001	850	69.03	33.97	27.70	18.99	0.65
1892	977	858	79.51	35.44	36.77	21.93	0.77
1893	897	770	92.90	46.81	45.59	18.60	0.89
1894	869	702	71.72	54.42	48.87	16.75	0.82
1895	864	765	89.44	34.95	53.92	24.49	0.82
1896	989	782	76.39	59.27	61.24	29.66	0.69
1897	1167	699	27.88	102.70	58.53	30.73	0.97
1898	1257	666	26.46	104.67	55.71	30.80	1.36
1899	1340	785	42.89	66.76	56.52	32.97	0.89
1900	1474	849	50.73	55.31	60.50	35.82	0.73
1901	1468	876	50.88	59.04	57.01	32.31	0.57
1902	1434	978	47.83	48.50	46.99	26.20	0.65
1903	1475	1022	64.28	72.02	46.86	25.97	0.71
1904	1525	1067	87.03	76.35	49.16	27.63	0.52
1905	1670	1186	65.58	74.94	57.36	35.96	0.91
1906	1856	1346	44.99	105.37	61.30	43.69	1.21
1907	1916	1329	61.92	131.42	57.33	43.80	0.95
1908	1804	1267	81.98	96.17	56.80	44.31	1.78
1909	1746	1446	105.05	43.67	55.48	44.59	2.25
1910	1945	1551	70.54	58.47	60.02	45.58	1.32
1911	2182	1598	39.92	61.27	64.82	46.49	1.05
1912	2397	1741	67.55	59.07	68.25	44.16	2.20
1913	2478	1859	94.90	67.87	63.29	35.80	2.87
1914	2168	1792	222.62	57.39	51.60	25.96	1.68
1915	3641	1781	31.43	451.95	53.60	34.48	3.71
1916	5514	2396	155.79	685.99	70.60	32.26	11.61
1917	6264	2959	371.88	552.45	84.13	53.34	13.10
1918	6187	3041	41.07	62.04	252.85	71.38	7.06
1919	7959	3916	368.19	76.53	239.02	89.41	20.00

5 Behavior

Merchandise exports as listed in column (1) of Table 1 exhibit salient behavior. There was growth to 1805–1806, with the United States advancing foreign trade in an environment of intermittent European conflict inhibiting belligerents' trade. Then occurred U.S. restrictive trade policy—especially the Embargo Act of December 22, 1807, which aimed to terminate foreign trade, and the Non-Intercourse Act of March 1,

Table 2 Adjustments to North-official merchandise exports (percent of initial value of exports)[a]

Item	*Percent*	
	Average (Years)	*Maximum (Year)*
(1) Recorded ship sales	0.03 (1868–1905)	0.14 (1874)
(2) Overvaluation of ad-valorem re-exports	1.00 (1790–1795, 1799–1833)	2.43 (1808)
(3) Addition to overland exports	4.05 (1790–1893)	10.88 (1846)
(4) General underreporting of exports[b]	2.06 (1790–1914)	2.22 (1846)
(5) Undervaluation of overland exports to Canada	0.87 (1790–1919)	3.52 (1819)

[a]Fiscal years, except (5) is for calendar years
[b]For 1914–1916 calendar years, average is 1.37 and maximum 2.00

Table 3 Merchandise and ship sales: comparisons (percentage deviation of existing series from new series)

Item	*1790–1819*	*1820–1860*	*1861–1899*	*1900–1918*
(1) merchandise exports	−4.97	−7.95	−1.77	−2.10
(2) merchandise imports	9.16	−4.90	−0.60	−0.78
(3) ship sales	−57.33	−10.18	−2.60	–

Note A negative (positive) sign means that the new series is larger (smaller) than the existing series. For discussion, see Sect. 4 in this Chapter; Sect. 7 in Chapter 7; Sect. 1.4 in Chapter 9

1809, a partial liberalization, which kept trade closed with Britain and France and their colonies. The British blockade during the War of 1812 was extremely effective, judging by the numbers. The adverse effect of war on trade is also seen in the figures for the early years of the Civil War–but not for World War I, when trade with the United States as a neutral again climbed, and when, even after the country entered the war, there was only a slight decline in exports.

One should bear in mind important features of U.S. exports *not* exhibited in the series. First, the division into domestic exports and re-exports is concealed in the aggregate figures. From 1796 to 1809, re-exports exceeded 40% of total exports in all years but one. Prior to 1835, the re-export share is above 15% in all but six years. From 1835, it is below

15% in all but three years. From 1881 to 1919, re-exports are less than 2 ½% in every year but one.[19] Re-exports to 1807 trend upward absolutely and relatively (except in 1803, when war broke out between Britain and France). As a neutral, the United States could re-export commodities between belligerents, taking the place of belligerent direct trade.[20] The re-export share fell not just because war ended but even more, as production of commodities such as cotton and manufactures increased and manifested in domestic exports.

Second, the tabulated series is in current dollars, thus embodying price change as well as volume. In the 1820s, because of price deflation, constant-dollar exports increased even though value fell.[21] Inflation during the Civil War means that the reduction in export volume was substantially greater than the series shows. Third, the movement of exports relative to the overall economy is considered not here but in Chapter 19 (Sect. 1.1). Fourth, exports of specific sectors of interest (cotton, tobacco, manufactures) are addressed in Chapter 20 (Sects. 1.4, 3).

Notes

1. North accepts the official series for 1820–1860; Simon takes the official series for 1861–1900 as the foundation for his adjustments. Trade-data fiscal-years end September 30 1790–1842, June 30 1843–1915 (with year 1843 nine months).
2. The contrary view is in FCN (1912, p. 43) and *Historical Statistics* (2006, pp. 5-463, 503).
3. Presumably, during the greenback period, ship sales continued to be recorded in currency dollars. Because merchandise exports are expressed in gold dollars (until at the end of Sect. 3.1.3), I divide ship sales by the greenback price of gold (Chapter 2, Appendix, Sect. A). Chapter 9 (Sect. 1) deals with ship sales.
4. "The principle established for the valuation of the exports by the ninety-third section of the act of March 2, 1799, is that each article shall be stated according to its actual value at the port and time of exportation"– Committee of Commerce and Manufactures, Senate Report, December 20, 1819 (ASPCN, vol. 2, p. 392). The rule is repeated in the Act of February 10, 1820: "That all articles exported shall be valued at their actual cost, or the values which they may truly bear at the time of exportation, in the ports of the United States from which they are exported."

5. Only 1790–1809 are employed here, but all years will be used in Chapter 7. Years 1790–1820 from ARSTR (1835, p. 31)–except that for 1800 the figure is incorrect, and North (1960, p. 591) repeats the error. The correct figure, which I use, is in various places (including later ARSTRs, and *Historical Statistics*), and the error as such is pointed out by Douglas A. Irwin (2003, p. 509). Years 1821–1825 from *Rates of Duty on Imports into the United States* (1891, pp. 305–306).
6. Regions in "Cape of Good Hope and beyond" are Cape of Good Hope, East Indies, Bourbon and Mauritius, Arabia, Sandwich Islands, Philippines, China, Asia generally, South Seas, Red Sea Ports. Total ad-valorem imports are extended beyond 1833, for Chapter 7.
7. The computation abstracts from the lag between import and re-export.
8. Reporting was also mandated for exports by water or land vehicle, if rail transport to the frontier was involved.
9. For the "exclusion" series, sources are ASPCN (vol. 2, pp. 453, 651) and MSCF (August 1901, pp. 612–613). For the "inclusion" series, sources are ASPCN (vol. 1) and MSCF (August 1901, p. 612), with 1793 linearly interpolated.
10. Source is ASPCN (vol. 2, p. 651) and MSCF (August 1901, pp. 612–613). "Exclusion" re-exports 1871–1872 are the difference between "inclusion" re-exports and estimated re-exports to Newfoundland and Labrador, with the latter zero 1790–1821.
11. Ontario and Quebec imports 1850–1871 for varying fiscal years are obtained from *Special Report* (pp. 252–257; 259, note) and extrapolated to 1849 via 1849–1850 figures in Province of Canada (1851, p. 436). Conversion to "fiscal year ended June 30" results in a series for 1850–1871. Imports of Nova Scotia, New Brunswick, and Prince Edward Island to the same end are developed from *Special Report* (pp. 252–257) and, for Nova Scotia and New Brunswick, extrapolation to 1849 via Ontario and Quebec. Manitoba imports exist only for January-June 1871 (*Special Report*, p. 257). The figure is doubled for fiscal-year 1871 and extrapolated to 1850 via Ontario-Quebec. British Columbia imports are given for 1872 (*Special Report*, p. 257) and extrapolated back in the same way. For lack of data, Alberta and Saskatchewan are excluded. They did not join Canada until 1905.
12. There is one year, 1859, for which the difference is (only slightly) negative. I make no adjustment for that year.
13. For some years, merchandise exports (inclusive of re-exports) to Spanish South America (which includes Mexico) are obtained directly. For other years, this series is extrapolated via exports amplified to include Spanish West Indies. Data source is FCN.
14. Exports in February 1916 were approximately $400 million, an increase averaging $55 million over the preceding two months, of which about

15% (midpoint of stated estimated range) were due to the new regulations. Thus underreporting prior to February 1916 is (0.15 x 55)/400 = about two percent. Mears (1935, pp. 505–506) should be credited with publicizing the regulations; but other authors have neglected both Mears and the regulations.

15. An adjustment is also made for the year 1916, adding two percent of exports in January 1916 (MSCF, January 1916, p. 3).
16. Notwithstanding his series, Simon does not perform the correction of this section.
17. Collecting figures for isolated years over 1784–1850, I interpolate missing years. Data sources are *Hunt's Merchant Magazine* (1841, p. 284), Taylor (1951, p. 133), and North (1965, pp. 244–245). Between 1819 and 1822, there was a general price deflation; rather than interpolating linearly, I interpolate with the wholesale price index (George F. Warren and Frank A. Pearson 1933, p. 25).
18. All data in this paragraph are from FCN. For 1871–1879, domestic exports to Canada include gold and silver, which are estimated as the product of "the average overland proportion of total domestic exports of gold and silver to Canada 1880-1884" (90.7%) and "total domestic exports of gold and silver," and then subtracted. Domestic exports are converted from mixed to gold dollars via the gold-dollar/mixed-dollar exchange rate.
19. Data source is *Historical Statistics* (2006, series Ee365–367).
20. Indirect shipment of British and European goods to the West Indies and of West Indies goods to Europe loomed large (Curtis P. Nettels 1962, pp. 235–236). Of course, the West Indies were largely territory of the belligerents.
21. This phenomenon is emphasized in Taylor (1951, pp. 192–193), and see Fig. 1 in Chapter 7.

References

Adams, Thurston M. 1944. *Prices Paid by Vermont Farmers for Goods and Services and Received by Them for Farm Products, 1790–1940*. Burlington: Vermont Agricultural Experiment Station.

American State Papers: Commerce and Navigation [ASPCN].

Annual Report of the Chief of Bureau of Foreign and Domestic Commerce. 1916.

Annual Report of the Secretary of the Treasury [ARSTR]. 1835.

Bullock, Charles J., John H. Williams, and Rufus S. Tucker [BWT]. 1919. The History of Our Foreign Trade Balance from 1789 to 1914. *Review of Economics and Statistics* 1 (July): 215–233.

Bureau of Statistics. 1896. *Commerce of the United States and Europe with American Countries, 1851–1895*. Washington: Government Printing Office.

Commerce and Navigation [CN]. 1867.

Department of Trade and Commerce. 1898. *Special Report on Trade Between Canada and the United States*. Ottawa: S. E. Dawson.

———. 1908. *Report, Canadian Trade*. Ottawa: S. E. Dawson.

Foreign Commerce and Navigation [FCN]. 1912.

——— . 1915.

——— . 1919.

[*Historical Statistics*] (1975). Bureau of the Census. *Historical Statistics of the United States, Colonial Times to 1970, Bicentennial Edition*. Washington: Government Printing Office.

———. 2006. *Historical Statistics of the United States, Millennial Edition*, ed. Susan B. Carter, Scott Sigmund Gartner, Michael R. Haines, Alan L. Olmstead, Richard Sutch, and Gavin Wright. Cambridge: Cambridge University Press.

Irwin, Douglas A. 2003. New Estimates of the Average Tariff of the United States, 1790–1820. *Journal of Economic History* 63 (June): 506–513.

Mears, Eliot G. 1935. The Foreign Trade Statistics of the United States. *Journal of the American Statistical Association* 30 (September): 501–516.

Monthly Summary of Commerce and Finance [MSCF].

Nettels, Curtis P. 1962. *The Emergence of a National Economy, 1775–1815*. New York: Holt, Reinhart and Winston.

North, Douglass C. 1960. The United States Balance of Payments, 1790–1860. In *Trends in the American Economy in the Nineteenth Century*, ed. William N. Parker, 573–628. Princeton: Princeton University Press.

———. 1965. The Role of Transportation in the Economic Development of North America. In *Les Grandes Voies Maritimes dans le Monde*, 209–246. Paris: S.E.V.P.E.N.

Powell, James. 2005. *A History of the Canadian Dollar*. Ottawa: Bank of Canada.

Province of Canada. 1851. *Tables of the Trade and Navigation of the Province of Canada for the Year 1850*. Toronto: Derbishire.

Rates of Duty on Imports into the United States. 1891.

Simon, Matthew. 1960. The United States Balance of Payments, 1861–1900. In *Trends in the American Economy in the Nineteenth Century*, ed. William N. Parker, 629–716. Princeton: Princeton University Press.

Sterns, Worthy P. 1898. The Beginnings of American Financial Independence. *Journal of Political Economy* 6 (March): 187–208.

Taylor, George Rogers. 1951. *The Transportation Revolution*. New York: Holt, Rinehart, and Winston.

The Balance of International Payments of the United States [BIPUS]. 1930. Annual.

Warren, George F., and Frank A. Pearson. 1933. *Prices*. New York: Wiley.

CHAPTER 7

Merchandise Imports

1 Basic Series

The plan for merchandise imports mirrors that for exports. For 1790–1819, North's revision of the official data in ARSTR (1835, pp. 32–33) is accepted for the basic series; for 1820–1919, the official series is taken.[1] North (1960, pp. 591–593) makes four adjustments to official figures. First, just as for exports, he corrects copying errors. Second, he follows Taylor (1951, p. 200) in rejecting the official figure for 1815 as too high and replacing it with the more-reliable alternative adopted by Taylor. Third, he improves the series of duty-free imports by applying an estimation technique superior to that of Treasury. Fourth, North includes the duty-free component in total imports, which, amazingly, the Treasury neglected to do.

2 Valuation

The Act of February 10, 1820 stated that all imports are to be valued f.o.b. the foreign port. Prior to that Act, only ad-valorem imports had their value recorded. Specific-duty imports had just quantity recorded and duty-free imports were ignored. While earlier legislation regarding valuation could pertain only to ad-valorem goods, nevertheless there was

L. H. Officer, *A New Balance of Payments for the United States, 1790–1919*, Palgrave Studies in American Economic History,
https://doi.org/10.1007/978-3-030-66099-4_7

adherence to the f.o.b. principle.[2] So one could infer that the f.o.b. valuation, which is adopted in this study, is obeyed by official import data even for 1790–1819; but the practice is not so simple and not readily discerned.

3 Adjustments

3.1 Deviation from F.O.B. Valuation

3.1.1 Ad-Valorem Imports

Overvaluation, 1790–1833: In Chapter 6 (Sect. 2.2) we developed ad-valorem imports for fiscal years 1790, 1795–1819, 1821–1833 (in fact, to 1861) and share of Cape-and-beyond for 1790–1833. Now we obtain ad-valorem imports for calendar years 1790–1794, 1818–1820, and convert to fiscal years 1791–1794, 1820, thus completing the series for 1790–1833 (and 1790–1861).[3] Multiplying the figures for 1791–1794, 1820 by the share of Cape-and-beyond, ad-valorem imports for that geographic region is completed 1790–1833. Other-region ad-valorem imports are the difference between total and Cape-and-beyond. Overvaluation of ad-valorem imports, in dollars, for fiscal years 1790–1794 and 1800–1832, is 20% of Cape-and-beyond *plus* 10% of other-region imports. Again, for 1795, 1799, and 1833: 1/2, 7/12 and 5/12 of the calculation applies; and again, for 1796–1798, there is no overvaluation.

Treasury Undervaluation of Pound, 1790–1873: From 1789 to 1873, ad-valorem imports from Britain and dependencies were valued at legal exchange rates: \$4.44 to March 3, 1833; \$4.80 to July 17, 1842; \$4.84 to March 3, 1873; \$4.8665 to May 27, 1921.[4] For each fiscal year 1790–1861, under-recording of imports due to Treasury undervaluation of the pound is calculated as the product of (1) the market exchange rate *minus* the legal exchange rate and (2) ad-valorem imports from Britain and dependencies.[5]

Overvaluation of Manufactured Imports, 1816–1818: During fiscal years 1816–1818 "a flood of [ad-valorem] imported goods were being dumped on the U.S. market at prices below their customhouse valuation" (North 1960, p. 601). A contemporary account states that, in November 1816, merchandise could not be sold "even at twenty and fifty per cent loss on the prime cost" (Norman S. Buck 1925, p. 138). I estimate the overvaluation as 35% (range midpoint) of ad-valorem imports from

England (representing ad-valorem manufactured imports, source ASPCN, vol. 2).[6]

Home Valuation, 1842: For the two months July–August 1842, c.i.f. valuation ("home valuation") replaced f.o.b. for ad-valorem imports.[7] In that year, home valuation was considered to be 20–30% above *foreign* valuation (Smith 1948, p. 89, note 64). Taking the midpoint (25%), overvaluation is 20% *home* valuation. So, for fiscal year (end September 30) 1842, overvaluation of ad-valorem imports due to home valuation is estimated as one-sixth of 20% ad-valorem imports.

3.1.2 Duty-Free Imports

North (1960, p. 593) argues that duty-free imports could have been valued even lower than f.o.b. in 1790–1820; but it seems prudent to assume that these imports were recorded f.o.b. Then a duty-free series is required only to estimate specific-duty imports for that time period (Sect. 3.1.3). For duty-free imports 1790–1795, I take North's figures.[8] For 1796–1804, the source is ARSTR (1835, p. 33–or the North computation described in note 8); for 1805–1819, North (1960, p. 592, column [5]). I estimate the figure for 1820, using North's technique for 1805–1819.[9]

3.1.3 Specific-Duty Imports

North (1960, pp. 593–594), weighs all the evidence and concludes that, during 1790–1820, specific-duty imports are valued between f.o.b. and c.i.f. I assume a midway valuation. Sterns (1898, p. 190, Note 2) sees in effect a c.i.f.-over-f.o.b. differential of 16.67% original estimate of imports (revised estimate at port-of-entry versus original estimate at port-of-shipment)—reasonably interpreted by North to apply to specific-duty goods. So I assume that specific-duty valuation is 8.34% over f.o.b., implying that overvaluation in fiscal years 1790–1820 is 7.7% of specific-duty imports (obtained as the basic import series less ad-valorem imports and duty-free imports).[10]

3.2 Legal Undervaluation

During the period July 1, 1883–July 31, 1890, the dutiable value of imported goods excludes transportation costs from point of origin (production) to point of shipment within the foreign country, resulting in valuation below f.o.b.[11] An official estimate (CN 1884, p. xi) is that this provision reduced the value of all imports by about five percent. I follow Simon (1960, pp. 642–643) in accepting the five-percent figure, and I compute overvaluation as five percent of the official (basic) series for fiscal years 1884–1891.[12]

3.3 Undervaluation of Overland Imports from Canada

Analogous to the undervaluation of overland exports to Canada (Chapter 6, Sect. 3.3), overland imports from Canada exclude inland freight from point of origin to the U.S. frontier. The matter was first mentioned in BIPUS (1926, p. 8), and BIPUS classifies the missing amount as a component of freight payments; but logically there is an undervaluation of f.o.b. (that is, at-border) imports. So, just as for the exports, I consider the issue from that standpoint and estimate undervaluation as the product of the freight rate and overland imports.[13]

The first Northern overland railroad was completed in 1853 (George P. de T. Glazebrook 1938, vol. 1, pp. 155–156). I make the adjustment only from that date.

Freight Rate: The freight rate from the Canadian point of origin to the border is estimated at three percent (BIPUS 1926, p. 8). It is extrapolated to 1907 via Canadian railway freight receipts per ton-mile and then to 1885 via 1907 overlap with Canadian Pacific Railway freight revenue per ton-mile.[14] Multiplication by the U.S.–Canada exchange rate (Chapter 2, Appendix, Sect. B) results in a U.S.-dollar series, and extrapolation using the U.S. inland freight rate (Chapter 6, Sect. 3.3) brings the series to 1852. For further computation, the series is converted to fiscal year 1853–1920; the calendar year equivalent is plotted ("imports from Canada") in Fig. 1 in Chapter 6.

Overland Imports: I obtain overland merchandise imports from the Northern border directly for 1880–1920 and via subtraction of gold and silver 1871–1879.[15] For earlier years, I extrapolate from 1871 to 1860, 1865, 1870, using a hitherto neglected source, imports in Northern border custom districts (SAUS 1923, p. 825). Employing imports of merchandise from BNA (MSCF, August 1901, p. 612) as interpolator, I estimate overland imports for 1861–1864, 1866–1869. I linearly interpolate the overland/total BNA imports ratio 1853–1860 (with ratio zero in 1852) and apply it to total BNA imports, to obtain overland imports for these years.[16]

The estimated undervaluation is converted from fiscal to calendar year.

4 Series

For fiscal years 1790–1915, f.o.b.-valuation imports are computed as the basic series *minus* overvaluation of ad-valorem imports *plus* undervaluation of ad-valorem imports from Britain and dependencies *minus* overvaluation of manufactured imports *minus* overvaluation due to home valuation *minus* overvaluation of specific-duty imports *plus* legal undervaluation *plus* undervaluation of overland imports.

5 Underinvoicing and Smuggling

North (1960, pp. 603–604) and Simon (1960, pp. 642–644) jointly adjust imports for "illegal undervaluation" (underinvoicing) and smuggling, adding two percent 1832–1846, four percent 1847–1860, three percent 1861–1875, two percent again 1876–1890, one percent 1891–1900. Unlike these authors and others, I separate underinvoicing and smuggling. A good reason for the separation is that underinvoicing logically pertains to ad-valorem imports, whereas smuggling applies to all dutiable imports. In contrast to all predecessors, I base my figures on an explicit model.

5.1 *Underinvoicing*

As benchmark figures for the underinvoicing-import ratio, I use two sources mentioned in Simon. First, Young (1874, pp. 351–352), writing in February 1874, by virtue of "careful examination of the subject during the past four years," postulates a three-percent addition to merchandise-import value "for undervaluation and smuggling as an ample allowance." Arbitrarily, I assign two percent to undervaluation and one percent to smuggling.[17] It is logical to apply the figure to fiscal year 1874, almost entirely prior to the Anti-Moiety Act (see below). Second, *Commercial Year Book* (1896, pp. 230–231) in effect estimates underinvoicing at 0.68 percent of total imports for fiscal-year 1895.[18]

I develop an inter/extrapolator variable: the product of (1) index of underinvoicing response to penalties and enforcement, (2) ad-valorem proportion of total imports, (3) average tariff rate. The product of (2) and (3) proxies the propensity to underinvoice. Variable (1) shifts this propensity.

Index of Underinvoicing, 1790–1919: Think of this index as the propensity-to-underinvoice emanating from legislation or administration. The index has assigned values 1.00 for January 1, 1790 to June 21, 1874; 0.75 for June 22, 1874 to June 9, 1890; 0.50 for June 10, 1890 to August 4, 1909; 0.25 for August 5, 1909 to October 3, 1913; zero for October 4, 1913 to December 31, 1919. The first period embodies the era of the notorious "moieties system," from the country's initial tariff law (July 4, 1789) to the Anti-Moiety Act.[19] The second period ends with the Customs Administration Act of 1890, which rationalized the law and "reduced the scale of undervaluation" (Simon 1960, p. 644).[20] The third and fourth periods are demarcated by the Payne-Aldrich Act, which "relieved many cases of manifest injustice where penalties would accrue for technical undervaluation," and the Underwood-Simmons Act, which "was an improvement over the old law" (Smith 1948, pp. 136, 137). The index is adjusted to the fiscal year 1790–1914.

Ad-Valorem Imports, 1790–1861, 1886: From Chapter 6 (Sect. 2.2), we have ad-valorem imports 1790–1861, after which they are combined with specific-duty imports in official statistics.[21] I obtain ad-valorem imports for 1886 by summing pure ad-valorem imports and the ad-valorem component of compound-duty imports (allocated via the ad-valorem share of duty collected on such imports—ARSTR 1886, p. xix).

Ad-Valorem Proportion of Dutiable Imports: For 1861 and 1886, calculated directly as per the information above. For 1867 and 1876, using data in Robert A. McGuire (1990, p. 635), the proportion is computed as the complement of "the pure-specific-duty share of dutiable imports *plus* half the compound-duty share of dutiable imports." For 1913–1914, the proportion is calculated as the "ad-valorem *plus* half the compound-duty" share of "total imports *minus* free imports."[22] The proportion is linearly interpolated for the missing years between 1861 and 1913.

Ad-Valorem Imports, 1862–1885, 1887–1914: Ad-valorem proportion of dutiable imports *times* dutiable imports, the latter in FCN 1924 (p. lxvii).

Ad-Valorem Proportion of Total Imports, 1790–1914: the ratio of ad-valorem imports to the basic import series (section 1).

Average Tariff Rate, 1790–1914: The average tariff rate is proxied, admittedly imperfectly, with tariff revenue ("duties") as the percentage of total imports (*Historical Statistics* 2006, series Ee429).[23]

Underinvoicing Series: From above, the ratio of underinvoicing to total imports is 0.02 in 1874 and 0.0068 in 1895. The inter/extrapolator variable now comes into play. As interpolator, the variable estimates the ratio of underinvoicing to total imports 1875–1894. As extrapolator, it carries the ratio back to 1790 and forward to 1914 (via 1874 and 1895 overlaps). Then the amount of underinvoicing of ad-valorem imports is the product of this ratio and the basic imports series 1790–1914, zero thereafter.

5.2 *Smuggling*

Except for liquor (due to Prohibition) and livestock, smuggling has been thought to be virtually zero after 1919 (United States Tariff Commission 1924, p. 679). Goldsmith makes no adjustment either for smuggling or for undervaluation. *Historical Statistics* has no allowance for smuggling or undervaluation after 1900 (that is, beyond North and Simon). BIPUS and also Lary do not incorporate estimates of smuggling or undervaluation. It is uncertain when smuggling essentially ceased; but it is reasonable to assume this happened with the "considerable additions to the free list" and "reduction of rates generally" associated with the Underwood-Simmons Act, say after June 1914 (United States Tariff Commission 1924, p. 756). So the ratio of smuggling to imports is 0.01 in 1874 (Sect. 5.1), zero in 1915, and is linearly interpolated 1875–1914. The average tariff rate is the logical extrapolator of this ratio, taking it back to 1790 via the 1874 overlap. The estimated amount of smuggling is the product of the ratio and basic-series imports 1790–1914.

6 Final Series

The underinvoicing and smuggling amounts are added to the f.o.b. series (Sect. 4), which is then converted to calendar year. The resulting series is in gold dollars, and is converted to currency dollars via multiplication by the greenback price of gold for 1862–1878. The final merchandise imports series is exhibited in column (2) of Table 1 in Chapter 6.

7 Comparisons

Table 1 exhibits the percentage alterations to the basic import series accounted for by the nine adjustments. The interpretation is the same

Table 1 Adjustments to North-official merchandise imports (percent of initial value of imports, fiscal years)

Item	*Percent*	
	Average (Years)	*Maximum (Year)*
(1) Overvaluation of ad-valorem imports	5.54 (1790–1795, 1799–1833)	8.67 (1813)
(2) Underinvoicing of ad-valorem imports	2.29 (1790–1914)	5.84 (1830)
(3) Smuggling of imports	0.87 (1790–1914)	2.03 (1830)
(4) Legal undervaluation of imports	4.43 (1884–1891)	5.00 (1884–1890)
(5) Overvaluation of specific-duty imports	3.58 (1790–1820)	5.87 (1812)
(6) Home valuation of ad-valorem imports	1.71 (1842)	1.71 (1842)
(7) Overvaluation of manufactured imports	9.94 (1816–1818)	12.09 (1816)
(8) Undervaluation of ad-valorem imports from Britain		
absolute values	5.76 (1790–1861)	39.32 (1813)
algebraic values	1.87 (1790–1861)	20.12 (1822)
(9) Undervaluation of overland imports from Canada	0.10 (1853–1920)	0.33 (1919)

as that of Table 2 in Chapter 6. Note that the effect of ad-valorem imports from Britain and dependencies (row [8]) could be an overvaluation (recorded as a negative undervaluation). This is especially true for the Bank Restriction Period, 1797–1821, during which time Britain was off the gold standard and the pound depreciated in the foreign-exchange market. Hence row (8) is divided into absolute values and algebraic values. The maximum absolute value, for 1813, is an *overvaluation* and reflects in part the low level of imports that took place during the British blockade. The low ("average") impact of underinvoicing and smuggling is in contradiction to the story of large-scale smuggling narrated by Andrew W. Cohen (2010).[24]

The new series is compared with the standard ("existing") merchandise-imports series in row (2) of Table 3 in Chapter 6. The standard series combines North (1960, pp. 591–592, last column; 605, col. [2]), Simon (1960, p. 643, col. [4]), and FCN; and is essentially incorporated in the *Historical Statistics* balance-of-payments table. Following methodology, comparisons are made after conversion of the standard series to calendar year, in conformity with the new series, and after subtraction of the gold-dollar premium from the 1861–1899 result. Similar to exports, the difference between the two series is most apparent in the antebellum period. Unlike for exports, in 1790–1819 the standard series is *higher*—almost ten percent higher—than the new series, which reflects new-series adjustments for overvaluation dominating those for undervaluation during that period.

8 Behavior

Much of the related discussion of exports (Chapter 6, Sect. 5) applies to the import series: effects of war, embodiment of price change as well as volume, relationship to overall economy postponed to Chapter 19 and discussion of specific sectors (here: coffee, sugar, manufactures) to Chapter 20. What is unique is the tariff. A reading of R. Elberton Smith (1948) and the majestic work of Frank W. Taussig (1923) indicates the following broad sweep: apart from the trade restrictions of 1808–1815, tariffs were moderate at first, followed by strong tariff protection, moderated 1846–1860, but provided generally high protection thereafter until 1913. The problem is that it is hard to isolate the effect of tariffs, given so many other influences—domestic and international—on imports.[25] And, of course, exports and imports are not independent of each other.

Another difficulty, applicable to the analysis of balance-of-payments flows in general, is the tendency to leap (or worse, creep) from association to causation. The objective of this book is data generation: construction of a new historical balance-of-payments table. While I indulge in some suggestive discussion of behavior and implications, I leave to others econometric use of the generated data series.

Appendix: Merchandise Price Indexes

Price indexes of exports and imports are used to obtain freight-rate series (Chapter 13, Sects. 2.3.1–2.3.2), to convert merchandise trade to constant dollars (Chapter 19, Appendix 1, Sect. A), and to construct terms-of-trade (Chapter 19, Sect. 3). Both export and import price indexes have four components, which Douglas Irwin assembles in *Historical Statistics* (2006, series Ee431–Ee441). Irwin neither adjusts nor links the component series; but I require integration into consistent calendar-year series appropriate for this study; and the same procedure is used for both exports and imports. First, I return to the original sources, for more significant digits.[26] Second, a continuous North-Simon series is generated for fiscal years 1790–1880, via overlapping years of the components. The North-Simon series is converted to calendar years 1790–1879 and linked to Lipsey via the 1879 year of overlap. The resulting series is changed from gold-dollar to currency via the greenback price of gold and transformed to base-year 1919 equaling unity.

The import and export price indexes are plotted in Fig. 1. There are spikes associated with wartime, especially for imports. Except for 1917–1919, the import index is uniformly above the export index. One should not simply conclude that this behavior does not augur well for the U.S. terms of trade in earlier years relative to the World War I period, because the movement of the U.S. terms of trade is another matter, requiring refined computation and analysis.[27]

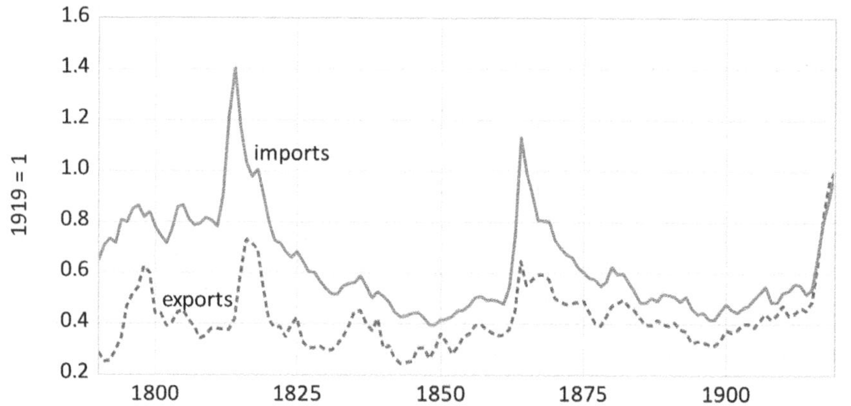

Fig. 1 Merchandise price indexes, 1790–1919. *Note* "Imports" and "exports" are price indexes of merchandise exports and imports, respectively. The time base is 1919 = 1

Notes

1. For fiscal years 1790-1819, North (1960, pp. 591–592, last column); for fiscal years 1820–1915, FCN (1912, pp. 43–44; 1915, p. 11); for calendar years 1914–1919, FCN (1918, p. 11; 1919, p. 11).
2. Acts of July 31, 1789; January 29, 1795; March 2, 1799; April 20, 1818. See United States Tariff Commission (1924, p. 282) and Smith (1948, pp. 47–48, 57–61).
3. Source is Young (1877, pp. xxvi–xxvii) and ARSTR (1819, p. 15; 1820, p. 20; 1821, p. 15).
4. Only the last rate has basis in current mint parity. Relevant Acts of Congress are dated July 31, 1789; July 14, 1832; July 17, 1842; March 3, 1873; May 27, 1921. See *Historical Statistics* (2006, p. 5-563).
5. Market exchange rate is the dollar-pound rate in Chapter 2, Appendix, Sect. B. Ad-valorem imports from Britain and dependencies are compiled 1790–1861 (ASPCN, vols. 1–2; CN), except that years 1792–1794 and 1820 are estimated as the share of Britain and dependencies in ad-valorem imports *times* ad-valorem imports. Share is directly computed for 1791, 1795, 1819, 1821, and linearly interpolated for the desired years. Consequent upon the Morrill Tariff Act of March 3, 1861, ad-valorem imports were not recorded separately; hence the undervaluation cannot be computed after fiscal-year 1861.
6. See also Observer (1820, pp. 20–22). From these accounts, I assume that dumping began in December 1815 and ended in September 1818.
7. Acts of March 3, 1833 and August 30, 1842. Home valuation was legislated almost a decade in advance! For the history, see Smith (1948, pp. 78–93).
8. Computed as col. (2) *plus* col. (3) *minus* col. (1) in North (1960, p. 591). Irwin (2003, p. 508, col. (4)) retains the stipulated numbers in ARSTR (1835, p. 32), but North (1960, p. 592) observes that the Treasury used different figures for 1790–1795 to arrive at total imports. I follow North, as his argument is persuasive.
9. That is, three *times* duty-free re-exports, the latter found in ASPCN (vol. 2, p. 467). Neither North nor Irwin (2003, p. 509) has a figure for 1820.
10. With valuation 1.083 f.o.b., f.o.b. is 1/1.083 valuation, whence overvaluation is (1-1/1.083) valuation, which is 0.077 valuation.
11. Acts of March 3, 1883 and June 10, 1890.
12. For July 1890, different from Simon; I must use the unadjusted official figure (*Summary Statement of Imports and Exports*, no. 1, July, 1880–1891, p. 7).
13. I restrict the adjustment to Canada, for two reasons. First, that is the only case of reliable data. Second, BIPUS 1926–1934 increases the Canada allowance to allow for inland freight to foreign seaports abroad or to incorporate Mexican overland trade.

14. Source is Urquhart and Buckley (1965, series S145 and S146).
15. Data from FCN. Gold and silver overland imports from Canada 1880–1909 are available directly in FCN. For 1871–1879, they are estimated via their 1880 overland proportion of total gold and silver imports from Canada.
16. For 1853, the ratio is taken arbitrarily as 25% of the interpolated value, as through traffic was not established until the third quarter (Norman Thompson and Major J. H. Edgar 1933, p. 384).
17. A justification is that smuggling involves full transportation cost, whereas underinvoicing is an add-on cost. Therefore, other things being equal, the act of underinvoicing is cheaper than that of smuggling.
18. Originally published in July 1895, the article estimates undervaluation at $5 million. With official imports $732 million for fiscal-year 1895, undervaluation is 5/732 = 0.68% of total imports, which logically applies to fiscal year 1895 (end June 30).
19. Under the moieties (French for "halves") system, government officials shared in the fines and penalties for violation of tariff laws, with one half the amount (after expenses) going to the government officials involved. For the history, see Smith (1948, pp. 45–47, 106–117), who writes: "the same government officers who administered and enforced the law had a vested interest in the initial violation of the law, followed by subsequent harsh, punitive measures" (p. 109).
20. On this Act, see Smith (1948, pp. 128–132).
21. Consequent upon the Morrill Act of March 2, 1861.
22. The data source is United States Tariff Commission (1924, p. 14). Proportions for fiscal-year 1913 (under the Tariff Act of 1909) and October 4, 1913–June 30, 1914 (initial period of Underwood-Simmons Tariff) are computed directly. The proportion for fiscal-year 1914 is the weighted (0.25, 0.75) average of the two.
23. An excellent summary of the biases of a related measure (ratio of tariff revenue to dutiable imports) is Irwin (1998, pp. 1015–1017).
24. "Americans avoided paying tariffs either by smuggling or by buying merchandise surreptitiously passed over the border. Black market sugar, opium, silk, diamonds, tobacco, art, manufactures, and many other goods flooded into the late nineteenth-century United States. Illegally imported goods from Europe, the Caribbean, and Asia filled store shelves, graced the dinner tables of fashionable houses, and swathed the bodies of chic women" (Cohen 2010, p. 374).
25. A skeptical view of the importance of tariff relative to domestic factors is Taylor (1951, pp. 194–195).
26. Original sources (for exports, imports) are: 1790–1815, North (1961, pp. 221, 229); 1815–1860, North (1961, p. 280, 2nd col., 3rd col.);

1860–1880, Simon (1960, pp. 650, col. (1); 652, col. (1)); 1879–1919, Robert E. Lipsey (1963, pp. 142–143, col. (1); 146, col. (1)).

27. For terms-of-trade history, see Chapter 19, Sects. 3 and 4.

References

Annual Report of the Secretary of the Treasury [ARSTR]. 1835.

The Balance of International Payments of the United States [BIPUS]. 1926. Annual.

Buck, Norman S. 1925. *Anglo-American Trade, 1800–1850*. New Haven: Yale University Press.

Cohen, Andrew W. 2010. Smuggling, Globalization, and America's Outward State, 1870–1909. *Journal of American History* 97 (September): 371–398.

Commerce and Navigation [CN]. 1884.

Commercial Year Book. 1896. Our International Balance Sheet, 225–231.

Foreign Commerce and Navigation [FCN]. 1912.

——— . 1915.

Glazebrook, George P. de T. 1938. *A History of Transportation in Canada*. Toronto: Ryerson.

[*Historical Statistics*]. 2006. *Historical Statistics of the United States, Millennial Edition*, ed. Susan B. Carter, Scott Sigmund Gartner, Michael R. Haines, Alan L. Olmstead, Richard Sutch, and Gavin Wright. Cambridge: Cambridge University Press.

Irwin, Douglas A. 1998. Changes in U.S. Tariffs: The Role of Import Prices and Commercial Policies. *American Economic Review* 88 (September): 1015–1026.

———. 2003. New Estimates of the Average Tariff of the United States, 1790–1820. *Journal of Economic History* 63 (June): 506–513.

Lipsey, Robert E. 1963. *Price and Quantity Trends in the Foreign Trade of the United States*. Princeton: Princeton University Press.

McGuire, Robert A. 1990. Deflation-Induced Increases in Post-Civil War US Tariffs. *Economic History Review* 43 (November): 633–645.

Monthly Summary of Commerce and Finance [MSCF].

North, Douglass C. 1960. The United States Balance of Payments, 1790–1860. In *Trends in the American Economy in the Nineteenth Century*, ed. William N. Parker, 573–628. Princeton: Princeton University Press.

———. 1961. *The Economic Growth of the United States, 1790–1860*. Englewood Cliffs: Prentice-Hall.

Observer. 1820. *A Review of the Trade and Commerce of New York*. New York: Van Winkle.

Simon, Matthew. 1960. The United States Balance of Payments, 1861–1900. In *Trends in the American Economy in the Nineteenth Century*, ed. William N. Parker, 629–716. Princeton: Princeton University Press.

Smith, R.Elberton. 1948. *Customs Valuation in the United States*. Chicago: University of Chicago Press.

Statistical Abstract of the United States [SAUS]. 1923.

Sterns, Worthy P. 1898. The Beginnings of American Financial Independence. *Journal of Political Economy* 6 (March): 187–208.

Taussig, Frank W. 1923. *The Tariff History of the United States*. New York: Putnam.

Taylor, George Rogers. 1951. *The Transportation Revolution*. New York: Holt, Rinehart, and Winston.

Thompson, Norman, and Major J.H. Edgar. 1933. *Canadian Railway Development*. Toronto: Macmillan.

United States Tariff Commission. 1924. *Dictionary of Tariff Information*. Washington: Government Printing Office.

Urquhart, Malcolm C., and Kenneth A.H. Buckley (eds.). 1965. *Historical Statistics of Canada*. Cambridge: Cambridge University Press.

Young, Edward. 1874. Foreign Indebtedness of the United States. *Monthly Report of the Chief of the Bureau of Statistics,* February: 351–352.

———. 1877. *Special Report on the Customs-Tariff Legislation of the United States*. Washington: Government Printing Office.

CHAPTER 8

Gold and Silver

1 Methodology

Gold and silver flows enter the balance of payments either as merchandise (nonmonetary, commodity) items or balancing (monetary, specie) items. Two decisions must be made. First, what are the time periods for which gold or silver are monetary versus nonmonetary? North and Simon avoid the issue, because they make no distinction between monetary and nonmonetary gold-and-silver movements. That approach means that the "balancing item" in the balance of payments incorporates either "all" or "none" of international gold and silver flows—not a useful characteristic of a balance-of-payments table.

The monetary-nonmonetary distinction of *Historical Statistics* (1960, pp. 558, 560; 1975, p. 859; 2006, p. 5-463) is clear from revealed preference: Gold is entirely merchandise 1790–1873 and divided into monetary versus nonmonetary 1874–1919, while silver is merchandise for all years.[1] This allocation is illogical and historically inaccurate. Rather, I treat gold and silver as monetary ***during the time when both coins circulated full-bodied***. The turning point was the Subsidiary Coinage Act of February 21, 1853, which provided for fiduciary coinage of silver pieces below a dollar, reducing their weight and limiting their legal-tender power to $5 (Officer 1996, pp. 20–21; 2002, p. 123, note 18). So both gold and silver are specie 1790–1852, gold alone 1853 onward.[2]

L. H. Officer, *A New Balance of Payments for the United States, 1790–1919*, Palgrave Studies in American Economic History,
https://doi.org/10.1007/978-3-030-66099-4_8

The second decision is how to distinguish monetary from nonmonetary flows of a specie metal. *Historical Statistics* (1960, p. 560) follows the official practice (established in Department of Commerce 1948, pp. 170–171) of treating the monetary gold stock (comprised of Treasury and Federal-Reserve-bank coin-and-bullion holdings, coin in national banks, and coin in circulation) as an international asset of the country. An increase in the monetary gold stock is a balancing debit, while net production (domestic production *minus* nonmonetary [industry and art] consumption) of gold is a merchandise credit, net consumption a debit. The (positive) difference between the two equals net international gold imports, though not shown directly as a balance-of-payments item. There is an internal logic to this scheme.[3] However, the scheme is arguably specious.[4] Further, there are two specific objections to the scheme. First, it treats domestic transactions as international. Second, it records *net* specie flows, whereas gross flows are sought—not only for their own sake but also the better to estimate freight and insurance (Chapter 13, Sects. 2 and 3; Chapter 16, Sect. 1.2).

2 Merchandise Silver, 1853–1919

Imports and exports of silver are obtained from FCN, converted to calendar year, and re-expressed in currency dollars during the greenback period.[5] These series are non-conventional merchandise flows, listed in columns (5) and (6) of Table 1 (Chapter 6).

3 Specie

3.1 Gold and Silver, 1790–1820

Any estimate of specie flows for 1790–1820 has to abstract from domestic production and consumption, generate the stock of specie at benchmark dates over time, interpolate annually between the benchmarks, and first-difference the result. North (1960, p. 599) estimates net specie movements using that approach; but superior data have since become known.[6] I aim to do better.[7]

First, one should justify the abstractions. It is reasonable to assume insignificant production of gold and silver 1790–1820.[8] Nonmonetary consumption is not so easily ignored. Seaman (1852, pp. 258–260) provides estimates of nonmonetary consumption of specie "over and above old metal used." His figures indicate annual average consumption net of production of $0.32 million both for 1820–1824 and 1824–1828. Projecting back to 1790; to the extent that nonmonetary consumption is non-varying, it does not affect the results of first-differencing the specie stock. This may be a weak reed; but I proceed ignoring nonmonetary consumption as well as domestic production.

End-of-year specie-stock benchmark figures: 1784, 1790–1807 (Samuel Blodget 1806, p. 66; per ARSTR 1855, p. 51); 1810 (average of two figures in Friedman and Schwartz 1970, p. 218); 1814–1815 (sum of banks and public–Gallatin 1831, p. 45; Secretary of the Treasury 1854, p. 63); 1820 (Treasury Department 1915, p. 45). Intervening years are linearly interpolated. The resulting specie-stock series is first-differenced. When the result is positive (negative), imports (exports) of specie are set equal to the change in stock. For lack of data, the gross flow must be equated to the net flow.

3.2 *Gold and Silver, 1821–1852*

Imports and exports of specie (gold and silver together) 1821–1853, from FCN (1911, pp. 43–44), are converted to calendar year.

3.3 *Gold, 1853–1919*

Imports and exports of gold for fiscal years 1853–1914 are from FCN (1911, p. 44; 1915, p. 11). Just as for merchandise, there is the issue of omitted overland exports to Canada that Simon (1960, pp. 644–645) again corrects, and in a similar manner (Chapter 6, Sect. 3.1.1). Here I follow Simon, but make improvements. He misinterprets the Canadian bullion series as restricted to gold, whereas it includes silver as well.[9] Also, he neglects to include re-exports in the U.S. series and takes the gold-dollar/Canadian-dollar exchange rate at par. And I extend Simon's 1861–1893 time period of correction to 1858–1893.[10]

On the Canada side, bullion imports from the United States are obtained from Department of Trade and Commerce (1898, pp. 252–257; 1908, p. 415), transformed to U.S. fiscal years 1858–1893, and converted to gold dollars (via division by the Canadian-dollar/gold-dollar exchange rate—Chapter 2, Appendix, Sect. B). On the U.S. side, the four series exports and re-exports of gold and silver to Canada, from FCN annual, are summed and compared to the Canada series. Where the Canada series is greater, the excess constitutes an addition to overland exports to Canada, and is added to gold exports.[11] Otherwise, there is no adjustment.[12]

Gold exports and imports are converted to calendar years 1853–1913, and directly recorded calendar-year figures 1914–1919 are attached (FCN 1918, p. 11; 1919, p. 11). As usual, multiplication by the greenback/gold exchange rate results in currency-denominated series.

Exports and imports of specie are listed in columns (3) and (4) of Table 1 in Chapter 6, and enter the official-settlements balance (Chapter 18, Sect. 2.4).

Notes

1. Goldsmith (1955, p. 1078) as well seems to adopt this procedure.
2. The Mint Act of June 28, 1834 (effective July 31) undervalued silver relative to gold, presumed to result in effective gold monometallism. However, there is evidence that "silver coins remained in common use in the United States until some time after the discovery of gold in California [1848]" (Thomas Senior Berry 1943, p. 488). In particular, I agree with David A. Martin (1973, pp. 825, 841) that 1853 is the date of switch from a bimetallic to a gold standard: "The Act of 1853 replaced bimetallism in the U.S. with...a subsidiary small silver coinage adjunct to a de facto gold standard...the Act of February 21, 1853...did terminate de facto bimetallism in the United States."
3. "If domestic consumption exceeds production [of gold], the excess is treated as an import or debit (-) in the merchandise account. It may be considered to be that part of the imported gold used as merchandise and not added to the monetary gold stock, or the part sold to the public from the monetary gold stock" (*Historical Statistics* 1960, p. 560).
4. Under this scheme, net exports of gold equal net production *minus* increase in stock. That is always true, but does not imply that net production and the increase in the gold stock logically enter the balance-of-payments table. An analogy is that merchandise exports of an ordinary commodity are production *minus* consumption *minus* change in stock—but does that equation mandate that net production and change in stock should enter the balance of payments, in lieu of the merchandise export itself?
5. Source is FCN (1911, p. 44; 1915, p. xi; 1918, p. xi; 1919, p. xi).
6. Very useful are the Friedman and Schwartz (1970, pp. 216, 218) compilation of figures of the specie stock and its components (Treasury, banks, public holdings) for 1790–1820, but they do not construct a best or even composite series of the specie stock.

7. Compared to an earlier try at estimating specie stock for 1790–1820 (Officer 2002, pp. 139–141), this time there are more-effective selection and more-accurate dating of benchmark figures.
8. Martin (1976, pp. 444–446) assumes that, prior to the overvaluation of gold in 1834, the percentage of domestic gold production deposited at the mints was between 10 and 33%. Taking his "middle" series, based on a 25% deposit ratio, then, for 1792–1823 (32 years), total production is computed as $188,000. Allocating this amount equally to the years, annual production is 0.188/32 = 0.005875 = $5875—so low that it is essentially zero. Silver production is also logically taken as zero 1790–1820. Silver production was "insignificant" 1792–1834 (*Annual Report of the Director of the Mint* [ARDM] 1910, p. 99). Further, Orris C. Herfindahl (1966, p. 328) notes that "the only mine producing sizable amounts of silver…was…discovered in 1836."
9. Canadian sources stipulate "bullion" or "coin and bullion," and Urquhart and Buckley (1965) state "gold" for the later period.
10. The ending year, 1893, is delineated by railroad reporting of exports (Chapter 6, Sect. 3.1).
11. I am assuming that the excess consists entirely of gold and not silver.
12. There are 11 such years, compared to nine for Simon.

References

Annual Report of the Secretary of the Treasury [ARSTR].

Berry, Thomas Senior. 1943. *Western Prices Before 1861.* Cambridge, MA: Harvard University Press.

Blodget, Samuel. 1806. *Economica: A Statistical Manual.* Washington.

Department of Commerce. 1948. *International Transactions of the United States During the War, 1940–1945.* Washington: Government Printing Office.

Department of Trade and Commerce. 1898. *Special Report on Trade Between Canada and the United States.* Ottawa: S. E. Dawson.

———. 1908. *Report, Canadian Trade.* Ottawa: S. E. Dawson.

Foreign Commerce and Navigation [FCN].

Friedman, Milton, and Anna Jacobson Schwartz. 1970. *Monetary Statistics of the United States.* New York: Columbia University Press.

Gallatin, Albert. 1831. *Considerations on the Currency and Banking System of the United States.* Philadelphia: Carey & Lea.

Goldsmith, Raymond W. 1955. *A Study of Saving in the United States*, vol. 1. Princeton: Princeton University Press.

Herfindahl, Orris C. 1966. Development of the Major Metal Mining Industries in the United States from 1839 to 1909. In *Output, Employment, and*

Productivity in the United States, ed. Dorothy S. Brady, 293–348. New York: Columbia University Press.

[*Historical Statistics*]. 1960. Bureau of the Census. *Historical Statistics of the United States, Colonial Times to 1957*. Washington: Government Printing Office.

———. 1975. Bureau of the Census. *Historical Statistics of the United States, Colonial Times to 1970, Bicentennial Edition*. Washington: Government Printing Office.

———. 2006. *Historical Statistics of the United States, Millennial Edition*, ed. Susan B. Carter, Scott Sigmund Gartner, Michael R. Haines, Alan L. Olmstead, Richard Sutch, Gavin Wright. Cambridge: Cambridge University Press.

Martin, David A. 1973. 1853: The End of Bimetallism in the United States. *Journal of Economic History* 33 (December): 825–844.

———. 1976. U.S. Gold Production Prior to the California Gold Rush. *Explorations in Economic History* 13 (October): 437–449.

North, Douglass C. 1960. The United States Balance of Payments, 1790–1860. In *Trends in the American Economy in the Nineteenth Century*, ed. William N. Parker, 573–628. Princeton: Princeton University Press.

Officer, Lawrence H. 1996. *Between the Dollar-Sterling Gold Points*. Cambridge: Cambridge University Press.

———. 2002. The U.S. Specie Standard, 1792–1932: Some Monetarist Arithmetic. *Explorations in Economic History* 39 (April): 113–153.

Seaman, Ezra C. 1852. *Essays on the Progress of Nations*. New York: Scribner.

Secretary of the Treasury. 1854. *Public Money*.

Simon, Matthew. 1960. The United States Balance of Payments, 1861–1900. In *Trends in the American Economy in the Nineteenth Century*, ed. William N. Parker, 629–716. Princeton: Princeton University Press.

Treasury Department. 1915. *Information Respecting United States Bonds, Paper Currency and Coin*. Washington: Government Printing Office.

Urquhart, Malcolm C., and Kenneth A.H. Buckley (eds.). 1965. *Historical Statistics of Canada*. Cambridge: Cambridge University Press.

CHAPTER 9

Ships and Slaves

1 Ship Sales

1.1 Methodology

Following North and Simon, I consider ship sales a current-account item separate from merchandise, whereas *Historical Statistics* (1975, p. 859) adds ship sales to merchandise exports.[1] It is only logical that ship sales are a unique component of goods exports, as the former does not involve freight or insurance. Ship sales are estimated as the product of volume (vessel tonnage sold to foreigners) and price (dollars per ton).

1.2 Volume

The official tonnage series of vessels sold to aliens is available for fiscal years 1813–1920 (*Historical Statistics* 1949, series K115). I extrapolate to 1797 via the ratio of "tonnage sold" to "merchant vessels built" five-year average 1813–1817 (*Historical Statistics* 2006, series Df613), after having linearly interpolated the year 1802 of the latter series.[2] Prior to 1797, there are no data on ships built; I extrapolate to 1790 via the 1797 overlap with merchandise exports (Chapter 6, Table 1, column (1)).[3] Then the entire series (number of tons) is converted to calendar-year 1790–1919 as needed.[4]

L. H. Officer, *A New Balance of Payments for the United States, 1790–1919*, Palgrave Studies in American Economic History,
https://doi.org/10.1007/978-3-030-66099-4_9

1.3 Price

For the price of ship sales (dollars per ton), I assemble comparable benchmark figures.

1790–1791: $34. This figure is stated in Tench Coxe (1794, p. 220) and applies to "about 1790" according to Sterns (1898, p. 193), "in 1791" according to Donald R. Adams (1980, p. 724).

1802: $47.50 (midpoint of range) and 1820: $60 (*Annals of Congress*, 16th Congress, 2nd session, pp. 1637 and 1646; dated January 15, 1803, and undated, but between January 15–February 2, 1821). Cited in Sterns (1898, pp. 193–194).

1830–1832: $45 and 1854–1856: $58.75. Midpoint of range in "early 'thirties," average of midpoints of price ranges for four shipyards in "mid-'fifties" (Hutchins 1941, pp. 202, 281).

1860: $52.31. Product of $58.75 and the 1860/1856 ratio of the price index of building materials (Warren and Pearson 1933, pp. 25–27).

1870: $68.95. Product of $52.31 and the 1870/1860 ratio of the price for ships in Maine, taking midpoints of ranges (Hutchins 1941, p. 389).

1919: $130.91. Ratio of the dollar value of ship sales (Vanderlip and Williams 1920, p. 20) to tonnage.

For interpolation between benchmark figures, I use the Adams "composite index" of shipbuilding cost (Adams 1980, p. 725, col. (5)) 1790–1807, extrapolated to 1919 via the 1807 overlap with the building-materials price index. The full series of the price of ships sold to foreigners is plotted in Fig. 1.[5] Peak prices occur during wartime and thereafter (1813–1820, 1863–1869, 1916–1919).

1.4 Series and Comparisons

Ship sales (export of ships), the product of volume and price, are listed in column (7) of Table 1 (Chapter 6). The peaks during major-war years and afterward are noticeable. Cost of shipbuilding relative to Britain was a fundamental determinant of sales, with the United States enjoying the advantage for wooden vessels (sailing ships), due to an abundance of lumber, but suffering the disadvantage when demand shifted to steamships, built with iron and steel which manifested British technological superiority.[6] There are nine years of ship exports exceeding $3 million 1854–1874, but sales do not reach that level again until World War I.

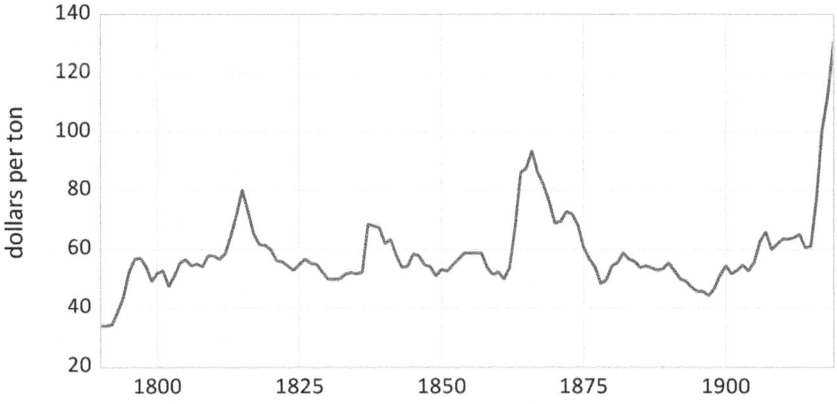

Fig. 1 Price of ships, 1790–1919. *Note* The series, expressed in dollars per ton, is the price of ships sold to foreigners

Comparison with the North (1960, pp. 600, 621) and Simon (pp. 699–705) series (each converted to calendar year, per protocol), is made in row (3) of Table 3 (Chapter 6).[7] The North–Simon series is on average more than 50% lower than the new series in 1790–1819, about ten percent lower in 1820–1860, but only about 2½% lower in 1861–1899 (after adjustment for the gold-dollar denomination of the Simon series).

2 Slave Imports

While ship sales are a credit item, forced immigration of enslaved persons ("slave imports") is a debit. Slave imports came on U.S. ships and on foreign ships—with U.S. ships disembarking slaves from Africa and from the Caribbean, foreign ships from Africa alone (Chapter 4, Sect. 3.1). Each debit is the product of the physical import (disembarkations) and the U.S. cost (applicable price per slave).

Import debits emanating from U.S.-ship disembarkations of Africans are the product of the disembarkations and the f.o.b. African price. That is the cost of the slaves to the U.S. slave-ship owners. Disembarkations are column (2) of Table 1 (Chapter 4); the African price is listed in Officer and Williamson (2020, Table A2.I, column (5)), and is graphed here ("Africa") in Fig. 2.[8] The debit series is column (1) in Table 1;

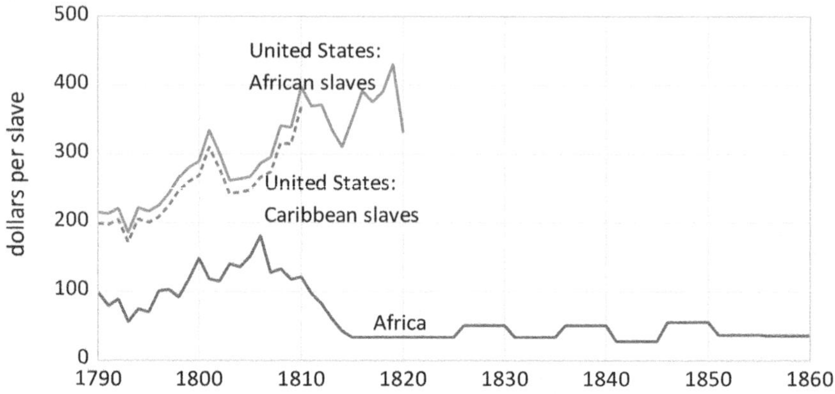

Fig. 2 Price of slaves: imports, 1790–1860. *Note* "United States: African slaves" and "United States: Caribbean slaves" are the U.S. selling price of newly arrived slaves from Africa and the Caribbean, respectively. "Africa" is the purchase price of slaves in Africa

it is the second component in Officer and Williamson (2020, Table 4, column (2)). This debit item is analogous to "merchandise imports transported on U.S. ships–imports f.o.b., with 'insurance and freight' domestic transactions."

Import debits from foreign-ship disembarkations of Africans are the product of the disembarkations and the U.S. price of disembarked slaves. That is the revenue earned by the foreign slave-ship owners. Disembarkations are column (4) of Table 1 in Chapter 4; the U.S. price is taken from Officer and Williamson (2020, Table A2.I, column (1)) and is graphed ("United States: African slaves") in Fig. 2. Officer and Williamson emphasize that, for the balance of payments, the U.S. price of African slaves must pertain to newly arrived African slaves rather than seasoned (established or trained) slaves. The debit series is column (3) in Table 1, and it is the first component in Officer and Williamson (2020, Table 4, column (2)). The merchandise analogy is "c.i.f. imports via foreign ships."

Caribbean slaves disembark only from U.S. ships (Chapter 4, Sect. 3.1–and see Officer-Williamson 2020, p. 186). The debit from these imports is again the cost of the slaves, the product of the disembarkations, and the f.o.b. Caribbean price of imported Caribbean slaves. Disembarkations are column (3) of Table 1 in Chapter 4; but the price of slaves (purchase

Table 1 Slave imports and non-imported purchases (thousands of dollars)

Year	*Imports*			*Non-imported purchases*
	U.S. ships		*Foreign ships*	
	African (1)	*Caribbean* (2)	*African* (3)	(4)
1790	17	11	0	366
1791	29	0	0	323
1792	153	8	106	632
1793	43	7	0	552
1794	22	0	0	594
1795	145	93	0	402
1796	484	19	0	462
1797	208	40	0	898
1798	17	69	116	455
1799	0	0	1	1172
1800	38	0	0	1312
1801	44	0	57	448
1802	5	0	222	1362
1803	75	24	139	1389
1804	581	285	1004	1506
1805	929	79	1082	1904
1806	1659	84	1942	2472
1807	3112	250	888	2201
1808	104	30	0	505
1809	0	0	0	59
1810	21	95	0	167
1811	0	0	0	76
1812	0	0	0	41
1813	25	0	0	5
1814	17	0	0	4
1815	14	0	0	3
1816	14	0	0	3
1817	14	0	0	3
1818	14	0	0	3
1819	14	0	0	3
1820	5	0	0	12
1821	0	0	0	5
1824	0	0	0	6

(continued)

Table 1 (continued)

Year	*Imports*			*Non-imported purchases*
	U.S. ships		*Foreign ships*	
	African (1)	*Caribbean* (2)	*African* (3)	(4)
1827	0	0	0	22
1829	0	0	0	71
1858	0	0	0	12
1860	0	0	0	4

price in the Caribbean) differs from that of Officer and Williamson (2020, p. 211), who assume that imported Caribbean slaves are at 90% the price of imported African slaves. Their series reflects only transport costs, whereas I develop a series that accounts for distribution costs in addition to transport costs.[9] The new price series ("United States: Caribbean slaves") is shown in Fig. 2. The debit series is in column (2) of Table 1. This series may be viewed as replacing the third component of Officer and Williamson (2020, Table 4, column (2)). The merchandise analogy is the same as for U.S.-ship disembarkations of Africans.

Total debits from slave imports, the sum of columns (1)–(3) of Table 1, differ from Officer-Williamson (2020) debits, column (2) of their Table 4, only because of the divergent Caribbean-slave price.

The slave-import costs that enter the balance of payments are the revenues or costs of slave-ship owners. But it should not be forgotten that business revenues or costs and resulting balance-of-payments entries are statistical constructs and narrowly construed from a humanistic standpoint. The costs to the enslaved persons in terms of liberty and dignity, to say nothing of the exploitation of their labor, do not enter the balance of payments but are opportunity costs nevertheless.

Very interesting in Fig. 2 is the widening differential of the U.S.-African price after 1806. The U.S./Africa price ratio is uniformly above 1.5, but from 1807 has a trend increase that peaks at 13 in 1819. In spite of the persistent and increasing price differential, suggestive of high profitability from slave imports, there is only a small amount of import debit [sum of columns (1)–(3) of Table 1] after 1807 (and especially after 1810)—further evidence that U.S. legislation making imports illegal became effective (Chapter 4, Sect. 3.2).

Notes

1. See North (1960, pp. 598–599, 619–620) and Simon (1960, p. 644).
2. North uses the eight-year average 1813–1820, and does not mention the year-1802 missing observation.
3. It is not clear how North estimates 1790–1796.
4. Source data 1790–1834 are for calendar years.
5. The series is richer than that of North (1960, pp. 598, 619)—described further in Simon (1960, p. 644)—and that of Officer–Williamson (2020, p. 212). All price series have the limitation that there is no explicit distinction between wooden and steam vessels.
6. See Cohn (2009, p. 61), Clinton H. Whitehurst Jr (1986, pp. 14–26), and Peter H. Lindert (2000, pp. 442–443).
7. Notwithstanding the slightly different year-definition for vessels sold, I adjust North according to the usual (merchandise) fiscal year, because that is how he (implicitly) interprets his ship-sales series, that is, having year-definition consistent with his other balance-of-payments series.
8. The final year of disembarkations is 1820; the African price is shown to 1860, for use in Chapter 17.
9. To estimate the "Caribbean purchase-price"/"U.S. sale-price" ratio I use data for the transAtlantic slave trade (E. Phillip LeVeen 1977, p. 164; David Eltis 1987, pp. 273–274) to obtain the ratio of total (shipping *plus* distribution) costs to shipping costs for 1790–1800, 1826–1835, 1836–1845, and 1856–1865, and linearly interpolate the missing years. For U.S. imports of Caribbean slaves, this ratio multiplies the Jamaican/U.S. transport-cost differential of five percent per David Eltis and David Richardson (2004, pp. 185–186), whereas Officer and Williamson double this differential. Thus the new Caribbean purchase price is computed as the product of (1–"0.05 *times* the aforementioned factor") and the U.S. African-slave price, replacing the Officer–Williamson product of (1–0.10) and that price.

References

Adams, Donald R., Jr. 1980. American Neutrality and Prosperity, 1793–1808: A Reconsideration. *Journal of Economic History* 40 (December): 713–737.

Cohn, Raymond L. 2009. *Mass Migration Under Sail*. Cambridge: Cambridge University Press.

Coxe, Tench. 1794. *A View of the United States of America*. Philadelphia: William Hall.

Eltis, David. 1987. *Economic Growth and the Ending of the Transatlantic Slave Trade*. New York: Oxford University Press.

Eltis, David, and David Richardson. 2004. Prices of African Slaves Newly Arrived in the Americas, 1673–1865: New Evidence on Long-Run Trends and Regional Differentials. In *Slavery in the Development of the Americas*, ed. David Eltis, Frank D. Lewis, and Kenneth L. Sokoloff, 181–218. Cambridge: Cambridge University Press.

[*Historical Statistics*]. 1949. Bureau of the Census. *Historical Statistics of the United States, 1789–1945*. Washington: Government Printing Office.

———. 1975. Bureau of the Census. *Historical Statistics of the United States, Colonial Times to 1970, Bicentennial Edition*. Washington: Government Printing Office.

———. 2006. *Historical Statistics of the United States, Millennial Edition*, ed. Susan B. Carter, Scott Sigmund Gartner, Michael R. Haines, Alan L. Olmstead, Richard Sutch, Gavin Wright. Cambridge: Cambridge University Press.

Hutchins, John G.B. 1941. *The American Maritime Industries and Public Policy, 1789–1914*. Cambridge, MA: Harvard University Press.

LeVeen, E.Phillip. 1977. *British Slave Trade Suppression Policies*. New York: Arno.

Lindert, Peter H. 2000. U.S. Foreign Trade and Trade Policy in the Twentieth Century. In *The Cambridge Economic History of the United States*, vol. 3, ed. Stanley L. Engerman and Robert E. Gallman, 407–462. Cambridge: Cambridge University Press.

North, Douglass C. 1960. The United States Balance of Payments, 1790–1860. In *Trends in the American Economy in the Nineteenth Century*, ed. William N. Parker, 573–628. Princeton: Princeton University Press.

Officer, Lawrence H., and Samuel H. Williamson. 2020. The Antebellum Slave Trade: Numbers and Impact on the Balance of Payments. *Research in Economic History* 36: 181–212.

Simon, Matthew. 1960. The United States Balance of Payments, 1861–1900. In *Trends in the American Economy in the Nineteenth Century*, ed. William N. Parker, 629–716. Princeton: Princeton University Press.

Sterns, Worthy P. 1898. The Beginnings of American Financial Independence. *Journal of Political Economy* 6 (March): 187–208.

Vanderlip, Frank A., and John H. Williams. 1920. The Future of Our Foreign Trade: A Study of Our International Balance in 1919. *Review of Economics and Statistics* 2 (April): 5–28.

Warren, George F., and Frank A. Pearson. 1933. *Prices*. New York: Wiley.

Whitehurst, Clinton H., Jr. 1986. *The U.S. Shipbuilding Industry: Past, Present, and Future*. Annapolis: Naval Institute Press.

PART IV

Movement of Funds

CHAPTER 10

Unilateral Transfers

1 Private

1.1 Immigrant Remittances via Money Transfers

1.1.1 Benchmark Figures

"Immigrant remittances via money transfers" are also termed "immigrant remittances via financial intermediaries" or simply "immigrant remittances." I begin with benchmark years, then develop inter/extrapolation series to fill the entire period. There are four benchmark figures, the most important of which is for the year 1907. This is the year on which the other benchmarks depend and the only year with an existing country-distribution of remittances. It is also a year with wide divergences among estimates and disagreement as to the correct figure. Charles F. Speare (1908, p. 110) has an estimate of $250 million, Paish (1910, p. 185) 150, Immigration Commission (1911, p. 276) 275, and BWT (1919a, p. 231) the range 150–200. The adopted figure is $175 million.

Rationale: Magee and Thompson (2006, pp. 549–553) present a model in which a multiplicative factor reduces *total* reported remittances via financial intermediaries and money orders. The parameters of the factor are the share of immigrant remittances in reported (immigrant *plus* commercial) remittances and the share of unreported remittances in total (reported *plus* unreported) remittances. Applying their two alternative sets of parameters to the Immigration Commission figure, the results are

L. H. Officer, *A New Balance of Payments for the United States, 1790–1919*, Palgrave Studies in American Economic History,
https://doi.org/10.1007/978-3-030-66099-4_10

153 and 194, averaging 173.5—close to 175, the midpoint of the BWT range.

For 1913: $225 million, the midpoint of the range 200–250 (Williams 1921, p. 197), itself founded on the BWT annual-average estimate for 1896–1914. For 1919: $569 million, computed from 1913 via the 1919/1913 index number of bank remittances (Williams 1921, p. 198). The final benchmark is for 1860: $4.6 million. There is a threefold justification. (1) This is the figure in Simon (1960, p. 682). (2) It is the truncated number ($4.669) in North (1960, pp. 615–618), who uses a radically different method. (3) Redoing North's computation with superior data, I obtain $4.6423, which rounds/truncates to $4.6.[1]

1.1.2 Interpolation 1908–1912, 1914–1918

I follow Dickens (1933, p. 279) in using total U.S.-issued international money orders as the interpolator series.[2] The years 1908–1912 are interpolated between 1907 and 1913, 1914–1918 between 1913 and 1919.

1.1.3 Interpolation 1861–1906

For 1860–1907, I develop an interpolator index with country components, and country weights computed as proportions of total remittances in 1907.[3] Of course, the best component series would involve a direct measure of remittances; but, for lack of data, a default index is necessary: the product of country-specific number of remitters and general "immigrant earning capacity." The index is a version of the formula in Rui Esteves and David Khoudour-Castéras (2011, pp. 449–451).

For the number of remitters, consider Europe first. I begin with official immigration for each European component country (or country group) 1820–1908, convert to proportion of total Europe (the residual constituting proportion for "other Europe"), and transform to calendar years 1820–1907.[4] The countries are Austria-Hungary, Balkans, Germany, Greece, Italy, Russia and Finland, Scandinavia, United Kingdom, and "other Europe." For each country, net immigrant admittances are the product of the immigration proportion and European net immigration admittances–the latter computed as "one *minus* the oceanic emigration-immigration ratio" *times* "European total (oceanic and transit) immigration admittances," these aggregate series from Sects. 5–6 of Chapter 3.

A similar procedure is followed for China and Japan, with immigration proportion relative to oceanic rest-of-world.[5] For China, Japan, and "other oceanic rest-of-world," net immigrant admittances are the product of the immigration proportion and oceanic rest-of-world net immigration (the latter, "one *minus* the oceanic emigration-immigration ratio" *times* "net total (oceanic and transit) admittances, oceanic rest of world." Canada is considered separately, with net immigration admittances computed as "one *minus* the Canadian emigration/immigration ratio" *times* Canada immigration admittances, again all from Chapter 3 (Sects. 5–6). Then "other-countries" net immigration admittances are the sum of "other Europe," "other oceanic rest-of-world," and Canada.

Finally, following Magee and Thompson (2006, pp. 559–560), the number of remitters for a given country is the moving sum of current-year and past-four-years net immigration admittances.

Immigrant earning capacity is a prospective concept, so pertains to the current year. It is measured as the product of the U.S. money wage and employment proportion (one *minus* 1/100th the unemployment rate).[6]

I move to individual-country indexes. In the case of two countries—the United Kingdom and Austria-Hungary—the indexes are direct remittance series, therefore clearly dominating the country default index. For the United Kingdom, the basic series 1848–1875 is immigrant remittances "via banks and mercantile houses" from the United States and BNA.[7] Via the 1875 overlap, the Magee and Thompson (2006, p. 574) U.S.-to-U.K. series 1875–1907 is linked to the basic series.[8] Then the entire series is converted from pounds to dollars. For Austria-Hungary, the remittance series 1880–1907 is in Matthias Morys (2005, p. 188) and converted to dollars via the dollar-crown exchange rate (Chapter 2, Appendix, Sect. B).[9] Per necessity, the series is extended to 1860 via the 1880 overlap with the Austria-Hungary default index.

International money orders issued in the United States to the specific country are judged superior to the default index, but only after there has been sufficient experience with the facility so that its use becomes routine and providing that there are at least ten usable calendar years. Germany (1885–1907), Italy (1885–1907), and Scandinavia (1890–1907) fall into that category.[10] For each country, linking to the default index carries the series back to 1860. For Russia-Finland, the Balkans, Greece, China, Japan, and other-countries, the default index must be used for the entire 1860–1907 period.

Each country's (or country-group's) component series is converted to an index number 1907 = 1; the series are weighted per note 3; and the interpolator index, thereby obtained for 1860–1907, interpolates total remittances 1861–1906 between 1860 and 1907.

1.1.4 Extrapolation 1790–1859

I adopt North's (1960, pp. 614–618) technique for the antebellum period, but only as an extrapolator and with superior immigration data.[11] Per Sect. 1.1.3, we have U.K. remittances 1848–1860. As extrapolator series 1790–1848: take the U.K. proportion of Europe immigration *times* European total immigration admittances, both lagged three years. This series extends U.K. remittances to 1790 via the 1848 overlap. For benchmark 1860, U.K. remittances are $2.6 million and therefore other-Europe $2.0 (4.6 - 2.6) million. The extrapolator series for other-Europe is "one *minus* the three-year-lagged U.K. proportion" *times* three-year-lagged European total immigration admittances; and, with the 1860 overlap, the extrapolator carries other-Europe back to 1790. The sum of U.K. and other-Europe remittances 1790–1859 completes the series.

1.1.5 Series and Comparisons

The complete series for immigrant remittances via money transfers is column (4) of Table 1. The series illustrates the fact that lots of immigrants involve lots of remittances! Comparison with North (1960, pp. 614–615, column (7)) and Simon (1960, pp. 686–687, column (3)) is shown in row (4) of Table 2. Both existing series are low compared to the new series. Simon especially underestimates remittances: almost 40% lower even after compensating for gold-versus-greenback valuation. The Magee-Thompson (2006, pp. 548, 558–559) disapproval of Simon's series apparently has operational validity.[12] There is no comparison for 1790–1819, absent any North estimate for that period.

1.2 Immigrant Remittances via Prepaid Tickets

Tickets prepaid by immigrants for their family or friends still in the home country are a form of immigrant remittances. All information on prepaid tickets pertains to European immigration; so I assume zero prepaid tickets for the rest of the world. The vast majority of immigrants traveled in steerage (Chapter 15, Sect. 2.1). Therefore prepaid tickets are measured as a proportion of European westbound steerage tickets.

Table 1 Unilateral transfers (millions of dollars)

Year	*Private receipts*			*Private payments*				*Govt*
	Immigrant funds (1)	*Head taxes* (2)	*Total* (3)	*Money transfers* (4)	*Prepaid tickets* (5)	*Emigrant funds* (6)	*Total* (7)	(8)
1790	0.82	0	0.82	0.05	0	0	0.06	0
1791	1.16	0	1.16	0.06	0	0	0.06	0
1792	1.41	0	1.41	0.13	0	0.01	0.14	0
1793	1.50	0	1.50	0.22	0	0.01	0.23	0
1794	1.12	0	1.12	0.31	0	0	0.32	−0.50
1795	1.05	0	1.05	0.33	0	0.01	0.34	−0.50
1796	1.07	0	1.07	0.30	0	0.01	0.31	−1.00
1797	0.72	0	0.72	0.24	0	0	0.24	0
1798	0.33	0	0.33	0.22	0	0	0.22	0
1799	0.32	0	0.32	0.24	0	0	0.24	0
1800	0.67	0	0.67	0.14	0	0	0.14	0
1801	2.45	0	2.45	0.02	0	0.01	0.04	0
1802	1.71	0	1.71	0.04	0	0.01	0.05	0
1803	0.53	0	0.53	0.13	0	0	0.13	−11.25
1804	0.65	0	0.65	0.66	0	0	0.66	0
1805	0.63	0	0.63	0.44	0	0	0.45	0
1806	0.52	0	0.52	0.09	0	0	0.10	0
1807	0.36	0	0.36	0.10	0	0	0.10	0
1808	0.26	0	0.26	0.10	0	0	0.10	0
1809	0.46	0	0.46	0.06	0	0	0.07	0
1810	0.43	0	0.43	0.05	0	0	0.06	0
1811	0.73	0	0.73	0.03	0	0.01	0.04	0
1812	0.50	0	0.50	0.04	0	0	0.05	0
1813	0.09	0	0.09	0.09	0	0	0.09	0
1814	0.15	0	0.15	0.16	0	0	0.16	0
1815	0.74	0	0.74	0.10	0	0.01	0.11	0
1816	1.47	0	1.47	0.02	0.01	0.01	0.03	0
1817	2.24	0	2.24	0	0.02	0.02	0.04	0
1818	2.81	0	2.82	0.12	0.03	0.02	0.17	0
1819	2.50	0.01	2.51	0.33	0.03	0.02	0.38	0
1820	1.44	0.01	1.45	0.51	0.02	0.01	0.55	0
1821	1.64	0	1.64	0.68	0.03	0.01	0.72	0
1822	2.41	0	2.41	0.59	0.05	0.02	0.66	0
1823	2.42	0	2.42	0.37	0.05	0.02	0.44	0
1824	1.63	0	1.63	0.38	0.03	0.01	0.43	0

(continued)

Table 1 (continued)

Year	Private receipts			Private payments				Govt
	Immigrant funds (1)	Head taxes (2)	Total (3)	Money transfers (4)	Prepaid tickets (5)	Emigrant funds (6)	Total (7)	(8)
1825	1.86	0	1.87	0.55	0.04	0.01	0.61	0
1826	1.77	0	1.77	0.54	0.04	0.01	0.60	0
1827	2.57	0	2.57	0.37	0.07	0.02	0.46	1.20
1828	2.98	0.02	3.00	0.47	0.09	0.02	0.58	0
1829	3.93	0.02	3.95	0.45	0.10	0.03	0.59	0
1830	4.83	0.02	4.86	0.67	0.08	0.04	0.80	0
1831	7.85	0.03	7.88	0.74	0.18	0.06	0.98	0.45
1832	8.93	0.04	8.98	0.77	0.23	0.07	1.07	0.22
1833	7.97	0.04	8.01	0.68	0.27	0.07	1.02	0
1834	9.27	0.06	9.33	1.55	0.37	0.07	2.00	0
1835	5.77	0.03	5.80	1.78	0.27	0.05	2.10	0.52
1836	10.15	0.05	10.20	1.35	0.46	0.08	1.90	3.98
1837	10.16	0.06	10.22	2.23	0.50	0.09	2.82	1.13
1838	4.46	0.03	4.49	1.44	0.22	0.04	1.70	1.03
1839	7.90	0.04	7.94	2.43	0.51	0.07	3.02	0
1840	10.08	0.05	10.13	2.39	0.28	0.51	3.18	0
1841	9.40	0.03	9.43	1.00	0.23	0.48	1.71	0
1842	12.39	0.04	12.44	1.82	0.31	0.70	2.83	0
1843	8.24	0.04	8.28	2.32	0.31	0.41	3.04	0
1844	9.86	0.05	9.91	2.36	0.58	0.50	3.44	0
1845	12.79	0.07	12.87	3.17	1.03	0.70	4.89	0
1846	16.27	0.11	16.38	1.94	1.96	0.97	4.87	0
1847	20.02	0.27	20.29	2.37	2.73	1.40	6.50	0
1848	17.39	0.33	17.72	3.25	2.22	1.50	6.96	0
1849	20.95	0.44	21.39	4.16	2.32	1.76	8.24	−5.50
1850	20.46	0.43	20.89	6.42	2.57	2.57	11.58	−4.30
1851	26.84	0.58	27.42	6.18	2.82	4.46	13.49	−3.40
1852	31.20	0.66	31.86	8.25	1.82	4.40	14.50	−3.20
1853	29.73	0.75	30.48	8.54	2.30	4.22	15.06	0
1854	40.00	0.81	40.81	10.16	3.25	4.91	18.35	−7.00
1855	16.16	0.38	16.54	7.18	1.22	2.18	10.61	0
1856	16.57	0.36	16.94	7.52	1.14	2.19	10.85	−3.00
1857	21.58	0.45	22.03	7.31	1.32	2.85	11.48	0

(continued)

Table 1 (continued)

	Private receipts			*Private payments*				*Govt*
Year	*Immigrant funds* *(1)*	*Head taxes* *(2)*	*Total* *(3)*	*Money transfers* *(4)*	*Prepaid tickets* *(5)*	*Emigrant funds* *(6)*	*Total* *(7)*	*(8)*
1858	9.89	0.20	10.09	3.88	0.50	1.42	5.81	0
1859	9.03	0.20	9.23	4.09	0.57	1.48	6.14	0
1860	11.32	0.26	11.58	4.60	0.79	3.51	8.91	0
1861	8.08	0.16	8.24	5.57	0.78	3.25	9.59	0
1862	9.77	0.17	9.94	5.85	0.87	3.68	10.40	0
1863	21.99	0.33	22.32	7.30	2.11	7.06	16.46	0
1864	29.85	0.39	30.24	9.42	2.69	8.56	20.68	0
1865	32.57	0.43	33.00	11.66	2.46	10.30	24.41	0
1866	33.52	0.52	34.04	14.36	3.02	13.01	30.40	0
1867	33.51	0.60	34.11	18.61	3.01	13.11	34.73	0
1868	37.35	0.63	37.98	24.72	3.67	15.17	43.56	−9.83
1869	37.79	0.78	38.57	32.64	4.36	16.82	53.82	0
1870	31.00	0.63	31.63	36.29	3.43	18.74	58.46	0
1871	29.87	0.43	30.30	38.07	3.73	21.92	63.72	0
1872	35.48	0.49	35.97	39.93	4.72	26.76	71.41	0
1873	28.01	0.44	28.45	39.33	4.13	24.47	67.94	17.64
1874	17.27	0.24	17.51	33.20	2.27	16.68	52.15	−2.09
1875	11.58	0.15	11.73	31.65	0.95	10.93	43.53	0
1876	9.07	0.01	9.08	31.20	1.00	8.38	40.58	0
1877	7.65	0	7.65	26.55	0.93	6.91	34.39	0
1878	8.47	0	8.47	22.57	0.96	7.70	31.23	−5.54
1879	15.91	0	15.91	21.88	2.10	15.05	39.03	0
1880	26.89	0	26.89	27.41	3.99	24.77	56.17	0
1881	33.63	0	33.63	41.38	5.60	29.17	76.14	0
1882	31.97	0.12	32.09	59.12	5.67	29.68	94.47	0
1883	25.67	0.23	25.90	68.86	4.07	24.28	97.21	0
1884	20.73	0.20	20.93	75.84	2.63	20.12	98.59	0
1885	16.12	0.18	16.30	72.81	1.78	15.67	90.26	0
1886	19.45	0.22	19.67	61.27	2.63	19.72	83.62	0
1887	24.96	0.27	25.23	53.25	3.57	27.09	83.91	0
1888	23.53	0.26	23.79	50.33	3.36	25.77	79.45	0
1889	20.36	0.24	20.59	50.97	2.74	24.57	78.28	0
1890	19.97	0.27	20.24	53.25	2.57	45.01	100.83	0

(continued)

Table 1 (continued)

Year	*Private receipts*			*Private payments*				*Govt*
	Immigrant funds (1)	*Head taxes* (2)	*Total* (3)	*Money transfers* (4)	*Prepaid tickets* (5)	*Emigrant funds* (6)	*Total* (7)	(8)
1891	19.96	0.31	20.27	53.93	3.12	64.38	121.42	0
1892	18.37	0.31	18.68	51.85	3.47	57.87	113.19	0
1893	16.18	0.25	16.43	44.83	3.69	51.21	99.72	0
1894	8.41	0.26	8.67	33.66	0.84	23.84	58.34	0
1895	9.82	0.38	10.20	30.33	1.15	30.61	62.09	0
1896	8.49	0.38	8.87	29.27	1.79	29.55	60.61	0
1897	5.72	0.31	6.03	25.86	1.25	20.56	47.67	0
1898	5.86	0.35	6.21	24.33	1.56	22.08	47.97	0
1899	7.91	0.47	8.38	27.81	2.55	33.00	63.36	−20.00
1900	10.34	0.56	10.90	33.54	3.58	49.30	86.41	0
1901	13.35	0.67	14.02	40.16	4.31	61.28	105.75	−0.10
1902	22.80	1.05	23.86	53.52	5.99	94.17	153.69	0
1903	42.76	1.51	44.27	72.73	7.77	135.80	216.30	0
1904	45.07	1.86	46.93	83.97	3.99	116.29	204.25	−10.00
1905	56.21	2.17	58.38	104.45	8.16	146.09	258.70	0
1906	64.16	2.54	66.69	141.73	10.55	175.57	327.86	0
1907	73.14	3.08	76.22	175.00	11.67	221.63	408.29	0
1908	29.38	3.33	32.71	169.62	3.36	69.09	242.08	0
1909	63.36	3.72	67.09	182.23	9.45	142.18	333.87	0
1910	89.19	3.92	93.11	218.95	12.27	197.77	428.98	0
1911	82.72	3.50	86.22	219.00	10.45	177.97	407.43	0
1912	107.82	4.04	111.86	214.63	13.10	246.28	474.02	0
1913	135.49	4.98	140.47	225.00	16.91	333.87	575.78	−0.25
1914	93.39	3.27	96.66	333.68	7.36	159.05	500.08	−0.25
1915	43.42	1.06	44.49	306.17	1.97	48.54	356.69	−0.25
1916	60.88	0.83	61.71	316.33	2.54	77.87	396.74	−0.25
1917	53.97	0.94	54.91	383.54	2.36	76.70	485.88	−25.25
1918	79.77	1.10	80.87	508.69	2.25	123.70	722.01	−0.25
1919	139.97	2.05	142.02	569.00	6.13	266.65	920.18	−95.15

For 1908–1913, the proportion of tickets prepaid is computed from Holland-America Line data in Keeling (2007, p. 171), with the 1911–1913 average projected to 1914–1919, and 1908 obtained via extrapolation using “Northern Europe lines” figures. For 1861–1899, I adopt Simon’s (1960, pp. 686–687, column (5)) figures converted to calendar years. The proportion for 1900–1907 is then linearly interpolated. For

Table 2 Unilateral transfers: comparisons (percentage deviation of existing series from new series)

Item	*1790–1819*	*1820–1860*	*1861–1899*	*1900–1918*
(1) Net government unilateral transfers	–	−36.56[a]	−65.46[b]	−75.12[c]
(2) Net private unilateral transfers	–	−27.45	−76.45[d]	−33.66
(3) Immigrant funds	–	−26.14	−12.99	–
Immigrant remittances via				
(4) Money transfers	–	−26.80	−38.08	–
(5) Prepaid tickets	–	–	36.64	–
(6) Emigrant funds	–	–	−26.55	–

[a]1827, 1831–1832, 1835–1838, 1849–1852, 1854, 1856
[b]1868, 1873–1874, 1878, 1899
[c]1901, 1904, 1913–1918
[d]1861–1869, 1873–1899
Note The negative signs mean that, with the exception of prepaid tickets, the new series are larger than the existing series. For discussion, see Sects. 1.1.5, 1.2, 1.3.2, 1.4.2, 1.7, and 2.5

1837–1860, I use unpublished figures provided by John Killick, after adjustment by the average Simon/Killick 1862–1864 ratio.[13] There is no evidence of the prepaid-tickets system until 1816 (Maldwyn A. Jones 1980, p. 904). So the prepaid proportion is zero 1790–1815. For 1816–1836, linearly interpolate between 1815 (zero) and 1837. Figure 1 exhibits the percentage of tickets that are prepaid. During the years encompassed by true data, variability is apparent along with upward trend. And one can infer that prepaid tickets were fully institutionalized by midcentury.

The prepaid-ticket proportion is the multiplier, ship revenue (both United States and foreign) from European steerage immigration (Chapter 15, Sect. 4) the multiplicand.[14] The resulting series—remittances in the form of prepaid tickets—is column (5) of Table 1. With the exception of three years (1817, 1846–1847), money transfers exceed prepaid tickets in amount, and the dominance increases over time. The literature emphasizes the rise of prepaid tickets, which is true in absolute terms but inaccurate relative to money transfers.

A comparison with Simon (the only predecessor series) is summarized in row (5) of Table 2. Although for 17 of the 39 years the deviation is negative, Simon (1960, pp. 686–687, column (8)) on average

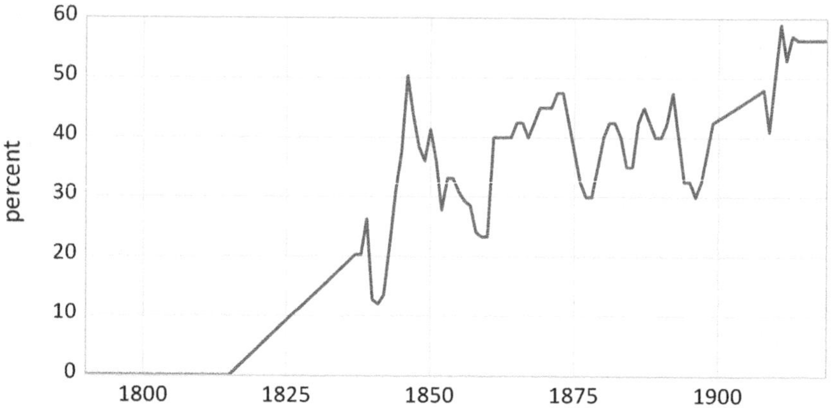

Fig. 1 Prepaid proportion of westbound steerage fares, 1790–1919. *Note* The series is the proportion of Europe westbound steerage tickets that is prepaid by immigrants already in the United States

overestimates the amount of prepaid-ticket remittances by a substantial percentage relative to the new series. The reason cannot be his proportion of prepaid fares; for I incorporate that series! Rather, the reason lies in Simon's multiplicand: official immigration, a poor series compared to ship fare revenue.

1.3 *Immigrant Funds*

1.3.1 Per Capita

1861–1919: Using data in Simon (1960, pp. 678–679), annually for 1861–1900, I construct average immigrant funds *per adult* ("old" and Canadian over-15, "new" and other over-15), convert from gold to current dollars, and transform to immigrant funds *per person* (whether youth or adult).[15] I accept Paish's (1910, p. 182) figure of \$50 for 1909. From ARCGI, I calculate official immigrant funds per person 1898–1920, and use the series to extrapolate the 1909 figure to 1920 and to interpolate 1900–1908. Then per-capita immigrant funds are transformed from fiscal to calendar years 1861–1919.

1847–1860: For 1840–1860, North (1960, p. 612) has German immigrants at \$100 per capita, Irish at \$25, all-other (including British) at \$75. North uses official immigration statistics to combine these figures; but, per note 4, the Irish-British distribution of antebellum official European immigration is flawed. Fortunately, a reliable source (beginning 1847) for the country distribution of immigrants exists: ARCENY. I compute the Irish and German proportions of immigrants 1847–1861 from this source.[16] These provide annual weights (all-other being the residual) to combine North's three per-capita amounts into one. I use the resulting series not in level form but only to extrapolate the 1861–1919 series to 1847 (via the 1861 overlap).

1790–1846: For 1820–1840, North (1960, p. 612) adopts a constant $75 per-capita figure for all nationalities. He bases the figure on £15 for English and Irish immigrants in 1837 (*Financial Register*, August 16, 1837, p. 59). I accept North's argument that many early immigrants were "settlers with some capital," whence the high figure of $75, that I extend to 1790. However, the final year logically is not 1840 but rather 1844, the year before the beginning of the Irish famine. So per-capita immigrant funds are taken as $75 1790–1844 and linearly interpolated 1845–1846.

1.3.2 Total and Comparisons

The per-capita series multiplies total (oceanic plus overland) immigrant admittances (Table 1, column (4), Chapter 3), to obtain immigrant funds–exhibited in column (1) of Table 1. Contrary to the conventional wisdom that immigrant funds and money-transfer remittances are largely offsetting, the former flow exceeds the latter (and often by a substantial multiple) in all years but three 1790–1869, and essentially equals the latter in these three years. Then the roles are reversed uniformly in all years 1870–1919, with money-transfer flows dominating immigrant funds.

Comparison with the North (1960, pp. 614–615, column (4)) and Simon (1960, pp. 678–679, column (10)) series is shown in row (3) of Table 2. Just as for money-transfer remittances, these predecessor series are low relative to the new series.

1.4 Emigrant Funds

1.4.1 Per Capita

Simon (1960, p. 689) has per-capita funds of $160 for "prosperous years" over 1861–1900. The figure is based on his estimate of the highest national per-capita immigrant remittances in calendar years 1907–1908. Jacob Viner (1924, p. 44) estimates $100 per capita for U.S. non-farmer emigrants to Canada. According to Paish (1910, p. 181), the average amount per emigrant is "probably not more than $200 per head," again for "normal" years (fiscal years 1904–1907), not the depression of fiscal-year 1908. Dickens (1933, p. 278) takes Paish's figure for the entirety of fiscal years 1897–1915, with the exception of 1908, to which he assigns a figure of $100.

With no other guidance, one must take a deep breath and do what seems reasonable. Paish's figure is too high in itself and Viner's too low for oceanic emigrants. I compromise with $150—the Viner-Paish average—which is close to Simon's $160 figure, apply it to 1904–1906 (normal years, per Paish), and extend "immigrant earning capacity" (Sect. 1.1.3) to extrapolate per-capita emigrant funds forward to 1919 and backward to 1790 via the 1904 overlap.[17]

1.4.2 Total and Comparison

The product of per-capita funds and total (land and oceanic) emigration (Table 1, column (5), in Chapter 3) yields emigrant funds, exhibited in column (6) of Table 1. Both in absolute level and relative to immigrant funds, the series is heavily determined by the emigration/immigration ratio, which is a stepwise variable (Chapter 3, Sect. 6). A result is that emigrant funds have some jumpiness (for example, 1839 to 1840). It is interesting that emigrant funds are uniformly less than immigrant funds to 1885, and uniformly greater thereafter. Even if per-capita emigrant funds were 20% less than assumed (so the 1904–1906 figure of $150 becomes $120), the switching-year simply shifts from 1886 to 1890, and only for one subsequent year (1915) do emigrant funds become less than immigrant funds.

The comparison in row (6) of Table 2 shows Simon (1960, p. 690, col (5)) below the new series. With the exception of prepaid tickets, that is a uniform result for North, Simon, and *Historical Statistics* private unilateral transfers.

1.5 Miscellaneous Transfers

<u>Collins Payment to Cunard:</u> The earliest shipping cartel agreement ever (or at least currently known to economic historians) was between the American Collins and British Cunard steamship companies. The arrangement, kept secret for over a century, ran 1850–1856, and involved price floors (for both passengers and cargo) and revenue pooling.[18] Under the

latter stipulation, Collins paid Cunard \$6898 in 1850, \$33,094 in 1851, \$25,509 in 1852, \$24,249 in 1854, and \$24,279 in 1855.[19]

Red Cross Remittances to Europe: From Williams (1921, p. 187), the amounts are \$23.272 million in 1917, \$87.376 in 1918, \$47.397 in 1919. Both cash and transfers in kind are covered.

Private Relief: Williams (1921, p. 198) estimates "immigrants' remittances and relief items other than those counted as government items" (in which he places Red Cross remittances) at \$600 million in 1919. With immigrant money transfers at \$569 million (Table 1, column (4)), "private relief" is computed as \$600 - \$569 = \$31 million.

1.6 Head Taxes

Revenue from head taxes on alien oceanic arrivals accrued to state and local governments until nonfederal immigrant legislation was deemed unconstitutional by Supreme Court decision of March 20, 1876.[20] The Immigration Act of 1882 instituted a federal head tax, periodically increased, on noncitizen arrivals at U.S. ports. Following Lary (1943, p. 212), head-tax revenue is classified as a private rather than government unilateral receipt. What follows is the first-ever assembling of government revenue from these "immigrant taxes."[21]

1.6.1 State and Local

There are six entities for which I could develop reliable head-tax revenue: five port cities (Philadelphia, New York, Boston, Baltimore, New Orleans) and the state of California.

Philadelphia: This is the only entity for which there are no direct data, and therefore for which revenue is estimated for all years as the product of the per-passenger tax and alien arrivals. Two taxes are involved, the state head tax (applicable 1828–1876) and the Philadelphia health tax (running 1818–1849 with a single rate and 1850–1876 with a differential child–adult rate).[22] I convert the state tax levy to an annual series and transform the 1850–1876 health tax to a per-person basis.[23] The per-passenger tax, running 1818–1876, is the sum of the two resulting series. Alien arrivals at Philadelphia are available 1856–1877 directly, 1820–1855 converted from total passengers to alien passengers via the U.S. alien/total passenger ratio, and 1818–1819 estimated via the 1820 overlap with the Grubb series.[24] The arrivals are transformed from fiscal to calendar year, incorporating Philadelphia's share of the alien-arrival

Table 3 Share of head-tax receipts (average percent over period)

Authority	*1818–1832*	*1833–1836*	*1837–1841*	*1842–1850*	*1851–1876*	*1877–1879*
New York	52.88	68.23	40.14	36.68	83.09	0
Pennsylvania[a]	47.12	16.69	26.48	15.28	2.63	0
Baltimore	0	15.08	20.88	9.26	2.96	0
Boston	0	0	12.50	17.52	4.26	0
New Orleans	0	0	0	21.26	4.31	0
California	0	0	0	0	2.76	100

[a]Includes Philadelphia hospital tax

adjustment for fourth-quarter 1832 (Chapter 3, Sect. 2.1.3) and of alien arrivals for fourth-quarter 1850 (data in Bromwell 1856, pp. 149, 152).

Remaining Places: When revenue is available directly, I assemble the data; missing years are estimated. I was able to assemble directly almost the entire series for New York receipts from commutation of bonds or head tax 1818–1876.[25] For Boston, the series is so obtained for 1837–1872.[26] Baltimore receipts from its head tax are available for intermittent years over 1833 (the year of inception of the tax) to 1876.[27] New Orleans revenue is available from 1842 (when the tax was instituted) to 1870, with missing years estimated.[28] Revenue for California is assembled for fiscal years 1852–1862 and 1868–1879.[29] Table 3 presents each authority's share of head-tax receipts for periods delineated by entities' taxes in effect. The dominance of New York, the main immigration port, is not unexpected.

1.6.2 Federal and Total

Receipts from the U.S. head tax on immigrants are obtained 1883–1887 from ARSTR and 1888–1920 from SAUS (1903, p. 34; 1912, p. 676; 1920, pp. 694–695). Total (federal, state and local) head-tax receipts are listed in column (2) of Table 1. Head taxes are a relatively small item, reaching a maximum of not-quite $5 million in 1913. The federal head tax itself—just as for the states, technically levied on all alien passengers (not just immigrants)—increased from 50 cents in 1882 to $8 in 1917.

1.7 *Totals and Comparisons*

Total private receipts, the sum of columns (1) and (2)—are shown in column (3) of Table 1, and total private payments—columns (4)–(6) ***plus*** Collins payment to Cunard, Red Cross remittances, and private relief (Sect. 1.5)—in column (7). Net receipts, column (3) ***minus*** column (7), are positive in "all years but five" in 1790–1866 and uniformly negative thereafter. From the 1890s, the trend in net receipts is clearly negative. Comparison with *Historical Statistics* (1975, series U16) is made in row (2) of Table 2.[30] The traditional series is substantially lower than the new series.

2 Government

2.1 *Foreign Aid and Tribute*

Conventional wisdom is that war reparations and foreign aid are the clearest manifestations of government unilateral transfers (think German reparations after World War I and the Marshall Plan after World War II). However, that statement does not apply to the period of the present study. Under the rubric of government unilateral payments, only in 1919 is there "foreign aid," taking the form of U.S. government relief of $94.9 million (Williams 1921, p. 201).[31] The closest to "war reparations" during our time period is the tribute paid to Barbary pirates, or to the North African rulers with whom they were in cahoots. The amount of $2 million is generally regarded as the total over 1794–1796, with about half of that occurring in 1796.[32] I adopt a $1 million payment in 1796, and split the remainder equally between 1794 and 1795. North, and therefore *Historical Statistics*, includes payments to the Barbary pirates.

2.2 *Indemnities*

Five transfer receipts relating to wartime damages suffered by the United States are discerned.[33] The Convention of 1826 resulted in British payment of $1,204,960 in 1827, "for slaves and other property" taken in the War of 1812. Per the Convention of 1830, in compensation for seizure of ships and cargoes, Denmark paid $449,250 in 1831 and $221,315 in 1832. Per the Claims Convention of 1832, for seizure of ships and cargoes during the Napoleonic Wars, the United States received from the Kingdom of Two Sicilies the amounts $516,333 in 1835,

$300,800 in 1836, and $291,400 in 1837.[34] The Convention of 1831, for similar reason, led to France paying $3,682,001 in 1836, $838,649 in 1837, and $1,033,520 in 1838. Finally, the Geneva Arbitration Tribunal vindicated the U.S. "*Alabama* claims" for damages caused by U.K.-built ships (especially the *Alabama*) sold to the Confederate Navy and used for privateering. Receipts from the British were $15.5 million in gold dollars, in 1873. Only the last two awards are included in the *Historical Statistics* table. North omits all indemnities, and Simon ignores all government unilateral transfers.

There is one instance of U.S. payment of wartime indemnity: $1,881,574 in gold, transferred to Britain in 1874, for damages suffered due to the Union blockade during the Civil War.[35]

2.3 *Fishing Rights*

Considered a U.S. unilateral payment (though there is a clear quid pro quo) is the $5.5 million in gold determined by the Halifax Fishing Commission, and paid to Britain in 1878, as compensation for fishing privileges in British North American waters.[36] This payment is not in *Historical Statistics*.

2.4 *Territorial Acquisition*

The purchase of territory is also traditionally treated as a unilateral transfer, even though a reciprocal transaction is involved. I separate contiguous from non-contiguous acquisitions.[37] With minor exception (possibly due to rounding amounts below $1 million to zero), all are included in *Historical Statistics*.

2.4.1 *Contiguous*

The Louisiana Purchase involved a payment of $11.250 million to France in 1803 by treaty. From a balance-of-payments perspective, the transaction is unusual in that the "unilateral-transfer" debit is the counterpart not of the usual commodity export or cash outflow but rather of a capital inflow—bonds issued by the United States and given to France.[38]

Spain's cession of Florida to the United States in 1819 did not involve the balance of payments; the quid pro quo was purely a domestic transaction: the United States taking responsibility for settling U.S.-citizen claims against Spain to a maximum of $5 million. Also, the annexation of the Republic of Texas in 1845 was outside the balance of payments.

The Guadalupe Hidalgo Treaty of 1848, which ended the Mexican-American War, had Mexico cede California, Nevada, Utah, and parts of Colorado, Arizona, and New Mexico to the United States in return for $15 million paid in annual installments *plus* interest, resulting in "unilateral payments" of $5.5, 4.3, 3.4, 3.2 million over 1849–1852.[39] The so-called Gadsden Treaty (after James Gadsden, the U.S. negotiator) at the end of 1853 involved the purchase of southern Arizona and New Mexico in return for payment of $7 million to Mexico in 1854 and $3 million in 1856.[40]

2.4.2 Non-contiguous

The Treaty for Alaska was signed and proclaimed in March and June 1867, and Alaska was transferred in October of that year. Yet payment to Russia did not take place until the second half of 1868! While the treaty called for payment of $7.2 million in gold, and that amount was paid by the Treasury to the Russian minister in the United States, only $7,035,000 was sent abroad and therefore enters the balance of payments.[41]

Following the Spanish-American War in 1898, the Treaty of Peace awarded the United States Puerto Rico and other islands in the West Indies, as well as Guam and the Philippines, in return for payment of $20 million consummated in 1899. A follow-up treaty with Spain stipulated the purchase of outlying Philippine islands (mistakenly omitted from the peace treaty) for the sum of $100,000, paid in 1901.

The Convention of 1903 with the Republic of Panama for the Canal Zone involved payment of $10 million in 1904 and $250,000 annually beginning nine years after ratifications exchanged (February 26, 1904), thus 1913–1919 for this study.

Via the Convention of 1916, Denmark ceded the Danish West Indies (U.S. Virgin Islands) to the United States in return for payment of $25 million, made in 1917.

2.5 Totals and Comparisons

Total government unilateral transfers in any year are shown in column (8) of Table 1. Gold-dollar figures are converted to currency dollars via the greenback/gold price. By happenstance, for every year, there are either only receipts, only payments, or no transfer. So gross receipts are the positive figures, gross payments the negative figures, and net receipts are the same display.

Government net (equivalent to gross) transfers are compared with *Historical Statistics* (1975, series U17) in Table 2, with the average annual deviation of *Historical Statistics* from the new series shown in row (1). The figures in *Historical Statistics* are much lower, mainly because the new series includes more transfers.[42] Comparison for 1790–1819 is not meaningful, because the numbers are small, rounded in *Historical Statistics* but not here.

Notes

1. North's technique applied to year 1860: exchange rate (Chapter 2, Appendix, Sect. B) *times* U.K. remittances (*Statistical Tables Relating to Emigration and Immigration* [*Statistical Tables*] 1880, p. 160) = 4.187 × 0.534476 = \$2.5746 million. "Other Europe" (Europe exclusive of Great Britain and Ireland) remittances = \$20 *times* year-1857 immigration = \$20 × 0.103384 million (*Historical Statistics* 2006; series Ad106 *minus* Ad107 *minus* Ad108) = \$2.0677 million. Summing U.K. and other-Europe: 4.6423. Both North's and Simon's approaches are criticized in Magee and Thompson (2006, pp. 547–548).
2. The source is *Report of the Postmaster-General* and *Annual Reports of the Post-Office Department*. Fiscal years are converted to calendar years.
3. The source of weights is Immigration Commission (1911, p. 276). Notwithstanding the Commission's overestimation of absolute amounts (Sect. 1.1.1), it is reasonable to take the country *proportions* as unbiased. Countries and percentage weights are: Italy 30.91; Austria-Hungary 27.27; U.K., Russia-Finland, Scandinavia (Norway, Sweden, Denmark), each 9.09; Germany 5.45; Greece, Balkans, Japan, China, each 1.82; all other (Europe and Asia) countries combined, 1.82.
4. Source is *Historical Statistics* (2006, series Ad106–Ad120). It has been pointed out by Cohn (2009, pp. 25–31) that the antebellum country distribution of European immigrants is flawed. The main criticism concerns the Britain (England, Scotland, Wales) versus Ireland division of U.K. immigrants. I avoid the issue here by combining Britain and Ireland into the United Kingdom as a single entity. A second criticism concerns the immigration *levels* of European countries, because of the existence of an unspecified-country category. I account for this category in developing

aggregate travel flows in Chapter 3 (Sect. 2.5), but do not do so here—because there is no necessary bias in country *proportions* computed from official immigration data.

5. Asia, Africa, North America, South America, and Oceania, less Canada and Mexico. Source is *Historical Statistics* (2006, series Ad92–96, Ad138, Ad143, Ad163–164).
6. Money wage 1800–1907 (1800–1859 for use in Sect. 1.4.1) is the average hourly earnings of production workers in manufacturing (Officer 2009, pp. 166–167). Unemployment rate 1900–1909 is from David R. Weir (1992, p. 341), 1869–1899 from J. R. Vernon (1994, p. 710), and 1860–1868 the average of Vernon's 1869 rate and Stanley Lebergott's (1971, p. 82) range-midpoint figure for 1860–1869.
7. The source is *Statistical Tables* (1880, p. 16). I agree with North (1960, p. 616) that "the amount from Canada would do little more than make up for unrecorded remittances from the United States." For 1863, the unallocated remittance from America and Australia combined is distributed separately according to the (earliest available year) 1875 remittances (Magee and Thompson 2006, pp. 574–575).
8. It is irrelevant which of two U.S.-to-U.K. series one takes, for the Magee-Thompson alternative series are proportional.
9. In private correspondence, Morys confirmed that, for these years, his series consists entirely of money transfers via banks and postal services, and that the transfers are exclusively or primarily from the United States.
10. The data source is that of note 2.
11. In *level* form, used by North and others, the technique has been subject to legitimate criticism—see note 1. The only good thing about the technique—sufficient for its use—is that, per North, it works as an empirical regularity! North's implicit abstraction from non-Europe remittances for the antebellum period is reasonable and is continued.
12. They find Simon's U.K. figures in effect too low after 1887.
13. The Killick data pertain to the Copes packet line. Killick's figure for 1861 is an outlier, so ignored.
14. Specifically, from Chapter 15, the multiplicand is ship revenue from westbound steerage fares of immigrants from Europe and transmigrants to Canada and the West Indies. The vessels involved are diverse sailing ships—(U.S.) packets, (British) Falmouth packets, U.S. and foreign traders—and U.S. and foreign steamships.
15. The last is accomplished via multiplication by "one *minus* the youth proportion of immigrants." For the data, see Chapter 15 (Sect. 3.1, especially note 21). Youth fare was half the adult fare.
16. ARCENY (1860, p. 288; 1861, p. 37). The suggestion to use ARCENY data for this purpose is made by Coleman (1972, pp. 297–298).

17. Following-up on note 6, the wage series is extrapolated to 1790 via the 1800 overlap with the unskilled wage-rate of Paul A. David and Peter Solar (1977, p. 59). I extend the unemployment rate to 1790, making liberal use of Lebergott's (1971) figures and narrative as follows: 1790–1839, 2%, and 1840–1859 4.5%—with exception years: 1818 and 1820, 3%; 1819, 4%; 1837 and 1858, 7%; 1838, 8%; 1857, 6%.
18. For histories, see Francis E. Hyde (1975, pp. 39–45) and Edward W. Sloan (1992, 1998).
19. The source is Hyde (1975, p. 44). Payment was in pounds; the amounts are converted to dollars.
20. The "head tax" was not necessarily directly imposed; often it was technically a fee paid in commutation of a bond. The essential history of state and local immigration regulation is Benjamin J. Klebaner (1958). Also pertinent is Gerald L. Neuman (1996, pp. 24–30).
21. If "taxes" are a misnomer for the state and local levies, then so is "immigrant," as *all* alien arrivals—nonimmigrants as well as immigrants—were subject to the fee or tax. In contrast, the federal "immigration head tax" is legitimately named; as the charge was always direct rather than in commutation of a bond and, further, the receipts were lodged in an "immigrant fund."
22. The Pennsylvania tax, from Klebaner (1958, p. 278), is $2.50 August 1828–April 1832 and August 1837–May 1842, $1.50 May 1832–July 1837 and June 1842–June 1849, and $1.00 July 1849–March 1876. The Philadelphia health tax, based on research kindly shared by John Killick, is $1.00 1818–1849, 50 cents for adults and 25 cents for children 1850–1876.
23. For the latter, the rate is the weighted average of the adult and child taxes, with the weights adult and child immigrant proportions. Age-recorded immigrants are in *Historical Statistics* (2006, series Ad227–Ad229); the proportions are converted to calendar year.
24. Data sources are Bromwell (1856, pp. 21, 25, 29), Bureau of Statistics (1903, p. 4366), Maffry (1939, pp. 6, 11), and Grubb (1990, p. 36, column (3)).
25. Sources are *Documents of the Board of Aldermen of New York*, vol. 1, 1834/35, p. 184 (attachment), for 1818–1829; *Annual Report of the Comptroller of City of New York*, and *Annual Statement* of same, for 1830–1847; ARCENY for 1847–1876. Years 1837, 1847, 1862, and 1872 are estimated as number of New York alien arrivals *times* commutation fee (assumed constant in 1836–1838) or head tax (Klebaner 1958, p. 291), with 1837 interpolated between 1836 and 1838. Arrivals are based on data in ARCENY (1873, p. 2), Bureau of Statistics (1903, p. 4366), and Maffry (1939, p. 6). For 1836–1838, alien arrivals at New

York are estimated as the alien/total U.S. arrivals ratio *times* total New York arrivals.

26. The source is *Annual Report of the Board of State Charities of Massachusetts*, January 1874, pp. 184–185, with conversion to calendar year as needed. Only a few hundred dollars were collected prior to 1837, and 1872 was the last year of the tax (Klebaner 1958, pp. 277, 283, 292).
27. Sources are *Ordinances of Baltimore*, Register's Statement; and *Annual Report of the Register*; with conversion to calendar year as required. Receipts for missing years are interpolated via a Baltimore alien-arrival series, constructed from data in Bromwell (1856, pp. 149, 152) and Bureau of Statistics (1903, p. 4366), the former for fourth-quarter 1850, as for Philadelphia. The Baltimore head tax was at $1.50 throughout the period (Klebaner 1958, p. 280).
28. Sources are *Report of the Board of Administrators of the Charity Hospital to the Legislature of the State of Louisiana*, and *Report of the Commissioners of Emigration,* Louisiana. Revenue is taken as zero in 1862–1863. A synthetic receipts series is constructed as per-passenger head tax (Klebaner 1958, pp. 293–294) *times* New Orleans alien arrivals (based on Bureau of Statistics 1903, p. 4366). This series constitutes revenue for 1876 and extrapolates 1860, 1865–1866, 1871–1875, via the 1859, 1867, 1870 overlap with revenue.
29. Source is *Annual Report*, *Biennial Report of the Controller of State.* Though the tax was instituted in 1850, no revenue was reported until 1852. The tax was abolished in 1874 per State Supreme Court decision; but revenue from a 70-cent "inspection charge" continued to 1879. Missing years 1863–1867 are interpolated between 1862 and 1868 via synthetic receipts: head tax *times* San Francisco immigrant arrivals 1862–1868 (Bureau of Statistics 1903, p. 4366). The head tax was constant, at $5, during that period (Klebaner 1958, pp. 294–295). After the interpolation, conversion is made to calendar year.
30. *Historical Statistics* (per North) has no figures for fiscal years 1790–1819. The years 1870–1872 are omitted from the comparison, because of opposite signs.
31. Red Cross remittances are classified as private transfers, and government loans enter the capital account.
32. See Sterns (1898, p. 200), James Schouler (1910, vol. 2, p. 18), North (1960, p. 601), Martha E. Rojas (2003, p. 165), Frank Lambert (2005, pp. 82, 84).
33. I make use of standard references on treaties and conventions: Moore (1898, vols. 1, 5), Malloy (1910, vols. 1–2). Amounts and timing of settlement of awards are obtained from ARSTR and from other reports and letters of the Secretary of the Treasury. I do not claim to include *all* indemnities (see Sterns 1898, p. 200).

34. The total is 37% less than Moore's (1898, vol. 5, p. 4581, note 1) receipts of $1,755,450; but I could find no further information of amounts paid under the indemnity. It may be that the discrepancy emanates from Moore's estimated exchange rate.
35. The award was $1,929,819; but there was a deduction for the U.S. share of the expenses of the Mixed Commission that determined the award. See *Papers Relating to the Foreign Relations of the United States*, 1874, pp. 571–572. This payment is not in *Historical Statistics*.
36. Source is Moore (1898, vol. 1, pp. 745, 748, 752), and see ARSTR (1879, p. 4).
37. The primary source of information is Douglas (1932). Also useful are Malloy (1910) and Thomas A. Bailey (1980). Further pertinent is *Message of the President of the United States*, January 19, 1852, p. 1; April 14, 1856, p. 76.
38. The stock was issued at the end of 1803 and assigned by France to British and Dutch financial houses, who thereby became the U.S. creditors. See Wilkins (1989, pp. 35–36).
39. North (1960, p. 622), and therefore *Historical Statistics*, has these amounts for fiscal years; I find that they are also for the corresponding calendar years.
40. See Garber (1959), in addition to sources cited in note 37. North, but not *Historical Statistics*, seems to omit the second payment.
41. The remainder was deposited in the minister's U.S. bank account. From there, some of the money went to U.S. citizens, some for the minister's expenses—there is not a full accounting. All this is beautifully described in Dunning (1912, esp. pp. 392–393).
42. Smith (1953, pp. 85, col. (8); 86, col. (13)) is to be commended for attention to government transfers, albeit his time period is only two decades. See Chapter 1, Sect. 3.3.1.

References

Annual Report of the Commissioner-General of Immigration [ARCGI].

Annual Report of the Commissioners of Emigration of the State of New York [ARCENY].

Annual Report of the Secretary of the Treasury [ARSTR].

Bailey, Thomas A. 1980. *A Diplomatic History of the American People*. Englewood Cliffs: Prentice-Hall.

Bromwell, William J. 1856. *History of Immigration to the United States*. New York: Redfield.

Bullock, Charles J., John H. Williams, and Rufus S. Tucker [BWT]. 1919a. The History of Our Foreign Trade Balance from 1789 to 1914. *Review of Economics and Statistics* 1 (July): 215–233.

Bureau of Statistics. 1903. *Immigration into the United States... from 1820 to 1903*. [Reprinted from *Summary of Commerce and Finance for June 1903*.] Treasury Department. Washington: Government Printing Office.

Cohn, Raymond L. 2009. *Mass Migration Under Sail*. Cambridge: Cambridge University Press.

Coleman, Terry. 1972. *Passage to America*. London: Hutchinson.

David, Paul A., and Peter Solar. 1977. A Bicentenary Contribution to the History of the Cost of Living in America. *Research in Economic History* 2: 1–80.

Dickens, Paul B. 1933. The Transition Period in American International Financing: 1897 to 1914. Ph.D., diss., George Washington University.

Douglas, Edward M. 1932. *Boundaries, Areas, Geographic Centers and Altitudes*. Washington: Government Printing Office.

Dunning, William A. 1912. Paying for Alaska. *Political Science Quarterly* 27 (September): 385–398.

Esteves, Rui, and David Khoudour-Castéras. 2011. Remittances, Capital Flows, and Financial Development During the Mass Migration Period, 1870–1913. *European Review of Economic History* 15 (December): 443–474.

Garber, Paul N. 1959. *The Gadsden Treaty*. Gloucester: Peter Smith.

Grubb, Farley. 1990. The Reliability of U.S. Immigration Statistics: The Case of Philadelphia, 1815–1830. *International Journal of Maritime History* 1 (June): 29–54.

[*Historical Statistics*]. 1975. Bureau of the Census. *Historical Statistics of the United States, Colonial Times to 1970, Bicentennial Edition*. Washington: Government Printing Office.

———. 2006. *Historical Statistics of the United States, Millennial Edition*, ed. Susan B. Carter, Scott Sigmund Gartner, Michael R. Haines, Alan L. Olmstead, Richard Sutch, Gavin Wright. Cambridge: Cambridge University Press.

Hyde, Francis E. 1975. *Cunard and the North Atlantic*. London: Macmillan.

Immigration Commission. 1911. *Immigrant Banks*. Washington: Government Printing Office.

Jones, Maldwyn A. 1980. Scotch-Irish. In *Harvard Encyclopedia of American Ethnic Groups*, ed. Stephan Thernstrom, 895–908. Cambridge, MA: Harvard University Press.

Keeling, Drew. 2007. Costs, Risks and Migration Networks Between Europe and the United States, 1900–1914. In *Maritime Transport and Migration: The Connections Between Maritime and Migration Networks*, ed. Torsten Feys and others, 113–173. St. John's: International Maritime Economic History Association.

Klebaner, Benjamin J. 1958. State and Local Immigration Regulation in the United States Before 1882. *International Review of Social History* 3: 269–295.

Lambert, Frank. 2005. *The Barbary Wars*. New York: Hill & Wang.

Lary, Hal B. 1943. *The United States in the World Economy*. Washington: Government Printing Office.

Lebergott, Stanley. 1971. Changes in Unemployment, 1800–1960. In *The Reinterpretation of American Economic History*, ed. Robert W. Fogel and Stanley L. Engerman, 73–83. New York: Harper & Row.

Maffry, August. 1939. *Overseas Travel and Travel Expenditures in the Balance of International Payments of the United States, 1919–1938*. Washington: Government Printing Office.

Magee, Gary B., and Andrew S. Thompson. 2006. 'Lines of Credit, Debts of Obligation': Migrant Remittances to Britain c.1875–1913. *Economic History Review* 59 (August): 539–577.

Malloy, William M. 1910. *Treaties, Conventions, International Acts, Protocols and Agreements*. Washington: Government Printing Office.

Moore, John B. 1898. *History and Digest of the International Arbitrations*. Washington: Government Printing Office.

Morys, Matthias. 2005. The Classical Gold Standard in the European Periphery: A Case Study of Austria-Hungary and Italy, 1870–1913. Ph.D. diss., London School of Economics and Political Science.

Neuman, Gerald L. 1996. *Strangers to the Constitution*. Princeton: Princeton University Press.

North, Douglass C. 1960. The United States Balance of Payments, 1790–1860. In *Trends in the American Economy in the Nineteenth Century*, ed. William N. Parker, 573–628. Princeton: Princeton University Press.

Officer, Lawrence H. 2009. *Two Centuries of Compensation for U.S. Production Workers in Manufacturing*. New York: Palgrave Macmillan.

Paish, George. 1910. *The Trade Balance of the United States*. Washington: Government Printing Office.

Rojas, Martha E. 2003. 'Insults Unpunished': Barbary Captives, American Slaves, and the Negotiation of Liberty. *Early American Studies* 1 (fall): 159–186.

Schouler, James. 1910. *History of the United States of America*. New York: Dodd, Mead.

Simon, Matthew. 1960. The United States Balance of Payments, 1861–1900. In *Trends in the American Economy in the Nineteenth Century*, ed. William N. Parker, 629–716. Princeton: Princeton University Press.

Sloan, Edward W. 1992. Collins versus Cunard: The Realities of a North Atlantic Steamship Rivalry, 1850–1858. *International Journal of Maritime History* 1 (June): 83–100.

———. 1998. The First (and Very Secret) International Steamship Cartel, 1850–1856. In *Global Markets: The Internationalization of the Sea Transport Industries Since 1850*, ed. David J. Starkey and Gelina Harlaftis, 29–52. St. John's, Newfoundland: International Maritime Economic History Association.

Smith, Walter B. 1953. *Economic Aspects of the Second Bank of the United States*. Cambridge, MA: Harvard University Press.

Speare, Charles F. 1908. What America Pays Europe for Immigrant Labor. *North American Review* 187 (January): 106–116.

Statistical Abstract of the United States [SAUS].

Statistical Tables Relating to Emigration and Immigration [*Statistical Tables*]. 1880. Reprinted in British Parliamentary Papers, vol. 25, 1971. Shannon: Ireland.

Sterns, Worthy P. 1898. The Beginnings of American Financial Independence. *Journal of Political Economy* 6 (March): 187–208.

Vernon, J.R. 1994. Unemployment Rates in Postbellum America: 1869–1899. *Journal of Macroeconomics* 16 (Fall): 701–714.

Viner, Jacob. 1924. *Canada's Balance of International Indebtedness, 1900–1913*. Cambridge, MA: Harvard University Press.

Weir, David R. 1992. A Century of U.S. Unemployment, 1890–1900: Revised Estimates and Evidence for Stabilization. *Research in Economic History* 14: 301–346.

Wilkins, Mira. 1989. *The History of Foreign Investment in the United States to 1914*. Cambridge, MA: Harvard University Press.

Williams, John H. 1921. The Balance of International Payments of the United States for the Year 1920. *Review of Economics and Statistics* 3 (June): 169–212.

CHAPTER 11

Capital

1 Methodology

There are three methods of estimating capital movements. The first is the direct recording of capital flows (called the "direct approach"). This is the ideal technique, providing it is sufficiently comprehensive—and that is a fair description of the approach in the modern balance of payments. This is the primary technique that I adopt—but lack of data means that the opportunities to do so are limited, and resort must be had to a default method.

The second method (termed the "residual approach") is to estimate *net* capital flow as the residual (net) balance of payments, after accounting for the current account (goods, services, income, unilateral transfers) and other noncapital items (gold flow, change in official reserves). This is the method used by North (1960, pp. 573–574) implicitly and Simon (1960, p. 629) explicitly. Net capital inflow is computed residually as the negative of the net balance of goods, services, unilateral transfers, and net gold-and-silver flow. The great advantage of the residual approach is that it automatically involves internal balance-of-payments consistency ("the balance of payments always balances"), albeit this consistency is by imposition. A related advantage is that cumulating residuals over time yields a series of net foreign liabilities that is consistent with the balance of payments.

L. H. Officer, *A New Balance of Payments for the United States, 1790–1919*, Palgrave Studies in American Economic History,
https://doi.org/10.1007/978-3-030-66099-4_11

However, there are three weaknesses of the approach. First, errors-and-omissions are incorporated entirely and exclusively in the capital-flow estimate, whereas in fact errors can apply to any balance-of-payments item and some items can be omitted in whole or part. Second, only the *net* capital flow is estimated. With no disaggregation, long-term capital flows cannot be separated from short-term, nor private from government. Third, defining net foreign liabilities as cumulative net capital inflow is fine for theory but abstracts from the empirical reality that the stock changes not only because of the balance-of-payments flow but also because of other factors, especially change in valuation. I find these weaknesses to be of overriding importance. So I reject the residual approach.[1]

The adopted, third, approach (called the "stock approach") is to obtain the asset or liability stock at various points of time and then first-difference to estimate the capital flow. This technique is used by various authors to test or justify the residual approach.[2] The innovations here are (1) assemble, either directly or by interpolation, continuous end-of-year series of the stock so that first-differencing results in an annual flow, and (2) do this on a disaggregate basis, so that estimates of capital flow by type and direction can be made.[3]

The main weaknesses of this approach are (1) uncertainty whether the stock estimates are based on market value or par value or book value or purchase price, to the extent that these valuations differ, and (2) time inconsistency of the estimates in this respect and possibly other respects. Fortunately, mainly due to the compilations of Wilkins and others, reasonably consistent end-of-year stock series can be generated and the technique made usable.[4] To an economist, market value is usually preferable to book or par value. However, to estimate capital flow, the stock of investment is valued better at par rather than at market prices. If the latter, a mere change in valuation would give rise to a false capital flow. Stock series are generated end-of-year 1789–1919 (131 observations).

I apply the direct method where data availability permits and the stock approach otherwise.

2 Long-Term Liabilities

2.1 *Stock*

The desired series is U.S. long-term liabilities (foreign long-term assets in the United States) at par value, in gold dollars, end-of-year 1789–1919. The proximate source for end-of-year 1789 to June 30, 1914 (and not only for total liabilities but also for two inter/extrapolator series: "foreign-owned federal-government securities" and "foreign-owned state-government securities") is the compilations, narratives, and notes of Wilkins (1989, pp. 32–33, 36, 48, 50–54, 76, 91–93, 111, 137, 147–150, 646 [note 99]); for end-of-year 1914–1919, it is Cleona Lewis (1938, pp. 546, 558) and Wilkins (2004, p. 63).[5] I exclude data which Wilkins (1989) judges unreliable or about which she states reservations. Wherever possible, I consult Wilkins' original sources to correct errors in her tables, to obtain a refined date of the estimate, or to find the full figure in cases of rounding. Generally, I take only worldwide figures. I reject data restricted to Britain, and convert figures for Europe to worldwide via the ratio of total-to-Europe liabilities (excluding life insurance) in Bacon (1900, p. 276). Otherwise, I use some judgment to adjust the Wilkins numbers or to make them precise in cases of a range or for selection where there are alternative estimates. For one year, I take figures not in Wilkins.[6]

The first step is assembling direct end-of-year figures, of which there are 25 years.[7] Second, foreign-owned federal-government securities serve as inter/extrapolator to obtain five more end-of-year figures.[8] Third, linear interpolation aided by foreign-owned state-government securities yields 11 years.[9] Fourth, the remaining missing years over 1789–1914 are log-linearly interpolated.[10] Finally, the years 1915–1917 are interpolated via an end-of-year series for 1914–1918 derived from foreign long-term capital figures in Williams (1921, p. 202, note h).[11] The full series of U.S. long-term liabilities is listed in column (4) of Table 1.

2.2 *Flow*

For 1897–1919, the inflow of foreign long-term capital is taken from Goldsmith (1955, p. 1082, column 2), who employs the "direct approach" with some approximations.[12] For 1790–1896, the inflow is the change in the stock of U.S. long-term liabilities. Multiplication by the greenback/gold exchange rate converts the 1862–1878 segment to

Table 1 International assets and liabilities (millions of gold dollars, end of year)

Year	*U.S. assets*			*U.S. liabilities*				
	Private		*Govt*	*Long-term*	*Short-term*			
	Direct	*Portfolio*			*Mercantile debt*	*Dollars abroad*	*Deposits at Fed*	*Net assets*
	(1)	*(2)*	*(3)*	*(4)*	*(5)*	*(6)*	*(7)*	*(8)*
1789	1.00	0.07	0	18	25	0	0	–41
1790	1.06	0.08	0	19	24	0	0	–41
1791	1.12	0.08	0	20	26	0	0	–44
1792	1.19	0.09	0	21	26	0	0	–46
1793	1.27	0.09	0	22	28	0	0	–49
1794	1.34	0.10	0	24	36	0	0	–59
1795	1.42	0.10	0	25	49	0	0	–73
1796	1.51	0.11	0	28	51	0	0	–78
1797	1.60	0.11	0	31	44	0	0	–73
1798	1.70	0.12	0	34	42	0	0	–74
1799	1.80	0.13	0	38	43	0	0	–79
1800	1.91	0.14	0	42	44	0	0	–83
1801	2.03	0.14	0	46	42	0	0	–86
1802	2.15	0.15	0	57	28	0	0	–83
1803	2.28	0.16	0	70	23	0	0	–91
1804	2.42	0.17	0	68	31	0	0	–96
1805	2.56	0.18	0	65	39	0	0	–102
1806	2.72	0.19	0	63	43	0	0	–103
1807	2.88	0.21	0	61	38	0	0	–96
1808	3.06	0.22	0	59	17	0	0	–73
1809	3.24	0.23	0	57	24	0	0	–77
1810	3.44	0.25	0	55	27	0	0	–78
1811	3.65	0.26	0	53	21	0	0	–70
1812	3.87	0.28	0	51	19	0	0	–65
1813	4.10	0.29	0	49	8	0	0	–52
1814	4.35	0.31	0	47	11	0	0	–54
1815	4.61	0.33	0	46	34	0	0	–74
1816	4.89	0.35	0	44	37	0	0	–76
1817	5.19	0.37	0	43	28	0	0	–65
1818	5.50	0.39	0	40	25	0	0	–59
1819	5.84	0.42	0	37	23	0	0	–54
1820	6.19	0.44	0	35	34	0	0	–63
1821	6.57	0.47	0	33	32	0	0	–58

(continued)

Table 1 (continued)

	U.S. assets			*U.S. liabilities*				
	Private		*Govt*	*Long-term*	*Short-term*			
Year	*Direct*	*Portfolio*			*Mercantile debt*	*Dollars abroad*	*Deposits at Fed*	*Net assets*
	(1)	*(2)*	*(3)*	*(4)*	*(5)*	*(6)*	*(7)*	*(8)*
1822	6.96	0.50	0	31	40	0	0	−63
1823	7.39	0.53	0	32	39	0	0	−64
1824	7.83	0.56	0	33	43	0	0	−68
1825	8.31	0.59	0	31	50	0	0	−72
1826	8.81	0.63	0	29	44	0	0	−64
1827	9.35	0.67	0	27	44	0	0	−61
1828	9.91	0.71	0	25	44	0	0	−58
1829	10.51	0.75	0	29	42	0	0	−59
1830	11.15	0.80	0	34	45	0	0	−67
1831	11.82	0.84	0	39	55	0	0	−82
1832	12.54	0.90	0	46	58	0	0	−91
1833	13.30	0.95	0	54	61	0	0	−101
1834	14.11	1.01	0	64	69	0	0	−117
1835	14.96	1.07	0	75	85	0	0	−144
1836	15.87	1.13	0	88	93	0	0	−164
1837	16.83	1.20	0	104	60	0	0	−146
1838	17.85	1.27	0	144	63	0	0	−189
1839	18.93	1.35	0	200	85	0	0	−265
1840	20.08	1.43	0	180	65	0	0	−224
1841	21.29	1.52	0	162	55	0	0	−194
1842	22.58	1.61	0	146	37	0	0	−158
1843	23.95	1.71	0	152	28	0	0	−155
1844	25.40	1.81	0	159	34	0	0	−165
1845	26.94	1.92	0	166	36	0	0	−174
1846	28.57	2.04	0	173	42	0	0	−185
1847	30.30	2.16	0	181	49	0	0	−198
1848	32.14	2.30	0	189	51	0	0	−206
1849	33.01	2.36	0	197	55	0	0	−217
1850	35.94	2.57	0	206	68	0	0	−235
1851	38.24	2.73	0	215	76	0	0	−249

(continued)

Table 1 (continued)

	U.S. assets			*U.S. liabilities*				
	Private		*Govt*	*Long-term*	*Short-term*			
Year	*Direct*	*Portfolio*			*Mercantile debt*	*Dollars abroad*	*Deposits at Fed*	*Net assets*
	(1)	*(2)*	*(3)*	*(4)*	*(5)*	*(6)*	*(7)*	*(8)*
1852	40.59	2.90	0	224	85	0	0	−266
1853	41.85	2.99	0	234	103	0	0	−292
1854	43.42	3.10	0	253	114	0	0	−320
1855	44.94	3.21	0	273	125	0	0	−350
1856	46.43	3.32	0	294	138	0	0	−383
1857	46.72	3.34	0	318	153	0	0	−420
1858	48.32	3.45	0	343	142	0	0	−434
1859	49.98	3.57	0	371	153	0	0	−470
1860	51.69	3.69	0	400	132	0	0	−476
1861	53.46	3.82	0	317	88	0	0	−348
1862	55.29	3.95	0	252	74	0	0	−266
1863	57.19	4.08	0	200	73	0	0	−212
1864	59.15	4.22	0	298	89	0	0	−323
1865	61.17	4.37	0	444	103	0	0	−482
1866	63.27	4.52	0	663	113	0	0	−707
1867	65.44	4.67	0	831	92	0	0	−853
1868	67.68	4.83	0	1043	99	0	0	−1069
1869	70.00	5.00	0	1360	121	0	0	−1406
1870	75.73	5.43	0	1175	149	0	0	−1243
1871	81.94	5.89	0	1411	184	0	0	−1507
1872	88.65	6.40	0	1500	191	0	0	−1596
1873	95.91	6.95	0	1500	190	0	0	−1587
1874	103.76	7.54	0	1500	165	0	0	−1554
1875	112.26	8.19	0	1500	149	0	0	−1529
1876	121.46	8.89	0	1500	142	0	0	−1512
1877	131.41	9.65	0	1106	149	0	0	−1114
1878	142.17	10.48	0	1049	154	0	0	−1050
1879	153.82	11.38	0	1154	177	0	0	−1166
1880	166.42	12.35	0	1269	202	0	0	−1293
1881	180.05	13.41	0	1477	202	0	0	−1485

(continued)

Table 1 (continued)

Year	*U.S. assets*			*U.S. liabilities*				
	Private		*Govt*	*Long-term*	*Short-term*			
	Direct	*Portfolio*			*Mercantile debt*	*Dollars abroad*	*Deposits at Fed*	*Net assets*
	(1)	*(2)*	*(3)*	*(4)*	*(5)*	*(6)*	*(7)*	*(8)*
1882	194.79	14.56	0	1719	204	0	0	−1713
1883	210.75	15.81	0	2000	201	0	0	−1975
1884	228.01	17.17	0	1949	188	0	0	−1892
1885	246.69	18.64	0	1900	182	0	0	−1817
1886	266.89	20.24	0	2130	190	0	0	−2032
1887	288.75	21.97	0	2387	198	0	0	−2274
1888	312.40	23.85	0	2676	204	0	0	−2544
1889	337.99	25.90	0	3000	220	0	0	−2856
1890	365.68	28.12	0	2910	234	0	0	−2750
1891	395.63	30.53	0	2823	245	0	0	−2642
1892	428.03	33.14	0	2739	243	0	0	−2521
1893	463.09	35.98	0	2657	222	0	0	−2379
1894	501.03	39.07	0	2577	209	0	0	−2246
1895	542.06	42.42	0	2500	217	0	0	−2133
1896	586.46	46.05	0	2600	237	0	0	−2204
1897	634.50	50.00	0	3000	250	0	0	−2566
1898	691.65	64.94	0	3145	242	1	0	−2631
1899	753.95	84.33	0	3384	250	2	0	−2798
1900	821.86	109.52	0	3642	276	3	0	−2991
1901	895.89	142.24	0	3919	282	5	0	−3168
1902	976.59	184.72	0	4218	294	6	0	−3356
1903	1064.55	239.90	0	4539	308	8	0	−3550
1904	1160.44	311.56	0	4884	323	9	0	−3744
1905	1264.97	404.62	0	5256	360	10	0	−3957
1906	1378.91	525.49	0	5656	408	12	0	−4172
1907	1503.11	682.45	0	6087	418	13	0	−4333
1908	1638.50	886.30	0	6087	400	15	0	−3977
1909	1787.01	883.31	0	6259	411	16	0	−4016
1910	1948.98	880.33	0	6437	445	17	0	−4070
1911	2125.64	877.35	0	6619	476	19	0	−4111

(continued)

Table 1 (continued)

	U.S. assets			U.S. liabilities				
	Private		Govt	Long-term	Short-term			
Year	Direct	Portfolio			Mercantile debt	Dollars abroad	Deposits at Fed	Net assets
	(1)	(2)	(3)	(4)	(5)	(6)	(7)	(8)
1912	2318.30	874.39	0	6806	515	20	0	−4149
1913	2528.43	871.44	0	6999	534	28	0	−4162
1914	2757.60	868.50	0	6259	482	37	0	−3151
1915	2947.64	1355.50	0	4734	601	45	0	−1076
1916	3150.77	2116.50	0	3565	791	53	0	858
1917	3367.90	2407.50	3657	3299	822	109	3	5199
1918	3600.00	2500.50	7686	3040	722	204	96	9724
1919	3879.50	2576.10	9591	2630	800	314	73	12,230

currency dollars. Long-term capital flow (inflow positive, outflow negative) is shown in column (1) of Table 2. The capital inflow toward the end of the Civil War and subsequently in the 1860s is noticeable, as is the capital outflow during World War I and afterward. The series is quite variable, as one would expect. I am not aware of any pre-existing gross long-term capital-flow series prior to 1897. Some analysis of the behavior of long-term capital is in Chapter 19, Sect. 1.2.

3 Long-Term Assets

3.1 Direct Investment

3.1.1 Stock

Stock, 1869–1919: The desired series are U.S. private direct and portfolio investment at par value (therefore in gold dollars), end-of-year 1789–1919. For both direct and portfolio stock, I begin with years 1869, 1897, 1908, 1914 (June 30), 1918–1919.[13] Turning to direct investment exclusively, end-of-year 1914 is linearly interpolated between midyear 1914 and end-of-year 1918, and the missing years over 1869–1919 are log-linearly interpolated.

Cumulated Flow, 1849–1857: Wilkins (1970, p. 31) writes "the data are not good enough to establish a schedule of the *value* of U.S. direct foreign investment in the years before 1860." Nevertheless, admittedly

Table 2 Capital (millions of dollars)

	Foreign capital[a]				*U.S. capital*[a]			
	Long-term	*Short-term*			*Private*		*Government*	
Year		*Mercantile debt*	*Dollars abroad*	*Deposits at Fed*	*Direct*	*Portfolio*	*Long-term*	*Short-term*
	(1)	*(2)*	*(3)*	*(4)*	*(5)*	*(6)*	*(7)*	*(8)*
1790	1	−1	0	0	0.06	0	0	0
1791	1	2	0	0	0.06	0	0	0
1792	1	0	0	0	0.07	0	0	0
1793	1	2	0	0	0.07	0.01	0	0
1794	1	8	0	0	0.08	0.01	0	0
1795	2	13	0	0	0.08	0.01	0	0
1796	3	2	0	0	0.09	0.01	0	0
1797	3	−7	0	0	0.09	0.01	0	0
1798	3	−2	0	0	0.10	0.01	0	0
1799	4	1	0	0	0.10	0.01	0	0
1800	4	1	0	0	0.11	0.01	0	0
1801	4	−2	0	0	0.12	0.01	0	0
1802	11	−14	0	0	0.12	0.01	0	0
1803	13	−5	0	0	0.13	0.01	0	0
1804	−2	8	0	0	0.14	0.01	0	0
1805	−2	8	0	0	0.15	0.01	0	0
1806	−2	4	0	0	0.16	0.01	0	0
1807	−2	−5	0	0	0.16	0.01	0	0
1808	−2	−21	0	0	0.17	0.01	0	0
1809	−2	7	0	0	0.19	0.01	0	0
1810	−2	3	0	0	0.20	0.01	0	0
1811	−2	−6	0	0	0.21	0.01	0	0
1812	−2	−2	0	0	0.22	0.02	0	0
1813	−2	−11	0	0	0.23	0.02	0	0
1814	−2	3	0	0	0.25	0.02	0	0
1815	−2	23	0	0	0.26	0.02	0	0
1816	−2	0	0	0	0.28	0.02	0	0
1817	−2	−23	0	0	0.30	0.02	0	0
1818	−3	−19	0	0	0.31	0.02	0	0
1819	−2	−23	0	0	0.33	0.02	0	0
1820	−2	−4	0	0	0.35	0.03	0	0
1821	−2	−2	0	0	0.38	0.03	0	0
1822	−2	7	0	0	0.40	0.03	0	0

(continued)

Table 2 (continued)

Year	*Foreign capital*[a]				*U.S. capital*[a]			
	Long-term	*Short-term*			*Private*		*Government*	
		Mercantile debt	*Dollars abroad*	*Deposits at Fed*	*Direct*	*Portfolio*	*Long-term*	*Short-term*
	(1)	*(2)*	*(3)*	*(4)*	*(5)*	*(6)*	*(7)*	*(8)*
1823	1	−1	0	0	0.42	0.03	0	0
1824	1	4	0	0	0.45	0.03	0	0
1825	−2	7	0	0	0.47	0.03	0	0
1826	−2	−6	0	0	0.50	0.04	0	0
1827	−2	0	0	0	0.53	0.04	0	0
1828	−2	−1	0	0	0.57	0.04	0	0
1829	4	−2	0	0	0.60	0.04	0	0
1830	5	4	0	0	0.64	0.05	0	0
1831	6	10	0	0	0.68	0.05	0	0
1832	7	3	0	0	0.72	0.05	0	0
1833	8	3	0	0	0.76	0.05	0	0
1834	10	8	0	0	0.81	0.06	0	0
1835	11	16	0	0	0.85	0.06	0	0
1836	13	8	0	0	0.91	0.06	0	0
1837	16	−33	0	0	0.96	0.07	0	0
1838	40	3	0	0	1.02	0.07	0	0
1839	56	22	0	0	1.08	0.08	0	0
1840	−20	−20	0	0	1.15	0.08	0	0
1841	−18	−11	0	0	1.22	0.09	0	0
1842	−16	−18	0	0	1.29	0.09	0	0
1843	6	−9	0	0	1.37	0.10	0	0
1844	7	6	0	0	1.45	0.10	0	0
1845	7	3	0	0	1.54	0.11	0	0
1846	7	6	0	0	1.63	0.12	0	0
1847	8	7	0	0	1.73	0.12	0	0
1848	8	2	0	0	1.84	0.13	0	0
1849	8	4	0	0	0.87	0.06	0	0
1850	9	13	0	0	2.93	0.21	0	0
1851	9	8	0	0	2.31	0.16	0	0
1852	9	9	0	0	2.35	0.17	0	0
1853	10	18	0	0	1.26	0.09	0	0
1854	19	11	0	0	1.56	0.11	0	0

(continued)

Table 2 (continued)

Year	Foreign capital[a]				U.S. capital[a]			
	Long-term	Short-term			Private		Government	
		Mercantile debt	Dollars abroad	Deposits at Fed	Direct	Portfolio	Long-term	Short-term
	(1)	(2)	(3)	(4)	(5)	(6)	(7)	(8)
1855	20	12	0	0	1.52	0.11	0	0
1856	22	13	0	0	1.49	0.11	0	0
1857	23	14	0	0	0.30	0.02	0	0
1858	25	−10	0	0	2.00	0.11	0	0
1859	27	10	0	0	1.66	0.12	0	0
1860	29	−21	0	0	1.71	0.12	0	0
1861	−83	−38	0	0	1.77	0.13	0	0
1862	−74	1	0	0	2.08	0.15	0	0
1863	−75	33	0	0	2.75	0.20	0	0
1864	200	32	0	0	3.98	0.28	0	0
1865	230	−6	0	0	3.19	0.23	0	0
1866	307	3	0	0	2.95	0.21	0	0
1867	233	−29	0	0	3.00	0.21	0	0
1868	296	7	0	0	3.13	0.22	0	0
1869	422	15	0	0	3.08	0.22	0	0
1870	−213	19	0	0	6.59	0.49	0	0
1871	264	37	0	0	6.93	0.52	0	0
1872	100	10	0	0	7.54	0.57	0	0
1873	0	−2	0	0	8.26	0.62	0	0
1874	0	−27	0	0	8.74	0.66	0	0
1875	0	−18	0	0	9.77	0.74	0	0
1876	0	−15	0	0	10.25	0.78	0	0
1877	−413	0	0	0	10.43	0.80	0	0
1878	−57	1	0	0	10.85	0.83	0	0
1879	105	23	0	0	11.65	0.90	0	0
1880	115	25	0	0	12.60	0.98	0	0
1881	208	0	0	0	13.63	1.06	0	0
1882	242	2	0	0	14.75	1.15	0	0
1883	281	−2	0	0	15.96	1.25	0	0
1884	−51	−13	0	0	17.26	1.36	0	0
1885	−49	−6	0	0	18.68	1.47	0	0
1886	230	7	0	0	20.21	1.60	0	0

(continued)

Table 2 (continued)

Year	*Foreign capital*[a]				*U.S. capital*[a]			
	Long-term	*Short-term*			*Private*		*Government*	
		Mercantile debt	*Dollars abroad*	*Deposits at Fed*	*Direct*	*Portfolio*	*Long-term*	*Short-term*
	(1)	*(2)*	*(3)*	*(4)*	*(5)*	*(6)*	*(7)*	*(8)*
1887	258	8	0	0	21.86	1.73	0	0
1888	289	6	0	0	23.65	1.88	0	0
1889	324	16	0	0	25.59	2.04	0	0
1890	−90	14	0	0	27.68	2.22	0	0
1891	−87	11	0	0	29.95	2.41	0	0
1892	−84	−2	0	0	32.41	2.62	0	0
1893	−82	−22	0	0	35.06	2.84	0	0
1894	−80	−12	0	0	37.93	3.08	0	0
1895	−77	8	0	0	41.04	3.35	0	0
1896	100	19	0	0	44.40	3.64	0	0
1897	0	13	0	0	5.00	5.00	0	0
1898	−8	−8	0.69	0	40.00	0.00	0	0
1899	−45	8	1.38	0	20.00	23.00	0	0
1900	−75	26	1.38	0	56.00	87.00	0	0
1901	−33	6	1.38	0	89.00	123.00	0	0
1902	−30	12	1.38	0	65.00	40.00	0	0
1903	20	14	1.38	0	81.00	−40.00	0	0
1904	59	15	1.38	0	80.00	−11.00	40	0
1905	56	37	1.42	0	46.00	93.00	0	0
1906	114	48	1.42	0	92.00	−46.00	0	0
1907	136	10	1.42	0	89.00	−24.00	0	0
1908	89	−18	1.42	0	48.00	87.00	0	0
1909	171	11	1.42	0	88.00	24.00	0	0
1910	345	34	1.42	0	124.00	−34.00	0	0
1911	171	31	1.42	0	95.00	28.00	0	0
1912	232	39	1.42	0	139.00	70.00	0	0
1913	252	19	8.09	0	138.00	27.00	0	0
1914	−432	−52	8.09	0	76.00	14.00	0	0
1915	−789	119	8.09	0	0	790.00	0	0
1916	−391	190	8.09	0	0	1064.00	0	0
1917	−36	31	56.21	3.34	0	594.00	3656.8	0
1918	0	−100	95.54	92.64	0	396.00	4028.8	0
1919	−215	78	109.19	−22.64	94.00	75.00	1901.7	426.3

[a]Increase in assets and increase in liabilities, both positive

with trepidation, I proceed in the best way that data allow: construct a cumulative-flow series for 1849–1857 and, subsequently, in conversion to change-in-stock, violate Wilkins' dictum that "flows do not stock make." I accept Wilkins' (1970, p. 28) assertion that "American funds spent on the Panama Railroad and on the Nicaraguan carriage–steamboat line were by far the most important pre-Civil War direct foreign investments of United States citizens," and usable data begin with these flows.

The annual series of cumulated direct-investment outflow 1849–1857 emanates from the following projects: Nicaragua Transit Company (1849–1851), Panama railroad (1850–1857), three Canadian railroads (1852), Canadian telegraph and cable (1854–1856)—and reaches $14.584 million in 1857.[14] I make the conservative assumption that this amount constitutes the entirety of U.S. direct investment over 1849–1857.

Cumulated Flow, 1858–1869: As extrapolator, I use total gold-dollar merchandise trade (exports plus imports—Chapters 6–7, Sects. 3.3 and 6). Total direct-investment flow 1858–1869 is estimated as the ratio "(total-trade 1858-1869)/(total-trade 1849-1857)" *times* $14.584 million.

Stock, 1848–1868: Direct-investment (end-of-year) 1857 is the 1869 figure *minus* the cumulated-flow 1858–1869. Direct-investment (end-of-year) 1848 is the 1857 figure *minus* the 1849–1857 cumulated flow ($14.584 million). Log-linear interpolation between 1857 and 1869 yields direct-investment stock 1858–1868. The stock for each (end-of) year 1849–1856 is the 1848 figure *plus* cumulated flow from 1849 inclusive to that year.

Stock, 1789–1847: When did U.S. foreign investment begin? No one knows. North (1960, pp. 587–588) writes: "In the late eighteenth century…there was…perhaps some…U.S. investment abroad." I impose $1 million for U.S. private long-term investment stock at the end of 1789. Direct investment 1790–1847 is log-linearly interpolated between 1789 and 1848.

Series: The entire series is shown in column (1) of Table 1. The series confirms the unanimity among scholars that there was little U.S. investment until well into the postbellum period. Wilkins (1970, p. 31) writes: "The statement in *Historical Statistics of the United States* [1960, series U193, note 5] that the U.S. direct foreign investment in the pre-Civil War years was 'negligible' is not disputed here. It seems true both in the absolute amount of money involved and on any realistic comparative basis."

In 1843 (the year to which the note pertains), U.S. direct investment is less than $25 million and only 16% of long-term liabilities. By 1860, it has doubled, but is still only 13% liabilities. In contrast, the doubling of direct investment in the 1890s brings it to over $750 million and 22% liabilities.

3.1.2 Flow

For 1897–1919, I adopt Goldsmith (1955, p. 1085, column 2).[15] For 1790–1896, the flow is computed as the change in the direct-investment stock, with two amendments.[16] First, $0.4 million is added to the 1858 figure, to account for surveying costs for a Honduras railroad that was never built.[17] Second, the 1862–1878 segment is multiplied by the greenback/gold exchange rate, to convert to current dollars. Direct-investment flow is shown in column (5) of Table 2. Interestingly, the series is always positive (never a net inflow). However, an outflow of $1 million is reached first only in 1838, $10 million only in 1876, and $100 million in 1910.

3.2 Portfolio Investment

3.2.1 Stock

Portfolio-investment stock figures are preset for end-of-year 1869, 1897, 1908, 1918–1919, and June 30, 1914 (Sect. 3.1.1). End-of-year 1914 is estimated by adding half the 1914 portfolio inflow (Goldsmith, p. 1085, column 3) to the June 30 figure. For 1915–1918, I first subtract the 1914 from the 1918 stock. Then I sum new foreign issues of securities 1915–1918 (Goldsmith 1955, p. 1085, column 3) and subtract that sum from the 1918-*minus*-1914 stock difference, yielding a negative residual. For each year 1915–1918, the stock is the previous-year stock *plus* new foreign issues *plus* one-quarter the (negative) residual.[18] Then, just as for direct investment, I log-linearly interpolate all missing years over 1869–1919. I extrapolate 1790–1868 via the direct-investment stock on the basis of the 1869 overlap.

The portfolio-investment stock series is listed in column (2) of Table 1. Until the end of the nineteenth century, portfolio is less than ten-percent direct investment. "The United State has been unique among the major investing countries in that the principal form of its investment has been, from the earliest times recorded, direct rather than portfolio investment" (Lipsey 2008, p. 479). And, in contrast: following the norm, U.S. capital *inflow* historically was portfolio-investment dominated (note 5).

3.2.2 Flow

For 1897–1919, I adopt Goldsmith (1955, p. 1085, column 3), again also used in *Historical Statistics* (1975, series U20). The years 1790–1896 are the first-difference of the portfolio stock, with 1862–1878 converted from gold to current dollars. The series is in column (6) of Table 2. World War I marks a tremendous outflow.

4 Short-Term Liabilities

4.1 Mercantile Debt

Stock: The most important U.S. short-term liability is mercantile debt to London. To estimate the end-of-year stock, I begin with 14 benchmark years from the compilations of Lewis (1938, pp. 442, 447, 522, 560), North (1960, pp. 588, 623, 626), and Platt (1984, p. 195).[19] Four additional years are generated as dollar-converted midpoints of period-averages of British short-term capital lent to the United States, and linearly interpolated to year-end.[20] Then the 1854–1856 segment is log-linearly interpolated, because this was a largely speculation-driven increase of short-term debt (note 19). The remaining years are estimated using the sum of current-dollar conventional merchandise exports and imports (Table 1, columns (1)–(2), Chapter 6) as interpolator.[21] To convert the series from currency dollars to gold dollars, I divide by the average of the current-year and subsequent-year greenback/gold rate (Chapter 2, Appendix, Sect. B).

The series is incomplete until debt default is incorporated. North (1960, p. 601) refers to debt default totaling \$70 million over fiscal years 1816–1819 (per Taylor 1951, p. 201). However, North adopts a contemporary estimate that is higher (\$100 million), in order to compensate for underestimation of an unrelated credit item and overvaluation of an unrelated debit item. In particular, he assigns \$20 million to each-year 1816 and 1817, \$30 million to 1818 and 1819. I reduce North's figures by 7/10th, and convert to calendar years 1815–1819. Subtracting this debt default, the above stock series is complete and listed in column (5) of Table 1.

Flow: Mercantile-debt flow is the first-difference of the current-dollar stock, and is shown in column (2) of Table 2. Mercantile debt is analyzed in Chapter 19, Sect. 1.2.

4.2 *Dollars Abroad*

Europe: Information on dollar holdings abroad is available for Europe, Cuba, the Dominican Republic, and Honduras. For Europe, I obtain two benchmark figures–based on Garber (1986), who provides evidence that "prior to World War I little U.S. currency was held in Europe…[W]ith the collapse of stable European currencies in 1914 and the major U.S. intervention starting in 1917, this situation must have changed" (Garber 1986, p. S150). The first U.S. forces arrived in France in June 1917. Therefore the first benchmark is end-of-May 1917, with assumed zero dollars in Europe until that date. The second benchmark is end-of-April 1923, with European stock of dollars estimated as $478.232 million. This figure is the cumulative U.S. net inflow of U.S. currency May 1923–June 1938 (Board of Governors 1943, p. 417); and Garber (1986, pp. S137–S138, S140–S142, S150) offers good justification for the arithmetic. The stock of U.S. paper currency in Europe for end-of-year 1917–1919 is linearly interpolated between the benchmarks.

Cuba: Logically, dollar bills in Cuba reached measurable level only with the Spanish-American War. U.S. forces invaded Cuba in June 1898; so I assume that, up to June 30, 1898, there are no dollar bills in Cuba. For end-of-year 1912, 1918–1919, I rely on data in Henry C. Wallich (1950, pp. 320, 324–325). For 1912, the dollar stock is midpoint dollars-and-coin range *minus* midpoint coin range. For 1918, per Wallich narrative, two-thirds the dollar-bills share are applied to the midpoint dollars-and-coin range. For 1919, I apply the average of the 1918 and 1920 dollar shares of currency-and-coin to the 1919 figure for currency-and-coin. Given the four benchmarks, the end-of-years 1898–1911, 1913–1917 are linearly interpolated.

Dominican Republic: I assume that there were zero dollars in the Dominican Republic through December 31, 1904, and that dollars appeared with the United States taking control of Dominican finances in 1905.[22] Data exist for end-of-April 1917 and end-of-year 1917, 1919 (ARDM 1917, p. 164; 1918, p. 168; 1920, p. 175). Linear interpolation yields 1905–1916 and 1918.

Honduras: The earliest figure I could find is $3.5 million end-of-1920 (ARDM 1921, p. 154). On April 1, 1918, U.S. banknotes began to circulate in Honduras throughout the country, per government arrangement with Banco Atlantida (ARDM 1919, p. 172). I assume zero dollar stock to end-of-1917, and linearly interpolate 1918–1919.

Total and Comparison: Summing the four series, the stock of dollars abroad is presented in column (6) of Table 1 and the associated capital inflow (change in the stock) in column (3) of Table 2. Previous estimates of the flow, for 1914–1918 total (Williams 1921, p. 201) and for individual years 1918–1919 (Goldsmith 1955, p. 1083, column 14), are noticeably below the new series.

4.3 *Deposits at Federal Reserve Banks*

Foreign deposits at Federal Reserve banks end-of-year 1917–1919 are shown in column (7) of Table 1, with the flow in column (4) of Table 2.[23] The latter series in rounded form is in Goldsmith (1955, p. 1083, column 9).

4.4 *Total*

Summing columns (2)–(4) of Table 2, total foreign short-term capital can be obtained—but it is a poor estimate of the total, largely because foreign deposits in U.S. commercial banks are omitted. Goldsmith (1955, p. 1083, column 10) provides both a total series and its deposit-component for 1914 onward; his total foreign short-term capital figures are incorporated in Jeffrey G. Williamson (1964, p. 151) and adopted, for 1914–1918, in *Historical Statistics* (1975, series U23). However, except for deposits in the Fed banks, the Goldsmith series is unreliable. It is based almost entirely on residual balance-of-payments flows (in the North-Simon vein), thus incorporating errors and omissions. So it is not surprising that *Historical Statistics* rejects Goldsmith for the "official period" when there are no official estimates (1919–1922), preferring a zero flow by default for these years. As for U.S. short-term capital, there are no data whatsoever—not even in Goldsmith (1955, p. 1085, column 7) until the official short-term capital series begins, in 1923.[24]

5 Government Capital

There are only a handful of entries in the government-capital flow series, columns (7) and (8) in Table 2. The figure for 1904 and total-figure for 1919 are taken from *Historical Statistics* (1975, series U18), with the sign reversed. Years 1917–1918 are Liberty Loans (Lewis 1938, p. 362).[25] Short-term capital is separated out only in 1919 (datum in Williams 1921,

p. 201). End-of-year net assets on government account, shown in column (3) in Table 1, are capital flow for 1917, the sum of 1917 and 1918 flows for 1918, Lewis' (1938, p. 450) figure for 1919.

Notes

1. As does Mira Wilkins (n.d.), in an excellent work that has a beautiful title ("Flows Do Not Stock Make") and that underlies her empirical research.
2. Simon (1960, pp. 706–707), and Lance E. Davis and Robert J. Cull (1994, pp. 108–111). Williamson (1964, pp. 234–243) provides a systematic empirical defense of the North-Simon residual-estimate.
3. The "short-term versus long-term" disaggregation that follows makes sense historically but admittedly not in the modern balance of payments. See Edelstein (2006, p. 5-468) and the references stated there.
4. For discussion and justification, see Wilkins (n.d., esp. pp. 13–14, 39–42; 1989, pp. 92, note a; 147, note a; 695, note 16; 697; 2004, pp. 624–625).
5. The ultimate sources in Wilkins (1989) are considered end-of-year, except where otherwise stated or where there is information to the contrary. It is likely that the data are in gold dollars, because at book value or par value (granted there may be some inconsistencies here). More serious is that the data pertain to securities alone. Therefore the direct-investment component of foreign investment in the United States is excluded, except to the extent that it is commingled with portfolio investment. (see Wilkins 1989, pp. 144–151). Fortunately, as Wilkins (1989, p. 145) states: "It has long been accepted that in the late nineteenth and early twentieth centuries, the value of foreign portfolio investment far exceeded that of foreign direct investment in the United States. My research confirms this." Lipsey (2000, pp. 698–699) provides an explanation of why "there was so little inflow of direct investment."
6. That is 1842, for which I make use of data and comments in Lewis (1938, pp. 518–520) and North (1960, pp. 620–625), in order to account for debt repudiations and scaling-down.
7. 1789, 1803, 1817, 1822, 1839, 1842, 1860, 1863, 1866, 1873–1876, 1880, 1883, 1885, 1889, 1895–1898, 1908, 1914, 1918–1919.
8. 1795, 1801, 1824, 1828, 1870.
9. 1833, 1837, 1853, 1868–1869, 1871–1872, 1877–1878, 1907, 1913. I assume that, although (amazingly) the entire federal debt was liquidated in January 1835 and thus became zero, there was sufficient time for foreign holdings of U.S. securities to reach stock equilibrium by mid-1838.
10. First, linear interpolation is applied in situations where an interpolation variable is involved or where conversion from within year to end-of-year

is performed. Then, for the remaining missing years, log-linear (exponential) interpolation of missing observations of a stock variable is logically superior to linear interpolation.

11. Williams' end-of-year figures for 1914, 1916, 1918 are taken directly; 1915 and 1917 are obtained by linear interpolation.
12. Goldsmith is also the source of the 1900–1919 segment of *Historical Statistics* (1975, series U22). Goldsmith's long-term capital-flow series rely heavily on Dickens (1933) for 1897–1914.
13. Source is Lewis (1938, pp. 442, 445, 605); except for 1918, for which it is Wilkins (2004, p. 64). For 1869, the 1897 direct-portfolio proportions are applied to the total.
14. The series is based on data and other information as follows. Nicaragua: Henry Clews (1888, p. 345), Lewis (1938, p. 315), Wilkins (1970, pp. 24, 31–32); Panama: Fessenden N. Otis (1867, pp. 18–66), Frederic M. Halsey (1914, p. 144; 1916, pp. 108, 111), Leland C. Derbyshire (1919, p. 72), Lewis (1938, p. 315), Davis and Cull (2000, p. 785); Canada railroads: Henry Y. Hind et al. (1864, pp. 192, 234), Peter Baskerville (1981, pp. 315–323); Canada telegraph and cable: Wilkins (1970, p. 21), Jean-Guy Rens (2001, pp. 15–17). For each investment project: where timing information is absent, I assume uniform expenditures over time.
15. Also the source for *Historical Statistics* (1975, series U19) 1900–1919.
16. Unlike the norm (including *Historical Statistics*) but following Goldsmith, I retain the sign of a change in the stock whether of an asset or a liability. So investment series are positive (negative) for an increase (decrease)—whether an asset or a liability. Thus the capital account is treated analogous to the other accounts.
17. See Halsey (1914, p. 138) and Lewis (1938, p. 315).
18. This technique redoes the figure for 1918, with the difference from that preset only $0.5 million.
19. The years are 1789, 1803, 1836–1837, 1839, 1843, 1853, 1857, 1869, 1897, 1899, 1908, 1914, 1919. For 1853, I take two-thirds the Lewis figure, based on North's argument that short-term debt piled up during the speculation of 1856–1857, that it was considerably less in prior years, and therefore that the Lewis figure is too high. End-of-year 1914 is interpolated between midyear-1914 and end-of-year 1919.
20. The years are 1864, 1867, 1871, 1876. Source is John J. Madden (1985, pp. 155–156).
21. For justification, see North (1960, p. 583), Madden (1985, ch. 2), and Platt (1984, pp. 143–144). The 1790 value of the interpolator series is repeated for 1789.
22. For the history, see Frank M. Pons (1998, pp. 287–295).
23. The source is Board of Governors (1943, p. 330).

24. Goldsmith (1955, p. 1085, column 7) and *Historical Statistics* (1975, series U21).
25. U.S.-government loans to allied governments under the Liberty Loan Acts.

References

Annual Report of the Director of the Mint [ARDM].

Bacon, Nathaniel T. 1900. American International Indebtedness. *Yale Review* 9 (November): 265–285.

Baskerville, Peter. 1981. Americans in Britain's Backyard: The Railway Era in Upper Canada, 1850–1880. *Business History Review* 55 (Autumn): 314–336.

Board of Governors of the Federal Reserve System. 1943. *Banking and Monetary Statistics, 1914–1941.* Washington.

Clews, Henry. 1888. *Twenty-Eight Years in Wall Street*. New York: Irving.

Davis, Lance E., and Robert J. Cull. 1994. *International Capital Markets and American Economic Growth, 1820–1914.* Cambridge: Cambridge University Press.

———. 2000. International Capital Movements, Domestic Capital Markets, and American Economic Growth, 1820–1914. In *The Cambridge Economic History of the United States*, vol. 2, ed. Stanley L. Engerman and Robert E. Gallman, 733–812. Cambridge: Cambridge University Press.

Derbyshire, Leland C. 1919. *Railroads of South and Central America.* Bloomington: Indiana University.

Dickens, Paul B. 1933. The Transition Period in American International Financing: 1897 to 1914. Ph.D., diss., George Washington University.

Edelstein, Michael. 2006. International Investment Position of the United States: 1843–1977. In *Historical Statistics*, pp. 5-467–469.

Garber, Peter M. 1986. Interwar Movements of Dollars to Europe and the US Currency Supply. *Journal of International Money and Finance* 5 (March): S135–S156.

Goldsmith, Raymond W. 1955. *A Study of Saving in the United States*, vol. 1. Princeton: Princeton University Press.

Halsey, Frederic M. 1914. *The Railways of South and Central America.* New York: Fitch.

———. 1916. *Railway Expansion in Latin America.* New York: Moody.

Hind, Henry Y., et al. 1864. *Eighty Years' Progress of British North America.* Toronto: Stebbins.

[*Historical Statistics*]. 1960. Bureau of the Census. *Historical Statistics of the United States, Colonial Times to 1957.* Washington: Government Printing Office.

———. 1975. Bureau of the Census. *Historical Statistics of the United States, Colonial Times to 1970, Bicentennial Edition*. Washington: Government Printing Office.

Lewis, Cleona. 1938. *America's Stake in International Investments*. Washington: Brookings.

Lipsey, Robert E. 2000. U.S. Foreign Trade and the Balance of Payments, 1800–1913. In *The Cambridge Economic History of the United States*, vol. 2, ed. Stanley L. Engerman and Robert E. Gallman, 685–732. Cambridge: Cambridge University Press.

———. 2008. Changing Patterns of International Investment in and by the United States. In *United States in the World Economy*, ed. Martin Feldstein, 475–517. Chicago: University of Chicago Press.

Madden, John J. 1985. *British Investment in the United States, 1860–1880*. New York: Garland.

North, Douglass C. 1960. The United States Balance of Payments, 1790–1860. In *Trends in the American Economy in the Nineteenth Century*, ed. William N. Parker, 573–628. Princeton: Princeton University Press.

Otis, Fessenden N. 1867. *History of the Panama Railroad*. New York: Harper.

Platt, Desmond C.M. 1984. *Foreign Finance in Continental Europe and the United States, 1815–1870*. London: Allen & Unwin.

Pons, Frank M. 1998. *The Dominican Republic*. Princeton: Markus Wiener.

Rens, Jean-Guy. 2001. *The Invisible Empire*. Montreal: McGill-Queen's University Press.

Simon, Matthew. 1960. The United States Balance of Payments, 1861–1900. In *Trends in the American Economy in the Nineteenth Century*, ed. William N. Parker, 629–716. Princeton: Princeton University Press.

Taylor, George Rogers. 1951. *The Transportation Revolution*. New York: Holt, Rinehart, and Winston.

Wallich, Henry C. 1950. *Monetary Problems of an Export Economy*. Cambridge, MA: Harvard University Press.

Wilkins, Mira. 1970. *The Emergence of Multinational Enterprise*. Cambridge, MA: Harvard University Press.

———. 1989. *The History of Foreign Investment in the United States to 1914*. Cambridge, MA: Harvard University Press.

———. 2004. *The History of Foreign Investment in the United States, 1914–1945*. Cambridge, MA: Harvard University Press.

———. n.d. *Flows Do Not Stock Make*. Miami: Florida International University.

Williams, John H. 1921. The Balance of International Payments of the United States for the Year 1920. *Review of Economics and Statistics* 3 (June): 169–212.

Williamson, Jeffrey G. 1964. *American Growth and the Balance of Payments, 1820–1913*. Chapel Hill: University of North Carolina Press.

CHAPTER 12

Income

1 Technique of Estimation

Ideally, there would be no need to *estimate* investment income; one would simply *count* the reported receipts and payments on investment account. However, for our time period, such data do not exist. Consequently, the way to estimate investment flow—done by all authors—is to sum the products of rate of return and investment stock. Then how one obtains the investment stock is crucial. Other things being equal, the greater the disaggregation, the better the estimate.

The North–Simon residual approach (Chapter 11, Sect. 1) yields as investment stock only *net* liabilities to foreigners, whence differential rates of return at home and abroad cannot be applied. Better is the approach of Dickens (1933, pp. 271–272), who separates stock of foreign investment in the United States and stock of U.S. investment abroad. I disaggregate even further, separating long-term from short-term capital. Also, I apply the earnings rate to average stock during the year, estimated as the average of the beginning-of-year (measured as end of previous year) and end-of-year stock—rather than simply the traditional beginning-of-year (North 1960, p. 599; Simon 1960, p. 698).

L. H. Officer, *A New Balance of Payments for the United States, 1790–1919*, Palgrave Studies in American Economic History,
https://doi.org/10.1007/978-3-030-66099-4_12

2 Payments

2.1 Long-Term Debt

To estimate income payments, long-term liabilities (column (4) in Table 1, Chapter 11) are the default multiplicand-series; but the direct-investment component of the stock is expressed better at current-share market prices than at par value. Barry Eichengreen (2000, pp. 476, 503) performs this revaluation for end-of-year 1900, 1908, 1912, 1914, 1919. I use the default series to interpolate the intermediate years.

For the rate of return 1790–1899, I take the figures in North (1960, pp. 599; 620, column (1)) and Simon (1960, pp. 696–697, column (11)) converted to calendar year. For 1908, based on Paish (1910, pp. 175–176), I compute a rate of 4.75%.[1] Pleasingly, this figure is also Dickens' (1933, p. 271) "standard rate for the earning on foreign investments in the United States" led one year. For January–June 1914, I accept 4.21%; and, from then to December 31, 1918, 4%—both from Williams (1921, p. 202, note h).[2] The rate for 1914 is the average, 4.105%. For 1919, I take 5%, the implicit interest rate in Vanderlip and Williams (1920, pp. 18–19).[3] Finally, the years 1900–1907 and 1909–1913 are linearly interpolated.[4] The rate of return for the entire period is graphed ("foreign in US") in Fig. 1.

The product of the rate of return and the stock is foreign income on long-term investments in the United States; but it is in gold dollars, because the stock of debt is measured at par value. So, for 1862–1878, the greenback/gold exchange rate converts income to current dollars.[5] Long-term income payments are listed in Table 1, column (2).

2.2 Short-Term Debt

Initial stock is mercantile debt without incorporation of debt default (Chapter 11, Sect. 4.1), and the average of the current and previous value is the initial average for the current year. Assuming that debt default occurs uniformly over each year 1815–1819, I subtract half the annual debt default ("half," representing "average" default during the year). Rate of return is the U.K. short-term interest rate.[6] Income is the product of rate of return and stock. The stock is in currency dollars, implicit in its construction; so the same applies to income. Short-term income payments are in column (3) of Table 1.

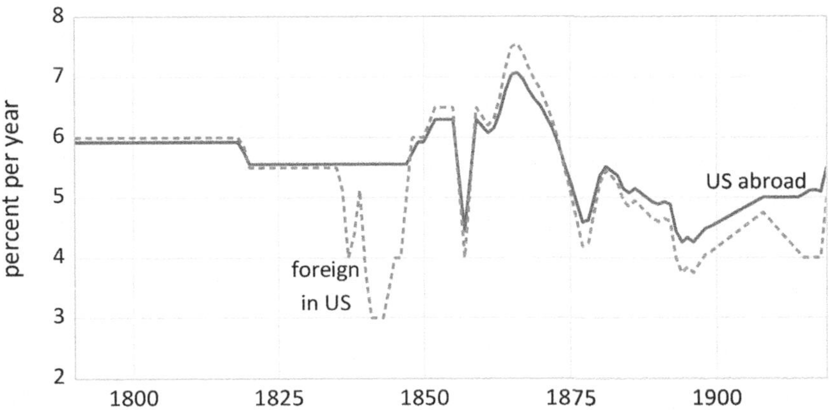

Fig. 1 Rates of return on investment, 1790–1919. *Note* "Foreign in US" is the rate of return on foreign long-term investment in the United States. "US abroad" is the rate of return on U.S. long-term investment abroad. Both series are expressed as percent of the stock per year

2.3 Total and Comparison

Total payments, in column (4) of Table 1, are compared with *Historical Statistics* (1975, series U13) in row (3) of Table 2. Compared to the new series, *Historical Statistics* underestimates income payments by more than a third in 1900–1918.

3 Private Receipts

Private long-term assets are the sum of direct and portfolio investment, columns (1)–(2) in Table 1 in Chapter 11. Just as for long-term debt, this is the default series—used to interpolate between the available years of the corresponding Eichengreen (2000, p. 476) series incorporating direct investment at market prices (end-of-year 1900, 1908, 1912, 1914, 1919), and to serve as the stock series 1790–1899. Again, for computation, the current year of the "stock of private long-term assets" is the average of the current and preceding end-of-year figures.

For the rate of return, I begin with 1908–1914 at 5%, Paish's (1910, p. 176) implicit figure ($75 million income on $1500 million capital) for

Table 1 Income (millions of dollars)

Year	Receipts	Payments		
	Long-term (1)	*Long-term* (2)	*Short-term* (3)	*Total* (4)
1790	0.07	1.08	1.22	2.30
1791	0.07	1.15	0.99	2.14
1792	0.07	1.23	1.03	2.26
1793	0.08	1.31	1.35	2.66
1794	0.08	1.39	1.61	3.00
1795	0.09	1.48	2.13	3.61
1796	0.09	1.60	2.51	4.12
1797	0.10	1.77	2.38	4.15
1798	0.10	1.95	2.13	4.09
1799	0.11	2.16	2.12	4.27
1800	0.12	2.38	2.17	4.55
1801	0.12	2.63	2.14	4.77
1802	0.13	3.08	1.75	4.83
1803	0.14	3.80	1.28	5.08
1804	0.15	4.13	1.36	5.49
1805	0.16	3.98	1.77	5.75
1806	0.17	3.84	2.07	5.91
1807	0.18	3.71	2.04	5.75
1808	0.19	3.58	1.39	4.97
1809	0.20	3.45	1.04	4.49
1810	0.21	3.33	1.29	4.62
1811	0.22	3.22	1.22	4.43
1812	0.24	3.10	1.00	4.10
1813	0.25	2.99	0.66	3.65
1814	0.27	2.89	0.46	3.35
1815	0.28	2.79	1.12	3.91
1816	0.30	2.69	1.86	4.55
1817	0.32	2.60	1.78	4.38
1818	0.34	2.47	1.56	4.03
1819	0.35	2.27	1.73	4.00
1820	0.36	2.00	1.83	3.82
1821	0.38	1.88	1.67	3.54
1822	0.40	1.76	1.45	3.21
1823	0.43	1.74	1.58	3.32
1824	0.45	1.80	1.44	3.24

(continued)

Table 1 (continued)

Year	Receipts	Payments		
	Long-term (1)	*Long-term* (2)	*Short-term* (3)	*Total* (4)
1825	0.48	1.76	1.81	3.57
1826	0.51	1.64	2.13	3.77
1827	0.54	1.52	1.44	2.96
1828	0.57	1.41	1.34	2.75
1829	0.61	1.47	1.44	2.92
1830	0.64	1.72	1.22	2.94
1831	0.68	2.01	1.86	3.87
1832	0.73	2.36	1.79	4.14
1833	0.77	2.75	1.63	4.38
1834	0.82	3.23	2.20	5.43
1835	0.87	3.81	2.85	6.66
1836	0.92	4.18	3.76	7.95
1837	0.97	3.85	3.39	7.23
1838	1.03	5.43	1.85	7.28
1839	1.09	8.82	3.81	12.63
1840	1.16	7.13	3.74	10.86
1841	1.23	5.13	2.93	8.07
1842	1.31	4.62	1.52	6.14
1843	1.38	4.48	0.70	5.18
1844	1.47	5.45	0.66	6.11
1845	1.56	6.50	1.04	7.54
1846	1.65	6.79	1.49	8.28
1847	1.75	8.86	2.68	11.54
1848	1.92	11.09	1.62	12.71
1849	2.07	11.58	1.23	12.81
1850	2.19	12.09	1.38	13.46
1851	2.43	13.14	2.19	15.33
1852	2.66	14.27	1.53	15.80
1853	2.78	14.89	3.45	18.34
1854	2.88	15.82	5.35	21.17
1855	2.98	17.07	5.26	22.33
1856	2.63	14.89	7.25	22.14
1857	2.22	12.25	9.45	21.70

(continued)

Table 1 (continued)

Year	Receipts	Payments		
	Long-term (1)	Long-term (2)	Short-term (3)	Total (4)
1858	2.73	17.35	3.85	21.20
1859	3.32	23.20	3.87	27.06
1860	3.37	24.46	5.85	30.32
1861	3.42	22.24	5.61	27.85
1862	4.06	20.32	2.33	22.65
1863	5.61	21.82	4.90	26.72
1864	8.59	36.20	10.44	46.65
1865	7.14	43.80	7.51	51.31
1866	6.64	58.88	10.26	69.13
1867	6.64	76.38	3.13	79.51
1868	6.75	93.61	2.45	96.06
1869	6.50	111.06	4.36	115.42
1870	5.85	99.03	4.86	103.89
1871	5.98	94.60	4.92	99.52
1872	6.32	103.07	8.22	111.29
1873	6.63	101.57	9.64	111.21
1874	6.62	91.74	6.82	98.56
1875	7.00	87.90	5.15	93.05
1876	6.89	77.77	3.05	80.82
1877	6.53	57.35	3.59	60.94
1878	6.85	46.16	4.97	51.13
1879	7.95	52.32	2.92	55.23
1880	9.24	63.60	4.40	68.00
1881	10.27	74.82	5.78	80.60
1882	10.97	85.48	6.85	92.33
1883	11.71	97.61	6.13	103.75
1884	12.14	97.75	4.67	102.42
1885	12.95	93.35	3.95	97.29
1886	14.22	99.74	3.96	103.70
1887	15.17	109.54	4.64	114.19
1888	16.17	120.26	4.77	125.04
1889	17.24	131.97	5.69	137.66
1890	18.52	135.93	8.30	144.23

(continued)

Table 1 (continued)

	Receipts	Payments		
Year	*Long-term* (1)	*Long-term* (2)	*Short-term* (3)	*Total* (4)
1891	20.20	133.30	6.30	139.60
1892	21.69	127.92	3.49	131.41
1893	21.34	107.91	4.95	112.86
1894	22.13	98.13	2.09	100.22
1895	24.37	97.73	1.71	99.44
1896	25.92	95.63	3.34	98.96
1897	28.78	109.20	4.33	113.53
1898	32.29	124.44	6.54	130.98
1899	36.03	133.85	7.82	141.67
1900	39.97	138.42	9.63	148.06
1901	44.65	146.16	8.83	154.99
1902	50.74	166.15	8.56	174.70
1903	57.88	188.54	10.26	198.80
1904	66.30	213.63	8.45	222.08
1905	76.31	241.70	8.74	250.44
1906	88.28	273.08	15.32	288.40
1907	102.73	308.14	18.47	326.60
1908	120.29	334.35	9.49	343.84
1909	136.58	330.05	9.29	339.34
1910	151.91	318.87	13.54	332.40
1911	168.86	307.40	13.41	320.81
1912	187.64	295.67	17.95	313.61
1913	207.82	271.61	22.93	294.54
1914	229.57	221.12	14.78	235.91
1915	278.27	176.25	19.82	196.07
1916	367.77	154.44	36.19	190.63
1917	455.78	146.34	38.62	184.97
1918	521.26	151.47	27.56	179.03
1919	634.07	187.36	26.48	213.84

1908 and Williams' (1921, p. 202) figure for interest on prewar investments during World War I. Williams is the most careful author for interest during the war period, stating 51/2% for wartime issues. Using his data on wartime issues of foreign loans, I create a series of average outstanding wartime issues of U.S. loans to foreigners 1915–1918.[7] The ratio of this series to the current-year "stock of private long-term assets" is the weight of wartime issues (rate 51/2%), its complement the weight of prewar

Table 2 Income: comparisons (percentage deviation of existing series from new series)

Item	*1790–1819*	*1820–1860*	*1861–1899*	*1900–1918*
(1) Net payments	27.96	41.03	26.49	–
(2) Private receipts	–	–	–	−15.83
(3) Payments	–	–	–	−36.14

Note A negative (positive) sign means that the new series is larger (smaller) than the existing series. For discussion, see Sects. 2.3–4

issues (rate 5%), in calculating the rate of return on U.S. investments abroad for 1915–1918. For 1919, I adopt the Vanderlip–Williams (1920, p. 518) rate of 51/2%.[8] Thus there is the rate of return for 1908–1919.

For 1790–1907, I construct an initial series and then link it to the 1908–1919 segment. Dickens' (1933, p. 271) in effect stipulates a differential "standard rate" of earnings on U.S. long-term investment abroad over earnings on foreign long-term investment in the United States. For 1897–1907, that differential is two percentage points—I project it to the 1790–1908 period. That differential pointedly is over the standard return, not the actual return. Therefore I adjust the differential for fiscal years 1820–1848, replacing North's (1960, pp. 619–620) actual interest rate on U.S. long-term debt (Sect. 2.1) with his "general rate" of 51/2%. With conversion to calendar years, an initial series of the rate of return on U.S. investments abroad for 1790–1908 results. It is linked to 1908–1919 via the 1908 overlap. The series is plotted ("US abroad") in Fig. 1.

The product of the rate of return and stock yields income receipts in gold dollars, as the stock is so denominated. Multiplication by the greenback/gold rate for 1862–1878 produces the current-dollar series, shown in column (1) of Table 1. The 1900–1918 comparison with *Historical Statistics* (1975, series U5), row (2) in Table 2, reveals that again *Historical Statistics* is lower, though by less than half the percentage for payments.

4 Net Payments

For 1790–1899, the comparison is limited to *net* payments—*Historical Statistics* (1975, series U13), which is based on the North–Simon residual approach to the capital account. The result, summarized in row (1) of

Table 2, indicates that *Historical Statistics* overestimates net payments relative to the new series, the opposite of the findings for the 1900–1918 gross series.

5 Government Receipts

Government interest receipts, on Liberty Loans, are not included in column (1) of Table 1. They are \$53.07, \$212.88, \$174.2 million in 1917–1919.[9] *Historical Statistics* (1975, series U6) begins with the 1919 official figure (\$175 million, possibly \$174.2 corrected or rounded up).

Notes

1. Paish has interest of \$300 million on total borrowed capital of \$6500 million, of which \$400 million is short-term and presumed to carry a lower interest rate than the rest. Thus the interest rate on long-term capital is underestimated at 300/6500 = 4.6% (assumes short-term and long-term capital have the same interest rate), overestimated at 300/6100 = 4.9% (ascribes zero interest to short-term capital), averaging 4.75%.
2. "Before the war," meaning the first half of 1914, Williams has interest of \$200 million on \$4500–\$5000 million foreign-owned capital. Taking the average base yields 200/4750 = 4.21%. Williams stipulates an interest rate of four percent from "the last half of 1914" to the end of 1918.
3. "Somewhat more than \$1,000,000,000 of our securities are still in foreign hands…the annual interest payable thereon is about \$50,000,000."
4. Dickens' (1933, p. 271) "standard rate" of five percent for earnings of foreign investment in the United States appears too high for 1908–1918, as does Wilkins' (1989, p. 149, note w) suggested five or six percent for 1895. Madden (1985, pp. 43, 383, 385, 388) provides disaggregate interest-rate data, but Simon's figures are better usable for our purpose.
5. Is the conversion to greenbacks (currency dollars) redundant, and therefore incorrect? Friedman and Schwartz (1963, p. 27) state that "throughout the suspension period, the Treasury made virtually all interest and principal payments on its debt in gold at the pre-Civil War monetary value" and "some private debt instruments required payment of interest or principal in gold." So, regarding nonfederal debt, some payments to foreigners were in greenback dollars rather than gold dollars (at a 1:1 rate). However, we measure the stock of debt at par value. So it is only logical to convert the payment to greenback dollars.
6. The source is the U.K. short-term rate, ordinary funds, "contemporary series," measuringworth.com (accessed 1 January 2016). Although

the "contemporary series" has a slight inconsistency, it provides greater accuracy for our purpose than the corresponding "consistent series."

7. Current-year and previous-year average of end-of-year figures from 1914 (zero) to 1918 ($1689.2 million).
8. Nothing in Williams (1921) is inconsistent with this rate.
9. Sources are Harold G. Moulton and Leo Pasvolsky (1932, p. 482) for 1917–1918, figures converted to calendar year; Williams (1921, p. 201) for 1919.

References

Dickens, Paul B. 1933. The Transition Period in American International Financing: 1897 to 1914. Ph.D., diss., George Washington University.

Eichengreen, Barry. 2000. U.S. Foreign Financial Relations in the Twentieth Century. In *The Cambridge Economic History of the United States*, vol. 3, ed. Stanley L. Engerman and Robert E. Gallman, 463–504. Cambridge: Cambridge University Press.

Friedman, Milton, and Anna Jacobson Schwartz. 1963. *A Monetary History of the United States 1867–1960*. Princeton: Princeton University Press.

[*Historical Statistics*]. 1975. Bureau of the Census. *Historical Statistics of the United States, Colonial Times to 1970, Bicentennial Edition*. Washington: Government Printing Office.

Madden, John J. 1985. *British Investment in the United States, 1860–1880*. New York: Garland.

Moulton, Harold G., and Leo Pasvolsky. 1932. *War Debts and World Prosperity*. New York: Appleton-Century.

North, Douglass C. 1960. The United States Balance of Payments, 1790–1860. In *Trends in the American Economy in the Nineteenth Century*, ed. William N. Parker, 573–628. Princeton: Princeton University Press.

Paish, George. 1910. *The Trade Balance of the United States*. Washington: Government Printing Office.

Simon, Matthew. 1960. The United States Balance of Payments, 1861–1900. In *Trends in the American Economy in the Nineteenth Century*, ed. William N. Parker, 629–716. Princeton: Princeton University Press.

Vanderlip, Frank A., and John H. Williams. 1920. The Future of Our Foreign Trade: A Study of Our International Balance in 1919. *Review of Economics and Statistics* 2 (April): 5–28.

Wilkins, Mira. 1989. *The History of Foreign Investment in the United States to 1914*. Cambridge, MA: Harvard University Press.

Williams, John H. 1921. The Balance of International Payments of the United States for the Year 1920. *Review of Economics and Statistics* 3 (June): 169–212.

PART V

Provision of Services

CHAPTER 13

Transportation

1 Components

Transportation excludes fares, the subject of Chapter 15. What is carried are commodities and slaves. The components of transportation are (1) oceanic waterborne freight (incorporating Great Lakes traffic, a small item) (2) carrying trade, divided into oceanic (commodities and slaves separately) and overland (railway only—for lack of data on wagon and motor-vehicle conveyances), (3) port charges (divided into freight, passenger ships, and slave ships), (4) charter payments (occurring only since World War I).

2 Waterborne Freight

2.1 Methodology

The first, and ideal, method of obtaining oceanic freight revenue would be via the assembling of income data, but is precluded by the absence of statistics.[1] The second approach is the "tonnage method," multiplying shipping tonnage by an estimate of shipping earnings per ton.[2] The third is the "freight-to-value method," multiplying waterborne trade (exports or imports) by the ratio of per-unit freight cost to per-unit price. For movement over time, the numerator and denominator in the ratio are the freight-rate index and trade price index, and the ratio is then termed

L. H. Officer, *A New Balance of Payments for the United States, 1790–1919*, Palgrave Studies in American Economic History, https://doi.org/10.1007/978-3-030-66099-4_13

the "freight factor."[3] I adopt the freight-to-value method for all years, although North uses the tonnage method for 1790–1819.[4]

2.2 *Preparatory Series: Waterborne Trade*

2.2.1 *Total Waterborne Trade*

Waterborne trade is obtained by subtracting *recorded* overland trade from total trade. The existence of *unrecorded* overland trade in this context is advantageous, unlike in Chapters 6 and 7.

Merchandise Exports: Overland exports were not recorded prior to 1871. Recorded overland domestic merchandise exports and re-exports of merchandise exports to Mexico for 1871–1919 are assembled from FCN and summed.[5] The result is added to overland merchandise exports to BNA/Canada (Chapter 6, Sect. 3.3), thus obtaining total recorded overland merchandise exports.[6] Waterborne merchandise exports, 1790–1919, are total *minus* overland, multiplied by the factor 1.02 (to allow for waterborne "general underreporting of exports"—Chapter 6, Sect. 3.2).[7]

Merchandise Imports: From FCN, overland merchandise imports from Mexico are obtained for 1871–1919.[8] For 1860, 1870–1871, merchandise imports for the Mexican Border District (considered here a proxy for overland imports) are listed in SAUS (1923, p. 824). The 1871–1919 series is extended to 1860 and 1870 via the 1871 overlap, and the intervening years interpolated using total merchandise import series from Mexico (MSCF, August 1901, p. 618). I assume that overland imports from Mexico were not recorded prior to 1860. Recorded overland imports from Mexico are added to overland imports from Canada (recorded from 1853—Sect. 3.3 of Chapter 7). Waterborne merchandise imports, 1790–1919, are the difference between total merchandise imports (excluding undervaluation of overland imports) and total overland imports.

Gold-and-Silver Exports: Overland domestic exports and re-exports of gold and silver to Canada and Mexico (four separate series) are available for 1871–1909, individually extrapolated to 1919 via the 1907–1909 average overland/total ratio, and logically assumed unrecorded (thus zero) 1790–1870. Source is FCN, and see note 5. The sum of the four series is subtracted from total specie and silver exports (sum of columns [3] and [5] in Table 1 in Chapter 6), yielding waterborne exports of gold and silver.[9]

Gold-and-Silver Imports: Overland imports from Canada 1871–1909 are from Chapter 7, Sect. 3.3. Overland imports from Mexico are in FCN 1880–1909; the years 1871–1879 are estimated per note 8. The series are assumed zero 1790–1870 and again individually extended to 1919 via the 1907–1909 overland/total ratio (data from FCN). The sum of the two series is subtracted from total specie and silver imports (sum of columns [4] and [6] in Table 1 in Chapter 6), resulting in waterborne imports of gold and silver.

2.2.2 *U.S.-Ship and Foreign-Ship Proportions*

Merchandise: The proportion of waterborne merchandise exports carried in U.S. ships and the proportion of waterborne merchandise imports in U.S. ships are obtained from James R. Soley (1894, pp. 522–538) for 1790–1820, *Merchant Marine Statistics* (1936, p. 91) for 1821–1858, and SAUS for the remaining years.[10] For 1790–1915, conversion from fiscal year to calendar year is made. Of course, the proportion of waterborne merchandise exports or imports carried in foreign ships is one *minus* the U.S. proportion.

Gold and Silver: Data in FCN for fiscal-years 1880–1909 are used to compute the proportion of waterborne gold-and-silver exports (domestic exports *plus* re-exports) carried in U.S. ships and the proportion of waterborne gold-and-silver imports in U.S. ships. Conversion is made to calendar-years 1880–1908. For 1790–1879, the U.S.-ship gold-and-silver exports proportion is estimated as the U.S.-ship merchandise-exports proportion *plus* the 1880 U.S.-ship gold-and-silver exports proportion *minus* the 1880 U.S.-ship merchandise-exports proportion. The same procedure is followed for 1909–1919, with the year 1908 instead of 1880. The entire protocol is repeated for U.S.-ship gold-and-silver imports.[11] Again the proportion of foreign-ship waterborne gold-and-silver exports or imports is one *minus* the U.S. proportion.

2.2.3 *Waterborne Trade by Ship Nationality*

Multiplying each of the eight total waterborne series by the corresponding (U.S., foreign) ship proportion, the result is the eight series waterborne (merchandise exports, merchandise imports, gold-and-silver exports, gold-and-silver imports) carried in (U.S., foreign) ships.

2.3 *Preparatory Series: Freight Rates*

2.3.1 *Merchandise Exports*

Freight-Rate Index: I begin with North's (1965, p. 236) freight-rate index for U.S. exports for 1814–1913, converting to currency dollars.[12] Then I develop an extrapolator series to carry this index back to 1790. North (1960, p. 595, column [3]) provides an early period (1790–1819) U.S.-shipping-earnings freight-rate index.[13] The index for 1790–1807 is composed only of British freight rates, denominated in pounds; therefore it is converted to dollars. For 1808–1813 the index is constant, but is here exchange-rate adjusted.[14] The index for 1814 is deemed dollar-denominated and accepted as is. Thus we have the extrapolator series 1790–1814, and the overlap for 1814 extrapolates the 1814–1913 index to 1790. The years 1914–1916 are extrapolated via the 1913 overlap with a freight-rate index constructed as an unweighted average of indexes constructed from wheat and cotton U.S.-outward freight rates (Johnson and Huebner 1920, p. 332). For the remaining years to 1919, I utilize United Kingdom or Continent inward freight rates from U.S. Atlantic ports. For 1916 (linking year) and 1917, the rate for grain is used. For 1917 (linking year) to 1919, an unweighted index number of the rates for grain and general cargo (1917 = 1) is computed.[15]

Freight Factor: Ratio of freight-rate index to price index of exports (Appendix, Chapter 7).

Freight Rate: For 1820–1860, there is the fiscal-year series in North (1960, pp. 607–608, column [3]). For fiscal year 1869, I compute a freight rate of 8.05% of exports, based on a four commodity-group weighted average.[16] The rate for 1873 is six percent (Young 1874, p. 352); for fiscal year 1914, five percent (National Foreign Trade Council 1917, p. 20); and for 1918, 31.2%.[17] Conversion to calendar year is performed as needed.[18] The freight factor extrapolates the freight rate to (1790–1819, 1919) via (1820, 1918) overlaps; and also serves as interpolator series to obtain missing years of 1790–1919.

2.3.2 *Merchandise Imports*

Freight-Rate Index: For 1820–1860 and 1860–1870 there are North indexes for U.S. imports, which I link via the 1860 overlap and convert to calendar year 1820–1869.[19] For the rest of the period, no index for U.S. imports exist, so resort must be had to other data. For 1870–1912, I adopt the Alexander K. Cairncross (1953, p. 176) index of U.K. outward freight rates, which is utilized by Simon for a shorter period. I extrapolate Cairncross to 1869 and 1913–1919 (1870 and 1912 overlaps) via the U.K. freight rate for coal, destination Jamaica and Eastern Latin America.[20] The extended Cairncross series is linked to the U.S. import freight-rate index via the 1869 overlap. The resulting index for 1820–1919 is converted from pound to dollar denomination and extrapolated to 1790 using the U.S.-export freight-rate index via the 1820 overlap. Clearly, all the extrapolator series in this paragraph leave much to be desired; but they are the best one can do, and Simon (1960, pp. 651, 653) defends Cairncross as much as one can.

Freight Factor: Ratio of freight-rate index to price index of imports (Appendix, Chapter 7).

Freight Rate: I assemble import freight rates for six benchmark years, beginning with North's (1960, p. 611) eight percent of imports for fiscal year 1859. For 1869 and 1873, sources are the same as for exports, with an import freight rate of 8.5% computed from a five-commodity weighted average and a stated rate of eight percent, respectively.[21] For fiscal years 1892 and 1914, rates of 3.6 and three percent are obtained.[22] For 1918 the rate is 13.6%, same source as for exports. Benchmark figures for 1859, 1869, 1892, 1914 are transformed to calendar year, using the technique in note 18. The freight factor extrapolates the freight rate to 1790–1858, 1919 via 1859, 1918 overlaps and also interpolates the remaining years over 1790–1919.

2.3.3 *Gold and Silver*

The freight rate on gold and silver is based on data for specie in Officer (1996, pp. 121–124), with the use of linear interpolation. Identical percentage charges in each direction, all specie flows paying the New York–London rate, and nonmonetary silver also paying this rate are assumed.[23]

2.3.4 *Comparisons*

The three freight-rate series are graphed in Fig. 1. The relatively low rate for specie is, of course, due to the high value/volume ratio. The downward trend in freight rates has been explained by technological innovation in ships themselves (sail to steam being one manifestation), productivity improvements in the construction of ships, and productivity improvements in the handling of ships and cargoes in ports (Simon 1960, p. 649; C. Knick Harley 1988). The influence of war in spiking freight

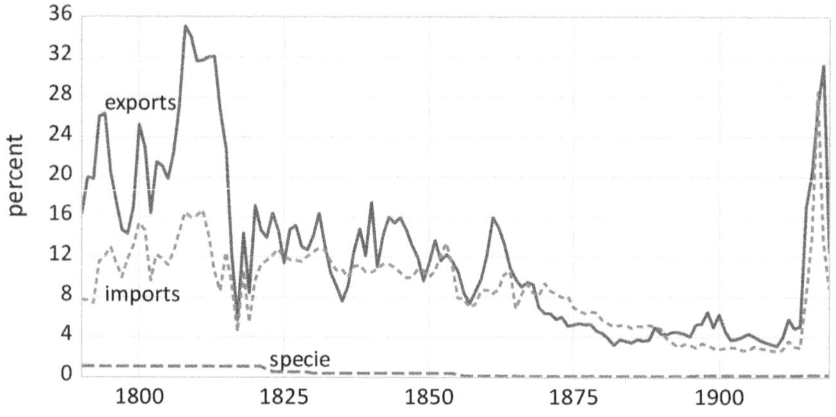

Fig. 1 Freight Rates, 1790–1919. *Note* "Exports" and "imports" are the oceanic freight rates for merchandise exports and imports, separately. "Specie" is the oceanic freight rate for gold and silver, and pertains to both exports and imports. The series are expressed as percent of value of exports or imports

rates is evident during the Napoleonic Wars, the Civil War, and the World War I. Relatively light goods imported and bulky cargoes exported is the explanation of the often-lower rate for merchandise imports compared to exports (Smith 1953, p. 86; Simon 1960, p. 653).

2.4 *Freight Income*

U.S. shipping earnings from exports, the credit item shown in column (1) of Table 1, are the sum of earnings from merchandise exports (the product of the export freight rate and merchandise exports in U.S. ships) and earnings from gold-and-silver exports (the product of the specie freight rate and gold-and-silver exports in U.S. ships). The share of gold and silver averages less than one percent over 1790–1919 and is less than two percent in any year. The corresponding debit (payments) item is *foreign shipping earnings from U.S. imports*, column (5) of Table 1, which is the sum of foreign-ship earnings from merchandise imports (the product of the import freight rate and merchandise imports in foreign ships) and from gold-and-silver imports (the product of the specie freight rate and gold-and-silver imports in foreign ships). The gold-and-silver

Table 1 Transportation (millions of dollars)

	Receipts				*Payments*			
	Shipping		*Port costs*		*Shipping*	*Port costs*		
Year	*Exports* (1)	*Carrying* (2)	(3)	*Total* (4)	*Imports* (5)	(6)	*Transit* (7)	*Total* (8)
1790	1.42	0.59	0.77	2.77	1.00	0.54	0	1.54
1791	2.15	0.60	0.73	3.48	0.96	0.88	0	1.83
1792	2.89	1.11	0.60	4.60	0.68	1.14	0	1.82
1793	5.84	1.25	0.58	7.68	0.62	2.18	0	2.80
1794	8.50	1.87	0.50	10.87	0.51	3.18	0	3.70
1795	9.71	2.45	0.54	12.71	0.71	4.26	0	4.97
1796	10.30	4.23	0.50	15.03	0.58	4.69	0	5.27
1797	7.64	5.15	0.46	13.25	0.61	3.83	0	4.44
1798	8.36	5.79	0.54	14.70	0.76	4.26	0	5.02
1799	11.44	7.95	0.71	20.10	0.96	5.40	0	6.36
1800	16.93	7.44	1.02	25.38	1.28	7.29	0	8.57
1801	17.70	6.98	1.12	25.80	1.35	7.70	0	9.05
1802	9.51	6.28	0.72	16.52	0.86	4.24	0	5.10
1803	11.16	4.59	0.88	16.62	1.09	4.40	0	5.49
1804	15.13	7.02	0.89	23.04	0.95	6.37	0	7.32
1805	17.17	9.93	0.84	27.94	0.94	7.65	0	8.59
1806	20.75	10.44	0.99	32.18	1.09	9.02	0	10.12
1807	21.10	8.00	0.96	30.06	1.04	8.82	0	9.87
1808	9.14	2.63	0.57	12.34	0.81	4.12	0	4.93
1809	16.38	3.15	1.04	20.57	1.11	5.84	0	6.95
1810	18.52	3.51	0.87	22.90	0.85	6.46	0	7.31
1811	15.01	2.00	0.96	17.97	0.83	4.84	0	5.67
1812	8.88	1.07	1.08	11.03	1.39	3.29	0	4.68
1813	4.56	0.30	0.84	5.70	0.43	1.17	0	1.60
1814	2.79	0.25	0.82	3.85	0.99	0.97	0	1.96
1815	9.76	1.29	1.88	12.93	3.09	4.28	0	7.37
1816	7.10	2.48	1.68	11.26	3.16	3.97	0	7.13
1817	3.85	2.72	0.60	7.16	0.82	2.26	0	3.09
1818	10.24	2.72	1.13	14.09	1.86	4.73	0	6.59
1819	4.98	2.65	0.51	8.14	0.91	2.54	0	3.45
1820	10.05	2.51	0.54	13.10	0.62	3.93	0	4.55
1821	7.19	1.84	0.50	9.53	0.59	3.49	0	4.09

(continued)

Table 1 (continued)

	Receipts				Payments			
	Shipping		Port costs		Shipping	Port costs		
Year	*Exports* (1)	*Carrying* (2)	(3)	*Total* (4)	*Imports* (5)	(6)	*Transit* (7)	*Total* (8)
1822	7.63	1.91	0.56	10.09	0.81	4.13	0	4.95
1823	9.94	2.49	0.55	12.98	0.75	4.57	0	5.32
1824	9.79	2.49	0.49	12.76	0.67	4.70	0	5.37
1825	8.86	2.22	0.42	11.50	0.56	4.72	0	5.29
1826	9.70	2.42	0.44	12.56	0.53	4.62	0	5.15
1827	9.55	2.42	0.53	12.51	0.63	4.59	0	5.22
1828	7.28	1.82	0.52	9.62	0.76	4.07	0	4.83
1829	7.59	2.17	0.47	10.24	0.62	3.96	0	4.58
1830	8.72	2.18	0.57	11.47	0.71	4.39	0	5.10
1831	9.83	2.46	0.98	13.27	1.34	5.48	0	6.82
1832	8.40	2.10	1.03	11.53	1.40	5.03	0	6.43
1833	7.30	1.83	0.90	10.03	1.17	4.66	0	5.83
1834	7.39	1.85	0.93	10.18	1.24	4.71	0	5.95
1835	7.07	1.77	0.94	9.78	1.58	5.24	0	6.82
1836	8.57	2.14	1.14	11.85	1.80	6.01	0	7.81
1837	11.12	2.78	1.21	15.10	1.77	6.20	0	7.97
1838	13.22	3.30	1.28	17.80	1.26	6.08	0	7.34
1839	11.27	2.82	1.55	15.63	1.81	6.17	0	7.98
1840	17.12	4.28	1.86	23.27	1.45	6.97	0	8.41
1841	9.53	2.38	1.27	13.18	1.47	5.40	0	6.86
1842	11.32	2.83	1.39	15.53	1.39	5.26	0	6.66
1843	11.38	2.84	1.58	15.80	1.69	4.86	0	6.54
1844	12.20	3.05	1.70	16.95	1.60	5.81	0	7.41
1845	13.36	3.34	1.66	18.36	1.60	6.27	0	7.87
1846	14.16	3.54	2.33	20.03	2.16	6.42	0	8.58
1847	13.56	3.39	2.69	19.64	2.77	6.99	0	9.77
1848	11.99	3.00	2.42	17.40	2.93	7.04	0	9.97

(continued)

share again averages less than one percent, and it exceeds one percent in only four years.

U.S. shipping earnings from imports are earnings from merchandise imports (the product of the import freight rate and merchandise imports in U.S. ships) *plus* earnings from gold-and-silver imports (the product of the specie freight rate and gold-and-silver imports in U.S. ships). These

Table 1 (continued)

	Receipts				*Payments*			
	Shipping		*Port costs*		*Shipping*	*Port costs*		
Year	*Exports* (1)	*Carrying* (2)	(3)	*Total* (4)	*Imports* (5)	(6)	*Transit* (7)	*Total* (8)
1849	9.45	2.36	2.56	14.37	3.53	6.67	0	10.21
1850	13.24	3.31	3.45	20.00	4.72	8.64	0	13.36
1851	17.08	4.27	4.40	25.75	5.93	11.94	0	17.86
1852	14.83	3.71	4.78	23.32	8.26	11.98	0	20.24
1853	18.98	4.75	6.21	29.94	11.32	14.70	0	26.02
1854	19.50	4.92	5.10	29.52	8.27	14.98	0	23.25
1855	19.62	4.99	3.98	28.59	6.79	13.35	0	20.14
1856	17.45	4.49	5.05	26.99	8.43	12.16	0	20.59
1857	15.47	4.02	4.40	23.89	6.13	9.10	0	15.23
1858	18.03	4.69	4.89	27.60	7.18	9.07	0	16.25
1859	22.06	5.73	7.36	35.15	10.98	11.07	0	22.06
1860	24.69	6.40	7.20	38.29	10.68	11.36	0	22.04
1861	21.21	5.54	7.21	33.96	9.47	8.61	0	18.08
1862	16.16	4.30	9.73	30.19	12.31	7.13	0	19.44
1863	12.64	3.45	16.35	32.43	28.41	7.82	0	36.23
1864	10.53	2.97	22.78	36.29	44.57	8.10	0	52.68
1865	13.00	3.67	18.92	35.60	27.12	6.59	0	33.71
1866	16.15	4.51	21.21	41.87	36.98	8.37	0	45.35
1867	14.70	4.19	20.23	39.12	35.06	8.43	0	43.48
1868	13.54	3.91	19.43	36.89	32.29	7.92	0	40.21
1869	11.77	3.56	18.65	33.99	32.45	7.47	0	39.92
1870	10.95	3.40	19.73	34.08	36.21	7.49	0	43.70
1871	9.96	3.19	21.86	35.01	39.80	7.02	0	46.82
1872	8.85	3.08	23.92	35.86	43.91	6.86	0	50.77
1873	9.66	3.35	24.16	37.17	39.74	6.93	0	46.67
1874	7.71	2.89	20.63	31.23	35.41	6.09	0	41.50
1875	7.89	2.99	18.11	28.99	28.22	5.51	0	33.73

(continued)

earnings are the result of domestic transactions, hence do not enter the balance of payments. However, the series "U.S. shipping earnings from imports" is utilized in Sect. 5.1 and in Chapter 20 (Sect. 1.2). And *foreign shipping earnings from U.S. exports*, calculated analogously to the three series above, are in Sect. 5.1.[24]

Table 1 (continued)

	Receipts				*Payments*			
	Shipping		*Port costs*		*Shipping*	*Port costs*		
Year	*Exports* (1)	*Carrying* (2)	(3)	*Total* (4)	*Imports* (5)	(6)	*Transit* (7)	*Total* (8)
1876	8.54	2.96	17.18	28.68	23.16	5.31	0	28.48
1877	8.37	2.79	16.45	27.62	20.33	4.98	0	25.31
1878	7.59	2.67	17.22	27.49	19.82	4.72	0	24.53
1879	5.57	2.31	20.53	28.41	26.21	4.25	0	30.46
1880	5.06	2.23	23.34	30.63	29.17	3.78	0	32.95
1881	4.22	2.12	22.76	29.09	29.34	3.55	0	32.89
1882	3.30	2.09	21.35	26.75	29.66	3.21	0	32.87
1883	3.93	2.07	22.96	28.96	29.51	3.37	0	32.88
1884	3.35	1.55	20.13	25.03	26.86	2.95	0	29.82
1885	2.85	1.36	18.57	22.77	24.80	2.63	0	27.44
1886	2.95	1.39	20.54	24.88	28.62	2.86	0.10	31.57
1887	2.62	1.22	21.82	25.65	30.51	2.85	0.09	33.46
1888	2.88	1.23	22.33	26.44	32.51	3.06	0.09	35.66
1889	4.14	1.72	25.90	31.75	32.96	3.48	0.09	36.54
1890	3.50	1.77	27.50	32.77	33.04	3.24	0.08	36.37
1891	3.53	2.05	28.11	33.69	26.28	2.95	0.09	29.33
1892	3.54	2.10	27.78	33.42	23.66	2.87	0.11	26.64
1893	3.35	1.83	24.00	29.18	18.38	3.54	0.09	22.02
1894	3.04	1.77	20.16	24.97	18.47	3.50	0.08	22.04
1895	2.80	1.74	21.08	25.62	20.11	3.67	0.09	23.88
1896	4.11	2.16	26.11	32.38	18.91	4.30	0.08	23.30
1897	4.14	2.59	27.46	34.19	19.31	3.52	0.09	22.92
1898	4.94	2.98	32.97	40.89	17.92	2.99	0.12	21.03
1899	4.39	2.91	29.82	37.11	19.44	2.95	0.14	22.53
1900	5.70	3.44	40.06	49.20	19.88	3.78	0.14	23.80
1901	4.02	3.45	34.92	42.38	21.57	3.08	0.13	24.77
1902	3.39	3.67	35.11	42.17	24.31	3.67	0.15	28.13

(continued)

3 Carrying Trade

3.1 Oceanic Merchandise and Specie

There are four components of carrying trade: merchandise, specie, slaves (these three oceanic), and rail transit; of which North and Simon recognize only the first two. Except for rail, carrying trade entering the

Table 1 (continued)

	Receipts				Payments			
	Shipping		Port costs		Shipping	Port costs		
Year	*Exports* (1)	*Carrying* (2)	(3)	*Total* (4)	*Imports* (5)	(6)	*Transit* (7)	*Total* (8)
1903	3.74	3.47	41.77	48.98	25.09	4.98	0.15	30.23
1904	4.81	3.28	38.98	47.08	23.36	5.16	0.19	28.72
1905	6.48	3.89	51.68	62.05	25.98	6.70	0.21	32.89
1906	6.29	4.05	62.09	72.43	33.98	7.45	0.22	41.65
1907	5.07	3.62	64.87	73.57	32.10	7.13	0.25	39.48
1908	4.16	3.60	46.82	54.58	29.18	5.09	0.25	34.52
1909	3.85	3.94	66.02	73.81	32.66	6.22	0.26	39.14
1910	4.04	3.97	77.23	85.25	33.47	6.13	0.26	39.86
1911	5.94	4.89	79.39	90.22	37.44	6.47	0.26	44.17
1912	10.23	6.75	108.79	125.77	52.68	8.90	0.28	61.86
1913	9.06	7.02	113.87	129.95	46.94	8.60	0.33	55.87
1914	9.68	6.68	76.65	93.01	41.10	8.11	0.33	49.53
1915	67.08	22.24	209.75	299.06	101.87	33.20	0.34	135.42
1916	140.68	39.54	382.15	562.37	224.89	72.66	0.47	298.02
1917	266.30	61.25	613.63	941.18	533.96	155.92	0.64	723.85
1918	324.08	67.70	575.91	967.69	253.09	142.43	0.73	516.73
1919	337.72	65.07	305.11	707.91	195.72	150.57	1.54	391.74

balance-of-payments is exclusively on U.S. carriers, giving rise to balance-of-payments credits. For carrying trade between foreign ports, North (1960, pp. 609–610) and Simon (1960, p. 654) together add 25% of export shipping earnings for 1820–1900.[25] I copy them and extend the percentage to 1913. For 1926, carrying trade is computable as 6.70% of export shipping earnings (BIPUS, 1926, p. 7). The proportion of shipping export earnings for carrying trade 1914–1919 is linearly interpolated between 1913 and 1926. For 1820–1919, merchandise carrying-trade shipping earnings are the carrying-trade/export-earnings proportion *times* merchandise-export shipping earnings, and gold-and-silver carrying-trade earnings are this proportion *times* gold-and-silver export shipping earnings (multiplicands in Sect. 2.2.3).

The carrying trade served a function similar to that of re-exports, and the two activities were more complementary than substitutive in the early nineteenth century.[26] From Chapter 6 (Sect. 2.2), I obtain fiscal-year re-exports and convert to calendar-year 1790–1824. For 1790–1819, merchandise carrying-trade shipping earnings are "average merchandise-carrying-trade-earnings/re-exports ratio 1820-1824" *times* re-exports, while gold-and-silver carrying-trade earnings are "average gold-and-silver-carrying-trade-earnings/re-exports ratio 1820-1824" *times* re-exports. Thus, for 1790–1919, commodity carrying-trade shipping earnings are the sum of merchandise and gold-and-silver carrying-trade earnings. The latter earnings are the first and second components of column (2) in Table 1.

North (1960, p. 609) points out: "The earnings of U.S. ships between foreign ports ... [in 1820–1860 was] considerably diminished from the years when the continental system and the British and French blockades gave the U.S. merchant marine a large share of the ocean-carrying trade..." Even during North's earlier period (1790–1819), the Embargo, Nonimportation, and Non–Intercourse Acts, as well as the War of 1812, with its British blockade of the U.S. coast, reduced the U.S. carrying trade—as did World War I—and U.S.-ship earnings on the country's own exports also reflect these forces.

3.2 *Slaves*

Recall that "carrying trade" means buying slaves at the origin, transporting them to the destination, and selling them at the destination (Sect. 4.1 of Chapter 4). For each destination, the corresponding credit (U.S. slave-ship revenue) is the product of the selling price and number of slaves successfully delivered. Per Chapter 4, carrying-trade destinations are: for African slaves, pre-U.S. Louisiana and Florida, Spanish America, Non-Spanish Caribbean, and Brazil; for creole slaves, Havana males and Havana females. The numbers of slaves disembarked are, in order, columns (1)–(6) in Table 2 in (Chapter 4).

Selling prices are as follows. The U.S. price (in Officer and Williamson 2020, Table A2.I, column (1); graphed in Fig. 2 in, Chapter 9) is used for Louisiana and Florida; the "Spanish America" price is in Officer–Williamson, Table A2.I, column (3), and graphed in Fig. 2. For the Non-Spanish-Caribbean price, Officer and Williamson, column (2), extend the Jamaica price of Eltis and Richardson (2004). I believe this price is too high for that purpose. Eltis–Richardson (2004, p. 185) increase Eastern Caribbean prices by six percent to generate the "Jamaican equivalent" price. I do the reverse, dividing the Officer–Williamson Jamaica price by 1.06 and graphing it ("Non-Spanish Caribbean") in Fig. 2.[27] The Brazil

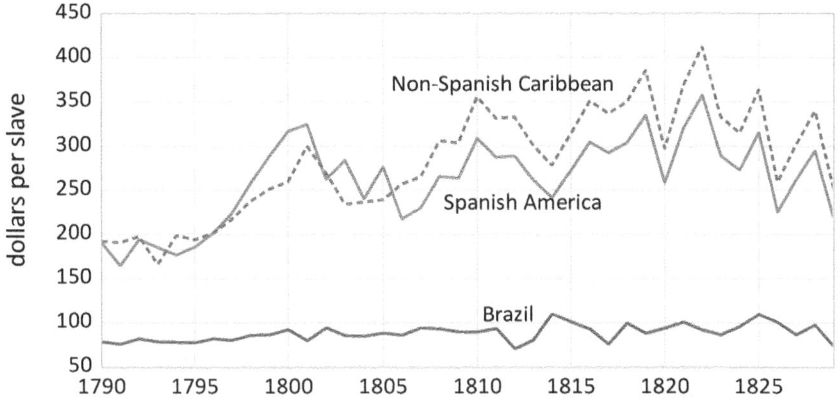

Fig. 2 Price of African slaves: Carrying trade, 1790–1829. *Note* "Non-Spanish Caribbean," "Spanish America," and "Brazil" are the selling prices of newly delivered African slaves in the three regions

price (for only the three years of positive disembarkation) is in Officer–Williamson, column (4); the full series to 1829 is shown in Fig. 2. The prices of creole males and females in Havana are in Officer–Williamson, columns (6) and (7).[28] As always, the revenue from the carrying trade excludes the human costs of enslavement.

Total carrying-trade credits earned by U.S. slave ships is the sum of the six component credits, and constitute the third component of column (2) in Table 1. The series (not shown here—but see Sect. 3.4 and, in particular, row [3] of Table 2) is very close to the Officer–Williamson (2020, Table 4, column [1]) equivalent—slightly less, for reason of the lower Non-Spanish-Caribbean price. Sharp reduction in slave carrying-trade credits after 1808 and elimination of credits after a last gasp in 1829 contradict the economic incentive of continuous substantial price differences between Africa and U.S. carrying-trade destinations in the antebellum period, suggestive of the effectiveness of laws outlawing the slave trade.

3.3 Rail Transit

Transit earnings of U.S. railroads were first included in the balance of payments in BIPUS (1926, p. 7); but related statistics go back to 1868,

Table 2 Components of carrying trade and port costs (average percent share over period)

Item	*1790–1807*	*1808–1860*	*1861–1899*	*1900–1919*
Carrying Trade				
(1) Merchandise	63.02	98.03	63.07	43.90
(2) Specie	0.44	0.44	0.37	0.25
(3) Slaves	36.54	1.14	0	0
(4) Rail transit	0	0.38	36.56	55.85
Port-Costs Earnings				
(5) Foreign-ships freight	91.81	91.14	79.45	63.82
(6) Foreign passenger ships	8.04	8.25	20.51	36.18
(7) Foreign slave ships	0.15	0.61	0.04	0
Port-Costs Payments				
(8) U.S.-ships freight	93.72	89.01	86.51	66.30
(9) U.S. passenger ships	6.21	10.97	13.49	33.70
(10) U.S. slave ships	0.07	0.02	0	0

and it is reasonable to assume that transit activity began in 1854, after the first overland railroad was completed (Sect. 3.3 of Chapter 7). The year-1926 transit credits of (a) $12.4 million on Canadian breadstuffs and (b) $3.6 million on Canadian trade other than breadstuffs are extrapolated to 1854–1919 via 1926 overlap with synthetic transit-earnings series: (a) freight rate on overland exports to Canada (Sect. 3.3 of Chapter 6) *times* breadstuffs hauled in transit by U.S. railroads, (b) same freight rate *times* other merchandise received from Canada for transit.[29] Total transit credits are the sum of breadstuffs and other merchandise, and are the fourth component of column (2) in Table 1.

On the debit side, the only carrying-trade item is transit payments to Canadian railways for carriage of U.S. imports through Canada, again initially appearing in the balance of payments in BIPUS (1926, p. 8), with amount of $2 million. Transit was mostly for imports from the Far East, with silk the most important commodity. Canada's first intercontinental railway was completed in November 1885 (Glazebrook 1938, vol. 2, p. 84). The 1926 figure is extrapolated to 1886 by virtue of the 1926 overlap with a synthetic debit series constructed as the product of the Canadian freight rate (Sect. 3.3 of Chapter 7) and raw-silk imports.[30] Rail-transit debits are listed in column (7) of Table 1, and in every year are less than one-fifth of rail-transit credits.

3.4 Total Credits and Comparisons

Total carrying-trade credits are in Table 1, column (2). The positive association with the French Revolutionary and Napoleonic Wars, and especially with World War I, is evident. Period average shares of the four components are in rows (1)–(4) of Table 2. Note that the first period ends in 1807 (rather than the usual, 1819), for a full estimate of slave activity prior to the 1807 Act. Slaves account for over one-third of carrying-trade earnings in 1790–1807. However, except for the last-gasp year (1829), the share of slaves falls below ten percent in every year after 1810. In contrast, the share of rail transit exceeds ten percent for the first time in 1864 and never falls below that level thereafter. Interestingly, during World War I the rail-transit share falls substantially, possibly due to the heavy use of railroads for carriage of war materiel to oceanic ports.

4 Waterborne Freight and Carrying Trade: Comparisons

Under the usual protocols (conversion to calendar year, gold-dollar correction), North and Simon oceanic freight income is compared with the commodity components of the new series in Table 3.[31] For fair comparison, only oceanic shipping and only commodity trade (no slaves,

Table 3 Transportation: comparisons (percentage deviation of existing series from new series)

Item	*1790–1819*	*1820–1860*	*1861–1899*	*1900–1918*
Transportation Services				
(1) Exports	89.14	−3.65	−15.94	−73.83
(2) Imports	4.53	−39.64	−7.38	36.80
Oceanic freight income				
(3) Exports and Carrying Trade	108.76	3.93	49.05	–
(4) Imports	–	−13.43	−2.58	–
Port Services				
Exports				
(5) Merchant ships	–	−67.75	−50.47	–
(6) Passenger steamships	–	–	14.52	–
Imports: (7) Merchant ships	45.75	−44.85	−26.13	–

Note A negative (positive) sign means that the new series is larger (smaller) than the existing series. For discussion, see Sects. 4, 5.4, 7

no rail) compose the new series. Yet North–Simon substantially overestimate credits 1790–1819 and 1861–1899 (row [3] of Table 3). In contrast, they underestimate debits (row [4]), especially in 1820–1860.

5 Port Charges

5.1 *Merchant Ships*

Foreign Ships: U.S.-port costs of foreign ships from freight ("foreign merchant ships")—a U.S. balance-of-payments credit—are the product of foreign-ship earnings and the port-costs/earnings ratio. Foreign shipping earnings are the sum of earnings from U.S. imports and U.S. exports, each merchandise and gold and silver. I adopt Simon's (1960, p. 654) formula for the ratio of port costs to earnings: 25 percent for sailing vessels and 33 1/3% for steamships, weighted by the sailing and steam proportions of foreign-ship tonnage *entering* U.S. seaports. Port charges as percent of earnings (all foreign merchant ships) are 25% 1790–1837, the Simon (1960, p. 655, column (3)) series converted to calendar year 1861–1899, and computed via the Simon formula 1838–1860, 1900–1919.[32]

U.S. Ships: Foreign-port costs of U.S. ships from freight ("U.S. merchant ships") are a balance-of-payments debit, estimated as the product of oceanic earnings and the port-costs/earnings ratio. U.S. shipping earnings are the sum of earnings from exports *and* imports, each merchandise and gold and silver, and also from commodity carrying-trade earnings (merchandise and gold and silver). Again I accept Simon's (1960, pp. 654–656) formula for the port-costs/earnings ratio: 20 percent for sailing vessels and 30% for steamships, weighted by the sailing and steam proportions of U.S.-ship tonnage *cleared from* U.S. seaports. Port charges as percent of earnings (all U.S. merchant ships) are 20% 1790–1846, the Simon (1960, p. 657, column [3]) series converted to calendar year 1870–1899, and computed via the Simon formula 1847–1869, 1900–1919.[33]

5.2 *Passenger Ships*

Port-costs/Revenue Ratios: I begin with the ratio for steamships. Using Cunard data that I project to all years and all steamship passenger lines, I estimate port expenses as 53.75% of passenger revenue.[34] For sailing ships, I adjust this figure as follows. For freight (Sect. 5.1), sail/steam port charges are 20%/30% = 2/3 earnings for U.S. ships in foreign ports, 25%/(33–1/3%) = 0.75 earnings for foreign ships in U.S. ports. Therefore, for U.S. passenger sailing-ships, the port-costs/revenue ratio is estimated as 2/3 × 53.75 = 35.8333% of passenger revenue; for foreign passenger sailing-ships, 0.75 × 53.75 = 40.3125% of passenger revenue.

Passenger Revenue: Via summing ship "basic revenue series" constructed in Chapter 15 (Sect. 4), four aggregate series 1790–1919 are obtained: (1) U.S. sailing-ship passenger revenue outbound from foreign ports, (2) U.S. steamship passenger revenue outbound from foreign ports, (3) foreign sailing-ship passenger revenue outbound from U.S. ports, (4) foreign steamship passenger revenue outbound from U.S. ports.

Port Costs: Foreign-port costs of U.S. passenger ships, a balance-of-payments debit, is the sum of 0.358333 *times* series (1) and 0.5375 *times* series (2). U.S.-port costs of foreign passenger ships, a U.S. credit, is the sum of 0.403125 *times* series (3) and 0.5375 *times* series (4).

5.3 *Slave Ships*

"Outfitting and provisioning" foreign slave-ships in U.S. ports (a credit) and same for U.S. slave-ships in foreign ports (a debit) are computed using the data and methodology in Officer and Williamson (2020, pp. 211–212). Except for rounding differences, the results are identical to columns (4) and (5) in their Table 4.

5.4 *Totals and Comparisons*

Total port-costs credits are listed in column (3) of Table 1, and debits in column (6). Average shares of the three components of each series (freight, passenger ships, slave ships) are shown in rows (5)–(10) of Table 2. The dominance of freight in carrying trade is notable for the antebellum period, but partially gives way to passenger ships in the last two periods. The insignificant share of slave-ship port costs in all periods is in contrast to the relatively high share of slaves in the carrying trade in 1790–1807.

Port-services credits and debits are compared with North and Simon in rows (5)–(7) of Table 3, under the usual protocols: conversion to calendar year and adjustment for gold dollar.[35] Except for early-period debits, North and Simon merchant-ship numbers are low relative to the new series. The opposite holds for passenger steamships, for which only Simon offers figures.

6 Charter Payments

Payments for foreign shipping chartered to the United States during World War I are included in Goldsmith (1955, p. 1078) and thence in *Historical Statistics* (1975, p. 859).[36] Goldsmith's figures are $87 million in 1917 and $174 in 1918, but both are based exclusively on one figure: the official number for the first half of 1918. Supplementing the last with other direct data, I estimate charter-hire payments as $33 million in 1917, $120 million in 1918, and $44 million in 1919.[37]

7 Totals and Comparisons

Total transportation credits (receipts, exports) and debits (payments, imports) are in Table 1, columns (4) and (8), respectively. They are compared with *Historical Statistics* in rows (1) and (2) of Table 3.[38] The divergence from the new receipts series is great in 1790–1819 and 1900–1918 but of opposite sign. The same is true for payments in 1820–1860 and 1900–1918. The inconsistency of the *Historical Statistics* table over time (Sect. 3.3.2 of Chapter 1) provides a general explanation of the anomalies.

Notes

1. See Van Pelt (1921, p. 401) and Lary (1943, p. 209).
2. For discussion of this method, see Douglass C. North and Alan Heston (1960, p. 267).
3. The third approach is described in Van Pelt (1921 p. 408) and North-Heston (1960, pp. 266–267).
4. "This method was used, not only because the data lend themselves to this method rather than the freight-divided-by-value method, but also because during that period U.S. ships received a large share of their earnings carrying cargo between foreign ports as a result of the Napoleonic War" (North 1960, p. 604). Rather, there is a virtue in consistency—a uniform approach (freight-to-value) throughout 1790–1919, and the carrying trade is better estimated separately.

5. For 1871–1879, gold and silver are included with merchandise; but gold-and-silver exports and re-exports are zero 1880–1882 and 1880–1881, respectively—therefore I assume both are zero 1871–1879. Domestic merchandise exports 1871–1879 are converted from gold dollars to currency.
6. At various stages in the computation described in this paragraph, gold-dollar or mixed-dollar denomination is converted to currency-dollar (via exchange rates, in Chapter 2, Appendix, Sect. A), and at various stages fiscal year is transformed to calendar year. Such adjustments are also made as needed in the computations for merchandise imports and gold-and-silver exports and imports.
7. As the subject here is waterborne trade, adjustments made for overland exports are excluded.
8. For 1871–1879, overland gold and silver are removed via its 1880–1881 average share of total gold-and-silver imports. Gold and silver imports 1825–1870 (for use below) are in FCN, 1871–1879 in SAUS (1880, p. 60).
9. For transportation, the distinction between specie and merchandise gold-and-silver is irrelevant.
10. SAUS (1895, pp. 399–400; 1913, pp. 318–319; 1920, pp. 380–381; 1924, p. 417).
11. Where the resulting proportion exceeds unity, it is replaced with unity. That is an issue only for pre-1841 exports.
12. The sources, the deflator, and no statement about year-definition suggest calendar year (see North 1965, pp. 216, 237–238). The low ratio of the series for 1864/1861 compared to that of the greenback price of gold (0.65 versus 2.03) indicates gold-dollar denomination.
13. Again considered calendar year, via component series (North 1960, p. 596; 1961, pp. 222–227). The series has base 1796–1800 = 100.
14. For 1790–1807, the conversion multiplicative-factor is an index of the dollar-pound exchange, 1796–1800 = 1. For 1808–1813, the constant number is multiplied by the ratio of the dollar-denominated freight-rate index to the pound-denominated freight-rate index, numerator and denominator each the sum of the 1807 and 1814 figures.
15. Source is Angier (1920, pp. 147, 151, 154, 159). Averages of highest and lowest rates are adopted, and conversion from shillings to dollars performed.
16. Freight rates in Wells (1869, p. xxx, note), trade figures in CN 1869.
17. See BWT (1919, p. 249) and Van Pelt (1921, pp. 402, 404).
18. For 1820–1842, 1843–1859, conversion is done in the regular way. For 1860, 1869, 1914, the freight rate is multiplied by the calendar-year/[converted] fiscal-year freight factor.

19. Sources are North (1960, pp. 607–608, column [8]) and Simon (1960, p. 652, column [2]).
20. Sources are (Angier 1920, pp. 6, 8), averages of highest and lowest rates, and Saif I. Shah Mohammed and Jeffrey G. Williamson (2004, p. 183).
21. For the latter, the alternatively presented rate of six percent is rejected, because specie is included.
22. Sources are *Commercial Year Book* (1896, p. 229) and National Foreign Trade Council (1917, p. 19).
23. The prewar rate shown in Officer ends August 3, 1914, the day before Britain declared war on Germany. The 1925 rate of 0.25% is the highest recorded rate over the full century 1830–1929; so that rate is deemed to apply to the World War I period to the end of 1919.
24. Analogous to U.S. shipping earnings from imports, foreign shipping earnings from U.S. exports do not *directly* enter the balance of payments.
25. The 25% figure emanates from the calculation/assumption that 20% of trade tonnage after satisfying the export trade was available for the carrying trade (Sterns 1899, p. 53). Assuming that carrying trade also constitutes 20% of total "export *plus* carrying-trade" income, carrying-trade income equals 25% of export income.
26. For 1790–1814, North (1961, p. 55) comments on "the strategic importance of the carrying and re-export trade to the American economy."
27. Admittedly, the factor would be too high to the extent that slaves are moved rather from Cuba or St. Dominque to Jamaica (the three areas grouped as Western Caribbean in Eltis–Richardson).
28. For the *purchase price* of these slaves (pertaining to a balance-of-payments debit), see Fig. 1 in Chapter 17.
29. Total merchandise received from Canada for transit by U.S. railroads 1868–1926 is in SAUS, various issues 1888–1928. With 1790–1853 zero, 1854–1867 linearly interpolated, and 1854–1917 converted from fiscal to calendar year, a full series 1854–1926 results. From MSCF (December 1901, p. 2545; October 1902, p. 1215; June 1903, p. 4641; June 1904, p. 4948), SAUS, and FCN, breadstuffs hauled in transit by U.S. railroads are obtained, converted to calendar year 1901–1926, and extrapolated to 1854 via 1901 overlap with total merchandise received for transit. Other merchandise for transit is total *minus* breadstuffs.
30. Imports are obtained from SAUS (1924, p. 445; 1931, p. 592) and converted to calendar year as needed, with *Historical Statistics* (2006, series Ee600) for 1916–1918.
31. The former series are, for exports and carrying trade, North (1960, pp. 595, column [4]; 607–608, column [7]) and Simon (1960, p. 650, column [8]); for imports, North (1960, pp. 607–608, column [11]) and Simon (1960, p. 652, column (6)).

32. Tonnage data exist only from 1864. For 1861–1863, Simon (1960, p. 655, col. [2]) assumes the steamship share is lower by one percentage point per year (from 29% in 1864). I continue this allocation to the past, stopping it at three percent in 1838, the first year of foreign steamship service on the Atlantic (Taylor 1951, p. 112) and thence zero. For 1899–1920 I obtain tonnage of foreign sailing vessels and steam vessels entering U.S. seaports (SAUS 1921, p. 436), converting to calendar-year 1900–1919 and then to sailing-steam proportions. North (1960, p. 611) takes 25% of earnings up to 1860, which ignores foreign steamship activity.
33. With tonnage data available only from 1870, Simon (1960, p. 657, cols. (1) - (2)) assumes a 70–30 sail/steam distribution for 1861–1869. That allocation is out of line with 1871–1875 going back in time, during which the steamship share steadily falls to 30% in 1871 (Simon implicitly considers the 1870 share of 33% an aberration). No U.S. steamship crossed the Atlantic to a European port until 1847 (John H. Morrison 1903, p. 408; Taylor 1951, p. 120). And U.S. steamship activity in Central America, South America, and the Pacific started later (Frederick E. Emmons 1985). I assume the steamship proportion is zero 1790–1846 and linearly interpolate 1847–1869, converting to calendar years. For 1899–1920 I obtain U.S. sailing vessels and steam vessels cleared from U.S. seaports (SAUS 1921, p. 436), converting to calendar-year 1900–1919 and then to sailing-steam proportions. Again, North (1960, p. 609, note to col. 13) assumes away steamship operations, as he takes 20% of earnings for all years.
34. For 1885–1914, Drew Keeling (1999, pp. 66–67) computes average "coal cost," "port and loading," and "wages and provisions," at 39, 19, and 35% of "voyage costs." He kindly shared unpublished information that, for 1900–1913 (extendible to 1885–1914), provisions average 48% of "wages and provisions" (equaling $0.48 \times 35 = 17\%$ of voyage costs) and "voyage costs" constitute 65% of voyage revenue. Thus port costs are $39 + 19 + 17 = 75\%$ of voyage costs for 1900–1913, with "ship repairs" another five percent (again per Keeling). So port costs total $(0.65 \times 75) + 5 = 53.75\%$ of revenue.
35. The series compared are, for row (5), North (1960, pp. 607–608, column [12]) and Simon (1960, p. 655, column [5]); for row [6], Simon (1960, p. 691, column [3]); for row (7), North (1960, pp. 595, column [5]; 607–608, column [6] [see p. 609, note to col. 13]) and Simon (1960, p. 657, column (5)).
36. Goldsmith obtains his data from BWT (1919, p. 250).
37. Source is United States Shipping Board *Annual Report* (1919, p. 136; 1920, p. 262). I take the figures for July 1917–June 1919 and July 1917–June 1920, obtain July 1919–June 1920 by subtraction, and assume uniform distribution over time.

38. *Historical Statistics* (1975, series U3 and U10). As usual, there is calendar-year conversion and gold-dollar adjustment.

References

Angier, E.A.V. 1920. *Fifty Years' Freights*. London: Fairplay.

The Balance of International Payments of the United States [BIPUS]. 1926. Annual.

Bullock, Charles J., John H. Williams, and Rufus S. Tucker [BWT]. 1919. The History of Our Foreign Trade Balance During the Great War. *Review of Economics and Statistics* 1 (July): 234–254.

Cairncross, Alexander K. 1953. *Home and Foreign Investment, 1870-1913*. Cambridge: Cambridge University Press.

Commerce and Navigation [CN].

Commercial Year Book. 1896. Our International Balance Sheet, 225–231.

Eltis, David, and David Richardson. 2004. Prices of African Slaves Newly Arrived in the Americas, 1673–1865: New Evidence on Long-Run Trends and Regional Differentials. In *Slavery in the Development of the Americas*, ed. David Eltis, Frank D. Lewis, and Kenneth L. Sokoloff, 181–218. Cambridge: Cambridge University Press.

Emmons, Frederick E. 1985. *American Passenger Ships*. Newark: University of Delaware Press.

Foreign Commerce and Navigation [FCN].

Glazebrook, George P. de T. 1938. *A History of Transportation in Canada*. Toronto: Ryerson.

Goldsmith, Raymond W. 1955. *A Study of Saving in the United States*, vol. 1. Princeton: Princeton University Press.

Harley, C. Knick. 1988. Ocean Freight Rates and Productivity, 1740–1913: The Primacy of Mechanical Invention Reaffirmed. *Journal of Economic History* 48 (December): 851–876.

[*Historical Statistics*]. 1975. Bureau of the Census. *Historical Statistics of the United States, Colonial Times to 1970, Bicentennial Edition*. Washington: Government Printing Office.

———. 2006. *Historical Statistics of the United States, Millennial Edition*, ed. Susan B. Carter, Scott Sigmund Gartner, Michael R. Haines, Alan L. Olmstead, Richard Sutch, and Gavin Wright. Cambridge: Cambridge University Press.

Johnson, Emory R., and Grover G. Huebner. 1920. *Principles of Ocean Transportation*. New York: Appleton.

Keeling, Drew. 1999. The Transportation Revolution and Transatlantic Migration, 1850–1914. *Research in Economic History* 19: 39–74.

Lary, Hal B. 1943. *The United States in the World Economy*. Washington: Government Printing Office.

Merchant Marine Statistics (1936). Washington: Government Printing Office.

Mohammed, Saif I. Shah, and Jeffrey G. Williamson. 2004. Freight Rates and Productivity Gains in British Tramp Shipping 1869–1950. *Explorations in Economic History* 41 (April): 172–203.

Monthly Summary of Commerce and Finance [MSCF].

Morrison, John H. 1903. *History of American Steam Navigation*. New York: Sametz.

National Foreign Trade Council. 1917. *Ocean Shipping*. Washington.

North, Douglass C. 1960. The United States Balance of Payments, 1790–1860. In *Trends in the American Economy in the Nineteenth Century*, ed. William N. Parker, 573–628. Princeton: Princeton University Press.

———. 1961. *The Economic Growth of the United States, 1790–1860*. Englewood Cliffs: Prentice-Hall.

——. 1965. The Role of Transportation in the Economic Development of North America. In *Les Grandes Voies Maritimes dans le Monde*, 209–246. Paris: S.E.V.P.E.N.

———, and Alan Heston. 1960. The Estimation of Shipping Earnings in Historical Studies of the Balance of Payments. *Canadian Journal of Economics and Political Science* 26 (May): 265–276.

Officer, Lawrence H. 1996. *Between the Dollar-Sterling Gold Points*. Cambridge: Cambridge University Press.

———, and Samuel H. Williamson. 2020. The Antebellum Slave Trade: Numbers and Impact on the Balance of Payments. *Research in Economic History* 36: 181–212.

Simon, Matthew. 1960. The United States Balance of Payments, 1861–1900. In *Trends in the American Economy in the Nineteenth Century*, ed. William N. Parker, 629–716. Princeton: Princeton University Press.

Smith, Walter B. 1953. *Economic Aspects of the Second Bank of the United States*. Cambridge, MA: Harvard University Press.

Soley, James R. 1894. The Maritime Industries of America. In *The United States of America*, ed. Nathaniel S. Shaler, 518–624. New York: D. Appleton.

Statistical Abstract of the United States [SAUS].

Sterns, Worthy P. 1899. The Foreign Trade of the United States from 1820 to 1840. *Journal of Political Economy* 8 (December): 34–57.

Taylor, George Rogers. 1951. *The Transportation Revolution*. New York: Holt, Rinehart, and Winston.

Van Pelt, Henry W. 1921. American Shipping Earnings and the Balance of Trade. *Federal Reserve Bulletin*, April, pp. 400–410.

Wells, David A. 1869. *Report of the Special Commissioner of the Revenue*, House of Representatives Ex. Doc., 41st Cong., 2d sess.
Young, Edward 1874. Foreign Indebtedness of the United States. *Monthly Report of the Chief of the Bureau of Statistics*, February: 351–352.

CHAPTER 14

Travel

1 U.S.-Citizen Tourist Expenditures

1.1 Overseas

1.1.1 Per-Capita Expenditures

U.S. tourism abroad is divided into three regions: Europe, "South America and Far East," "West Indies and Central America" (Chapter 3, Sect. 1.3).

Per-capita expenditures are the product of length of stay and daily expense, with cabin and noncabin passengers separately treated.[1] For Europe, I build on Simon (1960, pp. 668–671). He has the length of stay at 65 days 1873–1894, which I extend to calendar years and project to 1919.[2] For the earlier period, it is a reasonable assumption that the length of stay was higher, as Simon suggests. Almost certainly, major reduction occurred with revolutions in oceanic transportation. The packet (beginning 1818) eliminated the scheduling uncertainty of voyages, and the steamship (beginning 1838) eliminated the variability of duration of the westbound component of the round-trip voyage and completely replaced the packet for cabin accommodation in 1868 (Chapter 15, Sect. 2.2). I assume (doubling 65) 130 days 1790–1817, 120 in 1818, 100 in 1838. I extend 65 days back to 1868 and linearly interpolate missing years over 1790–1919. For noncabin passengers, I apply Simon's noncabin/cabin (50/65) ratio to the entire period.

L. H. Officer, *A New Balance of Payments for the United States, 1790–1919*, Palgrave Studies in American Economic History,
https://doi.org/10.1007/978-3-030-66099-4_14

Estimated daily expenses in gold dollars, separate for cabin and noncabin tourists in Europe, are in Simon (1960, pp. 669, 671). I convert the figures to calendar year and to currency dollars, 1860–1899. They are extrapolated to 1790 and 1919 using a price index of U.S. travel abroad (Appendix, Sect. B.1), with 1860 and 1899 overlaps. Finally, for cabin and noncabin separately, U.S.-citizen per-capita expenditures in Europe are calculated as the product of length of stay and daily expenses.

To estimate the corresponding series to the two other regions, I compute U.S.-citizen per-capita expenditures ratios for Europe/"South America and Far East" and Europe/"West Indies and Central America" for 1919.[3] That is the earliest available year and there is no cabin/noncabin breakdown. The ratios multiply both Europe cabin and Europe noncabin per-capita expenditures to obtain the corresponding "South America and Far East" and "West Indies and Central America" per-capita expenditures for 1790–1919.

1.1.2 Total Expenditures

Overseas expenditures in each of the three regions are the sum of cabin and noncabin "per-capita expenditures *times* number of U.S. cabin or noncabin tourists."[4] Total overseas expenditures of U.S.-citizen tourists are the sum of expenditures for the three regions, and are presented in column (4) of Table 1.

1.2 Overland

Expenditures of U.S. tourists in Canada 1900–1913 (Viner 1924, p. 85) are extrapolated to 1919 via 1913 overlap with Canada total tourist receipts (Knox 1939, p. 90), converted to U.S. dollars via the U.S./Canada exchange rate (Chapter 2, Appendix, Sect. B), and extended to 1790 using total overseas expenditures as extrapolator and 1900 year-of-overlap. To incorporate the inhibiting effect of war, I assume that expenditures were cut in half during the War of 1812 (Chapter 5, Appendix, Sect. C).

Expenditures of U.S. tourists in Mexico are estimated as the Mexico/Canada ratio of tourist receipts in 1938 (the earliest year of the Mexico figure) *times* U.S.-tourist expenditures in Canada.[5] Again I assume that, during the Mexican-American War, expenditures were halved.

Table 1 Travel (millions of dollars)

Year	*Receipts*			*Payments*		
	Tourists and transmigrants			*Tourists*		
	Oceanic (1)	*Canadian* (2)	*Total* (3)	*Overseas* (4)	*Overland* (5)	*Total* (6)
1790	0.22	0.04	0.26	0.38	0.13	0.51
1791	0.30	0.06	0.37	0.44	0.15	0.59
1792	0.38	0.08	0.46	0.48	0.16	0.64
1793	0.42	0.09	0.50	0.56	0.19	0.75
1794	0.32	0.06	0.38	0.74	0.26	0.99
1795	0.32	0.06	0.38	0.93	0.32	1.26
1796	0.35	0.07	0.42	0.97	0.34	1.31
1797	0.22	0.05	0.27	0.88	0.30	1.18
1798	0.10	0.02	0.12	0.94	0.32	1.26
1799	0.10	0.02	0.12	1.00	0.35	1.35
1800	0.21	0.04	0.25	1.59	0.55	2.14
1801	0.77	0.16	0.93	1.75	0.60	2.35
1802	0.43	0.09	0.52	1.44	0.50	1.94
1803	0.14	0.03	0.17	1.40	0.48	1.88
1804	0.17	0.04	0.21	1.68	0.58	2.26
1805	0.17	0.03	0.21	1.90	0.66	2.56
1806	0.14	0.03	0.16	2.34	0.81	3.15
1807	0.09	0.02	0.11	2.17	0.75	2.92
1808	0.06	0.01	0.08	0.93	0.32	1.26
1809	0.11	0.02	0.14	1.57	0.54	2.11
1810	0.11	0.02	0.13	1.67	0.58	2.25
1811	0.18	0.04	0.22	1.14	0.39	1.53
1812	0.13	0.02	0.15	0.88	0.22	1.11
1813	0.02	0.00	0.03	0.36	0.06	0.42
1814	0.04	0.00	0.05	0.37	0.06	0.43
1815	0.18	0.04	0.22	1.48	0.50	1.98
1816	0.37	0.08	0.45	2.00	0.69	2.69
1817	0.49	0.10	0.59	1.55	0.54	2.08
1818	0.48	0.10	0.58	1.45	0.50	1.95
1819	0.35	0.07	0.42	1.33	0.46	1.79
1820	0.19	0.04	0.23	1.35	0.47	1.82
1821	0.22	0.04	0.26	1.53	0.53	2.06
1822	0.38	0.08	0.46	1.14	0.39	1.53
1823	0.37	0.08	0.45	1.16	0.40	1.56
1824	0.20	0.04	0.24	1.21	0.42	1.63
1825	0.24	0.05	0.29	1.68	0.58	2.26
1826	0.22	0.04	0.26	1.80	0.62	2.43
1827	0.32	0.07	0.38	1.77	0.61	2.39

(continued)

Table 1 (continued)

Year	*Receipts*			*Payments*		
	Tourists and transmigrants			*Tourists*		
	Oceanic (1)	*Canadian* (2)	*Total* (3)	*Overseas* (4)	*Overland* (5)	*Total* (6)
1828	0.43	0.09	0.52	1.56	0.54	2.10
1829	0.57	0.12	0.69	1.12	0.39	1.50
1830	0.58	0.12	0.70	0.85	0.29	1.14
1831	0.93	0.19	1.12	0.72	0.25	0.97
1832	1.12	0.23	1.34	0.64	0.22	0.86
1833	1.27	0.26	1.53	0.71	0.24	0.95
1834	1.42	0.29	1.70	1.39	0.48	1.88
1835	1.02	0.21	1.22	1.90	0.66	2.55
1836	1.82	0.37	2.20	2.72	0.94	3.66
1837	1.95	0.40	2.35	3.39	1.17	4.56
1838	0.89	0.18	1.08	3.65	1.26	4.91
1839	1.56	0.32	1.88	4.00	1.38	5.39
1840	1.72	0.35	2.07	4.82	1.66	6.48
1841	1.43	0.29	1.72	4.38	1.51	5.89
1842	1.61	0.33	1.94	3.56	1.23	4.80
1843	1.01	0.21	1.22	3.05	1.05	4.10
1844	1.23	0.25	1.48	3.29	1.14	4.43
1845	1.87	0.38	2.26	2.81	0.97	3.78
1846	2.61	0.53	3.14	2.28	0.73	3.02
1847	3.64	0.74	4.38	2.12	0.65	2.76
1848	3.79	0.77	4.56	1.47	0.50	1.98
1849	4.31	0.88	5.18	1.65	0.57	2.21
1850	4.21	0.86	5.07	4.62	1.60	6.22
1851	5.81	1.18	6.99	14.38	4.97	19.34
1852	5.37	1.10	6.47	12.74	4.40	17.14
1853	5.11	1.04	6.15	16.18	5.59	21.77
1854	3.37	0.69	4.06	16.17	5.58	21.75
1855	4.16	0.85	5.01	12.93	4.47	17.40
1856	2.85	0.58	3.44	10.50	3.63	14.13
1857	2.68	0.55	3.23	9.35	3.23	12.58
1858	2.09	0.43	2.52	8.92	3.08	12.00
1859	1.55	0.32	1.87	14.31	4.94	19.25
1860	1.94	0.40	2.34	10.24	3.54	13.78
1861	1.25	0.26	1.51	8.33	2.88	11.21
1862	1.86	0.38	2.23	9.84	3.40	13.24
1863	1.43	0.29	1.72	13.44	4.64	18.08
1864	0.26	0.05	0.31	22.11	7.64	29.75
1865	0.52	0.11	0.62	23.12	7.99	31.11
1866	4.17	0.85	5.02	19.24	6.65	25.89
1867	3.53	0.72	4.25	19.21	6.63	25.84

(continued)

Table 1 (continued)

Year	Receipts			Payments		
	Tourists and transmigrants			Tourists		
	Oceanic (1)	Canadian (2)	Total (3)	Overseas (4)	Overland (5)	Total (6)
1868	6.00	1.22	7.23	17.31	5.98	23.29
1869	8.66	1.77	10.42	15.99	5.52	21.51
1870	10.04	2.05	12.09	17.48	6.04	23.51
1871	10.29	2.10	12.39	20.09	6.94	27.02
1872	7.02	1.43	8.45	20.53	7.09	27.62
1873	5.29	1.08	6.37	19.91	6.88	26.79
1874	5.06	1.03	6.09	19.20	6.63	25.83
1875	6.03	1.23	7.26	19.07	6.59	25.66
1876	8.15	1.66	9.81	18.51	6.39	24.90
1877	7.84	1.60	9.44	15.59	5.38	20.97
1878	8.44	1.72	10.16	18.83	6.51	25.34
1879	11.35	2.32	13.67	23.37	8.07	31.45
1880	12.09	2.47	14.56	21.59	7.46	29.05
1881	11.74	2.40	14.14	22.47	7.76	30.23
1882	16.27	3.32	19.59	27.56	9.52	37.08
1883	22.03	4.49	26.52	35.99	12.43	48.42
1884	22.93	4.68	27.60	40.80	14.09	54.89
1885	19.74	4.03	23.77	41.60	14.37	55.96
1886	14.98	3.06	18.04	44.26	15.29	59.54
1887	14.50	2.96	17.46	48.22	16.65	64.87
1888	13.31	2.72	16.03	43.48	15.02	58.49
1889	13.50	2.75	16.25	42.96	14.84	57.80
1890	12.48	2.55	15.03	44.85	15.49	60.34
1891	11.84	2.42	14.26	45.34	15.66	61.00
1892	19.11	3.90	23.00	45.93	15.86	61.79
1893	30.66	6.25	36.91	25.63	8.85	34.48
1894	14.34	2.92	17.26	38.73	13.38	52.11
1895	15.01	3.06	18.07	47.69	16.47	64.16
1896	14.41	2.94	17.35	47.05	16.25	63.30
1897	10.32	2.10	12.42	20.87	7.21	28.08
1898	9.99	2.04	12.03	12.10	4.18	16.28
1899	10.59	2.16	12.75	12.30	4.25	16.55
1900	12.26	2.50	14.76	18.82	6.50	25.32
1901	11.83	2.50	14.33	14.53	6.50	21.03
1902	11.70	3.75	15.45	17.38	9.75	27.13
1903	13.44	3.75	17.19	51.82	9.75	61.57
1904	12.17	5.00	17.17	77.65	13.00	90.65
1905	19.13	5.00	24.13	89.63	13.00	102.63
1906	41.79	6.25	48.04	93.60	16.25	109.85
1907	82.83	6.25	89.08	106.56	16.25	122.81

(continued)

Table 1 (continued)

Year	Receipts			Payments		
	Tourists and transmigrants			*Tourists*		
	Oceanic (1)	*Canadian* (2)	*Total* (3)	*Overseas* (4)	*Overland* (5)	*Total* (6)
1908	48.35	7.50	55.85	110.29	19.50	129.79
1909	103.20	7.50	110.70	129.93	19.50	149.43
1910	93.48	8.75	102.23	140.54	22.75	163.30
1911	69.12	8.75	77.87	142.41	22.75	165.16
1912	73.05	10.00	83.05	145.16	25.99	171.15
1913	86.27	10.00	96.27	150.87	26.00	176.87
1914	74.78	11.25	86.02	121.67	29.69	151.35
1915	39.77	7.82	47.59	66.11	31.58	97.69
1916	48.83	7.86	56.68	49.33	38.95	88.29
1917	85.43	8.45	93.88	95.94	46.88	142.82
1918	228.31	9.18	237.48	120.37	56.02	176.39
1919	281.47	13.47	294.94	118.38	61.85	180.23

Total overland expenditures (Canada and Mexico combined) are column (5) of Table 1.

1.3 Total

Total U.S. tourist expenditures (imports of travel services) are listed in column (6) of Table 1. For comparisons, see Chapter 15 (Sect. 4).

2 Foreign Tourist and Transmigrant Expenditures

2.1 Overseas

2.1.1 Per-Capita Expenditures

Again I begin with Simon (1960, pp. 671–675). Using his data directly, I compute the ratio of per-capita expenditures of “alien oceanbound tourists and distant-land transmigrants” to per-capita expenditures of U.S. travelers in Europe, cabin and noncabin separately, for (converted) calendar years 1873–1893. These ratios multiply Europe cabin and noncabin U.S.-citizen per-capita expenditures (Sect. 1.1.1), to obtain per-capita expenditures of cabin and noncabin "alien oceanbound tourists and distant-land transmigrants" for that time period. From Simon, I construct an extrapolator series "combined cabin plus noncabin alien oceanbound tourists and distant-land transmigrants per-capita expenditures" converted to current dollars and calendar years 1861–1873, 1893–1899. This series extends per-capita expenditures of both cabin and noncabin "alien cabin oceanbound tourists and distant-land transmigrants" back to 1861 and forward to 1899 via 1873 and 1893 overlaps, thus complete for calendar years 1861–1899.

The third group of alien travelers is transmigrants to Canada and West Indies. Simon data produce per-capita expenditures, cabin and noncabin passengers together, converted to current dollars and for calendar years 1861–1899.

Finally, a price index for foreign travel expenditures in the United States, developed in the Appendix (Sect. B.3), extrapolates the three alien-travel per-capita expenditures series back to 1790 and forward to 1919 on the basis of 1861 and 1899 overlaps.

2.1.2 Total Expenditures

Per-capita expenditures of "alien oceanbound tourists and distant-land transmigrants," cabin, are multiplied by the number of these cabin travelers; noncabin, by the number of these noncabin travelers (numbers computed from Chapter 3, Sect. 2.4, and Chapter 15, Sects. 2.1 and 4). Similarly, per-capita expenditures of alien transmigrants to Canada and West Indies are multiplied by the number of such transmigrants. The sum of the three products constitutes total expenditures of alien oceanbound tourists and transmigrants, listed in column (1) of Table 1.

2.2 Canada

Expenditures of Canadian tourists in United States 1900–1913 (Viner 1924, p. 86) are extrapolated to 1919 via 1913 overlap with Canadian-tourist total expenditures (Knox 1939, p. 90), converted to U.S. dollars, and extended to 1790 using expenditures of alien oceanbound tourists and transmigrants as the extrapolator series (1900 overlap). The series is reduced by 50% during the War of 1812. The final series is in column (2) of Table 1. There are no data to estimate the expenditures of Mexican tourists.

2.3 *Total*

Total foreign tourist expenditures in the United States (exports of travel services) are listed in column (3) of Table 1. Again for comparisons, see Chapter 15 (Sect. 4).

Appendix: Travel Price Indexes

A Weighting Pattern

Three price indexes are constructed: U.S. travel overseas (represented by United Kingdom), U.S overland travel (represented by Canada), foreign travel in United States. Though U.S. overland is not required in this chapter, all three indexes are utilized in Chapter 19 (Appendix 1, Sect. B.2). A common weighting pattern is adopted: food 40%, alcohol 10%, rent 25%, transportation 25%—except that, absent a price index for alcohol, food is 50% for Canada.[6] Each set of component indexes, and therefore the overall index, is set at base-year 1919 = 1.

B Component Indexes

B.1 U.S. Travel Overseas (United Kingdom)
Primary U.K. data are cost-of-living indexes in Charles H. Feinstein (1972, p. T134; 1991, pp. 170–171; 1998, p. 640), with indexes from the three sources linked for consistent series over time.[7] The transportation index for 1854–1870 is the ratio of railway passenger receipts to passenger-journeys (Brian R. Mitchell 1988, pp. 545–546), with 1868 linearly interpolated.[8] The travel index for 1790–1853 excludes transportation; it is linked to the comprehensive travel index via the 1854 overlap. Multiplication by the dollar/pound exchange rate makes the index dollar-denominated, and explains the spike during the Civil War period. The index is then divided by its 1919 value, to reestablish base-year 1919 = 1. The index ("UK") is graphed in Fig. 1.

B.2 U.S. Travel Overland (Canada)
Cost-of-living indexes for food and rent in Canada are available 1913–1919, conjoined with an earlier index 1900, 1905, 1910–1913. A foodstuffs wholesale price index interpolates intervening years of the food index and extends that index back to 1848 via the 1900 overlap (Urquhart and Buckley 1965, series J129, J131, J140, J142, J165). The

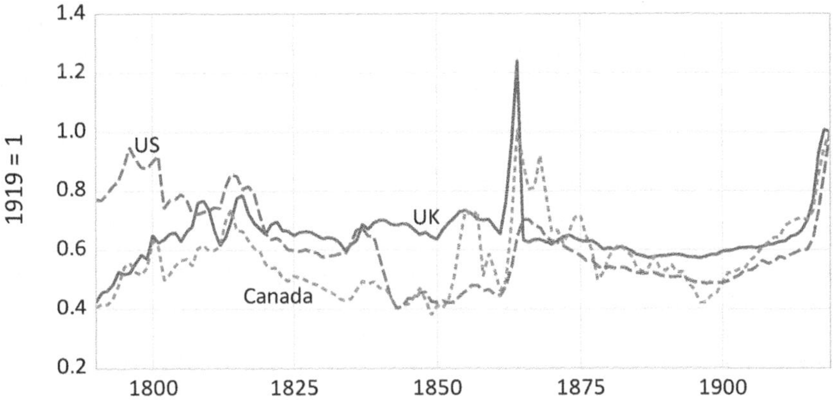

Fig. 1 Travel price indexes, 1790–1919. *Note* "UK" is the price index for American overseas travel, "Canada" the price index for American overland travel. "US" is the price index for foreign travel in the United States. All series are based at 1919 = 1

rent index exists for only 1900–1919. Transportation is measured by railroad receipts per passenger-mile, available directly 1907–1919 and linked to the ratio of passenger earnings to passengers carried 1875–1907 via the 1907 overlap (Urquhart and Buckley 1965, series S44, S54, S148).[9] The three-component indexes (food, rent, transportation) are converted to calendar year.

The complete travel price index is constructed directly 1900–1919. It is extended to 1875 via 1900 overlap with the index of food and transportation, then to 1848 via 1875 overlap with the foodstuffs index. Multiplication by the U.S./Canada exchange rate results in the U.S.-dollar denominated index 1848–1919, and again is responsible for the spike during the Civil War. For extension to 1790, the extrapolator series is the average of the U.S. and dollar-denominated U.K. consumer price indexes (base-year 1848, the year of overlap for the extrapolation).[10] The index ("Canada") is plotted in Fig. 1.

B.3 Foreign Travel in the United States

B.3.a Food

The U.S. food price index is a composite series with component indexes linked by year of overlap. Always "preferred data" are retail (consumer price indexes), with sources for food *Historical Statistics* (1975, series E137) 1913–1919, Lebergott (1996, Table A7, series 2) 1900–1913, Paul H. Douglas (1930, p. 36) 1890–1900, Clarence D. Long (1960, p. 158) 1880–1890, Leonard J. Kloft (1995, p. 278) 1851–1880. For the earlier period, I resort to the food wholesale price index of Warren and Pearson (1933, pp. 25–26) 1790–1851.[11]

B.3.b Alcohol

The retail price index of alcohol for 1900–1919, in Lebergott (1996, Table A7, series 5), begins the series. To extend the series, benchmark figures for 1809, 1834, 1836, 1839, 1844, 1849, 1854, 1859, 1869, 1879, 1889, 1899 are constructed from data in Dorothy S. Brady (1966, pp. 106, 108).[12] That exhausts retail information. For inter/extrapolation, I develop a wholesale price index of "spirits" for 1790–1900.[13] This index interpolates the intervening years of the benchmark figures and extrapolates the retail price index back to 1899. Using that year of overlap, the benchmark series extrapolates the retail price index to 1809. The wholesale price index extends the retail price index to 1790 via the 1809 overlap.

B.3.c Rent

The rent index is a composite of indexes in *Historical Statistics* (1975, series E150) 1913–1919, Albert Rees (1961, p. 74) 1890–1913, Long (1960, p. 159) 1880–1890, Kloft (1995, p. 286) 1851–1880, and the New York City index of Robert A. Margo (1996, p. 623) 1831–1851, the indexes linked by applicable year of overlap.[14] The construction-cost index (with substitution, combined index) of Adams (1975, pp. 811–812, column (7)) 1790–1831 extrapolates the rent index to 1790 via the 1831 overlap.[15]

B.3.d Transportation

The transportation price index has two components: purchased local transportation and purchased intercity transportation, obtained for 1900–1919 in Lebergott (1996, Table A7, series 57 and 58).[16] For the earlier years, I generate price series corresponding to the domestic-passenger series in Chapter 5: omnibus, street railway, stagecoach, and railroad.

For omnibus, I take the New York fare (dollars per passenger), assembled as 0.125 for 1811–1837, 0.0625 for 1847–1853, 0.06 for 1854–1860, 0.10 for 1865–1889.[17] Using the overall consumer price index (Officer 2007, pp. 143–144) as interpolator, I obtain 1838–1846 and 1861–1864.

The street-railway fare was typically five cents throughout the nineteenth century, not only in New York but also for the country in general. The fare (again dollars per passenger) that I adopt is 0.05 for 1852–1863 and 1871–1900, 0.0522 for 1864, 0.06 for 1865–1869, 0.0575 for 1870.[18] Thus there is the series 1852–1900.

A stagecoach fare series requires creativity. Seymour Dunbar (1937, p. 750) observes that the "Boston and Hartford" fare was $10 in 1783–1800, the "Boston to New York" fare $11 in 1832. With road-mile distances about 102 (Boston to Hartford) and 220 (Boston Commons to New York Central Park), the cost-per-mile is approximately 9.8 and five cents, respectively.[19] Taylor (1951, p. 142) has the average rate for stagecoach travel in general at about seven cents per mile in 1815–1819, the Boston–Worcester turnpike fare at five cents per mile in the early 1830s (take as 1832) and 6.5 cents per mile in 1850. The concurrence of the Dunbar and Taylor figures for 1832 suggests that the Boston–Worcester fare can represent all fares in 1850. These numbers enable assembly of an average stagecoach fare (dollars per mile): 0.10 in 1790–1800, 0.07 in 1815–1819, 0.05 in 1832, 0.065 in 1850. I use the consumer price index to interpolate 1801–1814, 1820–1831, 1833–1840.

In contrast, there are good data for a railroad fare (dollars per mile). The source for 1891–1901 is *Historical Statistics* (2006, series Df955); for 1880 and 1890, Fishlow (1966, p. 585, column (3)), with Henry C. Adams (1895, pp. 617–618) interpolating 1881–1889. The preceding figures are converted from fiscal year ending June 30 to calendar year 1880–1900. An index of passenger revenue per mile for Vermont railroads (Thurston M. Adams 1944, p. 49) is obtained for 1857–1881 and extended to 1830 (the first year of railroad service) via North's (1965, p. 245) intermittent freight-rate figures.[20] I take Fishlow's figures. (1966, p. 585, column (3)) for 1839, 1849, 1859, 1870 as benchmarks, and use the extended Adams series to convert them from average fiscal year ending November 15 to calendar year, and then to interpolate and extrapolate to complete the series 1830–1900.

Using the omnibus and street-railway passenger numbers (Chapter 5, Sects. 1–2) as weights, a price index of local transportation (omnibus and street-railway fares) is constructed for 1852–1889. For 1811–1851 and 1890–1900, the omnibus and street-railway fare series, respectively, are used alone—permissible as both series are identically denominated

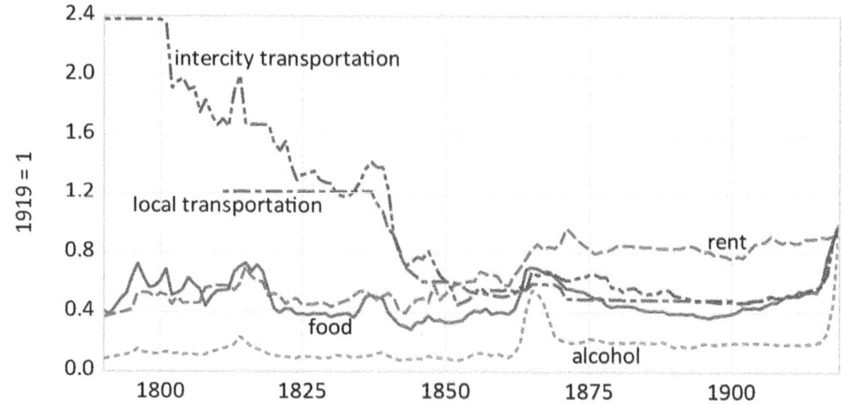

Fig. 2 Consumer price indexes, 1790–1919. *Note* The five series are components of the price index for foreign travel in the United States. The series are based at 1919 = 1

(dollars per passenger). The resulting 1811–1900 series extrapolates Lebergott's local-transportation series to 1811 via the 1900 overlap.

A similar construction is used for intercity transportation. Using stagecoach and railroad passenger-miles (Chapter 5, Sects. 3–4) as weights, an index of stagecoach and railroad fares is constructed for 1830–1840. The stagecoach fare alone and railroad fare alone constitute the series for 1790–1829 and 1841–1900.[21] The 1790–1900 series extrapolates Lebergott's intercity-transportation price series to 1790 via the 1900 overlap.

For lack of information, I assume that, for foreign travelers, intercity and intracity transportation are of equal importance. So, for 1811–1919, the transportation index is an equally weighted average of the local and intercity indexes. For 1790–1810, the transportation index is extrapolated via 1811 overlap with the intercity index.

B.3.e Total Index

Components of the price index for foreign travel in the United States are graphed in Fig. 2. The U.S. travel price index ("US") is plotted in Fig. 1. All have base 1919 = 1.

Notes

1. Recall from Chapter 3 (Sect. 1.1) that "tourists" incorporate *all* travelers temporarily abroad. Also note that passenger fares are separate from travel expenditures and generated in Chapter 15.
2. World War I could have shortened length of stay (minimize exposure to danger: do your business abroad quickly, then return) or could have increased it (stay abroad longer to accomplish the objective with fewer trips, thus reducing exposure to attacks at sea).
3. Expenditures abroad are total balance-of-payments expenditures *minus* payments to foreign vessels. Data source is Maffry (1939, pp. 77, 82). Per-capita expenditures are expenditures abroad divided by the number of US-citizen tourists outbound to the region (the denominator, from Chapter 3, Sect. 1.3).
4. The six US-citizen tourist (travel) series—cabin and noncabin, for the three regions—are generated in Chapter 15 (Sects. 2.1 and 4).
5. Source for Mexico is *Statistics on the Mexican Economy* (1966, p. 214); for Canada, Dominion Bureau of Statistics (1949, p. 175). The Mexican number is in U.S. dollars; the Canadian figure is converted via the exchange rate (Board of Governors 1943, p. 665).
6. Inspiration for the weighting pattern comes from Lebergott (1996, pp. 90; 267, notes 132–133). It is strange that Lebergott excludes food from his U.K. index.
7. For 1788–1867, the Feinstein (1998, p. 640) data are five-year averages; I take the figures to pertain to the midyear, then interpolate linearly. For 1868–1870, the data are averages of the three years, which I apply to all years.
8. The inconsistency in the series before versus after the missing year 1868 would affect the ratio less than the numerator or denominator, so is ignored. However, the inconsistency in receipts from 1853 to 1854 specifically affects the ratio; hence I do not use the 1843–1853 data. See Mitchell (1988, p. 550, notes d–e).
9. While the railroad data have issues of consistency over time (Urquhart and Buckley 1965, pp. 516–517), for our use the inconsistencies are not serious. I do not utilize the series of streetcar fares (Urquhart and Buckley 1965, series J136), as it exists only from 1913.
10. The U.S. index is in Officer (2007, pp. 142–144); the U.K. index is in Feinstein (1998, p. 653), then multiplied by the dollar/pound exchange rate.
11. The missing year 1792 is interpolated via Anne Bezanson et al. (1936, p. 394) wholesale price index for total foods.
12. Figures are constructed as equally weighted price indexes of "rum and whiskey," "malt liquors," and "vinous liquors." For 1809, only the first

two indexes are available; the two-component index is linked to the three-component index via the 1834 overlap.

13. Sources are, for 1860–1900, Christopher Hanes (1998, pp. 205–206); for 1790–1860, linked via 1860 overlap, Warren and Pearson (1933, pp. 25–26), with the BGH (1936, p. 393) "wines" index serving to interpolate the missing year 1792.
14. The Brady rent index (Gallman and Weiss 1969, p. 292) is rejected, because it behaves contradictorily to the Rees, Long, and Margo indexes.
15. There are two objections to the use of a construction-cost series to represent the rent level. First, rent is determined by the stock of housing, not (per construction cost) the flow (Margo 1996, p. 605). In response, David and Solar (1977, pp. 44, 56 [note 1]) provide justification that, for the first half of the nineteenth century, rent was closely related to the capitalized value of housing. Second, construction cost does not allow for change in productivity. There are two counters to the latter criticism: The Adams index picks up productivity improvements associated with shifts in factor proportions, and "the sources of productivity improvement in construction do not appear to have been important before the mid-1830s" (Robert E. Gallman and Paul W. Rhode 2019, p. 81).
16. The modes are street railways for local, steam railroads for intercity (Lebergott 1996, pp. 88, 266 [note 118]).
17. Data are in Taylor (1966a, p. 47), Middleton (1967, p. 13), Edwin Williams (1833, p. 160; 1834, p. 172), *Glance at New York* (1837, p. 260), Orville L. Holley (1847, p. 55), George C. Foster (1849, p. 63), John Disturnell (1876, p. 172), *New York Times* (June 16, 1853, p. 6; December 27, 1856, p. 4; September 30, 1870, p. 4). Rest-of-country fares do not systematically differ from the New York fare.
18. Data sources are Charles W. Cheape (1980, p. 25), Taylor (1966b, p. 52), Holt (1972, p. 336), Boris S. Pushkarev et al. (1982, p. 5), Durand (1905, p. 10), McShane and Tarr (1997, p. 111), Alexander Easton (1859, pp. 22, 24), *New York Times* (various issues). The 1864 and 1870 fares are monthly averages based on the timing of fare changes in New York (*New York Times*, October 12, 1864, p. 4; October 8, 1870, p. 4).
19. It is good confirmation that the "Boston to New York" $11 fare in 1832 and "this rate being about five cents a mile" are stated by George G. Crocker (1900, pp. 5–6).
20. North's figures are for 1833, 1848, 1851–1852, 1854, 1856, 1858. The Warren–Pearson (1933, pp. 25–26) wholesale price index interpolates 1834–1847 and extrapolates the 1833 figure to 1830–1832. Years 1849–1850, 1853, 1855 are linearly interpolated.
21. Absence of data prevents extending the stagecoach series past 1840. For the same reason, water transportation taken by foreign travelers within the country is not incorporated.

References

Adams, Donald R., Jr. 1975. Residential Construction Industry in the Early Nineteenth Century. *Journal of Economic History* 35 (December): 794–816.

Adams, Henry C. 1895. Statistics of Steam Railroad Transportation. In *Report on Transportation Business in the United States at the Eleventh Census*, 591–620. Washington: Government Printing Office.

Adams, Thurston M. 1944. *Prices Paid by Vermont Farmers for Goods and Services and Received by Them for Farm Products, 1790–1940*. Burlington: Vermont Agricultural Experiment Station.

Bezanson, Anne, Robert D. Gray, and Miriam Hussey [BGH]. 1936, 1937. *Wholesale Prices in Philadelphia, 1784–1861*. Philadelphia: University of Pennsylvania Press.

Board of Governors of the Federal Reserve System. 1943. *Banking and Monetary Statistics, 1914–1941*. Washington.

Brady, Dorothy S. 1966. Price Deflators for Final Product Estimates. In *Output, Employment, and Productivity in the United States*, ed. Dorothy S. Brady, 91–115. New York: Columbia University Press.

Cheape, Charles W. 1980. *Moving the Masses*. Cambridge, MA: Harvard University Press.

Crocker, George G. 1900. *From the Stage Coach to the Railroad Train and the Street Car*. Boston: W. B. Clarke.

David, Paul A., and Peter Solar. 1977. A Bicentenary Contribution to the History of the Cost of Living in America. *Research in Economic History* 2: 1–80.

Disturnell, John. 1876. *New York As It Was and As It Is*. New York: Van Nostrand.

Dominion Bureau of Statistics. 1949. *The Canadian Balance of International Payments 1926 to 1948*. Ottawa: Edmond Cloutier.

Douglas, Paul H. 1930. *Real Wages in the United States, 1890–1926*. Boston: Houghton Mifflin.

Dunbar, Seymour. 1937. *A History of Travel in America*. New York: Tudor.

Durand, Edward D. 1905. Street and Electric Railways. In Bureau of the Census, *Street and Electric Railways 1902*, 3–235. Washington: Government Printing Office.

Easton, Alexander. 1859. *A Practical Treatise on Street or Horse-Power Railways*. Philadelphia: Crissy & Markley.

Feinstein, Charles H. 1972. *National Income, Expenditure and Output of the United Kingdom, 1855–1965*. Cambridge: Cambridge University Press.

———. 1991. A New Look at the Cost of Living 1870–1914. In *New Perspectives on the Late Victorian Economy*, 151–179. Cambridge: Cambridge University Press.

———. 1998. Pessimism Perpetuated: Real Wages and the Standard of Living in Great Britain During and After the Industrial Revolution. *Journal of Economic History* 58 (September): 625–658.

Fishlow, Albert. 1966. Productivity and Technological Change in the Railroad Sector, 1840–1910. In *Output, Employment, and Productivity in the United States*, ed. Dorothy S. Brady, 583–646. New York: Columbia University Press.

Foster, George C. 1849. *New York in Slices*. New York: W. F. Burgess.

Gallman, Robert E., and Paul W. Rhode. 2019. *Capital in the Nineteenth Century*. Chicago: University of Chicago Press.

———, and Thomas J. Weiss. 1969. The Service Industries in the Nineteenth Century. In *Production and Productivity in the Service Industries*, ed. Victor R. Fuchs, 287–352. New York: Columbia University Press.

Glance at New York. 1837. New York: A. Greene.

Hanes, Christopher. 1998. Consistent Wholesale Price Series for the United States, 1860–1900. In *Business Cycles Since 1820*, ed. Trevor, J.O. Dick, 176–209. Cheltenham: Edward Elgar.

[*Historical Statistics*]. 1975. Bureau of the Census. *Historical Statistics of the United States, Colonial Times to 1970, Bicentennial Edition*. Washington: Government Printing Office.

———. 2006. *Historical Statistics of the United States, Millennial Edition*, ed. Susan B. Carter, Scott Sigmund Gartner, Michael R. Haines, Alan L. Olmstead, Richard Sutch, Gavin Wright. Cambridge: Cambridge University Press.

Holley, Orville L. 1847. *A Description of the City of New York*. New York: J. Disturnell.

Holt, Glen E. 1972. The Changing Perception of Urban Pathology. In *Cities in American History*, ed. Kenneth T. Jackson and Stanley K. Schultz, 324–343. New York: Alfred A. Knopf.

Kloft, Leonard J. 1995. Problems and Issues in Constructing National and Regional Price Indices for the United States: 1851–1880. Ph.D. diss., University of Iowa.

Knox, Frank A. 1939. *Dominion Monetary Policy, 1929–1934*. Ottawa: Royal Commission on Dominion-Provincial Relations.

Lebergott, Stanley. 1996. *Consumer Expenditures*. Princeton: Princeton University Press.

Long, Clarence D. 1960. *Wages and Earnings in the United States, 1860–1890*. Princeton: Princeton University Press.

Maffry, August. 1939. *Overseas Travel and Travel Expenditures in the Balance of International Payments of the United States, 1919–1938*. Washington: Government Printing Office.

Margo, Robert A. 1996. The Rental Price of Housing in New York City, 1830–1860. *Journal of Economic History* 56 (September): 605–625.

McShane, Clay, and Joel A. Tarr. 1997. The Centrality of the Horse in the Nineteenth-Century American City. In *The Making of Urban America*, ed. Raymond A. Mohl, 105–130. Wilmington: Scholarly Resources.

Middleton, William D. 1967. *The Time of the Trolley*. Milwaukee: Kalmbach.

Mitchell, Brian R. 1988. *British Historical Statistics*. Cambridge: Cambridge University Press.

North, Douglass C. 1965. The Role of Transportation in the Economic Development of North America. In *Les Grandes Voies Maritimes dans le Monde*, 209–246. Paris: S.E.V.P.E.N.

Officer, Lawrence H. 2007. An Improved Long-Run Consumer Price Index for the United States. *Historical Methods* 40 (summer): 135–147.

Pushkarev, Boris S., Jeffrey M. Zupan, and Robert S. Cumella. 1982. *Urban Rail in America*. Bloomington: Indiana University Press.

Rees, Albert. 1961. *Real Wages in Manufacturing, 1890–1914*. Princeton: Princeton University Press.

Simon, Matthew. 1960. The United States Balance of Payments, 1861–1900. In *Trends in the American Economy in the Nineteenth Century*, ed. William N. Parker, 629–716. Princeton: Princeton University Press.

Statistics on the Mexican Economy. 1966. Mexico: National Financiera.

Taylor, George Rogers. 1951. *The Transportation Revolution*. New York: Holt, Rinehart, and Winston.

———. 1966a. The Beginnings of Mass Transportation in Urban America: Part I. *Smithsonian Journal of History* 1 (Summer): 35–50.

———. 1966b. The Beginnings of Mass Transportation in Urban America: Part II. *Smithsonian Journal of History* 1 (Fall): 31–54.

Urquhart, Malcolm C., and Kenneth A.H. Buckley (eds.). 1965. *Historical Statistics of Canada*. Cambridge: Cambridge University Press.

Viner, Jacob. 1924. *Canada's Balance of International Indebtedness, 1900–1913*. Cambridge, MA: Harvard University Press.

Warren, George F., and Frank A. Pearson. 1933. *Prices*. New York: Wiley.

Williams, Edwin. 1833, 1834. *New York As It Is*. New York: J. Disturnell.

CHAPTER 15

Fares

1 Methodology

Passenger-ship revenue, emanating from fares, is needed for three purposes. First, directly as balance-of-payments items (this chapter). U.S-ship revenue from foreigners is a credit, while foreign-ship revenue from U.S. residents is a debit. Second, total ship revenue outbound ("total" meaning from both U.S. and foreign residents) to estimate passenger-ship port costs (Chapter 13, Sect. 5.2). In particular, total U.S.-ship revenue outbound from foreign ports and total foreign-ship revenue outbound from U.S. ports—for port-costs debits and credits, respectively. Third, grand-total U.S.-ship revenue (outbound from both U.S. and foreign ports) to examine the shipping sector (Chapter 20, Sects. 1.2, 2.2–2.3).

To generate these series, two sets of series need to be integrated via linking series. The first set is the *number of oceanic passengers* to/from the United States by travel group and origination/destination, constructed in Chapter 3. The series are U.S. citizens (round-trip), separately for Europe, West Indies and Central America, South America and Far East; foreign tourists and transmigrants to distant lands (inbound and outbound); transmigrants to Canada and West Indies (inbound); immigrants (inbound), separately for Europe and rest of world; emigrants (outbound), separately for Europe and rest of world.[1]

L. H. Officer, *A New Balance of Payments for the United States, 1790–1919*, Palgrave Studies in American Economic History,
https://doi.org/10.1007/978-3-030-66099-4_15

The second set of series is ***per-passenger fares***, of which the basic series are for Europe: four accommodation-direction categories (cabin and steerage, each inbound and outbound), each for four ship types (three sailing ships—traders, Falmouth packets, [U.S.] packets—and steamships). Traders were either "irregular" or "regular," neither with fixed schedules but the latter having fixed routes. The two types of traders are combined here. Falmouth packets were British government mail ships, with monthly sailings between Falmouth and New York; but the route was indirect—via Bermuda in the winter and Halifax in the other seasons. And there was room for only a few passengers. U.S. packets, termed simply "packets," were passenger-oriented and involved scheduled monthly sailings between the U.S. and European port. They were the first "liners," each of which was composed of several vessels owned and operated by a private management company.[2] Rest-of-world fares are derived from the Europe series but do not distinguish between type of sailing ships.

There are five groups of linking series (or parameters), all in the nature of ***passenger proportions***.

1. Accommodation Proportions (cabin versus steerage): varying for U.S.-citizen tourists, foreign tourists and distant-land transmigrants combined, immigrants and "transmigrants to Canada and West Indies" combined, and emigrants.
2. Ship-Type Proportions (sailing-ship versus steamship): varying for Europe and rest of world; for Europe, varying for cabin and steerage.
3. Sailing-Ship-Type Proportions (U.S. packet versus other sailing-ship [traders and Falmouth packets]): Europe, varying for cabin and steerage.
4. Ship Nationality Proportions (United States versus foreign): varying for cabin and steerage; for Europe, varying for packets, other sailing ships, and steamships; for rest of world, varying for sailing-ships combined and steamships.
5. Foreign Sailing-ship Proportions (traders versus Falmouth packets): Europe.

2 Linking Series (Passenger Proportions)

2.1 Accommodation

U.S. Tourists: Cabin proportions are calendar-year-converted from figures in ARCGI (1920, p. 227) for 1910–1919, ARCENY for 1871 and 1874–1889. Intervening years are linearly interpolated. In view of the traditional elite characteristics of international tourism, it is likely that the cabin proportion increases as one goes back in time.[3] There is a huge percentage jump in U.S. tourists in 1850 over 1849, followed by a tremendous absolute jump 1850 to 1851 (series (1), Table 1, Chapter 3), and the new higher level is broadly maintained. I infer 100% "elite travel" (unity cabin proportion) 1790–1849, with a shift to "mass travel" (positive noncabin share) beginning 1850, and I linearly interpolate the cabin proportion between 1849 (unity) and 1871. Here and everywhere below, the steerage proportion 1790–1919 is the complement of the cabin.[4]

Foreign Tourists and Distant-Land Transmigrants: Cabin proportion 1873–1919 is estimated as the U.S.-tourist proportion *plus* Simon's (1960, pp. 671, 674–675) "alien-traveler *minus* U.S.-tourist cabin-proportion" figure converted to calendar-year 1873–1893, and extended to 1894–1919 via the 1891–1893 average. Travel data (column (2) in Table 1, Chapter 3) show a distinctly higher level for 1851–1853 compared to past years; so again (and for symmetry) I assume 100% cabin 1790–1849 and linearly interpolate 1850–1872.

Immigrants and Transmigrants to Canada and West Indies: For steamships from Europe, I accept Keeling's (2012, pp. 286–287) one-percent first-class proportion for 1899–1914 and expand it to cover 1890–1919. Keeling's second-class proportion is 10 and 19% for fiscal years 1899 and 1914 (the latter extended to 1915–1919). I take these figures for calendar year also, and linearly interpolate 1900–1913. It is reasonable to assume that second-class substituted from steerage, not from first-class. So cabin proportion is 0.01 *plus* the estimated second-class proportion 1899–1919. For second class in 1890, I take the 1890/1900 ratio of "second-class percentage of second and third classes" (Keeling, 2012, p. 52) and multiply by the (linearly interpolated) 1900 second-class proportion of all immigrants. I compute second-class proportion for Cunard "Liverpool to New York" 1886–1890 (Keeling 2008, pp. 29–30) and cabin proportion of alien passengers New York 1880–1886 (ARCENY), and use the former and latter, respectively, to extrapolate the cabin proportion to 1886–1889 (1890 overlap) and then

1880–1885 (1886 overlap). The first steamship carriage of immigrants in the Liverpool–New York route was in 1853 (Albion 1938, p. 267), for which I assume zero cabin (100% steerage). Linear interpolation of the cabin proportion 1854–1879 and 1891–1898 completes the series.

For sailing ships, I assume 100% steerage throughout.[5] For rest of world, I apply the Europe proportions, separately for sailing ships and steamships.

Emigrants: The cabin proportion of alien outbound passengers equals the weighted average of the cabin proportion of "foreign tourists and distant-land transmigrants" and the cabin proportion of "emigrants."[6] For 1910–1919, with data for all other components available, the equation yields the cabin proportion of emigrants. Cabin proportion is assumed zero 1790–1853. For 1854–1909 cabin proportion is extrapolated via the steamship cabin proportion of "immigrants and transmigrants to Canada and West Indies" (1910 overlap). The assumption (again) is no Europe versus rest-of-world differential, and also no sailing-ship divergence from steamship.

Comparisons: Fig. 1 shows the cabin proportions of each travel group 1850–1919. (Figures are either unity or zero 1790–1849.) Naturally, migrants have less cabin than tourists; but the cabin proportion for migrants increases with the availability of second-class accommodation.

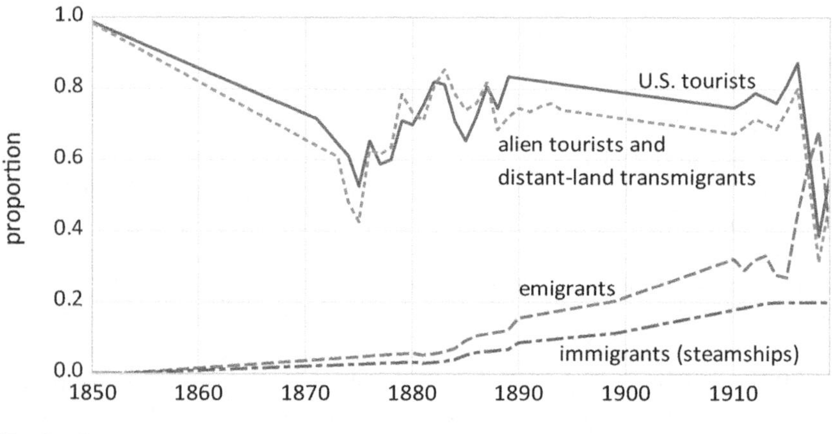

Fig. 1 Passenger cabin proportions, 1850–1919. *Note* The series are the respective cabin proportions of each travel group. For each series, the residual (from unity) is the proportion of noncabin for that travel group

The higher cabin proportion of emigrants versus immigrants reflects greater wealth.

2.2 *Sailing-Ship Versus Steamship*

Europe Cabin: For 1790–1837, with no steamship service, the steamship proportion is zero. For 1839–1840, it is 0.50, based on Albion's (1938, pp. 260–261) observation that "the passenger trade see-sawed back and forth between steamships and packets." The figure is reduced to 0.375 in 1838, as steamship service began in April (Albion 1938, p. 258; C. R. Vernon Gibbs 1957, p. 34). In 1846 the proportion is 0.50 again: "By 1846 the number of passengers crossing the Atlantic under steam drew level with that under sail" (Gibbs 1957, p. 31). "About half of the ocean passengers, he [a contemporary] estimated, were travelling by packets and half by steamships" (Albion 1938, p. 263). For 1841–1844, I take the proportion as 0.25—half the 1840 and 1846 figure, as this was a difficult time for steamships (Albion, p. 259); for 1845, 0.375, as an additional steamship temporarily provided service on the New York run. For 1848–1855, DKW (2017, p. 54) provide figures for the Cunard and Collins lines combined. I add 15 percentage points, to conform with Albion, Gibbs, and ARCENY. For 1864–1867, I use ARCENY data to compute the proportion. For 1868–1870 ARCENY has proportion exceeding 0.99. Therefore the proportion is taken as unity 1868–1919. Linear interpolation covers the remaining years. Of course, sailing-ship proportion is the complement of the steamship.

Europe Steerage: The first steamship carriage of immigrants was in October 1853 (Albion 1938, p. 267). Steamship proportion 1856–1873 is from ARCENY. After 1873, the steamship share exceeds 99%. So the proportion is zero 1790–1852, unity 1874–1919, and linearly interpolated 1853–1855 (with adjustment for a zero proportion over most of 1853).

Rest of World: I ignore the antebellum intermittent steamship service. After the Civil War, the first regular steamship service was to Brazil in 1865 (Emmons 1985, pp. 73, 75). In 1890 the steamship share of worldwide passengers departing U.S. ports was over 99%, for both cabin and steerage (FCN 1890, pp. 816–817). I conservatively assume that the essential unity steamship proportion began in 1878, some years after it did for Europe. Thus steamship proportion, for both cabin and

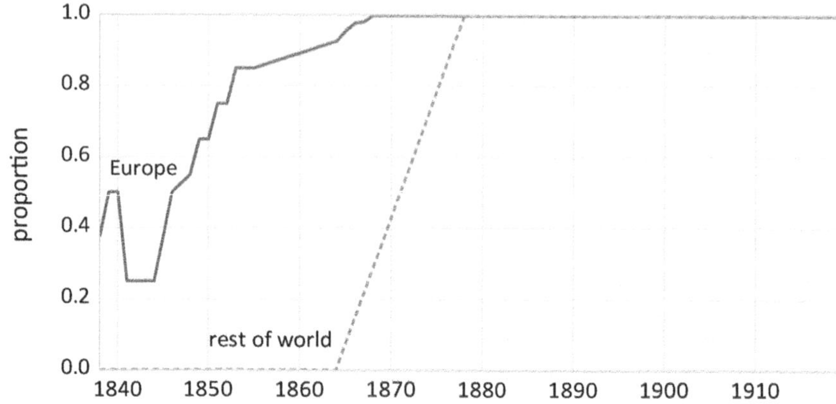

Fig. 2 Steamship share of cabin passengers, 1838–1919. *Note* "Europe" and "rest of world" are the steamship proportions of cabin passengers. For each series, the residual (from unity) is the sailing-ship proportion of cabin passengers to the region

steerage, is zero 1790–1864, unity 1878–1919, with 1865–1877 linearly interpolated.

Comparisons: The steamship proportion of cabin passengers 1838–1919 and steerage passengers 1853–1919 is shown in Figs. 2 and 3, respectively. Recall that steamship share is zero for the prior years.

2.3 *Packet Versus Other Sailing-Ship, Europe*

Cabin: To aid in estimating the packet (always meaning "U.S. packet") proportion of sailing-ship passengers, I construct a series of the number of New York packet sailings between New York and Liverpool/London.[7] Prior to 1818, the packet did not exist, so its share is zero. "At the outset, the liners [packets] managed to lure most of the cabin passengers away from the regular traders" (Albion 1938, pp. 247–248). I assume the packet share is 0.55 in 1818–1821 (with annual sailings constant). I also assume, with a constant number of sailings 1828–1832, that equilibrium share is reached in 1828, and is constant at 0.90 to the end of the packet period (1875), after which it is zero. For 1825–1826, the proportion (0.7761) is computed from data in Albion (1938, p. 248). Linear interpolation takes care of 1822–1824 and 1827.

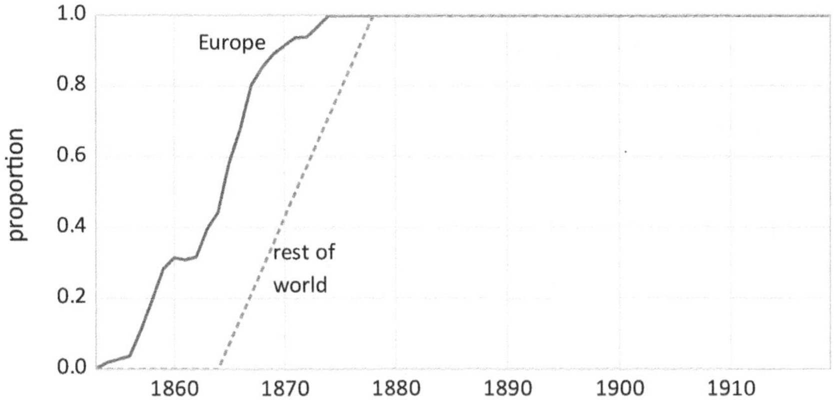

Fig. 3 Steamship share of steerage passengers, 1853–1919. *Note* "Europe" and "rest of world" are the steamship proportions of steerage passengers. For each series, the residual (from unity) is the sailing-ship proportion of steerage passengers to the region

Steerage: Packet proportion of sailing-ship steerage passengers is zero 1790–1817 and 1876–1919, just as for cabin. A figure of 0.1268 packet proportion New York–Liverpool for 1826 (Albion 1938, p. 248) is extendible to all other U.S.–U.K. routes but is an underestimate when incorporating New York–Havre. The Havre-packet proportion (versus traders) had to be high, with typical steerage passenger numbers "a hundred or more" versus only six for Liverpool in 1826 (Albion 1938, p. 248). Havre sailings to New York in 1826 are 29% of Havre, Liverpool, London. Out of ignorance, I make the Havre-packet share of "Havre and Liverpool-London" (to New York) passengers 0.50, which is about four times the Liverpool share. A weighted average yields a packet proportion of 0.23 for that year. For 1848 and 1849, the U.S.-ship (equals U.S. sailing-ship) proportion of immigrants arrived at New York port (ARCENY 1848, p. 38; 1849, p. 42) is allocated equally to packets and traders. For 1852–1875 the packet proportion is unity.[8] Linear interpolation is applied for intervening years.

Comparison: Fig. 4 shows the packet proportion of passengers for Europe (United Kingdom and Continent), cabin and steerage. The complement is the proportion for U.S. traders, foreign traders, and Plymouth packets together.

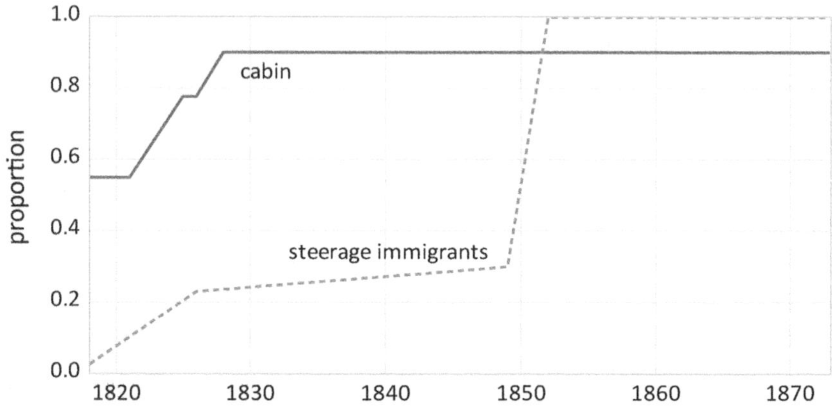

Fig. 4 Packet share of passengers, 1818–1873. *Note* "Cabin" is the U.S.-packet proportion of all sailing-ship cabin passengers for Europe; the residual (from unity) is the proportion of U.S. traders, foreign traders, and Falmouth packets together. A similar statement applies to "steerage immigrants"

2.3.1 Trader Sailing-Ship Nationality: Europe

With packets 100% United States, the U.S.-ship (U.S.-traders) passenger proportion of the remaining sailing ships (U.S. traders, foreign traders, Falmouth packets—termed "traders" for this purpose) is in order. The share is taken as zero (or inapplicable) 1876–1919. The proportion for 1848–1849 (0.42, 0.43) is implicit in the above discussion (Sect. 2.3). The proportion is extrapolated back to 1790 and forward to 1873 via the U.S.-ship proportion of waterborne merchandise trade (Chapter 13, Sect. 2.2.2). Figure 5 graphs the series. The complement is the foreign trader (including Falmouth packet) share of the remaining sailing ships. In comparison, North (1960, pp. 618–619) assumes, for 1820–1860, that *all* tourist travel (United States and alien) is on U.S. ships.

2.4 Foreign Sailing-Ships: Europe

The Falmouth-packet proportion of foreign sailing-ship passengers is, of course, zero when there was no such service: December 1812–April 1815 (suspension due to War of 1812) and after 1827 (service terminated).[9] For 1790–1812, 1815–1827, Falmouth packets could carry 144 passengers annually and foreign traders 4080 *times* the above foreign trader

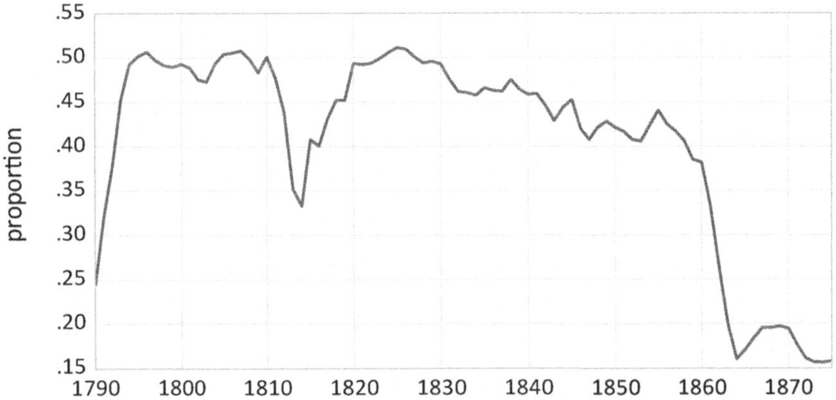

Fig. 5 U.S.-ship share of trader passengers, 1790–1875. *Note* The series is the U.S.-traders proportion of "sailing-ship passengers not transported by U.S. packets." The residual (from unity) is the foreign-traders and Falmouth-packets proportion

share of sailing ships remaining after the U.S. share (Sect. 2.3.1).[10] The Falmouth packet share never reaches seven percent in any year.

2.4.1 Sailing-Ship Nationality: Rest of World

Traditionally, U.S. sailing ships were "in a strong position in the South American and West Indian trades" (Hutchins 1941, p. 237). And U.S. ships set sailing-ship speed records worldwide during "the Clipper ship era" (1843–1860)—Taylor (1951, p. 111). Absent data, one can only guess at the U.S.-versus-foreign passenger shares outside Europe; but the U.S. proportion was certainly very high: I assume 0.90, for 1790–1889. I make no distinction between type of sailing ship for rest of world.

2.4.2 Steamship Nationality: Europe

1838–1892: The U.S. proportion of steamship passenger service is reasonably assumed zero until 1850.[11] The situation changed in 1850, with the rise of the U.S. Collins line. For 1851–1852, the U.S. proportion is deemed 0.60, the rounded Collins share of "Collins and the British Cunard."[12] I extend the figure to 1853–1854, reduce it to 0.23 in 1850—based on the average number of months the four Collins ships were in service (Bonsor 1975, pp. 201–208). For 1855 I increase Collins to 0.90, reflecting the fact that, with the Crimean War, Cunard withdrew from New York but retained Boston service (Bonsor 1975, pp. 82–83). Using ARCENY data, the U.S.-ship proportion of steamship passengers 1857–1864 is estimated as the U.S.-ship proportion of steamship arrivals, 1865–1870 as the U.S.-ship proportion of passenger arrivals.[13] The loss of a Collins ship in January 1856 and the launching of a superior Cunard ship were "the beginning of the end for the Collins line" (Albion 1939, p. 330). For 1856, the U.S. proportion is estimated as the average of the figures for 1854 (the "normal" Collins share) and 1857. As and after Collins collapsed (in early 1858), the U.S. share fell precipitously, reaching 0.015 in 1870. Subsequently, for 1871–1892, I assume a zero U.S. proportion.[14] Note that there is no cabin-steerage nationality distinction until 1893.

1893–1919: I continue to use U.S. registry as the criterion for U.S. nationality. One could instead make a case for crew nationality or direct-ownership or ultimate-ownership (holding-company) location. Certainly for U.S.-flag slave ships during 1835–1860 (Officer and Williamson 2020, pp. 193, 212) and Liberian/Panamanian flag-of-convenience merchant vessels in the postwar twentieth century, registry is a misleading principle. However, for the postbellum period to the end of World War I, registry is an appropriate criterion, as it was a good indicator of operational management location and, at least for U.S. versus foreign-flag ships, is correlated with predominant crew nationality. Then seven ships are classified as United States: *New York*, *Paris*, *St. Louis*, *St. Paul* of the American Line; *Finland*, *Kroonland*, *Samland* of Red Star. U.S.-ship years of service are 1893–1918 for the American Line, 1902–1915 for Red Star.[15]

Official data permit construction of American and Red Star individually, total eastbound passenger numbers, cabin and steerage separately: 1893–1894 and 1900–1919 for American, 1902–1915 for Red Star. Via use of series of westbound American cabin volume 1893–1914 (DKW 2017, p. 60) and both American and Red Star steerage volumes 1895–1913 (provided by Drew Keeling), I construct eastbound-westbound-total cabin and steerage series for each line.[16] Keeling provided four total figures over 1900–1913—for the U.S.-flag component of American and Red Star passengers, cabin and steerage—which I allocate annually via the total cabin or steerage volume for the line, and then use the latter to extrapolate 1893–1899, 1914–1918 (via 1900, 1913 overlap) for

American, 1914–1915 (via 1913 overlap) for Red Star. The American—Red Star total constitutes the numerator for the U.S.-ship proportion of cabin and steerage passengers (separately). Denominators, for cabin and steerage, are total U.S.-ship and foreign-ship passengers all-lines, and are based on official departures data.[17]

2.4.3 Steamship Nationality: Rest of World

Using the official sources, through a tedious liner-by-liner count of passengers departed on U.S. ships versus foreign ships, for fiscal years 1890–1895 and 1910–1920, I generate the U.S.-ship proportion of passengers departed on steamships from U.S. seaports for oceanic non-Europe.[18] Then I linearly interpolate 1896–1909. Absent earlier data, U.S. share 1865–1889 is the average proportion 1890–1892, with zero share prior to 1865.[19] I make no steerage-cabin differential.

2.5 Comparisons

Figure 6 graphs U.S. steamship passenger shares. The series contradict the North (1960, pp. 618–619) and Simon (1960, p. 668) extreme assumptions of 100% and zero U.S.-ship tourist share for 1820–1860 and 1861–1900, respectively.

3 Fares

3.1 Methodology

The ideal fare concept is ship revenue per passenger, but revenue-based fare series are limited in availability. Advertised fares are more prevalent, and shipping-conference minimum fares are in the same vogue.[20] Revenue per equivalent-adult passenger, advertising fares, and conference minimum fares have denomination ***dollars per adult passenger***, and must be changed to ***dollars per passenger*** (over all passengers), to enable multiplication by number of passengers to obtain ship revenue. Per-passenger fare is the weighted average of adult and youth fares, with weights the adult and youth proportions of passengers. With youth-fare half adult-fare, the formula reduces to: per-passenger fare equals adult-fare *times* "one *minus* half the youth proportion of passengers." The youth proportion is generated 1790–1919 separately for cabin, immigrant steerage, and nonimmigrant steerage.[21]

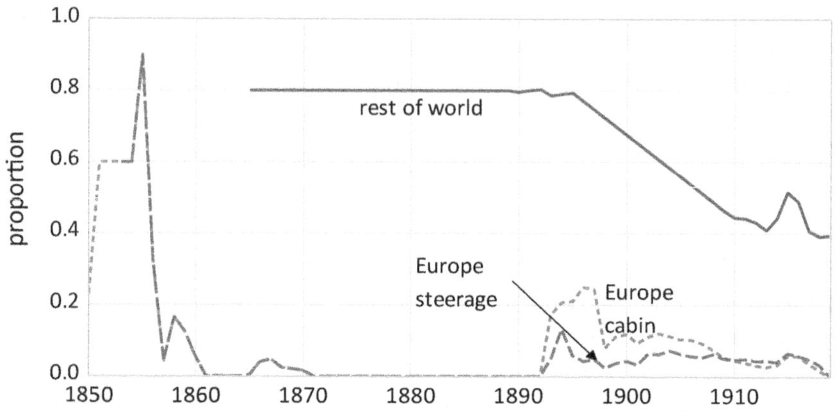

Fig. 6 U.S.-ship share of steamship passengers, 1850–1919. *Note* "Rest of world" is the U.S.-ship proportion of steamship passengers (cabin and steerage together) departing for oceanic non-Europe, with the residual the foreign-ship proportion. "Europe cabin" is the U.S.-ship proportion of cabin passengers departing for Europe, and "Europe steerage" similarly for steerage passengers. The residuals of "Europe cabin" and "Europe steerage" are the respective foreign-ship proportions. Observe that, for Europe, from the late-1850s onward, the foreign-ship share is dominant

An "immigration head tax" (Chapter 10, Sect. 1.6) was assessed on *all* aliens—not just steerage, also cabin; not just immigrants, also nonimmigrants. Paid by the steamship company and expressed as dollars per passenger, the tax was not an add-on; rather, it was included in the advertised fare faced by all travelers. Thus it was assessed on westbound (inbound) non-citizens.[22] To obtain ship revenue per passenger (the fare series), the product of (1) head-tax rate and (2) alien proportion of passengers is subtracted from the advertised fare.

1. The head-tax rate pertains to the two port cities Philadelphia and New York. The Philadelphia per-passenger tax rate (sum of state head tax and city health tax) for 1818–1876 is constructed in Chapter 10 (Sect. 1.6.1). For New York fares, the state head tax 1847–1876 is conjoined with the U.S. head tax 1882–1919 to create an annual series.[23] For both cities, the annual series involves a weighted average of monthly figures for years of rate change.

2. For steerage passengers, the alien proportion of passengers is calculated as the complement of the U.S.-citizen proportion.[24] For steamship cabin passengers, the expansion of second class in the 1880s found a market in immigrants and it is reasonable to assume the alien proportion decreases going backward in time.[25] For sailing-ship cabin passengers, recall the above (Sect. 2.1) assumption that immigrants traveled 100% steerage 1790–1874. But alien nonimmigrants could travel by cabin. The alien proportion is estimated as the ratio of "foreign tourists and distant-land transmigrants" to "same *plus* U.S.-citizen tourists to Europe" (Chapter 3, Sects. 1.3.1, 1.3.3, 2.2, 2.4).

3.2 Europe—Sailing Ship

3.2.1 Cabin Eastbound

Packets: Weighted average of New York to Liverpool (1818–1867), New York to London (1824–1867), New York to Havre (1822–1867), and (Copes-Line) Philadelphia to Liverpool (1822–1867) fares, with weights proportional to round-trip sailings 1818–1835 and to number of ships 1836–1862, with the 1862 weighting pattern extended to 1863–1873.[26] Converted from adult to per-passenger basis.

Falmouth Packets: Fares for 1810 and 1815, applicable both eastbound and westbound, are extended back to 1790 and forward to 1827, with linear interpolation in between.[27] Converted from pounds to dollars and from adult to per-passenger.

Traders: Benchmark figures for 1806 (projected back to 1790), 1817–1819, 1830–1839 (one datum) are converted to dollars and to per-passenger as needed.[28] Linear interpolation yields 1807–1816. The packet fare serves to interpolate 1820–1829 and to extrapolate 1840–1867 via the average 1830–1839 overlap.

3.2.2 Cabin Westbound

Packets: Weighted average of Liverpool to New York, London to New York, Havre to New York, and Liverpool to Philadelphia fares, weights same as for eastbound.[29] Converted from pounds to dollars and from adult to per-passenger. Each component series is adjusted for the head tax.

Traders: The only new datum is for 1819 (Killick spreadsheet, row 6, converted to dollars). For 1790–1806 and 1830–1839, eastbound fare adjusted for head tax.[30] Years 1807–1818 linearly interpolated, 1820–1829 interpolated via packet westbound fare, 1840–1867 extrapolated using packet westbound fare via 1830–1839 overlap.

3.2.3 *Steerage Westbound*

Packets: Lacking Havre data, weighted average of "Liverpool to Philadelphia" (1822–1873) and "London or Liverpool to New York" (1818–1873—converted to per-passenger) fares, weights derived from above (Sect. 3.2.1), each component adjusted for head tax. Basic data converted from pounds to dollars.[31]

Falmouth Packets: Fares for 1810 and 1815 are extended back to 1790 and forward to 1827, with linear interpolation in between.[32] Converted from pounds to dollars and from adult to per-passenger.

Traders: I develop separately U.K.-to-U.S. and Continent-to-U.S. fare series. Benchmark years for U.K.-to-U.S. are 1806, 1816–1821, 1827, 1830–1853.[33] Linear interpolation yields intervening years, and the 1806 figure is projected back to 1790. The series is transformed to per-passenger, extrapolated to 1873 via 1853 overlap with London/Liverpool packet fare, converted to dollars, and adjusted for the New York head tax.

Turning to the Continent, European fares were generally higher than United Kingdom. As a representative series, I take Bremen or North Germany to the United States, with 17 benchmark years between 1798 and 1870, extending the end-point fares to 1790 and 1873.[34] Using Holland-to-U.S. fares (Grabbe 2001, pp. 296–297), I extrapolate ten more years, via 1819 overlap.[35] Remaining years are linearly interpolated. The resulting series is completed with adjustments to per-passenger fare and for the head tax.[36]

The U.K.-to-U.S. and Bremen/North Germany-to-U.S. series, 1790–1873, are weighted 60–40.[37]

3.2.4 *Steerage Eastbound*

Packets: Westbound steerage fare multiplied by the Liverpool–Philadelphia eastbound/westbound steerage adult-fare ratio, converted to per-passenger.[38]

Plymouth Packets and Traders: Respective westbound steerage fare, replacing immigrant with nonimmigrant per-passenger adjustment.

3.3 Europe—Steamship

Cabin Eastbound: The basis is dollar-converted Cunard first-cabin revenue-based New York to Liverpool adult-equivalent fares 1882–1914 provided by Drew Keeling.[39] The series is extrapolated to 1838 using the first-cabin steamship New York to U.K. minimum fare via the average overlap for 1882–1886.[40] Years 1915–1916 extrapolated from 1914, using Anchor Line advertised fares (85/70, "1915-1916"/1914) in *New York Times*. Years 1917–1918 obtained as ten-percent increase over 1916, per *New York Times* (January 7, 1917, p. 5). Year 1919 computed as monthly average (see *New York Times*, August 20, 1919, p. 2; August 28, 1919, p. 11). Resulting series is converted to per-passenger.

The series embodies the assumptions that Cunard represents all lines, New York represents all Eastern ports, minimum first-class represents all cabin (first class and second class), and United Kingdom represents all Europe. All four assumptions are alleviated by multiplying the series (1838–1919) by the ratio of the per-passenger average all-cabin (first-cabin and second-cabin combined) all-lines U.S.-to-Europe fare (computed as receipts per passenger) to the per-passenger Cunard fare (yielding the "per-passenger resulting series").[41]

Cabin Westbound: Same basis and source (Keeling) as for cabin eastbound, 1882–1914, Liverpool to New York, head tax excluded (Keeling 2008, pp. 18–19). For extension, I construct a series of dollar-converted head-tax-removed U.K.-to-New York advertised (or announced) first-cabin steamship fare 1838–1860, and consider the series integrated.[42] Both segments are converted from adult to per-passenger, and, using the eastbound series, the integrated series is interpolated 1861–1881 and extrapolated to 1919 via 1914 overlap. The same four assumptions as for cabin eastbound are implicit, and are corrected by the eastbound adjustment ratio.

Steerage Eastbound: Same basis and source (Keeling) as for cabin eastbound, 1882–1914, New York to Liverpool. I extend this series to 1866–1873 via assembling a series of Cunard advertised fare, New York to Liverpool, and converting it from advertising to per-revenue.[43] Then I construct advertised steerage eastbound fares: annual multiple-lines average 1853–1886, and extended Anchor Line 1914–1919 (similar to cabin eastbound).[44] These segments are used to interpolate the extended Cunard series 1874–1881 and to extrapolate the series to 1853–1865 and

1915–1919 (via 1866 and 1914 overlaps), so that the full period 1853–1919 encompasses this series, which is then converted to per-passenger. The 1894 ratio of "five-ports all-lines" to "Cunard New York" average steerage fare adjusts the series for the assumptions that Cunard represents all lines, New York represents all Eastern ports, and United Kingdom represents all Europe.[45]

Steerage Westbound: Same basis and source (Keeling), 1882–1914, Liverpool to New York, head tax excluded.[46] I assemble a series of Cunard advertised fare, Liverpool to New York, correct for head tax, and use the resulting series to extrapolate Keeling 1860, 1863, 1866–1867, 1875–1877, via average "1882, 1884-1885" overlap.[47] I also assemble a series of "various-lines excluding Cunard" average advertised fare, Liverpool to New York, correct for head tax, and extrapolate Keeling 1853–1859, 1868–1873, 1880–1881 via 1860, 1867, 1882 overlaps.[48] Because of a rate-cutting war during 1874–1875, the fare for these years is constructed as monthly averages. For 1915–1919, the head-tax-adjusted Anchor line steerage-eastbound fare extends the series via 1914 overlap. Remaining years (1861–1862, 1864–1865, 1878–1879) are linearly interpolated. The entire series 1853–1919 is converted to per-passenger, and the eastbound adjustment factor for assumptions is applied.

3.4 *Europe—Comparisons*

Figures 7, 8, 9, and 10 compare packet, trader, Falmouth-packet, and steamship fares for eastbound cabin, westbound cabin, eastbound steerage, and westbound steerage. Notable are the high Falmouth-packet fares and the closeness of steerage fares (relative to cabin) on the part of packets, traders, and steamships, during the period when all three ship-types were in operation.

3.5 *Rest of World*

For the year 1920 (considered a more-normal year than 1919, the earliest available year), I compute average fare (per-passenger revenue), for individual passenger groups, as the ratio of total (U.S. *plus* foreign) ship revenue to the number of *departures* (for U.S.-citizens and emigrants) or *arrivals* (for immigrants).[49] In Sect. 4, I use the non-Europe/Europe average-fare ratio to estimate the non-Europe fare series from the corresponding Europe series. The computation results in U.S. citizens to

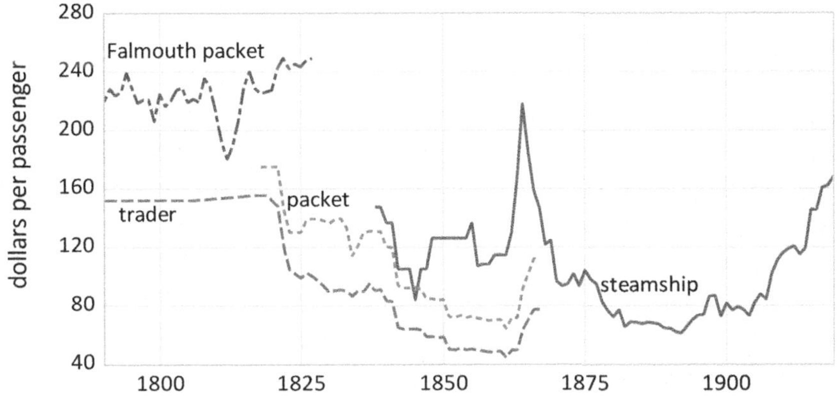

Fig. 7 Europe fares: eastbound cabin, 1790–1919. *Note* "Steamship" is the U.S. and foreign steamship fare. "Falmouth packet," "trader," and "packet" are the fares for Falmouth packets, U.S. and foreign traders, and U.S. packets. Fares are for eastbound (United States to Europe) cabin. Fares are dollars per passenger, which is lower than dollars per adult passenger

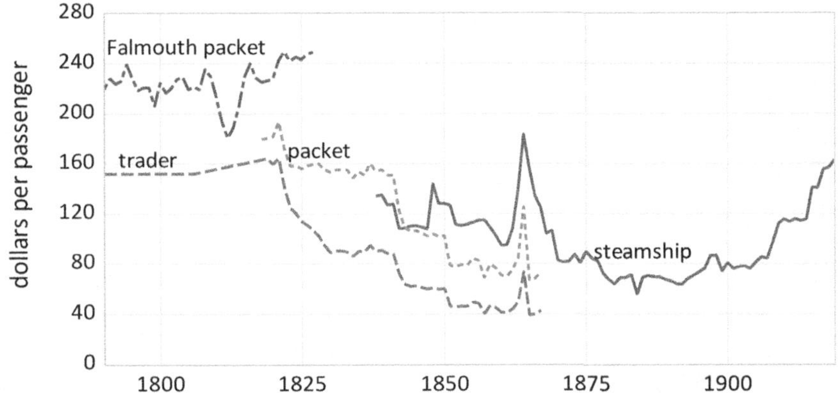

Fig. 8 Europe fares: westbound cabin, 1790–1919. *Note* "Steamship" is the U.S. and foreign steamship fare. "Falmouth packet," "trader," and "packet" are the fares for Falmouth packets, U.S. and foreign traders, and U.S. packets. Fares are for westbound (Europe to United States) cabin. Fares are dollars per passenger, which is lower than dollars per adult passenger

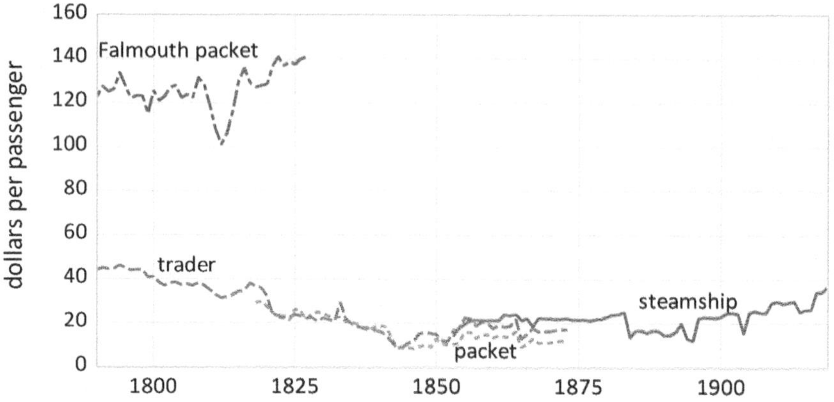

Fig. 9 Europe fares: eastbound steerage, 1790–1919. *Note* "Steamship" is the U.S. and foreign steamship fare. "Falmouth packet," "trader," and "packet" are the fares for Falmouth packets, U.S. and foreign traders, and U.S. packets. Fares are for eastbound (United States to Europe) steerage. Fares are dollars per passenger, which is lower than dollars per adult passenger

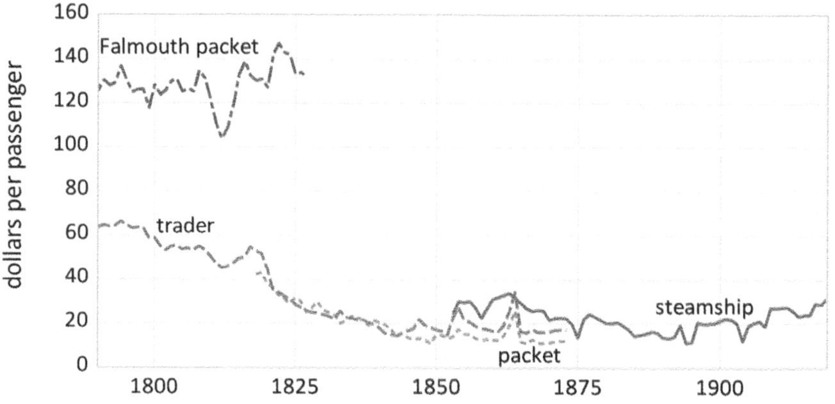

Fig. 10 Europe fares: westbound steerage, 1790–1919. *Note* "Steamship" is the U.S. and foreign steamship fare. "Falmouth packet," "trader," and "packet" are the fares for Falmouth packets, U.S. and foreign traders, and U.S. packets. Fares are for westbound (Europe to United States) steerage. Fares are dollars per passenger, which is lower than dollars per adult passenger

"South America and Far East" and "West Indies and Central America" having 1.3503 and 0.4176 the U.S.-citizen Europe fare, immigrants from rest of world having 0.7973 the immigrant Europe fare, and emigrants to rest of world 0.8071 the emigrant Europe fare.

4 Revenue

From the above information, I construct 82 basic revenue series, each specified, per Sect. 1, as the product of (A) number of oceanic passengers in the travel group under consideration, (B) passenger proportion, and (C) pertinent per-passenger fare. There are nine travel groups.[50] The passenger proportion is the product of applicable sub-proportions:

(1) accommodation proportion (cabin, steerage for each travel group), (2) sailing-ship versus steamship proportion (Europe cabin, Europe steerage, rest of world) (3) packet versus other sailing-ship [traders and Falmouth packets] proportion (Europe cabin, Europe steerage), (4) U.S.-ship versus foreign-ship proportion (Europe packet, other sailing-ship, steamship: cabin, steerage; rest-of-world sailing-ship, steamship) (5) foreign trader versus Plymouth-packet proportion (Europe).

I make simplifying assumptions as follows: Foreign tourists and transmigrants are from Europe; distant-land transmigrants have "South America and Far East" as destination; transmigrants to "Canada and West Indies" have Canada as destination.[51] Some further abstractions—that infants pay half-fare along with older minors, that there is no round-trip discount, and that all U.S. citizens return from overseas—could bias the revenue series upward. Still other assumptions—the exclusion of tips, steward fees, and direct payments for extra goods and services—could bias the series downward.

The 82 revenue series are summed into eight groups, constituting the columns of Table 1, as follows. U.S. sailing-ship revenue (1) from U.S. residents (14 series), (2) from foreign residents (nine series); U.S. steamship revenue (3) from U.S. residents (ten series), (4) from foreign residents (eight series); foreign sailing-ship revenue (5) from U.S. residents (14 series), (6) from foreign residents (nine series); foreign steamship revenue (7) from U.S. residents (ten series), (8) from foreign residents (eight series).[52] Columns (2) *plus* (4) are fares credits, columns (5) *plus* (7) fares debits. The other columns are domestic transactions for the respective country.

Table 1 Ship revenue (millions of dollars)

Year	U.S. ships				Foreign ships			
	Sailing ships		Steamships		Sailing ships		Steamships	
	U.S. residents (1)	Foreign residents (2)	U.S. residents (3)	Foreign residents (4)	U.S. residents (5)	Foreign residents (6)	U.S. residents (7)	Foreign residents (8)
1790	0.08	0.21	0	0	0.17	0.58	0	0
1791	0.11	0.38	0	0	0.16	0.74	0	0
1792	0.13	0.55	0	0	0.16	0.74	0	0
1793	0.16	0.69	0	0	0.16	0.61	0	0
1794	0.20	0.55	0	0	0.18	0.46	0	0
1795	0.26	0.52	0	0	0.23	0.42	0	0
1796	0.27	0.52	0	0	0.23	0.44	0	0
1797	0.24	0.34	0	0	0.19	0.26	0	0
1798	0.23	0.16	0	0	0.20	0.06	0	0
1799	0.26	0.14	0	0	0.21	0.08	0	0
1800	0.36	0.30	0	0	0.31	0.23	0	0
1801	0.40	1.02	0	0	0.36	1.03	0	0
1802	0.32	0.67	0	0	0.30	0.71	0	0
1803	0.29	0.22	0	0	0.29	0.19	0	0
1804	0.36	0.27	0	0	0.33	0.22	0	0
1805	0.44	0.26	0	0	0.38	0.19	0	0
1806	0.51	0.22	0	0	0.44	0.13	0	0
1807	0.47	0.15	0	0	0.39	0.10	0	0
1808	0.20	0.11	0	0	0.14	0.07	0	0
1809	0.29	0.19	0	0	0.27	0.09	0	0
1810	0.32	0.17	0	0	0.30	0.14	0	0
1811	0.24	0.26	0	0	0.23	0.23	0	0
1812	0.18	0.16	0	0	0.21	0.15	0	0
1813	0.06	0.03	0	0	0.10	0.03	0	0
1814	0.06	0.05	0	0	0.08	0.02	0	0
1815	0.23	0.21	0	0	0.31	0.18	0	0
1816	0.30	0.44	0	0	0.42	0.56	0	0
1817	0.28	0.66	0	0	0.34	0.79	0	0
1818	0.52	0.72	0	0	0.16	0.70	0	0
1819	0.50	0.57	0	0	0.15	0.52	0	0
1820	0.53	0.32	0	0	0.14	0.27	0	0
1821	0.59	0.32	0	0	0.16	0.25	0	0
1822	0.39	0.54	0	0	0.09	0.41	0	0

(continued)

Table 1 (continued)

Year	U.S. ships				Foreign ships			
	Sailing ships		Steamships		Sailing ships		Steamships	
	U.S. residents (1)	*Foreign residents (2)*	*U.S. residents (3)*	*Foreign residents (4)*	*U.S. residents (5)*	*Foreign residents (6)*	*U.S. residents (7)*	*Foreign residents (8)*
1823	0.40	0.53	0	0	0.07	0.37	0	0
1824	0.43	0.28	0	0	0.06	0.19	0	0
1825	0.64	0.35	0	0	0.07	0.22	0	0
1826	0.69	0.32	0	0	0.07	0.19	0	0
1827	0.72	0.42	0	0	0.05	0.27	0	0
1828	0.67	0.59	0	0	0.03	0.28	0	0
1829	0.48	0.78	0	0	0.02	0.30	0	0
1830	0.38	0.80	0	0	0.02	0.26	0	0
1831	0.33	1.21	0	0	0.02	0.51	0	0
1832	0.30	1.38	0	0	0.02	0.62	0	0
1833	0.34	1.72	0	0	0.02	0.75	0	0
1834	0.63	1.63	0	0	0.04	0.90	0	0
1835	0.86	1.15	0	0	0.04	0.59	0	0
1836	1.25	1.89	0	0	0.06	0.96	0	0
1837	1.49	1.97	0	0	0.07	1.01	0	0
1838	1.03	0.83	0	0	0.04	0.43	0.63	0.07
1839	0.90	1.45	0	0	0.04	0.76	0.91	0.16
1840	1.11	1.65	0	0	0.10	0.85	1.01	0.19
1841	1.46	1.54	0	0	0.10	0.71	0.46	0.09
1842	1.01	1.79	0	0	0.09	0.90	0.31	0.09
1843	0.78	1.06	0	0	0.06	0.60	0.27	0.06
1844	0.84	1.40	0	0	0.06	0.77	0.30	0.08
1845	0.66	1.93	0	0	0.08	1.14	0.35	0.15
1846	0.49	2.54	0	0	0.10	1.77	0.44	0.30
1847	0.51	3.77	0	0	0.16	2.98	0.45	0.42
1848	0.40	3.63	0	0	0.15	2.65	0.41	0.58
1849	0.41	4.04	0	0	0.18	2.97	0.53	0.79
1850	1.00	5.05	0.35	0.18	0.19	1.86	1.18	0.59
1851	1.73	7.46	3.11	0.71	0.16	1.23	2.07	0.48
1852	1.60	7.16	2.52	0.62	0.05	0.05	1.68	0.42

(continued)

Table 1 (continued)

	U.S. ships				*Foreign ships*			
	Sailing ships		*Steamships*		*Sailing ships*		*Steamships*	
Year	*U.S. residents (1)*	*Foreign residents (2)*	*U.S. residents (3)*	*Foreign residents (4)*	*U.S. residents (5)*	*Foreign residents (6)*	*U.S. residents (7)*	*Foreign residents (8)*
1853	1.41	7.30	3.56	0.67	0.04	0.03	2.37	0.45
1854	1.58	9.97	3.47	0.59	0.04	0.04	2.31	0.39
1855	1.16	4.09	4.38	0.95	0.03	0.03	0.49	0.11
1856	1.03	3.91	1.16	0.25	0.03	0.03	2.47	0.52
1857	0.90	3.99	0.16	0.06	0.02	0.03	3.41	1.35
1858	0.70	1.68	0.53	0.17	0.03	0.02	2.66	0.85
1859	0.88	1.51	0.65	0.17	0.04	0.02	4.64	1.23
1860	0.89	1.83	0.23	0.12	0.03	0.02	3.90	2.06
1861	0.71	1.11	0	0	0.02	0.02	3.57	1.28
1862	0.71	1.22	0	0	0.02	0.01	4.31	1.48
1863	0.96	2.65	0	0	0.02	0.02	6.38	3.19
1864	1.23	3.54	0	0	0.03	0.01	9.89	3.58
1865	0.69	1.38	0.05	0.03	0.02	0.01	11.84	4.89
1866	0.62	1.34	0.45	0.33	0.02	0.02	10.21	6.89
1867	0.55	0.99	0.54	0.42	0.02	0.02	9.77	7.48
1868	0.28	0.76	0.30	0.37	0.01	0.02	8.34	9.29
1869	0.24	0.68	0.33	0.48	0.01	0.02	8.21	11.09
1870	0.22	0.50	0.35	0.42	0.01	0.01	8.44	9.17
1871	0.20	0.40	0.33	0.30	0.01	0.01	9.83	10.15
1872	0.25	0.49	0.45	0.38	0.01	0.01	10.83	11.65
1873	0.15	0.28	0.55	0.45	0.01	0.01	10.45	10.58
1874	0	0	0.62	0.43	0	0	8.31	6.92
1875	0	0	0.68	0.58	0	0	7.09	4.19
1876	0	0	0.71	0.74	0	0	6.97	5.36
1877	0	0	0.66	0.67	0	0	5.95	5.36
1878	0	0	0.75	0.68	0	0	6.35	5.38
1879	0	0	0.75	0.79	0	0	8.66	8.94
1880	0	0	0.75	0.82	0	0	9.91	13.36
1881	0	0	0.99	1.15	0	0	11.72	16.95
1882	0	0	1.03	1.24	0	0	12.59	17.96

(continued)

Table 1 (continued)

Year	*U.S. ships*				*Foreign ships*			
	Sailing ships		*Steamships*		*Sailing ships*		*Steamships*	
	U.S. residents (1)	*Foreign residents (2)*	*U.S. residents (3)*	*Foreign residents (4)*	*U.S. residents (5)*	*Foreign residents (6)*	*U.S. residents (7)*	*Foreign residents (8)*
1883	0	0	1.04	1.25	0	0	14.14	16.00
1884	0	0	0.80	1.14	0	0	11.06	12.53
1885	0	0	0.78	0.95	0	0	11.03	10.01
1886	0	0	0.92	0.75	0	0	12.22	10.72
1887	0	0	1.01	0.77	0	0	14.23	12.97
1888	0	0	1.18	0.70	0	0	12.79	12.52
1889	0	0	1.33	0.69	0	0	12.22	11.26
1890	0	0	1.32	0.67	0	0	15.70	11.53
1891	0	0	1.36	0.57	0	0	18.66	12.71
1892	0	0	1.67	0.82	0	0	18.12	13.77
1893	0	0	3.09	3.35	0	0	13.25	16.28
1894	0	0	4.09	1.92	0	0	9.47	5.74
1895	0	0	5.09	2.07	0	0	12.28	7.53
1896	0	0	5.52	2.45	0	0	13.56	9.96
1897	0	0	3.00	1.85	0	0	8.26	6.97
1898	0	0	1.27	1.04	0	0	8.14	8.04
1899	0	0	1.51	1.34	0	0	9.44	9.99
1900	0	0	2.44	1.88	0	0	14.68	13.93
1901	0	0	2.02	1.67	0	0	16.80	15.97
1902	0	0	3.43	2.77	0	0	23.59	21.24
1903	0	0	6.44	3.74	0	0	37.34	28.07
1904	0	0	6.53	2.61	0	0	32.86	18.25
1905	0	0	8.63	4.01	0	0	50.90	32.04
1906	0	0	9.93	5.70	0	0	62.75	44.26
1907	0	0	10.15	7.21	0	0	68.16	54.15
1908	0	0	7.41	3.36	0	0	43.98	22.97
1909	0	0	9.73	7.16	0	0	77.98	64.30
1910	0	0	10.52	6.49	0	0	100.31	67.17
1911	0	0	9.92	4.71	0	0	92.21	49.27
1912	0	0	10.70	5.12	0	0	114.18	64.19

(continued)

Table 1 (continued)

	U.S. ships				Foreign ships			
	Sailing ships		*Steamships*		*Sailing ships*		*Steamships*	
Year	*U.S. residents (1)*	*Foreign residents (2)*	*U.S. residents (3)*	*Foreign residents (4)*	*U.S. residents (5)*	*Foreign residents (6)*	*U.S. residents (7)*	*Foreign residents (8)*
1913	0	0	11.24	5.83	0	0	134.78	79.34
1914	0	0	7.97	4.41	0	0	70.71	45.58
1915	0	0	6.50	3.47	0	0	30.09	19.40
1916	0	0	7.28	4.34	0	0	32.20	24.53
1917	0	0	9.14	4.77	0	0	43.33	31.18
1918	0	0	11.89	7.92	0	0	49.30	50.06
1919	0	0	7.87	7.49	0	0	71.85	76.57

Table 2 Travel and fares: comparisons (percentage deviation of existing series from new series)

Item	*1790–1819*	*1820–1860*	*1861–1899*	*1900–1918*
(1) Exports	–	−32.97	−37.08	−53.94
(2) Imports	–	2.12	7.31	34.78

Note A negative (positive) sign means that the new series is larger (smaller) than the existing series. For discussion, see Sect. 4

Comparison with North–Simon—*Historical Statistics* is presented in Table 2. Because these sources combine travel and fares, the comparisons do likewise.[53] On the export (credit) side, the traditional series are much too low; but the finding is reversed—albeit more moderately—on the import (debit) side.

Notes

1. "Inbound" means inbound to the United States, called "westbound" with respect to Europe. "Outbound" means outbound from the United States, "eastbound" with respect to Europe.
2. For further discussion of the types of sailing ships, see Albion (1938, pp. 15–20; 1939, pp. 38–44), Taylor (1951, pp. 104–107), and Gibbs

(1957, pp. 27–29). Though there were different types of steamships; for our purpose, it is not feasible to distinguish between them.

3. See DGW (2012, p. 165). Simon (1960, pp. 670, 672) notes that, relative to 1873–1894, "for 1861-72...[there were] more cabin or wealthier passengers."
4. Everywhere, I equate steerage with "noncabin" accommodation.
5. For the pre-steamship period, the assumption is consistent with discussion in Albion (1938, pp. 247–249) and Gibbs (1957, p. 31). For the steamship period, ARCENY data show packet all-passenger cabin proportion less than one percent in 1863–1869, less than 1½% in 1870.
6. Weights are respective proportions of alien outbound passengers (columns (2) and (5) in Table 1, Chapter 3). The cabin proportion of alien outbound passengers is from ARCGI (1920, p. 226), converted to calendar year.
7. The series is based on data in Albion (1938, pp. 20, 30–35) and Carl C. Cutler (1961, pp. 389–392, 394—for Havre–New York).
8. A sample of ten packet voyages in 1852 is 0.9960 steerage (Albion 1938, p. 267), suggestive that virtually all immigrants had shifted from traders to packets.
9. See Albion (1938, p. 17) and John S. Olenkiewicz (2013).
10. Use is made of Albion's (1938, pp. 16–18, 248) figures on the number of voyages and number of passengers per voyage carried by traders and the Falmouth packets. For 1812 and 1815, the Falmouth-packet annual share is reduced by 1/12 and 1/3.
11. There was a British steamship monopoly, that faced only minor U.S.-ship involvement. See Albion (1939, pp. 318–325), Gibbs (1957, pp. 29–31, 35, 37–100).
12. The figure is unambiguous; but authorities differ on applicable period (Gibbs 1957, p. 102; Albion 1939, p. 328; N. R. P. Bonsor 1975, pp. 78, 204).
13. There are no arrivals at New York, hence estimated zero U.S. share, during the years 1861–1864 of the Civil War period.
14. Due to absence of data, I abstract from the American ("Keystone") Line, operating 1873–1886. Also omitted, for 1892 onward, is the Atlantic Transport Line, a British-American concern, for lack of U.S.-registry ship passenger data. See Gibbs (1957, pp. 258, 264–267) and Bonsor (1979, pp. 920–924, 938–942, 1075–1097).
15. For this entire paragraph, I benefitted greatly from Drew Keeling sharing his knowledge. A useful background is Keeling (2012, esp. pp. 70–74). For histories of the seven ships and their lines, see Bonsor (1978, ch. 98; 1979, ch. 101).
16. U.S. ports are New York and Philadelphia. Official data sources are *Immigration and Passenger Movement* 1893–1895, MSCF various issues

1900–1905, ARCGI 1906–1920. Converted to calendar year. For American Line, total cabin passengers 1915–1919 and total steerage passengers 1893–1894, 1914–1919 are extrapolated via eastbound figures. For Red Star, this is so for 1915 cabin and 1914–1915 steerage.

17. Departures to Europe directly obtained 1893–1895, 1900–1905 (sources in note 16); extrapolated 1906–1920 (1905 overlap) via total passengers departed (ARCGI, 1913, pp. 134–135; 1920, p. 227); interpolated via same, for other years. For cabin, the outbound figure is doubled. For steerage, a Keeling unpublished series of New York all-lines inbound passengers 1893–1913 is extrapolated to 1919 via New York immigrant-arrivals figures in SAUS (1920, p. 106), and added to the official departures series. Conversion to calendar year as needed.
18. Identifiable U.S. ships versus foreign ships. Destinations included are West Indies, Central America, South America, and Far East. Origination Canada or Mexico border stations or seaports excluded. For 1898–1920, Hawaii, Puerto Rico, Philippines considered U.S. territory. Equal allocation of figures with multiple destinations. Sources: for 1890–1892, ARSTR and Treasury Statements; for 1893–1920, per note 16.
19. The 1865 positive-share start date emanates from information in E. Mowbray Tate (1986, ch. 1, esp. pp. 23, 27), Hutchins (1941, chs. 15–16, esp. pp. 528–529), and Emmons (1985—see Sect. 2.2).
20. Excellent discussion of these historical fare concepts is DKW (2017, pp. 21–35). Based on New York–U.K. cabin fares, they conclude that there is "statistical consistency" and "correspondence and agreement" in the three fare concepts.
21. For cabin and nonimmigrant steerage, the youth proportion is calculated from departures data in SAUS (1907, pp. 72–73; 1920, p. 107) and ARCGI (1920, p. 227). The years 1869 and 1896–1897 are linearly interpolated, and 1790–1867 estimated as the 1868–1870 average. The youth proportion of immigrants is generated from *Historical Statistics* (2006, series Ad226, Ad227, Ad230), with the 1820–1822 average projected to 1790–1819. Conversion to calendar year as needed. I ignore zero fare for infants.
22. I am indebted to Drew Keeling for sharing his knowledge regarding this issue.
23. The New York head tax begins at $1.00 May 5, 1847; increases to $1.50 April 11, 1849; $2.00 April 13, 1853; $2.50 May 14, 1867; and ends at $1.50 April 1871 to March 20, 1876, when it was declared unconstitutional. Sources are ARCENY (1875, pp. 15–16; 1847–1860, pp. 30, 32; 1876, p. 5), Kapp (1870, p. 98), Klebaner (1958, p. 292). The U.S. head tax went steadily upward, starting at $0.50 (Act of August 3, 1882), continuing to $1.00 effective October 1, 1894 (Act of August 18, 1894),

then \$2.00 (Act of March 3, 1903), \$4.00 (Act of February 20, 1907), and \$8.00 (Act of February 5, 1917).

24. Data sources for the U.S.-citizen proportion are ARCENY for 1880–1890, Keeling (2012, p. 287) for 1899–1919 (extended from 1899–1914). Linear interpolation is used for 1891–1898 and the oceanic emigration/immigration ratio (Chapter 3, Sect. 6) extrapolates 1790–1879 via the 1880 overlap. "Westbound steerage passengers [who] were U.S. citizens…were overwhelmingly naturalized citizens returning from visits to the European origins they previously migrated from" (Keeling 2012, p. 287). Therefore one would expect the U.S.-citizen proportion to decline going back in time (as does the emigration/immigration ratio).
25. Estimating the cabin proportion directly, data sources are ARCENY 1880–1890 and ARCGI (1905, p. 73) for 1894–1919 (one figure for all years). With proportion zero 1790–1852, linear interpolation is used for 1853–1879 and 1891–1893.
26. Data sources are as follows. Weights: Albion (1938, esp. pp. 274, 284–286), Cutler (1961) compilation kindly provided by John Killick, and Killick (2000, pp. 65, 68). New York to Liverpool fare: Albion (1938, pp. 233–235), Gibbs (1957, p. 30), DKW (2017, p. 52). New York to London fare: DKW (2017, p. 52), with interpolation via New York-to-Liverpool for missing years of service. New York to Havre fare: *New York Annual Register* [NYAR] 1830–1837, *New York State Register* [NYSR] 1843–1845, *The Albion* 1842–1855. Philadelphia to Liverpool fare: Killick (2014, p. 191, first column); spreadsheet (rows 2, 24) provided by Killick, with linear interpolation of missing years. Philadelphia-to-Liverpool extrapolates other fares to 1856–1867 via 1855 overlap.
27. Data from Tony Pawlyn (2003, p. 128) and John Beck (2009, p. 146).
28. Sources are John Melish (1815, vol. 1, p. iv); Killick spreadsheet, row 24 (for pre-packet per-passenger fare); Frank C. Bowen (1930, p. 25). Midpoint of ranges. Melish westbound figure is extended eastbound, justified by Falmouth two-way fare for New York direct.
29. Fare data sources are as follows. Liverpool to New York: Albion (1938, pp. 233–235), Gibbs (1957, p. 30), *The Albion* 1839–1853, NYAR 1830–1840, NYSR 1843–1845. London to New York: assumed identical to Liverpool series. Havre to New York: eastbound series applied. Liverpool to Philadelphia: Killick (2014, p. 191, 4th column) and spreadsheet (row 6); linear interpolation for missing years. Liverpool-to-Philadelphia extrapolates the other series to 1867 via 1853 or 1855 overlap.
30. The head-tax element (1830–1839) is a weighted average of New York and Philadelphia adjustments, with weights proportional to New York and Philadelphia weights in packet eastbound cabin fare.

31. Data for Liverpool to Philadelphia fare from Killick (2014, p. 191, last column; spreadsheet, row 19, for 1818–1821—pre-packet but utilized below). Year 1865 linearly interpolated; 1868 figure extended to 1869–1873. London/Liverpool to New York: Benchmark figures for 1820, 1826, 1832, 1840, 1849, 1851, 1859–1863 from John Talbot (1820, p. 398), Calvin Colton (1832, p. 186), Edith Abbott (1926, p. 64), Hansen (1945, p. 198), Philip Taylor (1971, p. 94); converted to per-passenger. Intervening years interpolated via Liverpool-to-Philadelphia fare, which also serves as extrapolator to obtain 1818–1819 and 1864–1873 (via 1820 and 1863 overlap).
32. Data from Pawlyn (2003, p. 128) and Beck (2009, p. 146).
33. Sources are Melish (1815, p. v), *Niles' Weekly Register* (July 20, 1816, p. 346), John Noble (1819, p. 55), Talbot (1820, p. 399), Bowen (1930, p. 24), William F. Adams (1932, p. 161), Hansen (1945, pp. 180–181, 198, 249), North (1960, p. 613), Taylor (1971, p. 94), Jones (1973, p. 16), Brinley Thomas (1973, p. 96), Gould (1979, p. 612), Coleman (1972, pp. 22–23). Where range, midpoint taken.
34. The years are 1798, 1819, 1833, 1839–1843, 1846, 1848, 1851–1852, 1854–1855, 1857, 1860, 1870. Data sources are Engelsing (1961, pp. 117–119), Wegge (1998, p. 975, note 37), Grabbe (2001, pp. 295–297), with figures converted to dollars at the rate 1 thaler = $0.70 (Wegge 1998, p. 974, note 35). Midpoint of range taken.
35. The years are 1802–1806, 1816–1817, 1820, 1827, 1831. Grabbe figures are averages of two numbers, or midpoint of range.
36. Conversion to per-passenger based on information in Engelsing (1961, p. 119); head-tax adjustment per note 30.
37. In 1853, 362,545 alien passengers officially arrived at the United States by sea from the United Kingdom and Continental Europe combined (Bromwell 1856, p. 161). One cannot accept Bromwell's nativity figures to separate these two regions, because many Europeans (particularly Germans) traveled to North America via British ports (especially Liverpool). Instead, I use official statistics of passengers departing U.K. ports. In 1853 (the earliest-year of data availability), 217,210 passengers left U.K. ports for the United States (Parliamentary Papers 1882, p. 22). So relative weights are 217,210/362,545 = 0.5991 for the United Kingdom, 1–0.5991 = 0.4009 for Europe.

    Ideally the weights should incorporate only steerage passengers, but cabin passengers are also included. It is unclear in which direction there is a bias, or if there is a bias. Also, steamships likely carried few steerage passengers in 1853, their first year carrying passengers across the Atlantic—but that may not matter.

38. Eastbound/westbound ratio calculated from Killick (2014, p. 191, 2nd and 6th columns), with linear interpolation of 1865 and projection from 1822 and 1868 to 1790–1821 and 1869–1873.
39. Excel file February 17, 2012 and (for 1882) email June 13, 2017. The methodology is in Keeling (2008).
40. Source is DKW (2017, pp. 52–57), with gold-dollar converted to currency. Fares for 1842 and 1847 estimated from surrounding packet and *Great Western* fares. For 1848–1855, Cunard fare; for 1856–1914, average of steamship-line fares.
41. Source of the numerator is *Commercial Year Book* (1896, pp. 229–230). Ports are New York, Boston, Philadelphia, and Baltimore. The year is 1894.
42. For various years, fares of individual steamships (*Sirius*, *Great Western*, *Royal William*, *Great Britain*), Cunard and Collins lines. Sources are Bowen (1930, pp. 29, 73), David B. Tyler (1939, p. 48), Hyde (1975, p. 40), Gibbs (1957, pp. 33, 44–45, 53–54, 361–362), Bonsor (1975, p. 78). Years 1854–1856 and 1858–1859 are interpolated.
43. Sources are *Appleton's European Guide Book* (1870, p. 14) and *New York Times* (various issues). The conversion factor is the 1894 ratio of the Keeling basis series to the "Cunard fare per liner-agent" (*Commercial Year Book* 1896, p. 230), the latter taken as an advertised rate.
44. For 1853–1886, I aimed for multiple-month observations yearly. Sources are: *New York Herald* 1853–1861, *New York Times* 1862–1865, *New York Tribune* 1866–1886. In this, I thank Drew Keeling for access to his compilation and Tom Weiss for providing the data file underlying the series in DGW (2012). For 1913–1916, annual average of Anchor advertised fare is directly assembled from *New York Times* (various issues). The Anchor series is extended to 1917–1919 via general information on steerage (or third-class) fares for New York (or North American ports in general) to Europe or England (*New York Times*: April 25, 1915, p. 28; January 7, 1917, p. 5: August 20, 1919, p. 2; August 28, 1919, p. 11).
45. Same source as for cabin eastbound, with another port (New Orleans).
46. For this entire paragraph, I am indebted to Drew Keeling for information and advice.
47. Data sources for the assembled series and for 1874–1875 below are Hyde (1975, pp. 64, 96–97, 104); Cunard Steamship Company (1877, p. 31); *The Times*, *New York Times*, *New York Tribune*, *New York Herald* (all, various issues). Pound fares converted to dollars.
48. Source of this fare series is the newspapers per note 47. Lines are Inman, Guion, Galway, Vanderbilt, White Star, National, Anchor, Glasgow & New York.
49. The data source is Maffry (1939, pp. 37–38, 77–78). Alien residents are not included in this exercise.

50. Three for U.S. tourists (Europe, West Indies and Central America, South America and Far East), two for foreign tourists and transmigrants (foreign tourists and distant-land transmigrants, transmigrants to Canada and West Indies), two each for immigrants and for emigrants (Europe, rest of world).
51. Thus both groups of transmigrants take the Europe-to-U.S. westbound passage, the distant-land group also takes a one-way journey to South America or Far East, and the Canada group has no subsequent oceanic journey. The Europe eastbound fares are used as basis for the second leg of the distant-land group (see Sect. 3.5), because the Pacific is a relatively peaceful ocean, thus more akin to the eastbound rather than westbound Atlantic passage fare. "Because of the prevailing westerly winds on the North Atlantic: the sailors called the eastward passage, going downhill all the way and the westbound trip, all uphill...Even today the record-breaking liners make faster eastbound than westbound trips, though the difference now is relatively negligible" (Aliber 1938, p. 9).
52. For example, the revenue series comprising (1) U.S. sailing-ship revenue from U.S. residents are as follows. (a) U.S. packets, U.S. traders; each cabin, steerage: U.S. tourists to Europe, emigrants to Europe. (b) U.S. sailing ships; cabin, steerage: U.S. tourists to West Indies and Central America, U.S. tourists to South America and Far East, emigrants to rest of world. Total = (a) + (b) = (4 × 2) + (2 × 3) = 14 series.
53. Sources are North (1960, pp. 614–615, columns (8), (9)), Simon (1960, pp. 673, column (5), 674–675, column (14)), *Historical Statistics* (1975, series U4, U11)—for travel-*plus*-fare exports, imports. In addition to the usual adjustments for calendar year and gold dollar, the North component is expanded to include his implicit computation of immigrant fares in U.S. ships, which he places in immigrant funds (see North 1960, p. 613). Following North's logic, the addition to fiscal-years 1820–1860 exports is $15 *times* total immigrants (*Historical Statistics* 1975, series C89). The new series in the comparison for exports is the sum of column (3) in Table 1 in Chapter 14 and columns (2) and (4) in Table 1; for imports, it is the sum of column (6) in Table 1 in Chapter 14 and columns (5) and (7) in Table 1.

References

Abbott, Edith. 1926. *Historical Aspects of the Immigration Problem*. Chicago: University of Chicago Press.

Adams, William F. 1932. *Ireland and Irish Emigration to the New World*. New Haven: Yale University Press.

Albion, Robert G. 1938. *Square-Riggers on Schedule*. Princeton: Princeton University Press.

———. 1939. *The Rise of New York Port*. New York: Scribner's.

Annual Report of the Commissioner-General of Immigration [ARCGI].

Annual Report of the Commissioners of Emigration of the State of New York [ARCENY].

Appleton's European Guide Book. 1870. London: Longmans, Green.

Beck, John. 2009. *A History of the Falmouth Packet Service*. Exton: South West Maritime History Society.

Bonsor, N.R.P. 1975, 1978, 1979. *North Atlantic Seaway*. New York: Arco.

Bowen, Frank C. 1930. *A Century of Atlantic Travel*. Boston: Little, Brown.

Bromwell, William J. 1856. *History of Immigration to the United States*. New York: Redfield.

Coleman, Terry. 1972. *Passage to America*. London: Hutchinson.

Colton, Calvin. 1832. *Manual for Emigrants to America*. London: Westley & Davis.

Commercial Year Book. 1896. Our International Balance Sheet, 225–231.

Cunard Steamship Company. 1877. *Official Guide*. London: Sutton Sharpe.

Cutler, Carl C. 1961. *Queens of the Western Ocean*. Annapolis: United States Naval Institute.

Dupont, Brandon, Alka Gandhi, and Thomas Weiss [DGW]. 2012. The Long-Term Rise in Overseas Travel by Americans, 1820–2000. *Economic History Review* 65 (February): 144–167.

Dupont, Brandon, Drew Keeling, and Thomas Weiss [DKW]. 2017. First Cabin Fares from New York to the British Isles, 1826–1914. *Research in Economic History* 33: 19–63.

Emmons, Frederick E. 1985. *American Passenger Ships*. Newark: University of Delaware Press.

Engelsing, Rolf. 1961. *Veröffentlichungen aus dem Staatsarchiv der Freien Hansestadt Bremen*. Bremen: Schunemann.

Gibbs, C.R.Vernon. 1957. *Passenger Liners of the Western Ocean*. New York: De Graff.

Gould, John D. 1979. European Inter-Continental Emigration 1815–1914: Patterns and Causes. *Journal of European Economic History* 8 (Winter): 593–679.

Grabbe, Hans-Jürgen. 2001. *Vor der großen Flut*. Stuttgart: Franz Steiner.

Hansen, Marcus Lee. 1945. *The Atlantic Migration, 1607–1860*. Cambridge, MA: Harvard University Press.

[*Historical Statistics*]. 1975. Bureau of the Census. *Historical Statistics of the United States, Colonial Times to 1970, Bicentennial Edition*. Washington: Government Printing Office.

———. 2006. *Historical Statistics of the United States, Millennial Edition*, ed. Susan B. Carter, Scott Sigmund Gartner, Michael R. Haines, Alan L. Olmstead, Richard Sutch, Gavin Wright. Cambridge: Cambridge University Press.

Hutchins, John G.B. 1941. *The American Maritime Industries and Public Policy, 1789–1914*. Cambridge, MA: Harvard University Press.

Hyde, Francis E. 1975. *Cunard and the North Atlantic*. London: Macmillan.

Jones, Maldwyn A. 1973. The Background to Emigration from Great Britain in the Nineteenth Century. *Perspectives in American History* 7: 3–92.

Kapp, Friedrich. 1870. *Immigration and the Commissioners of Emigration*. New York: Douglas Taylor.

Keeling, Drew. 2008. The Voyage Abstracts of the Cunard Line as a Source of Transatlantic Passenger Fares, 1883–1914. *Business Archives Sources and History* 96 (November): 15–36.

———. 2012. *The Business of Transatlantic Migration Between Europe and the United States, 1900–1914*. Zurich: Chronos.

Killick, John. 2000. An Early Nineteenth-Century Shipping Line: The Cope Line of Philadelphia and Liverpool Packets, 1822–1872. *International Journal of Maritime History* 12 (June): 61–87.

———. 2014. Transatlantic Steerage Fares. British and Irish Migration, and Return Migration. *Economic History Review* 67 (1): 170–191.

Klebaner, Benjamin J. 1958. State and Local Immigration Regulation in the United States Before 1882. *International Review of Social History* 3: 269–295.

Maffry, August. 1939. *Overseas Travel and Travel Expenditures in the Balance of International Payments of the United States, 1919–1938*. Washington: Government Printing Office.

Melish, John. 1815. *Travels Through the United States of America*. Philadelphia.

Monthly Summary of Commerce and Finance [MSCF].

New York Annual Register [NYAR].

New York State Register [NYSR].

Noble, John (1819). *Noble's Instructions to Emigrants*. Boston.

North, Douglass C. 1960. The United States Balance of Payments, 1790–1860. In *Trends in the American Economy in the Nineteenth Century*, ed. William N. Parker, 573–628. Princeton: Princeton University Press.

Officer, Lawrence H., and Samuel H. Williamson. 2020. The Antebellum Slave Trade: Numbers and Impact on the Balance of Payments. *Research in Economic History* 36: 181–212.

Olenkiewicz, John S. 2013. *British Packet Sailings, Falmouth–North America: 1755–1826*. Internet, accessed March 8, 2018.

Parliamentary Papers. 1882. *Tables Showing the Progress of British Merchant Shipping*, vol. 62.

Pawlyn, Tony. 2003. *The Falmouth Packets*. Cornwall: Truran.
Simon, Matthew. 1960. The United States Balance of Payments, 1861–1900. In *Trends in the American Economy in the Nineteenth Century*, ed. William N. Parker, 629–716. Princeton: Princeton University Press.
Statistical Abstract of the United States [SAUS].
Talbot, John. 1820. *History of North America*. Leeds: Davies.
Tate, E. Mowbray. 1986. *Transpacific Steam*. New York: Cornwall.
Taylor, George Rogers. 1951. *The Transportation Revolution*. New York: Holt, Rinehart, and Winston.
Taylor, Philip. 1971. *The Distant Magnet*. London: Eyre & Spottiswoode.
Thomas, Brinley. 1973. *Migration and Economic Growth*. Cambridge: Cambridge University Press.
Tyler, David B. 1939. *Steam Conquers the Atlantic*. New York: Appleton-Century.
Wegge, Simone A. 1998. Chain Migration and Information Networks: Evidence from Nineteenth-Century Hesse-Cassel. *Journal of Economic History* 58 (December): 957–986.

CHAPTER 16

Financial

1 Marine Insurance: Rates

1.1 Merchandise

Simon (1960) sets the tone for financial transactions, and in the main I follow him. To do so for marine insurance, data on rates are readily available for the postbellum period but require creativity to take the figures back from 1861 or 1870. An important fact is that marine insurance has two components: (1) marine risk, which is the "normal" or "peacetime" rate, and (2) war-risk. There are separate marine-risk rates for sailing-ships and steamships, but war-risk is the same. As does Simon, I assume that rates are identical for United States and foreign vessels, justified by Simon (1960, p. 656, note 55). Differing from Simon, I have separate rates for merchandise and specie (with the specie rate assumed the same for sailing ships and steamships). All rates are in percentage terms.

1.1.1 Sailing Ships

1790–1816: The primary source is Albion and Pope (1942, p. 70). They present inclusive percentage rates (marine-risk *plus* war-risk) for four regions of U.S. trade (Britain, Mediterranean, West Indies, Far East) for 1792–1815. Where there is a range, I take the midpoint. The table has missing observations and missing years. Figures for 1792 (with no war-risk) are here projected back to 1790. To complete the table, I begin with

L. H. Officer, *A New Balance of Payments for the United States, 1790–1919*, Palgrave Studies in American Economic History,
https://doi.org/10.1007/978-3-030-66099-4_16

Kingston's (2011, p. 179) comparable-region data converted to annual averages, followed by interpolation and other extrapolation, with special computations for 1815 and 1816.[1] The desired annual rate 1790–1816 is the four-region average, except that Britain is excluded 1813–1814. The years 1794–1795 are linearly interpolated.

1825, 1835, 1845, 1860: New York insurance rates, average of 15–16 foreign ports (or regions) in Albion (1939, p. 412). Peacetime, so war-risk zero.

1820, 1830, 1859, 1861–1864: Peacetime rate is average of New York rates to foreign ports in *Annual Report of the Chamber of Commerce of the State of New York* [ARCC], adjusted (multiplied) by the Albion/ARCC 1860 overlap. Exceptions are 1864, for which the ARCC average is unadjusted, and 1863, which (because of insufficient data) is the average of the 1862 and 1864 rates. For 1861–1864, war-risk premium is added.[2]

1817–1819, 1821–1824, 1826–1829, 1831–1834, 1836–1844, 1846–1858: linearly interpolated.

1866–1869, 1871–1899: ARCC rate per Simon (1960, p. 659 or 660, column (3)), adjusted to calendar year.

1870, 1900–1919: Average New York rate to foreign ports, ARCC.

1.1.2 Steamships

1870, 1900–1919: Average New York rate to foreign ports, ARCC.

1871–1899: ARCC rate per Simon (1960, p. 659 or 660, column (5)) adjusted to calendar year.

1837–1870: Instead of Simon's (1960, p. 661, Cols. 3 and 5) assumed constant and arbitrary peacetime rate (for 1861–1870), I apply the steam-sail percentage-point peacetime differential rate, which is −0.53 percentage point in 1870 (computed from ARCC 1869–1870, p. 146) and assumed half that in 1854, apparently the first year of a differential rate.[3] I linearly interpolate the differential between 1854 and 1870 and add it to the sailing-ship inclusive rate. For earlier years, the sailing-ship rate is applied to steamships.

1.1.3 U.S. Ships

Average sailing-ship and steamship marine-insurance rates, weighted by the sailing-ship and steamship tonnage proportions of U.S. vessels cleared from U.S. seaports.[4]

1.1.4 Foreign Ships

Average sailing-ship and steamship marine-insurance rates, weighted by the sailing-ship and steamship tonnage proportions of foreign vessels entering U.S. seaports.[5]

1.2 Specie

Insurance rate New York to/from London for 1827–1830, 1835–1848, 1851, 1868, 1882, 1892, 1896, 1905–1913 is in Officer (1996, p. 125). Intervening years are interpolated via the average U.S.-ship and foreign-ship merchandise rate. Years 1790–1826 and 1914–1919 are extrapolated via 1827 and 1913 overlaps with this rate.

1.3 Presentation

The merchandise-rate series for foreign vessels and for U.S. vessels, as well as the specie rate, are graphed in Fig. 1, with wartime risk very noticeable as spikes. The difference between U.S.-ship and foreign-ship rates,

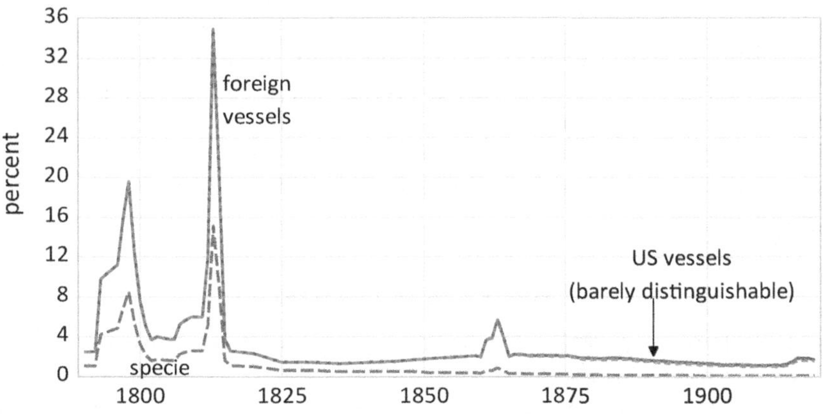

Fig. 1 Marine-insurance rates, 1790–1919. *Note* "US vessels" and "foreign vessels" are average marine-insurance rates for merchandise on United States and foreign ships, respectively. The series differ because U.S. ships and foreign ships have differing proportions of steamship/sailing-ship tonnage. "Specie" is the rate for gold and silver

zero 1790–1853, is uniformly positive from 1854—but is hard to discern, because the level is so low.

2 Marine Insurance: Payments and Receipts

What enters the balance of payments are U.S.-companies insurance of U.S.-ship exports and foreign-companies insurance of foreign-ship imports. It is fair to assume that foreign (British) companies insured the totality of U.S. imports. Therefore marine-insurance payments are calculated as the sum of (a) 1/100th the foreign-ships merchandise rate *times* merchandise imports in foreign ships, and (b) 1/100th the specie rate *times* gold and silver imports in foreign ships.[6]

Initially, British companies also dominated marine insurance for U.S.-exports, whether on British or U.S. ships. Consistent with other studies, I assume an initial British monopoly that gradually waned to the favor of U.S. companies, until the U.S. share becomes 100% in 1841.[7] I construct a U.S.-share variable that is zero 1790–1791, unity 1841–1919, and linearly interpolated 1792–1840. Marine-insurance receipts are the "U.S. proportion" *times* the sum of (a) 1/100th the U.S.-ships merchandise rate *times* merchandise exports in U.S. ships, and (b) 1/100th the specie rate *times* gold-and-silver exports in U.S. ships.

Marine-insurance receipts and payments are listed in columns (1) and (2) of Table 1. Comparison with Simon (1960, pp. 659, column (7); 660, column (7)) shows, on average, a Simon overestimate for receipts but little difference for payments (Table 2, rows (3) and (4)). As always, the comparison is corrected for fiscal-year and gold valuation of the existing (Simon) series.

3 Bankers' Commissions

Simon (1960, pp. 692–694) develops a series of commissions paid to foreign (largely London) bankers for his fiscal years, 1861–1900. The series is: 1/2% "imports c.i.f." *plus* 1/40% "exports c.i.f." *plus* miscellaneous commissions (assumed constant at $100,000 annually). I adopt the Simon technique using the new data, and extend the computation to the full 1790–1919 period. I improve on Simon methodologically as follows (1) exclude overland trade and carrying trade, (2) include specie trade, and (3) allow miscellaneous commissions to vary over time.

Table 1 Miscellaneous services (millions of dollars)

	Receipts	*Payments*		
Year	*Marine insurance*	*Marine insurance*	*Bankers' commissions*	*Military expenditures*
	(1)	*(2)*	*(3)*	*(4)*
1790	0	0.32	0.13	0
1791	0	0.34	0.20	0
1792	0.01	0.23	0.18	0
1793	0.09	0.55	0.20	0
1794	0.20	0.44	0.27	0
1795	0.42	0.59	0.40	0
1796	0.67	0.57	0.43	0
1797	0.99	0.96	0.40	0
1798	1.62	1.25	0.38	0
1799	1.34	0.94	0.43	0
1800	0.91	0.63	0.51	0
1801	0.78	0.47	0.52	0
1802	0.47	0.33	0.39	0
1803	0.50	0.36	0.39	0
1804	0.72	0.32	0.52	0
1805	0.91	0.31	0.65	0
1806	1.04	0.33	0.71	0
1807	1.32	0.39	0.63	0
1808	0.50	0.29	0.34	0
1809	1.04	0.43	0.37	0
1810	1.34	0.33	0.39	0
1811	1.15	0.30	0.25	0
1812	1.43	1.16	0.29	0
1813	2.27	1.41	0.08	0
1814	1.06	2.42	0.18	0
1815	0.77	0.94	0.58	0
1816	0.75	0.88	0.73	0
1817	0.89	0.46	0.51	0
1818	0.94	0.43	0.56	0
1819	0.79	0.40	0.46	0
1820	0.79	0.15	0.38	0
1821	0.68	0.12	0.42	0
1822	0.71	0.14	0.51	0
1823	0.73	0.12	0.47	0
1824	0.74	0.09	0.51	0

(continued)

Table 1 (continued)

Year	*Receipts*	*Payments*		
	Marine insurance	*Marine insurance*	*Bankers' commissions*	*Military expenditures*
	(1)	*(2)*	*(3)*	*(4)*
1825	0.79	0.07	0.57	0
1826	0.68	0.07	0.51	0
1827	0.69	0.08	0.51	0
1828	0.63	0.10	0.52	0
1829	0.67	0.08	0.45	0
1830	0.71	0.09	0.48	0
1831	0.71	0.15	0.63	0
1832	0.74	0.16	0.61	0
1833	0.80	0.14	0.62	0
1834	0.93	0.17	0.71	0
1835	1.07	0.20	0.88	0
1836	1.13	0.25	0.98	0
1837	1.11	0.23	0.77	0
1838	1.16	0.16	0.70	0
1839	1.27	0.24	0.82	0
1840	1.39	0.20	0.63	0
1841	1.28	0.20	0.67	0
1842	1.19	0.19	0.53	0
1843	1.07	0.24	0.55	0
1844	1.22	0.22	0.65	0
1845	1.31	0.24	0.68	0
1846	1.52	0.36	0.74	5.85
1847	1.70	0.47	0.85	9.37
1848	1.70	0.46	0.87	0.78
1849	1.69	0.57	0.93	0
1850	2.08	0.82	1.15	0
1851	2.33	1.00	1.27	0
1852	2.43	1.24	1.42	0
1853	2.99	1.59	1.68	0
1854	3.30	1.39	1.64	0
1855	3.73	1.63	2.17	0
1856	4.22	2.08	2.44	0
1857	4.35	1.75	1.82	0

(continued)

Table 1 (continued)

Year	*Receipts*	*Payments*		
	Marine insurance	*Marine insurance*	*Bankers' commissions*	*Military expenditures*
	(1)	*(2)*	*(3)*	*(4)*
1858	4.43	1.98	1.77	0
1859	4.82	2.60	1.99	0
1860	4.04	2.39	1.92	0
1861	5.02	4.20	1.51	0
1862	4.38	5.41	1.52	0
1863	5.98	15.78	2.54	0
1864	4.30	16.80	3.51	0
1865	2.84	7.88	3.19	0
1866	4.13	9.73	3.60	0
1867	3.59	8.13	3.25	0
1868	3.27	7.94	3.33	0
1869	3.56	8.00	3.50	0
1870	3.71	7.84	3.41	0
1871	3.39	9.31	3.84	0
1872	3.27	10.50	4.23	0
1873	3.41	9.96	4.13	0
1874	3.16	8.67	3.70	0
1875	3.18	7.98	3.41	0
1876	3.31	7.03	3.12	0
1877	3.16	6.05	2.91	0
1878	2.70	5.37	2.74	0
1879	2.25	7.18	3.53	0
1880	2.15	8.95	4.30	0
1881	2.01	9.33	4.30	0
1882	1.89	9.82	4.27	0
1883	1.97	9.73	4.19	0
1884	1.77	9.03	3.88	0
1885	1.56	8.75	3.75	0
1886	1.45	9.65	4.11	0
1887	1.29	10.03	4.40	0
1888	1.33	9.94	4.46	0
1889	1.40	10.10	4.59	0
1890	1.31	10.28	4.80	0

(continued)

Table 1 (continued)

Year	Receipts	Payments		
	Marine insurance	*Marine insurance*	*Bankers' commissions*	*Military expenditures*
	(1)	*(2)*	*(3)*	*(4)*
1891	1.32	9.82	4.85	0
1892	1.25	9.63	4.85	0
1893	1.15	8.28	4.43	0
1894	1.06	7.34	4.15	0
1895	1.03	8.14	4.39	0
1896	1.14	8.17	4.63	0
1897	1.09	7.13	4.48	0
1898	1.05	6.75	4.35	23.68
1899	1.19	7.81	4.78	25.80
1900	1.20	8.13	5.03	21.08
1901	1.12	8.21	5.14	20.52
1902	1.10	8.96	5.57	20.31
1903	1.14	9.11	5.91	25.00
1904	1.39	9.41	6.15	26.42
1905	1.77	10.25	6.74	24.57
1906	1.80	11.50	7.76	23.92
1907	1.56	11.45	7.85	25.26
1908	1.36	10.84	7.32	27.14
1909	1.30	12.47	7.92	26.98
1910	1.43	13.42	8.52	26.35
1911	1.66	13.65	8.82	25.59
1912	2.00	14.39	9.59	25.25
1913	2.09	15.13	10.04	25.22
1914	2.41	15.11	9.28	24.41
1915	5.90	17.48	11.29	22.91
1916	12.76	25.56	14.57	30.55
1917	18.06	29.79	18.61	205.48
1918	19.04	29.82	16.78	1018.00
1919	44.72	34.05	21.59	757.00

"Imports c.i.f." are waterborne imports (merchandise, gold and silver) in U.S. vessels and in foreign vessels *plus* foreign shipping earnings from imports [Chapter 13, Sects. 2.2 and 2.4] *plus* marine-insurance payments. "Exports c.i.f." are waterborne exports (merchandise, gold and silver) in U.S. vessels and in foreign vessels *plus* U.S. shipping earnings from exports [Chapter 13, Sects. 2.2 and 2.4] *plus* marine-insurance receipts.

Table 2 Marine insurance and bankers' commissions: comparisons (percentage deviation of existing series from new series)

Item	*1861–1899*
(1) Total exports	3.84
(2) Total imports	−1.60
(3) Marine-insurance receipts	6.61
(4) Marine-insurance payments	−0.86
(5) Bankers' commissions payments	−2.59

Note A negative (positive) sign means that the new series is larger (smaller) than the existing series. For discussion, see Sects. 2–4

As indicator of the growth of international transactions, hence a logical extrapolator of miscellaneous commissions, "merchandise trade" is generated as the sum of conventional merchandise exports and imports (columns (1) and (2), Table 1 in Chapter 6). Miscellaneous commissions in any year 1790–1919 are constructed as the product of (a) the ratio of $100,000 to annual average merchandise trade over 1861–1900 and (b) merchandise trade in that year.

Bankers' commissions are shown in column (3) of Table 1. Notwithstanding the steps I take to improve on Simon, there is only a 21/2% difference on average between Simon's series and the new series (row (5) in Table 2).[8]

4 Comparisons

Total financial exports and imports per *Historical Statistics* (1975, series U7 and U14) are compared with the new series (marine-insurance receipts, sum of marine-insurance payments and bankers' commissions) for 1861–1899 in rows (1) and (2) of Table 2.[9] *Historical Statistics* overestimates exports by almost four percent and underestimates imports by about 11/2%, on average. These are not much of a difference, but remember that we always adjust for gold dollars.

Notes

1. Taking weighted averages of his two sources, I convert Kingston's (one-way) figures to annual averages for 1796–1798, 1800–1801 for U.K., Northern Europe, West Indies (Hispaniola and Cuba), and Asia. As his figures are only war-risk (Kingston, p. 177, note 57), I add peacetime rates per Albion-Pope. Extrapolating via overlap with adjoining year, I obtain

Albion-Pope figures for missing cells Britain 1800, Mediterranean 1796 and 1798, Far East 1798 and 1800. Then linear interpolation takes care of 1793 West Indies and Far East, 1799 all except West Indies, and 1808 all regions. Mediterranean and West Indies 1813–1814 are extrapolated via 1812 overlap with Far East. For 1815, the Albion-Pope Britain rate (only figure available) is multiplied by their "four-region average"/Britain ratio for 1792, both years deemed zero war-risk. For 1816, Albion (1939, p. 412) has the same rate for Britain Isles and West Indies as the Albion-Pope rate for 1792. For the Mediterranean, I average three subregions; for Asia, I adopt half the round-trip rate. For all data ranges, I take the midpoint.

2. For 1861–1862, average of rates for four foreign-port groups (ARCC 1862–1863, p. 217). For 1864, I multiply the 1862 figure by the 1864/1862 war-risk ratio in George W. Dalzell (1940, p. 239). The 1863 rate is 2/3 the ARCC January–August 1863 four-port-group figure and 1/3 the 1864 rate.
3. "Steamers were somewhat grudgingly accorded lower rates than sailing vessels (in 1854 the New York Board expressly singled out the Collins and Cunard liners for preferred treatment), albeit underwriters still distrusted propellers" (C. Bradford Mitchell 1970, p. 16).
4. For the weights, see Chapter 13 (Sect. 5.1, U.S. Ships).
5. For the weights, see Chapter 13 (Sect. 5.1, Foreign Ships).
6. The waterborne trade series are derived in Chapter 13 (Sect. 2.2).
7. "Brokers' commissions and marine insurance...were for the most part in the hands of the British...the expansion of shipping induced the growth of U.S. merchants and marine insurance so that...this item becomes a smaller debit" (North 1960, pp. 599–600); "the twenty years following 1840 may be jointly characterized as the 'golden period' of American marine insurance" (Solomon Huebner 1905, p. 258). Marine-insurance premiums of Insurance Company of North America jumps over six-fold from 1833–1842 to 1843–1852 (Thomas H. Montgomery 1885, p. 163). Founded in 1792, this was the first U.S. marine-insurance company.
8. As usual, the Simon (1960, p. 692, column (5)) series is converted to calendar year and the comparison is adjusted to currency dollars.
9. The *Historical Statistics* series are based on Simon. Comparison is not made with North, because he simply assumes a debit of four percent of imports 1790–1812, two percent 1813–1819, and implicitly zero 1820–1860 (North 1960, p. 600).

References

Albion, Robert G. 1939. *The Rise of New York Port*. New York: Scribner's.

———, and Jennie B. Pope. 1942. *Sea Lanes in Wartime*. New York: Norton.

Annual Report of the Chamber of Commerce of the State of New York [ARCC].

Dalzell, George W. 1940. *The Flight from the Flag*. Chapel Hill: University of North Carolina Press.

[*Historical Statistics*]. 1975. Bureau of the Census. *Historical Statistics of the United States, Colonial Times to 1970, Bicentennial Edition*. Washington: Government Printing Office.

Huebner, Solomon. 1905. The Development and Present Status of Marine Insurance in the United States. *Annals of the American Academy of Political and Social Science* 26 (September): 241–272.

Kingston, Christopher. 2011. Marine Insurance in Philadelphia During the Quasi-War with France, 1795–1801. *Journal of Economic History* 71 (March): 162–184.

Mitchell, C.Bradford. 1970. *A Premium on Progress*. New York: Newcomen Society.

Montgomery, Thomas H. 1885. *A History of the Insurance Company of North America*. Philadelphia: Review.

North, Douglass C. 1960. The United States Balance of Payments, 1790–1860. In *Trends in the American Economy in the Nineteenth Century*, ed. William N. Parker, 573–628. Princeton: Princeton University Press.

Officer, Lawrence H. 1996. *Between the Dollar-Sterling Gold Points*. Cambridge: Cambridge University Press.

Simon, Matthew. 1960. The United States Balance of Payments, 1861–1900. In *Trends in the American Economy in the Nineteenth Century*, ed. William N. Parker, 629–716. Princeton: Princeton University Press.

CHAPTER 17

Military and Slaves

1 Military Expenditures Abroad

Direct Data: U.S. military expenditures abroad are a debit item, not unlike civilian travel expenditures in terms of what enters the balance of payments—another instance in which human costs and political impacts are poorly reflected in the economic measure. Significant amount first occurred during the Mexican-American War. North (1960, p. 622) has $8 million for each fiscal year 1847–1848. Based on time of war for each year, I allocate the $16 million total to calendar years 1846–1848.[1] W. H. Allen (1904, p. 278) sees annual military expenditures abroad as $25 million, which I apply to the year 1903. The most-reliable data are for 1918–1919, in *Historical Statistics* (1975, series U12).

Figure for 1917: Synthetic military expenditures abroad 1917–1918 are the product of the U.K. cost-of-living index and average armed forces overseas.[2] I convert the latter series to calendar-year monthly averages.[3] Military expenditures abroad in 1917 are the 1917/1918 synthetic-expenditures ratio *times* military expenditures abroad in 1918.

Zero Expenditures: The Spanish-American and Philippine-American Wars began the era of "U.S. imperialism" (continuous stationing of U.S. forces abroad). There was use of U.S. armed forces abroad in almost all years since 1798 (Barbara S. Torreon and Sofia Plagakis 2018); but the "imperialist" phase of U.S. military activity abroad began with the

L. H. Officer, *A New Balance of Payments for the United States, 1790–1919*, Palgrave Studies in American Economic History,
https://doi.org/10.1007/978-3-030-66099-4_17

Spanish-American War.[4] So, except for the Mexican-American War, I assume zero military expenditures abroad until 1898.

Inter/Extrapolated Years: The inter/extrapolation series is total military expenditures.[5] Military expenditures abroad 1898–1902 are extrapolated via the 1903 overlap, and 1904–1916 interpolated between 1903 and 1917. The complete series "military expenditures abroad" is in column (4) of Table 1 (Chapter 16).

2 Non-imported Slave Purchases

Another debit item is the purchase cost of slaves that embarked on U.S. ships but were not imported into the United States. They were either successfully landed in third countries ("carrying trade") or thwarted from adding to ship revenue (via pirates, privateers, accident, or natural disaster). Following Officer and Williamson (2020), U.S. purchases of African and creole slaves are considered separately.

Slaves that embarked U.S. ships in Africa are enumerated in column (1) of Table 1 (Chapter 4). Successful imports of these slaves are listed in column (2) of the table. The number of non-imported African slaves, column (1) *minus* column (2), is multiplied by the Africa price (Fig. 2 in Chapter 9), yielding the purchase cost of African slaves.

For the carrying trade of creole slaves, the numbers of male and female slaves landed in Havana from U.S. ships are separately considered and shown in columns (5)–(6) of Table 2 in Chapter 4. The *sale price of each in Cuba* (Sect. 3.2 of Chapter 13) requires conversion to *purchase price elsewhere in the Caribbean*. Eltis and Richardson (2004, pp. 185–186) apply a differential transport cost of zero between Cuba and Jamaica, six percent between the Eastern Caribbean and Jamaica. Using the same technique as for U.S. Caribbean imports (Chapter 9, note 9), the purchase price of creole male (female) slaves is the product of (1–0.06 *times* the {"shipping-plus-distribution"/shipping} cost factor) and the male (female) Havana sale price. In contrast, Officer and Williamson (2020, p. 211) simply divide the sale prices by 1.10. It turns out that the price series here, graphed in Fig. 1, are virtually the same as in Officer–Williamson. Multiplying the male and female numbers by the applicable purchase price, and summing, the result is the purchase cost of non-imported creole slaves.[6]

U.S.-ship purchases of slaves not imported into the United States are the sum of the purchase cost of Africans and the purchase cost of creoles.

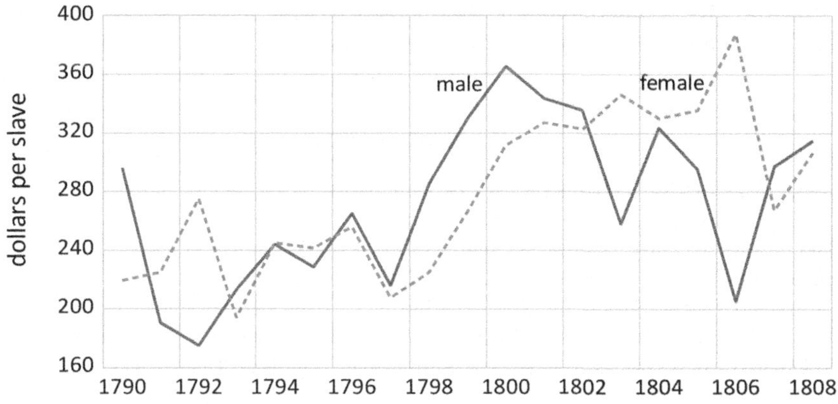

Fig. 1 Price of creole slaves: carrying trade, 1790–1808. *Note* The series are the purchase price of creole male or female slaves in the Caribbean

The series is shown in column (4) of Table 1 (Chapter 9). It differs from the corresponding series in Officer–Williamson (2020, Table 4, column (3)) by little more than rounding error. As always, the full cost would include that borne by the enslaved themselves, and the latter does not enter the balance of payments.

Notes

1. The United States declared war on May 13, 1846; war ended February 2, 1848, with the Treaty of Guadalupe.
2. The U.K. dollar-denominated cost-of-living index is the Feinstein (1995, p. 265) series multiplied by the dollar/pound exchange rate. Armed forces overseas for midyear 1917–1919 are computed from *Historical Statistics* (2006, series Aa6 *minus* Aa7).
3. The United States entered the war April 6, 1917. For the purpose at hand, armed forces overseas are deemed zero until May 1. These several weeks allow time for mustering of troops and shipping them to Britain (prior to transport to France).
4. "The Spanish-American War in 1898 made the U.S. Navy the most important branch of the armed services, because it connected the new American empire" (Anni P. Baker 2004, p. 17).
5. Sum of Army and Navy outlays, converted to calendar year. Source is *Historical Statistics* (1975, series Y458 and Y459).

6. Note the assumption, for the creole carrying trade (and per Officer–Williamson), that embarkations equal disembarkations.

References

Allen, W.H. 1904. What Becomes of Our Trade Balances? *Sewanee Review* 12 (July): 268–296.

Baker, Anni P. 2004. *American Soldiers Overseas*. Westport: Praeger.

Eltis, David, and David Richardson. 2004. Prices of African Slaves Newly Arrived in the Americas, 1673–1865: New Evidence on Long-Run Trends and Regional Differentials. In *Slavery in the Development of the Americas*, ed. David Eltis, Frank D. Lewis, and Kenneth L. Sokoloff, 181–218. Cambridge: Cambridge University Press.

Feinstein, Charles H. 1995. Changes in Nominal Wages, the Cost of Living and Real Wages in the United Kingdom over Two Centuries, 1780–1990. In *Labour's Reward*, ed. Peter Scholliers and Vera Zamagni, 3–36, 258–266. Aldershot: Edward Elgar.

[*Historical Statistics*]. 1975. Bureau of the Census. *Historical Statistics of the United States, Colonial Times to 1970, Bicentennial Edition*. Washington: Government Printing Office.

———. 2006. *Historical Statistics of the United States, Millennial Edition*, ed. Susan B. Carter, Scott Sigmund Gartner, Michael R. Haines, Alan L. Olmstead, Richard Sutch, Gavin Wright. Cambridge: Cambridge University Press.

North, Douglass C. 1960. The United States Balance of Payments, 1790–1860. In *Trends in the American Economy in the Nineteenth Century*, ed. William N. Parker, 573–628. Princeton: Princeton University Press.

Officer, Lawrence H., and Samuel H. Williamson. 2020. The Antebellum Slave Trade: Numbers and Impact on the Balance of Payments. *Research in Economic History* 36: 181–212.

Torreon, Barbara S., and Sofia Plagakis. 2018. *Instances of Use of United States Armed Forces Abroad, 1798–2018*. Congressional Research Service.

PART VI

Implications

CHAPTER 18

Aggregates and Balances

Parts III, IV, and V (Chapters 6–17) generate the items in the balance-of-payments table. This chapter aggregates the items in meaningful ways and constructs the various balances.

1 Aggregates

1.1 Goods

Components of "goods" are merchandise (conventional and silver), ships and slaves. So exports of goods are conventional merchandise, merchandise silver, and ships; while imports of goods are conventional merchandise, merchandise silver, and slaves. Table 1 exhibits the average share of each component, separately for exports and imports. The dominance of merchandise is not unexpected; but the extremely low shares of slaves and ships even in the early period are a surprise from this vantage point.

Comparisons of total exports and total imports of goods with *Historical Statistics* (1975, series U2 and U9) are shown in rows (1) and (2) of Table 2.[1] Only three of the eight period-average deviations exceed two percent in magnitude. For exports, *Historical Statistics* is too low in 1790–1819 but too high in 1861–1899. In contrast, *Historical Statistics* overestimates imports by over ten percent in 1790–1819. It is not

L. H. Officer, *A New Balance of Payments for the United States, 1790–1919*, Palgrave Studies in American Economic History,
https://doi.org/10.1007/978-3-030-66099-4_18

Table 1 Components of trade in goods (average percent share over period)

Item	*1790–1807*	*1808–1860*	*1861–1899*	*1900–1919*
Exports				
(1) Merchandise	97.23	98.44	95.35	97.06
(2) Silver	0	0.14	4.05	2.85
(3) Ships	2.77	1.41	0.60	0.09
Imports				
(4) Merchandise	99.24	99.78	97.86	97.41
(5) Silver	0	0.21	2.14	2.59
(6) Slaves	0.76	0.01	0	0

Table 2 Total goods and total services: comparisons (percentage deviation of existing series from new series)

Item	*1790–1819*	*1820–1860*	*1861–1899*	*1900–1918*
(1) Exports of goods	−4.37	1.40	5.22	1.27
(2) Imports of goods	10.20	1.81	0.46	−0.84
(3) Exports of services	66.79	−13.97	−19.13	−66.73
(4) Imports of services	−38.54	−30.98	−4.55	3.72

Note A negative (positive) sign means that the new series is larger (smaller) than the existing series. For discussion, see Sects. 1.1, 1.2

surprising that divergences have relatively high magnitude in 1790–1819, the worst period for data availability; but the existence of substantial deviation in only one other period is remarkable—given this study's consistent and complete methodology in goods trade (Chapters 6–9), in contrast to *Historical Statistics*.

Pleasingly, the conundrum is removed if *algebraic* are replaced by *absolute* deviations. Then (still following comparison protocol), for 1820–1860, the average percentage deviation of *Historical Statistics* from the new series is over 6½% for both exports and imports; and, for 1861–1899, the deviation reaches 14% for exports and 17% for imports. Note that taking absolute deviations simply involves changing the sign of negative deviations to positive. Therefore a period-average of absolute deviations cannot be less than the corresponding average of algebraic deviations. In other words, absolute deviations prevent cancelation of positive and negative deviations (see Sect. 2 of Chapter 2).

1.2 Services

Shares of the components of services, exports, and imports separately, are exhibited in Table 3. For both exports and imports, the reduction in the share of transportation over time is notable. In contrast, shares of travel exports and ship-revenue and military-expenditures imports increase. It is surprising that, in the antebellum period, ship revenue—considered of great importance in the literature—is so low a proportion of services exports (and see Chapter 20, Sect. 2.2).[2]

Total exports and total imports of services are compared with *Historical Statistics* (1975, sums of series U3, U4, U7; U10, U11, U12, U14) in rows (3) and (4) of Table 2, under the usual protocol. The differences between the new and established series are substantial. For exports, *Historical Statistics* exceeds the new series by two-thirds in 1790–1819, but falls short of the new series by an equal proportion in 1900–1918. Computing ***absolute*** deviations, the difference in 1861–1899 jumps to 36 and 29% for exports and imports, while the difference in 1900–1918 climbs to 20% for imports.

Table 3 Components of trade in services (average percent share over period)

Item	*1790–1807*	*1808–1860*	*1861–1899*	*1900–1919*
Exports				
(1) Transportation	90.51	78.43	66.30	63.49
(2) Travel	2.91	7.06	25.77	32.17
(3) Ship Revenue	3.39	7.27	2.54	2.78
(4) Financial[a]	3.19	7.23	5.39	1.56
Imports				
(5) Transportation	58.42	58.73	36.28	23.42
(6) Travel	16.80	26.50	37.46	34.78
(7) Ship revenue	3.03	3.04	10.99	18.57
(8) Financial[b]	11.04	10.08	13.76	7.64
(9) Military expenditures	0	1.42	1.52	15.59
(10) Slave purchases[c]	10.71	0.24	0	0

[a] Marine insurance
[b] Marine insurance and bankers' commissions
[c] Not imported

1.3 Net Assets

U.S. net assets, traditionally termed the "international investment position" of the United States, are shown in column (8) of Table 1 in Chapter 11.[3] Note that the United States is a net debtor until 1916. I take the negative of net assets to obtain net liabilities, and perform comparison of "net liabilities" with two predecessors. Lewis (1938) provides direct stock estimates for five years over 1843–1914, and the comparison is made in row (1) of Table 4.[4] *Historical Statistics* (2006, series Ee22) adopts the residual-based net-liabilities series of North and Simon. This series measures the change in net liabilities as the net capital inflow, which itself is calculated as negative net goods, services, income, and unilateral transfers, allowing for debt default. In Chapter 11 (Sect. 1), I reject this "residual approach" to estimating the capital account. Comparison of the calendar-year-converted *Historical Statistics* series with the new net-liabilities series is made in row (2) of Table 4.

With the exception of 1900–1918, results show that predecessors on average overestimate U.S. net liabilities—and by substantial percentages, except for the postbellum Lewis figures. An implication is that the conventional wisdom describing the United States as a "substantial international net debtor" until World War I (Lipsey 2008, p. 480), based as it is on North–Simon and Lewis, may require that the adjective "substantial" be replaced with "moderate."

Table 4 Net International Liabilities: comparisons (percentage deviation of existing series from new series)

Predecessor	*1789–1819*	*1820–1860*	*1861–1899*	*1900–1918*
(1) Lewis figures[a]	–	29.25[b]	4.91[c]	−0.88[d]
(2) *Historical Statistics* series[e]	19.37	16.82	33.09	–

Note The one negative sign means that, for only that period, the new series is larger than the existing series. For discussion, see Sect. 1.3

[a]End of year, except June 30 for 1914

[b]1843

[c]1869, 1897. Not adjusted for gold dollar

[d]1908, 1914

[e]End of year

2 Balances

2.1 Merchandise and Goods

The balance of merchandise (net exports of conventional merchandise, or "trade balance") is exhibited in column (1) of Table 5. The balance of goods—merchandise balance *plus* net exports of silver *plus* ship exports *minus* slave imports—is shown in column (2). The two balances are close in level and movement. The "trade-balance" narrative of the literature is confirmed: largely deficits (with the 1840s the main exception) until the mid-1870s—then principally surpluses, associated with the development of the manufacturing sector.[5]

2.2 Goods and Services

The balance of services is net transportation exports *plus* net travel exports *plus* net passenger-fares credits *plus* net financial credits *minus* military expenditures abroad *minus* purchases of non-imported slaves. What is listed in Table 5, column (3), is the balance of goods and services, which is the goods balance *plus* the services balance. The statement that "the overall net balance of exports minus imports of goods and services, which had swung both positive and negative across the nineteenth century, had become positive, and was to stay that way" (Lindert 2000, p. 409) remains true, except that Lindert sees the turning point as "around 1900," whereas it is 1891 in this study.

For a given aggregate, let CR denote credits and DR debits. Then the balances presented in Table 5 are calculated as (CR–DR) or (X–M), the "level difference" between credits and debits (or, exports and imports) of the aggregate. Call this the "level balance" or just the "balance." I suggest an alternative definition of balance, which I term the "normalized balance," thus: 100 times (CR–DR)/(CR + DR) or (X–M)/(X + M). The "normalized balance" is the "level balance" divided by the sum of "the aggregates differenced for the level balance." In other words, the "normalized balance" is the balance expressed as percent of the "credits *plus* debits" *constituting the level balance*. (Alternatively, for a specified balance, "credits *plus* debits" *on current account* may be used as the denominator.) From some standpoints, the normalized balance is better conducive than the level balance for comparisons.

Figure 1 exhibits the normalized "goods" balance and the normalized "goods and services" balance.[6] There is clear co-movement; but

Table 5 Balances: Net Credits (millions of dollars)

Year	*Merchandise* (1)	*Goods* (2)	*Goods and Services* (3)	*Current Account* (4)	*Official Settlements* (5)	*Statistical Discrepancy* (6)
1790	−2	−2	−2	−3	0	−3
1791	−10	−9	−9	−9	7	−13
1792	−8	−8	−6	−7	2	−7
1793	−5	−5	−1	−2	2	0
1794	−10	−9	−4	−6	2	1
1795	−18	−17	−11	−14	−3	3
1796	−11	−10	−2	−6	−3	1
1797	−13	−12	−5	−9	−1	−13
1798	−1	0	8	5	−2	7
1799	4	6	17	13	3	15
1800	−14	−11	3	−1	1	3
1801	−3	0	15	13	−1	16
1802	0	2	11	8	−1	5
1803	−6	−3	4	−11	−1	−3
1804	−9	−8	4	−1	2	3
1805	−19	−17	−2	−8	1	−3
1806	−23	−23	−7	−12	1	−11
1807	−25	−26	−11	−16	2	−25
1808	−28	−28	−22	−27	4	−53
1809	−6	−3	9	5	4	6
1810	2	6	20	16	4	14
1811	16	20	32	28	−2	21
1812	−15	−12	−7	−10	−2	−13
1813	11	14	19	15	−2	4
1814	−11	−10	−10	−13	−2	−10
1815	−37	−36	−33	−36	2	−18
1816	−41	−39	−38	−41	0	−43
1817	4	5	8	6	0	−18
1818	−7	−6	1	0	0	−22
1819	−6	−5	−2	−3	0	−29
1820	4	4	12	9	0	2
1821	−9	−8	−4	−7	−4	−7
1822	−23	−22	−18	−19	−6	−8
1823	−7	−7	0	0	−1	0
1824	−5	−5	2	0	0	4
1825	−6	−5	−1	−2	−1	4

(continued)

Table 5 (continued)

Year	*Merchandise* (1)	*Goods* (2)	*Goods and Services* (3)	*Current Account* (4)	*Official Settlements* (5)	*Statistical Discrepancy* (6)
1826	−9	−8	−2	−4	2	−15
1827	−10	−9	−3	−2	0	−5
1828	−20	−19	−15	−15	0	−18
1829	0	0	6	7	3	5
1830	−1	−1	6	8	4	12
1831	−27	−26	−19	−15	−1	2
1832	−15	−14	−7	−3	1	5
1833	−3	−3	3	7	7	10
1834	1	1	7	10	14	13
1835	−21	−21	−18	−19	7	−1
1836	−37	−37	−32	−27	8	−15
1837	−10	−10	−3	−1	7	−25
1838	1	2	9	6	10	39
1839	−19	−18	−13	−20	−2	58
1840	31	31	43	40	−1	0
1841	7	7	11	12	−4	−14
1842	30	31	38	43	6	1
1843	38	39	46	48	14	30
1844	8	8	16	18	−2	31
1845	4	4	15	17	−2	27
1846	30	31	39	44	11	45
1847	28	29	34	38	6	45
1848	3	3	16	16	−4	28
1849	−11	−10	0	−3	−1	9
1850	−30	−29	−19	−26	−13	6
1851	−39	−38	−37	−39	−31	6
1852	−55	−54	−56	−55	−30	−8
1853	−67	−66	−73	−73	−30	−16
1854	−56	−54	−57	−60	−46	13
1855	−136	−135	−135	−148	−49	−69
1856	−139	−139	−142	−158	−51	−74
1857	−19	−20	−19	−28	−49	58
1858	−18	−20	−18	−32	−49	30
1859	−29	−28	−35	−55	−57	38
1860	−34	−32	−30	−54	−21	−27

(continued)

Table 5 (continued)

Year	*Merchandise* (1)	*Goods* (2)	*Goods and Services* (3)	*Current Account* (4)	*Official Settlements* (5)	*Statistical Discrepancy* (6)
1861	−22	−20	−17	−43	−4	−161
1862	−12	−5	−11	−30	−45	−60
1863	−138	−120	−156	−171	−108	−110
1864	−230	−202	−270	−299	−148	76
1865	−125	−104	−151	−187	−92	126
1866	−138	−116	−158	−217	−63	153
1867	−127	−103	−146	−219	−63	45
1868	−149	−126	−160	−265	−64	99
1869	−124	−105	−137	−261	−32	204
1870	−78	−61	−97	−222	−48	−376
1871	−150	−125	−171	−298	−56	52
1872	−164	−132	−188	−328	−43	−183
1873	−43	−10	−60	−187	−29	−169
1874	18	44	−3	−131	−38	−130
1875	55	78	40	−78	−44	−63
1876	149	169	141	36	−13	23
1877	235	249	228	147	2	−279
1878	283	292	269	197	2	126
1879	228	233	197	126	39	203
1880	217	222	185	97	87	137
1881	151	160	118	5	50	148
1882	78	88	41	−102	4	121
1883	84	96	46	−118	−6	150
1884	101	116	63	−105	−1	−187
1885	89	105	48	−111	−3	−183
1886	17	29	−43	−197	5	13
1887	−20	−9	−91	−248	28	−34
1888	−34	−18	−95	−260	−13	23
1889	15	32	−39	−218	−28	122
1890	60	70	−8	−214	−37	−282
1891	151	161	87	−134	−35	−207
1892	120	135	73	−132	−44	−209
1893	127	155	143	−32	−46	−128
1894	168	201	151	23	−17	−93
1895	99	129	63	−64	−54	−122

(continued)

Table 5 (continued)

Year	*Merchandise* (1)	*Goods* (2)	*Goods and Services* (3)	*Current Account* (4)	*Official Settlements* (5)	*Statistical Discrepancy* (6)
1896	207	239	179	54	−17	143
1897	467	496	475	349	75	277
1898	591	617	592	452	78	318
1899	555	580	545	365	24	262
1900	625	650	619	436	5	241
1901	592	617	580	378	8	132
1902	456	477	425	171	1	48
1903	453	474	376	63	8	50
1904	458	480	354	31	−11	9
1905	484	507	371	−4	9	−58
1906	511	529	400	−61	60	−4
1907	587	601	498	−58	70	−45
1908	538	552	413	−19	14	−96
1909	300	314	193	−277	−61	−144
1910	395	410	254	−262	−12	40
1911	584	603	428	−45	21	14
1912	656	682	502	14	−8	86
1913	619	650	466	−56	−27	84
1914	376	404	269	−141	−165	−542
1915	1859	1882	1923	1693	421	−179
1916	3118	3168	3315	3157	524	1376
1917	3306	3350	3244	3111	229	−1317
1918	3146	3335	2760	2674	−118	−1637
1919	4043	4212	3811	3532	285	1149

the goods-and-services balance appears greater algebraically in the earlier years, with the goods balance correspondingly higher toward the end of the full period.[7]

2.3 *Current Account*

The current-account balance is the goods-and-services balance *plus* net income credits *plus* net unilateral-transfer receipts. Alternatively, it is current-account credits *minus* current-account debits.[8] The current-account (level) balance is in column (4) of Table 5. The series is broadly consistent with the narratives of Lipsey (1963, p. 578) and Michael Edelstein (2006, pp. 5-441 to 442), that there were generally deficits

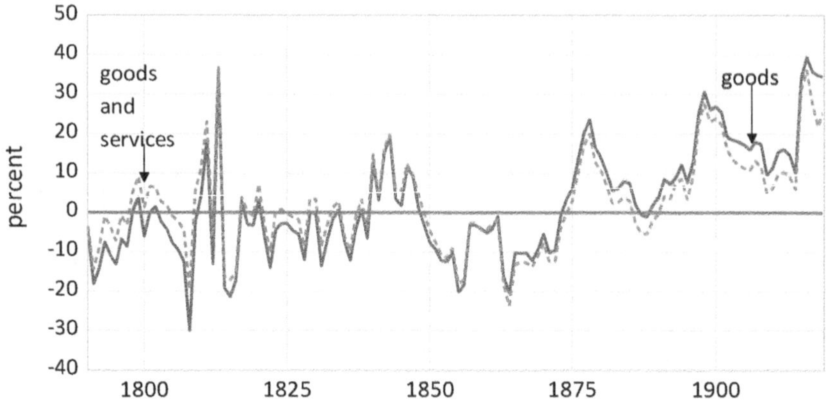

Fig. 1 Normalized balances: goods and services, 1790–1919. *Note* The "goods" balance is expressed as the percent of exports *plus* imports of goods, the "goods and services" balance as the percent of exports *plus* imports of goods and services

until the late 1890s, followed by years of surpluses—except that the new series has deficits in all but one year of the decade 1905–1914. Edelstein (2006, Table Ee-A) shows the annual average current-account balance of the *Historical Statistics* series for decades 1790–1799 to 1910–1919. Applying the same statistic to the new series, one finds that the averages are the same in sign but that the new series is distinctly greater *in magnitude* in nine of the 13 decades and is barely lower in another.

Edelstein also computes the average ratio of the current-account balance to GDP for decades beginning 1840–1849. Prior to 1840, the "Millennial Edition GDP series" (*Historical Statistics* 1975, series Ca10) that he utilizes exists for the isolated years 1800, 1810, 1820, 1830; and I thereupon extend his calculation. I compute the ratio of the new current-account-balance to the Louis D. Johnston and Samuel H. Williamson (measuringworth.com) GDP series, to correspond to Edelstein, and find again that the signs are in conformity and that the new ratio exceeds that of Edelstein in magnitude in nine of the 12 cases.

The normalized current-account balance is the "level balance" as a percent of current-account credits *plus* debits, and is shown in Fig. 2.

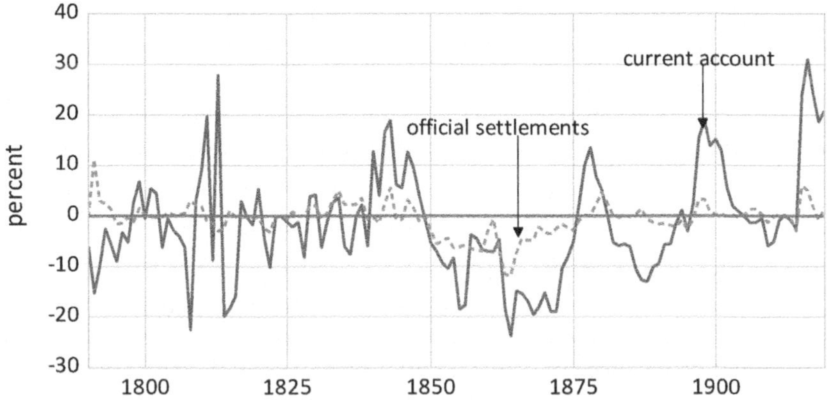

Fig. 2 Normalized balances: current account and official settlements, 1790–1919. *Note* The "current account" and "official settlements" balances are each expressed as the percent of current-account credits *plus* debits

2.4 Official Settlements

For our time period, *Historical Statistics* (1975, series U24) measures the official-settlements balance as the change in the monetary gold stock; but data are provided only from 1874.[9] My measure of official settlements begins in 1790, and is composed of the sum of (A) *the negative* of the sum of (1) net specie exports (thus including silver as well as gold until 1853) 1790–1919, (2) increase in earmarked gold held in the United States for foreign central banks and governments (net of gold held under earmark abroad for the Federal Reserve Banks) 1916–1919, (3) increase in foreign deposits at Federal Reserve Banks 1917–1919; and (B) government short-term capital outflow 1919.[10]

The official-settlements balance is exhibited in column (5) of Table 5. The low level relative to the current account is noticeable. In only 16 of the 130 years 1790–1919 is the magnitude of official settlements greater than the current-account balance. This finding is supported in the graph of the two normalized balances, both with respect to the sum of current-account credits and debits (Fig. 2). Official settlements are much closer to the zero line. One can infer that both the specie standard and the occasional paper standards under which the United States operated during 1790–1919 worked efficiently to remove imbalances.[11]

Conspicuous periods of balance-of-payments difficulty are the 1850s and the greenback period. Interestingly, the deviation of the *Historical Statistics* official-settlements balance from the new series over 1874–1919 averages only 1.4% of new-series current-account credits *plus* debits, and in only two years does it exceed three percent (and then barely).[12]

2.5 Financial Services

Financial services consist of investment income, marine insurance, and bankers' commissions. The financial-services balance is net income *plus* net marine-insurance *minus* bankers'-commissions debit. Figures 3 and 4 exhibit this balance for 1790–1860 and 1861–1919. The balance is in continuous deficit until near the end of the period. The issue is: how fast, over 1790–1919, did the United States reduce its dependence on London for financial services. The answer: not fast at all. The graphs show a trend deterioration in the level balance, reaching an algebraic minimum in 1907.[13] An upward trend follows; but not until 1915 does the balance become positive—then increasingly so.[14]

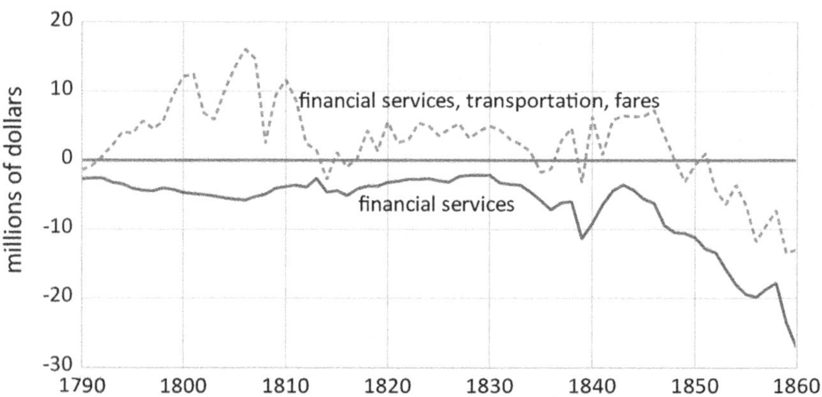

Fig. 3 Financial, transportation, fares balances, 1790–1860. *Note* Balance on "financial services" is net income credits *plus* net marine-insurance credits *minus* bankers'-commissions debits. Balance on "financial services, transportation, fares" is balance on financial services *plus* net transportation credits *plus* net passenger-fares credits. The 1790–1860 period is covered in this figure, the 1861–1919 period in Fig. 4

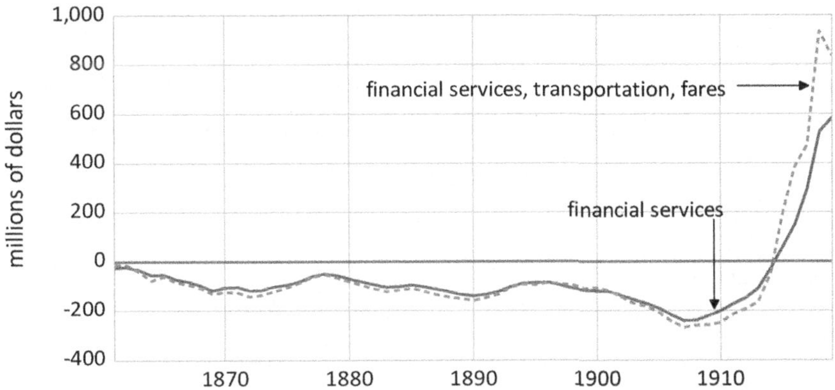

Fig. 4 Financial, transportation, fares balances, 1861–1919. *Note* See note to Fig. 3

2.6 Financial Services, Transportation, Fares

The "financial-transportation-fares" balance augments the financial-services balance with net transportation credits and net passenger-fares credits. The two balances are shown together in Figs. 3 and 4. The additions reduce the financial-services deficit or transform it to a surplus, throughout the antebellum period. Then they worsen the deficit 1863–1896 and again 1902–1914. Transportation and fares relate to oceanic shipping, which will be revisited in Chapter 20 (Sects. 1.2 and 2.2).

2.7 Statistical Discrepancy

I define statistical discrepancy as total measured credits ***minus*** total measured debits, or net measured credits.[15] I interpret this balance as the "unexplained residual" of the balance-of-payments table.[16] Statistical discrepancy is column (6) of Table 5. Throughout the antebellum period, annual statistical discrepancy is below $75 million in magnitude. From 1861 to 1913, it reaches $300 million in only two years. Only with World War I does the discrepancy climb above $1 billion.

For 13 decadal periods, Table 6 shows that the average level statistical discrepancy is quite low—less than $15 million in a majority of the periods. The table also provides averages of the ***normalized*** discrepancy,

Table 6 Statistical discrepancy (average over period)

Period	*Millions of Dollars*	*Percent of Current-Account Credits and Debits*	
		Algebraic Values	*Absolute Values*
1790–1799	−0.89	−3.05	6.30
1800–1809	−6.26	−4.54	7.71
1810 –1819	−11.38	−5.55	11.43
1820–1829	−3.84	−2.10	3.68
1830–1839	9.69	3.62	6.16
1840–1849	20.16	6.06	7.00
1850–1859	−1.58	0.01	4.10
1860–1869	34.61	0.02	10.28
1870–1879	−79.55	−5.09	10.26
1880–1889	31.09	1.45	5.80
1890–1899	−4.09	−0.45	8.86
1900–1909	13.22	0.84	2.41
1910–1919	−92.62	−0.97	5.80

defined as a percent of current-account credits *plus* debits. For algebraic values, only one figure exceeds six percent in magnitude, and that barely. Absolute values are a tougher test. Now the normalized discrepancies average over ten percent in three periods. One would expect statistical discrepancy to be higher in magnitude in earlier periods, when data are poorer. That does not appear to be generally true. In fact, neither algebraic nor absolute values show a pattern over time.

Whether the level and behavior of the residuals are consistent with a reliable balance-of-payments table is a matter of judgment. My belief is that the series in this volume are sufficiently reliable for most scholarly purposes. One must remember that all balance-of-payments series in this study are determined independent of the residual. Unquestionably, statistical discrepancy would be lower if I followed the North–Simon-Goldsmith (and thence *Historical Statistics*) practice of assigning all or part of the measured residual to capital flow.

Notes

1. As always for comparisons, in this chapter and elsewhere, conversion to calendar year and adjustment for the gold dollar are made.

2. Note that ship revenue means revenue *earned* by shipping, with ship sales included in goods.
3. Sum of columns (1)–(3) *minus* sum of columns (4)–(7).
4. Source is Lewis (1938, pp. 442, 445, 450, 520). For 1843, Lewis shows only gross liabilities, "not less than 225 million dollars." For that year, *Historical Statistics* (2006, series Ee23) states that gross assets are "less than $50 million," which I take as $25 million—whence net liabilities of $200 million. For 1914, to conform to Lewis, I convert the new series to midyear by averaging the 1913 and 1914 figures.
5. For the literature, see North (1961a, p. 81; 1961b, p. 196), Lipsey (1963, pp. 577–578; 2000, p. 692), Michael Edelstein (2006, pp. 5-441 to 442). For manufacturing, see Chapter 20, Sect. 3.
6. "Goods" credits consist of merchandise, silver, and ships; debits are merchandise, silver, and slaves. Both credits and debits of "services" incorporate transportation, travel, ship revenue, and marine insurance; but debits also include bankers' commissions, military expenditures, and non-imported slave purchases.
7. Note that, while the "level balance" of goods and services identically equals the balance of goods *plus* the balance of services, this equation is not true for the normalized balances.
8. Current-account credits and debits each emanate from goods, services, income, and unilateral transfers. Income receipts are long-term private and government; income payments are long-term private and short-term private. Unilateral transfers, both credits and debits, are private and government. Former convention included income in services rather than as a separate item (for example, *Historical Statistics* 1975).
9. The applicable correct definition is stated in *Historical Statistics* (1960, p. 560), not in *Historical Statistics* (1975, p. 861).
10. Change in earmarked gold is taken from Board of Governors of the Federal Reserve System (1943, p. 536), with the sign reversed (making an earmark increase comparable to a gold export—see, for example, BIPUS 1927, p. 50). Government short-term capital outflow is the purchase of foreign currencies, column (8) of Table 2 (Chapter 11).
11. For history of these standards, see Officer (1996, ch. 3).
12. A nod to the official gold-stock series; but note that the difficult periods are largely prior to the comparison years. For the comparison, the *Historical Statistics* series is converted to calendar year as needed, and its sign is reversed.
13. I do not normalize the financial-services or subsequent (Sect. 2.6) balance, because the level-balance coverage is limited (in particular, merchandise trade is excluded).

14. Existing literature limits the financial sector to investment income, but has broadly similar findings. See Lipsey (2000, p. 692) and Edelstein (2006, pp. 5-442 to 443).
15. Remember that *all* capital-account items are defined as change in stock (increase in assets positive, just as is increase in liabilities). Then net measured credits are current-account balance *plus* balance of long-term capital (gross long-term capital inflow *minus* long-term capital outflow [direct investment abroad *plus* portfolio investment abroad *plus* government long-term capital]) *plus* balance of private short-term capital (increase in mercantile debt *plus* dollars abroad) *plus* balance of government short-term capital (increase in foreign deposits at Federal Reserve Banks *minus* increase in government short-term capital) *plus* net specie outflow (net exports of specie *plus* increase in net earmarked gold).
16. Arguably, the principal items omitted from the table are short-term capital movements in the forms of foreign deposits in U.S. banks and U.S. deposits in foreign banks. But there is no basis to make the leap that statistical discrepancy reflects *primarily* the net flow of these items.

References

Board of Governors of the Federal Reserve System. 1943. *Banking and Monetary Statistics, 1914–1941*. Washington.

Edelstein, Michael. 2006. International Transactions and Foreign Commerce. In *Historical Statistics*, 5-441 to 444.

[*Historical Statistics*]. 1960. Bureau of the Census. *Historical Statistics of the United States, Colonial Times to 1957*. Washington: Government Printing Office.

———. 1975. Bureau of the Census. *Historical Statistics of the United States, Colonial Times to 1970, Bicentennial Edition*. Washington: Government Printing Office.

———. 2006. *Historical Statistics of the United States, Millennial Edition*, ed. Susan B. Carter, Scott Sigmund Gartner, Michael R. Haines, Alan L. Olmstead, Richard Sutch, Gavin Wright. Cambridge: Cambridge University Press.

Lewis, Cleona. 1938. *America's Stake in International Investments*. Washington: Brookings.

Lindert, Peter H. 2000. U.S. Foreign Trade and Trade Policy in the Twentieth Century. In *The Cambridge Economic History of the United States*, vol. 3, ed. Stanley L. Engerman and Robert E. Gallman, 407–462. Cambridge: Cambridge University Press.

Lipsey, Robert E. 1963. Foreign Trade. In *American Economic Growth*, ed. Lance E. Davis, and others, 548–581. New York: Harper & Row.

———. 2000. U.S. Foreign Trade and the Balance of Payments, 1800–1913. In *The Cambridge Economic History of the United States*, vol. 2, ed. Stanley L. Engerman and Robert E. Gallman, 685–732. Cambridge: Cambridge University Press.

———. 2008. Changing Patterns of International Investment in and by the United States. In *United States in the World Economy*, ed. Martin Feldstein, 475–517. Chicago: University of Chicago Press.

North, Douglass C. 1961a. *The Economic Growth of the United States, 1790–1860*. Englewood Cliffs: Prentice-Hall.

North, Douglass C. 1961b. The United States in the International Economy, 1790–1850. In *American Economic History*, ed. Seymour E. Harris, 181–206. New York: McGraw-Hill.

Officer, Lawrence H. 1996. *Between the Dollar-Sterling Gold Points*. Cambridge: Cambridge University Press.

CHAPTER 19

Structure

1 Openness

1.1 Trade

Did the U.S. economy become more or less open over time? The usual way to measure openness is to take ratios of trade to GDP. Previous authors confined trade to merchandise. It is more logical to include trade of both goods and services in the numerator. Figure 1 exhibits the ratios of goods-and-services total exports and total imports to GDP.[1] There is co-movement of the two ratios, and both show a trend decline until about 1910; but the subsequent sharp jump in the export ratio, with World War I, is not followed by imports. The conventional data and narrative are not inconsistent with these findings.[2] However, our ratios are naturally higher, with trade inclusive of services. This makes the United States much more of an open economy throughout 1790–1913 than, for example, the figures shown in Lipsey (2000, p. 691).

An even higher level of openness is achieved by taking the ratio of total credits and debits on current account to GDP, shown in Fig. 2. A variant is the ratio of total (exports *plus* imports) goods-and-services trade to GDP, with both numerator and denominator measured in *real* terms.[3] The graphs in Fig. 2 are broadly similar to those in Fig. 1; but the levels are higher.

L. H. Officer, *A New Balance of Payments for the United States, 1790–1919*, Palgrave Studies in American Economic History,
https://doi.org/10.1007/978-3-030-66099-4_19

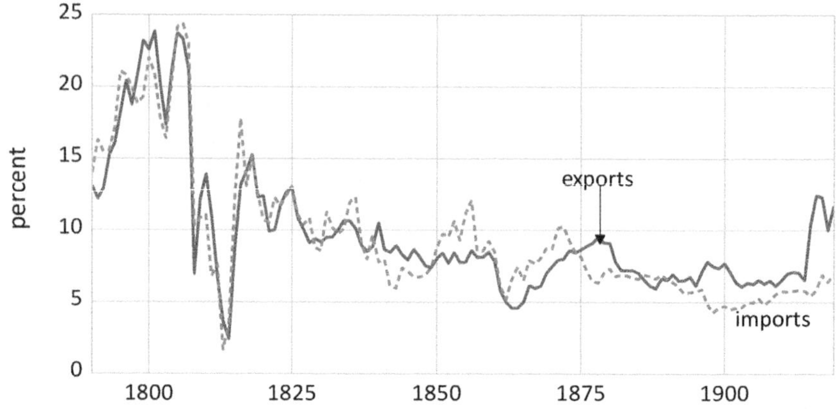

Fig. 1 Trade-GDP ratios, 1790–1919. *Note* "Exports" and "imports" are goods-and-services exports and imports, respectively, expressed as percent of GDP

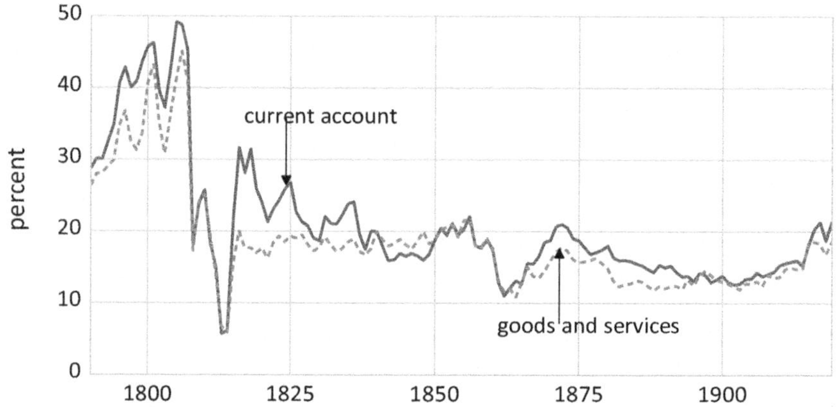

Fig. 2 Ratios of credits and debits to GDP, 1790–1919. *Note* "Goods and services" and "current account" are credits *plus* debits on goods-and-services and current account, respectively, expressed as percent of GDP

In all measures, openness drops sharply in 1808, after the Embargo Act, and never again reaches the high level of the pre-Embargo years.

1.2 *Capital*

Another approach to openness is financial dependence, with measures involving capital. A flow statistic is the ratio of the foreign long-term capital inflow (column (1), Table 2, Chapter 11) to gross private plus public fixed investment ("gross domestic investment)."[4] This "flow ratio" is graphed in Fig. 3. The level is generally low—averaging less than three percent over 1790–1919, compared to a higher average ratio of over five percent for 1799–1900 on the part of Davis and Cull (2000, p. 735); but they use different data and their measure is for *net* domestic investment.

There appears to be the absence of a trend in the "flow ratio," but there are prominent spikes. Indeed, the range is −51 to 50%![5] Consistent with other data (for example, Lipsey 2000, p. 696), the findings are in agreement that "in the aggregate, foreign capital cannot have played a major role [in American growth]" (Davis and Cull 2000, p. 809) and "The role of foreign capital appears to have been that of accommodating

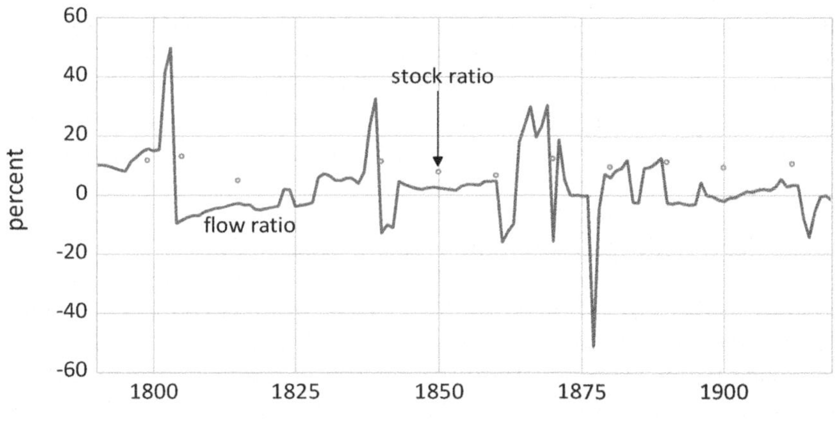

Fig. 3 Relative foreign-owned captial: stock and flow ratios, 1790–1919. *Note* "Flow ratio" is foreign long-term capital inflow expressed as percent of domestic gross fixed investment. "Stock ratio" is gross long-term liabilities to foreigners expressed as percent of domestic structures-and-equipment capital stock

capital needs for sharp bursts in U.S. growth or in the growth of particular sectors, especially capital-intensive ones" (Lipsey 2008, p. 514).

An alternative measure of openness in this sphere is the percent of the relevant domestic capital stock that is owned by foreigners. Lipsey (2000, p. 695; 2008, p. 477) computes the ratio of net foreign liabilities to the domestic capital stock, for 11 years spanning 1799 to 1912.[6] Lipsey's figures show a distinct downward movement, interrupted temporarily in 1840 and 1870; and the average is only 4.2%. Some of Lipsey's figures are cited approvingly by Edelstein (2006, pp. 5-442).

For the same years as Lipsey, I construct a conceptually superior series. The numerator is logically gross (not net) liabilities to foreigners; and I use long-term (not all) liabilities to foreigners, with direct investment at market prices (Chapter 12, Sect. 2.1). To correspond, rather than the entire capital stock, the denominator consists only of structures and equipment.[7] Plotted as 11 individual points in Fig. 3, the series averages 9.9% (more than double that of Lipsey) and exhibits no apparent trend.[8] If openness is gauged via my stock measure, the United States was more open than the conventional wisdom—and openness did not decrease—throughout 1799–1912.

Another indicator of U.S. financial openness is the stock of short-term debt financing merchandise trade. Going back to colonial times, "the British short-term capital market supplied working capital to American importers and exporters" (Platt 1984, p. 144). To measure this dependence, Fig. 4 plots the ratio of "stock of mercantile debt to foreigners" (column (5), Table 1, Chapter 11) to "sum of merchandise exports and imports" (column (1) *plus* column (2), Table 1, Chapter 6). Notwithstanding spikes or higher levels associated with the Jefferson Embargo, the War of 1812, and the Civil War, there is a distinct downward trend in the debt/trade ratio, from the global-maximum 55% in 1790.

World War I witnessed "a remarkable extension of American banks into foreign fields" (BWT 1919, p. 234), with the debt/trade ratio falling in half from 12.8% in 1914 to the global-minimum 6.4% in 1919. "All the while [from 1896 to 1913], the balance-of-payments strength of the United States was growing, and along with it resentment of foreign-exchange dependence on London, which financed U.S. trade even with third parties" (Officer 1996, p. 63—and see Chapter 18, Sect. 2).

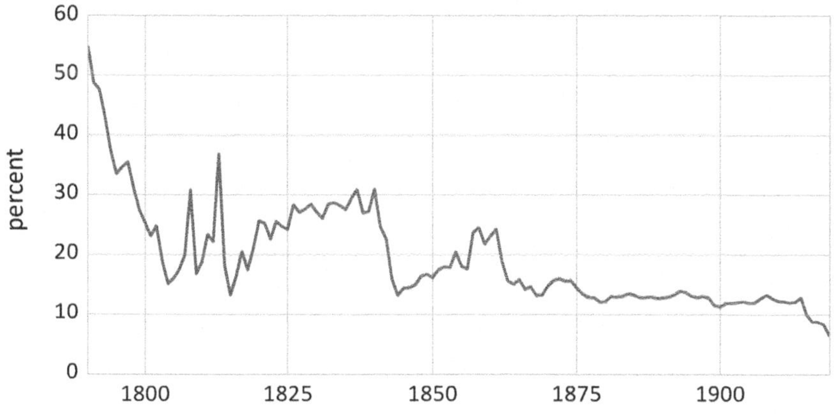

Fig. 4 Ratio of short-term mercantile debt to trade, 1790–1919. *Note* The series is the stock of mercantile debt to foreigners expressed as percent of "merchandise exports plus imports"

2 Goods-Versus-Services Economy

Did the U.S. transition from a goods economy to a services economy or vice versa, *relative to the rest of the world* (the U.S. international-transactions partners)? Comparing the balance of services with the balance of goods is one approach. The balance of goods is column (2) of Table 5 in Chapter 18, and the balance of services is column (3) *minus* column (2). The results are remarkable. Until 1852, the balance of services is in surplus in all but one year (1814), and that year it is trivially negative. From 1862 onward, the balance of services is in continuous deficit. In contrast, the balance of goods is in deficit in all but 11 years 1790–1839. After a run of surpluses in the 1840s, it is in deficit again until 1873—but thereupon, except for 1887–1888, uniformly in surplus. Most tellingly, the balance of goods exceeds the balance of services in only ten years until 1872, but in every year thereafter. The suggestion is that the United States may have had a comparative advantage in services relative to goods until the early 1870s, but that this relationship reversed itself in the final quarter of the nineteenth century.

The switch of the United States from comparative advantage in services to that in goods is also illustrated via comparison of the share of services in real exports of goods and services versus the share of services in real

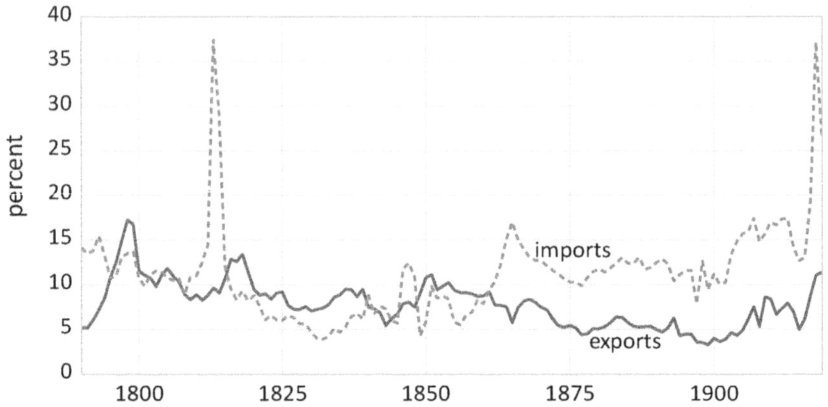

Fig. 5 Share of services, 1790–1919. *Note* "Exports" is the percent of services in real exports of goods and services, "imports" the percent of services in real imports of goods and services

imports of goods and services. These shares presumably shed light on the U.S. goods-services production structure. The underlying real-trade series are constructed in Appendix 1, and the shares are exhibited in Fig. 5.

The peaks in the import graph are associated with the War of 1812 and the end of World War I. Interesting is the result for the antebellum period versus thereafter. During the antebellum period, the share of services in imports exceeds that of exports in only 22 of the 71 years. From 1861 onward, the services proportion of imports is *uniformly* higher than that of exports. The structure of the U.S. economy became strongly goods-oriented rather than services-oriented *relative to its trading partners*, and remained there throughout the postbellum period. The conventional statement that the United States became an "industrial power" (Lipsey 2000, p. 717) is supported in the behavior of international transactions.

3 Terms of Trade

Terms of trade (TT) are defined as the ratio of the price of exports to the price of imports. For given volumes of exports and imports, TT increasing enhances the welfare of the country. Lipsey (2000, p. 718) provides figures for the U.S. TT for 14 periods 1789–1913. His series has three deficiencies, absent here. First, as are all existing historical TT, Lipsey's are confined to merchandise trade.[9] A complete measurement requires that goods involve non-merchandise as well as merchandise items, and that services also are included. Second, Lipsey shows only period averages, whereas a continuous annual series is preferred. Third, as is the norm, Lipsey's TT are essentially a ratio of Laspeyres index numbers with disjoint changes in weights over time. In contrast, I use implicit deflators, which have the advantage of incorporating continuous changing weights of components.

So, in Fig. 6, I present the first-ever goods TT, services TT, and combined goods-and-services TT, for 1790–1919 (based 1790 = 100).[10] Lipsey (2000, p. 717) writes: "On the whole, the picture is one of long-term improvement in the terms of trade—perhaps an increase of two-thirds from the founding of the country to World War I." The 1904–1913/1789–1798 ratio for his merchandise series is 1.71. For my goods series the ratio is 1.66—almost exactly his "two-thirds" assessment. There is a marked difference for services, with the ratio only 0.57—a TT *decrease* of over 40%; while goods-and-services together have a ratio of 1.45.

TT of goods have an upward trend from the 1820s—and, after 1866, never fall below 160. From a global maximum of 128 in 1793, TT of services fall to 72 in 1815; after which they are below 60 in all but seven years until World War I. Terms-of-trade movement in conjunction with the balances of goods and services suggests that the United States was fortunate indeed to experience a shift in revealed comparative advantage

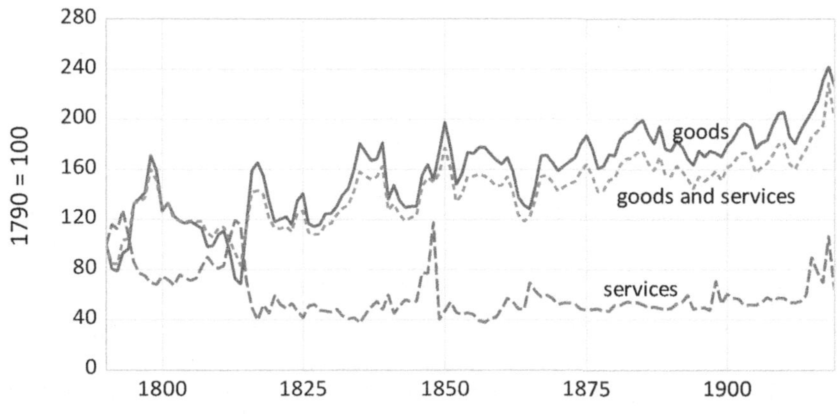

Fig. 6 Terms of trade: goods and services, 1790–1919. *Note* "Goods," "services," and "goods and services" are the terms-of-trade for goods, services, goods and services combined. Terms of trade are the ratio of price of exports to price of imports. The series are denominated on base 1790 = 100

from services to goods! And U.S. businesspersons and merchants were wise to respond to price incentives in their import-export trade of goods and services.

For decomposition of the goods-and-services TT, consider Sect. 4.

4 Goods-and-Services Ratios

Exports and imports of goods-and-services combined can each be aggregated in current-dollar and constant-dollar denomination (per steps (1) and (2) in note 10). Figure 7 exhibits the current-dollar and the constant-dollar goods-plus-services export/import ratio.[11] Note that a value of unity indicates balanced trade in goods and services. The graphs show the balance of trade as a ratio, for both current-dollar and constant-dollar denomination. With the unity line denoting balanced trade, the United States has a *continuous* current-dollar surplus only from 1891 onward, but has a "real" surplus throughout 1790–1919 in all but three years (1855–1856, 1868). Note that these statements are relative to the year-1919 imposed equality of current-dollar and constant-dollar ratios (at 1.70, a surplus in both nominal and real terms).

For another interpretation of Fig. 7, take the ratio of the current-dollar series to the constant-dollar series. That ratio can be re-expressed as the

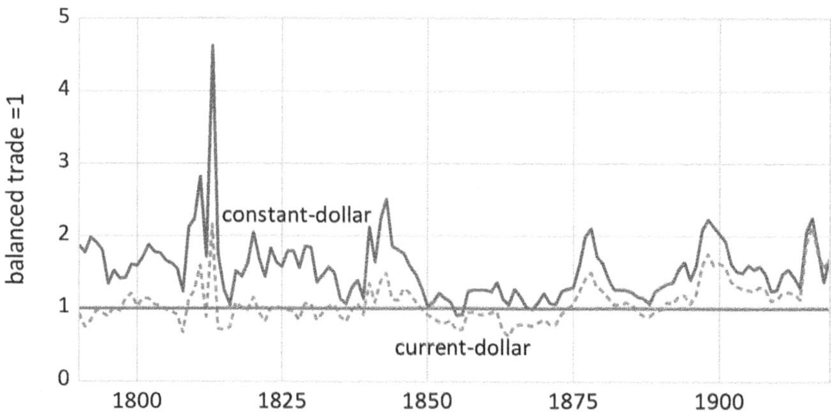

Fig. 7 Export/import goods-and-services ratios, 1790–1919. *Note* "Current-dollar" is goods-and-services exports divided by goods-and-services imports. "Constant dollar" is constant-dollar goods-and-services exports divided by constant-dollar goods-and-services imports

exports goods-and-services deflator divided by the imports goods-and-services deflator; it is the goods-and-services TT normalized at 1919 = 1. The imposed equality of the constant-dollar ratio to the current-dollar ratio in 1919 is another way of stating that (originally based) TT are unity in that year (step (4) in note 10).

Movements of the TT are associated with divergence between the current-dollar and constant-dollar series. For analyzing the balance of payments, the current-dollar ratio is pertinent; for examining real GDP, the constant-dollar ratio applies. Figure 7 is an indicator that, *even with the balance in ratio form*, it is dangerous to assume that the current-dollar balance is representative of the constant-dollar balance.

Appendix 1: Constant-Dollar Goods and Services

To the best of my knowledge, a systematic set of constant-dollar series for the U.S. historical goods-and-services account has not previously been published. In this Appendix, individual items in goods and services—developed in *current dollars* in Chapters 6–9, 13–17—are re-expressed in *constant (1919) dollars*. Two alternative techniques are utilized. Either a price index (base 1919 = 1) deflates the current-dollar series, or a direct physical measure of the item is applied. In the latter case, the physical measure is converted to constant-dollar form via linking to the current-dollar figure for 1919. Thus all constant-dollar series are expressed in "millions of 1919 dollars" (corresponding to current-dollar series in "millions of current dollars").

A. Goods

Exports: Real exports of conventional merchandise are current-dollar exports divided by the price index of merchandise exports. Real exports of merchandise silver are current-dollar exports divided by the price of silver (*Historical Statistics* 1975, series M270). Real exports of ships are derived physically via tonnage sold to foreigners. Constant-dollar exports of goods are the sum of the three real components.

Imports: Real imports of conventional merchandise are current-dollar imports divided by the price index of merchandise imports. Real imports of merchandise silver are current-dollar imports divided by the price of silver. Current-dollar imports of slaves are total revenues from U.S.-ship and foreign-ship imports of slaves, that is, the sum of columns (1–3) in Table 1 (Chapter 9). I convert year-1807 current-dollar imports to constant (1919) dollars via multiplication by the 1919/1807 ratio of the wholesale price index.[12] For the other years, that resulting figure is multiplied by the ratio of the number of imported slaves to the number in 1807.[13] Thus a physical measure of slave imports extends the "constant-dollar" 1807 figure to the other years, and, as with the current-dollar measure, does not account for the value of the damaged and destroyed lives of the enslaved persons themselves. Again, constant-dollar imports of goods are the sum of the three constant-dollar components.

B. Services

B1. Transportation

Deflators are developed using four sets of weights: 1860 weights for 1790–1860, 1879 weights for 1860–1879, 1913 weights for 1879–1913, 1919 weights for 1913–1919, with one-year linking of the resulting series segments. The year 1860 is the final antebellum year; 1879 marks the end of the greenback period, and 1913 is the final normal year before World War I. The weight of an item is the proportion of its value in total transportation exports or imports, as the case may be, and the corresponding price index is based at 1919 = 1.

For exports, the items and price indexes are (a) merchandise freight earnings: freight rate for merchandise exports; (b) specie freight earnings: specie freight rate; (c) port-costs earnings: wholesale price index; (d) transit earnings: overland-exports freight rate. For imports, they are (a) merchandise freight payments and charter payments: freight rate for merchandise imports; (b) specie freight payments: specie freight rate; (c) port-costs payments: U.K. wholesale price index; (d) transit payments: freight rate for inland imports from Canada.[14]

B2. Travel

Exports of travel services are deflated by the price index for foreign travel expenditures in the United States. Imports (U.S. travel expenditures abroad) are deflated by the current-year weighted average of U.S.-resident-travel United Kingdom and Canada indexes, with weights the proportions of U.S.-citizen expenditures overseas versus in Canada and Mexico.

B3. Passenger-Ship Revenue

Rather than constructing price deflators to be applied to the current-dollar series of passenger-ship revenue (fares), I obtain the corresponding "real" series via physical measure: number of passengers. This yields constant-dollar series of greater precision, albeit the procedure lacks an index-number basis. The number of one-way passengers represents "real" oceanic passenger service (ship revenue). A round-trip counts as two one-way trips.

U.S. steamship constant-dollar revenue from foreign residents is set equal to current-dollar revenue in 1919 and extrapolated to earlier years via number of foreign passengers on U.S. steamships (1919 overlap, of course). Foreign steamship constant-dollar revenue from U.S. residents is similarly derived.

The above technique cannot be applied to sailing-ship revenue, because there is zero such revenue in 1919. The solution is to express sailing-ship revenue in 1860 dollars, then extrapolate to 1919 dollars via an inflator factor. The inflator series is steamship per-passenger revenue, dollars per one-way trip, constructed as the ratio of all steamship revenue (U.S. and foreign steamships, revenue from U.S. and foreign residents) to all steamship passengers (U.S. and foreign steamships, number of U.S. and foreign passengers). The inflator factor is the 1919/1860 ratio of the inflator series.

Thus U.S. sailing-ship constant-dollar revenue from foreign residents is set equal to current-dollar revenue in 1860, extrapolated to other years (forward and back, 1860 overlap) via the number of U.S. sailing-ship foreign passengers (resulting in a constant-1860-dollar series), and multiplied by the inflator factor (for the constant-1919-dollar series). Foreign sailing-ship constant-dollar revenue from U.S. residents is similarly generated.

U.S.-ship constant-dollar revenue from foreign residents is the sum of U.S. steamship and U.S. sailing-ship constant-dollar revenues. Foreign-ship constant-dollar revenue from U.S. residents is the sum of foreign steamship and foreign sailing-ship constant-dollar revenues.

B4. Financial Transactions

Deflators for financial transactions are ideally based on the wage rate in the financial sector of the country providing the services. The second best is a clerical or white-collar wage of the country, and the third best the unskilled or manual-worker wage. Where a wage rate is not available (or, for consistency), weekly or annual earnings are adopted.

For exports, the deflator begins with Lebergott's (1996, Table A7, series 46) deflator for personal expenditures on finance 1900–1919. Linked to it via 1900 overlap is a clerical-wage series constructed as follows. Railways clerical average annual earnings 1890–1900 (Douglas 1930, p. 361) are extended to 1860, 1869, 1879, 1889 (1899 overlap) via weekly wage of clerks and weekly wage in retail trade (Lebergott 1964, pp. 300–301; Barger 1960, p. 329).[15] Average hourly earnings of manufacturing production workers (Officer 2009, p. 166) 1859–1889 interpolates 1861–1868, 1870–1878, 1880–1888. Monthly wage of white-collar workers 1822–1860 (Margo 2000, Table 5B.4), monthly wage of clerks in iron-producing firms 1800–1822 (Jeffrey F. Zabler 1972, p. 112), and the David and Solar (1977, p. 59) unskilled wage 1790–1800 extrapolate the series to 1790 (via 1860, 1822, 1800 overlaps).[16]

For imports, a weighted average of men and women clerk's pay for 1911–1919 is generated from data in Guy Routh (1980, pp. 7, 90), using Feinstein's (1995, pp. 264–265) manual-worker earnings as wage interpolator.[17] Linked via 1911 overlap is a clerical-earnings series developed from Jeffrey G. Williamson's (1982, p. 48, series 9H) figures for 15 years over 1781–1911, with intervening years interpolated by Feinstein's (1998, pp. 652–653) manual-worker earnings series.[18] The resulting series for 1790–1919 is denominated in U.S. dollars, via the dollar-pound exchange rate.

B5. Military Expenditures Abroad

Armed forces overseas are extrapolated from 1917–1919 to 1846–1848, 1898–1916 via 1917 overlap with total military personnel on active duty (*Historical Statistics* 2006, series Ed26). Constant-dollar is set equal to current-dollar military expenditures abroad in 1919 and extrapolated to the earlier years via armed forces overseas. With no direct data, constant-cost military expenditures are estimated by the number of personnel stationed overseas. The implicit assumption is that the cost of maintaining a soldier overseas in earlier years is the same, adjusted for inflation, as it was in 1919. (See Sect. 1 of Chapter 17).

B6. Non-imported Slave Purchases

Just as for imports, I convert year-1807 current-dollar non-imported slave purchases to constant (1919) dollars via multiplication by the 1919/1807 ratio of the wholesale price index. For the other years, the resulting figure is multiplied by the ratio of "the number of U.S-ship purchased slaves not imported into the United States" to "this number in 1807."[19]

B7. Totals

Constant-dollar exports of services are the sum of constant-dollar transportation exports, travel exports, U.S.-ship passenger revenue, and financial exports. Constant-dollar imports of services are the sum of constant-dollar transportation imports, travel imports, foreign-ship passenger revenue, financial imports, military expenditures abroad, and non-imported slave purchases.

Appendix 2: Gross Domestic Investment

Gross domestic investment is composed of gross producers' durables and gross construction. For 1909–1919, the Kuznets (undated, Tables T-12, column (1); T-9, column (5)) series remain unsurpassed. For the earlier years, producers' durables and construction are considered in detail.

A. Gross Producers' Durables: 1790–1908

Years with reliable current-dollar figures serve as benchmarks: 1839, 1844, 1849, 1854, 1859, from Gallman (1966, p. 34, column (1)); 1869, 1879, 1889, 1899–1909, from Gallman and Paul W. Rhode (2019, p. 111).[20] I am cognizant that the Gallman "interpolation and extrapolation procedures are useful for determining long-run trends but, as Gallman noted, problematic for analyzing business-cycle fluctuations" (Gallman and Rhode 2019, p. 114). So I take care that the figures between benchmarks are not merely trend-based estimates but also incorporate cyclical movements.

Therefore, to estimate the remaining years, I construct a cycle-friendly synthetic producers'-durables series: the product of (1) machinery industrial production and (2) the implicit price deflator for producers' durables.[21] The synthetic series interpolates the current-dollar series between the benchmark years and extrapolates the current-dollar series to 1790 via the 1839 overlap.

B. Gross Construction: 1790–1908

For 1790–1862, construction is the sum of three components: canals, railroads, and other construction. For 1863–1908, only railroad and nonrailroad construction are distinguished.

B1. Canals: 1790–1862

Total canal investment (construction) for 1815–1860 is in Harvey H. Segal (1961, pp. 208–209), for 1861 in Segal (1956, p. 108).[22] The wage for "common labor" on the Erie Canal is unchanged 1852–1862 (Smith 1963, p. 304); hence I am comfortable estimating canal construction in 1862 as the 1862/1861 mileage ratio times construction in 1861. For 1790–1815 and 1861–1862, I obtain the mileage of completed canals from Walter Isard (1942, p. 150) and Christopher T. Baer (1981, pp. 58–59).[23] I generate synthetic canal investment for 1790–1815 as the product of the David-Solar unskilled wage and the completed-canals mileage. The synthetic series extrapolates investment to 1790 via the 1815 overlap.

B2. Railroads: 1790–1908

Current-dollar railroad construction 1828–1860 is in Fishlow (1965, pp. 385, 389).[24] The figures for 1860 and 1869–1909 are the product of constant [1860]-dollar construction and a railroad-construction price index (1860 = 1). Constant-dollar construction equals current-dollar construction in 1860, and is the Gallman and Rhode (2019, p. 108) series 1869–1909. Per Fishlow (1965, p. 390), the price index—generated 1860–1909—has weights "building and materials" 0.1, "iron rail" 0.3, and "unskilled labor" 0.6; but I use different component price indexes.[25] A synthetic current-dollar railroad-construction series is the product of the railroad-construction price index and railroad mileage built (*Historical Statistics* 2006, series Df882).[26] This series interpolates current-dollar construction 1861–1868 between 1860 and 1869.

B3. Other Construction: 1790–1862

The current-dollar figure for 1839 is in Gallman (1966, p. 61). Figures for 1844, 1849, 1854, and 1859 are the product of constant [1860]-dollar "other gross new construction" (Gallman and Rhode 2019, p. 107) and a price index (1860 = 1) of construction costs (Brady 1966, pp. 110–111).[27] The foundation of an inter/extrapolator series is current-dollar total (residential plus nonresidential) building (Manuel Gottlieb, 1965, p. 417) for 1850–1869. The Gottlieb series is extrapolated to 1830 via 1850 overlap with the total value of building permits, Riggleman series as adjusted by Isard (Miles L. Colean and Robinson Newcomb 1952, pp. 226–227) 1830–1850. Pleasingly, both series exclude railroad and canal construction; unfortunately, they also exclude bridges, roads, and like construction.

For 1785–1830, lumber and wood constituted three times the cost of metal in construction (Adams 1975, p. 797). The Davis "wood and paper" and "metals" industrial-production indexes are weighted 0.75 and 0.25 accordingly, for 1827–1830; and the resulting index is extended to 1790 via total industrial production (1827 overlap). The product of this index and the Adams (1975, pp. 811–812, column (7)) "construction-cost index (with substitution)" serves to extrapolate the Gottlieb-Isard series to 1790 via the 1830 overlap. The extended Gottlieb-Isard series interpolates inter-benchmark years of "other construction" 1839–1859, and extrapolates "other construction" back to 1790 and forward to 1862, via 1839 and 1859 overlaps.

B4. Nonrailroad Construction: 1863–1908

Railroad current-dollar gross construction, 1869–1909 is the product of constant [1860]-dollar railroad construction (Gallman and Rhode 2019, p. 108) and an index of cost of road, rebased to 1860 = 1 (Melville J. Ulmer 1960, pp. 275–276, column (8)). Nonrailroad construction is the difference between total gross new construction (Gallman and Rhode 2019, p. 109) and railroad construction 1869–1909, the sum of canal and "other construction" for 1862, and then interpolated 1863–1868 via the Gottlieb-Isard series.

B5. Total Series and Components

Table 1 shows the series of gross domestic investment. The shares of the components are graphed in Fig. 8. For 1863–1908, "other construction" includes canal investment. The spike in producers' durables occurs during the Civil War.

Table 1 Gross domestic investment (millions of dollars)

Year	*Investment*
1790	11
1791	12
1792	13
1793	15
1794	17
1795	19
1796	23
1797	22
1798	22
1799	23
1800	26
1801	28
1802	26
1803	27
1804	26
1805	28
1806	30
1807	32
1808	30
1809	36
1810	39
1811	43
1812	44
1813	48
1814	58
1815	63
1816	51
1817	50
1818	53
1819	49
1820	51
1821	53
1822	55
1823	55
1824	61
1825	64
1826	66
1827	68
1828	79
1829	70

(continued)

Table 1 (continued)

Year	*Investment*
1830	67
1831	87
1832	133
1833	157
1834	163
1835	198
1836	331
1837	199
1838	172
1839	171
1840	155
1841	178
1842	146
1843	137
1844	182
1845	236
1846	307
1847	372
1848	323
1849	292
1850	347
1851	403
1852	472
1853	566
1854	572
1855	537
1856	584
1857	684
1858	536
1859	574
1860	598
1861	516
1862	600
1863	777
1864	1105
1865	968
1866	1025
1867	1189
1868	1265
1869	1382

(continued)

Table 1 (continued)

Year	*Investment*
1870	1353
1871	1401
1872	1917
1873	1961
1874	1510
1875	1007
1876	966
1877	808
1878	1252
1879	1440
1880	1900
1881	2452
1882	2610
1883	2348
1884	2168
1885	2001
1886	2494
1887	2703
1888	2655
1889	2560
1890	3474
1891	3059
1892	3543
1893	2867
1894	2521
1895	2622
1896	2271
1897	2541
1898	2791
1899	3165
1900	3804
1901	4019
1902	4565
1903	4495
1904	4204
1905	4839
1906	5898
1907	6369
1908	5117
1909	5965

(continued)

Table 1 (continued)

Year	*Investment*
1910	6267
1911	5781
1912	6553
1913	7241
1914	5519
1915	5527
1916	7414
1917	9392
1918	11,714
1919	12,590

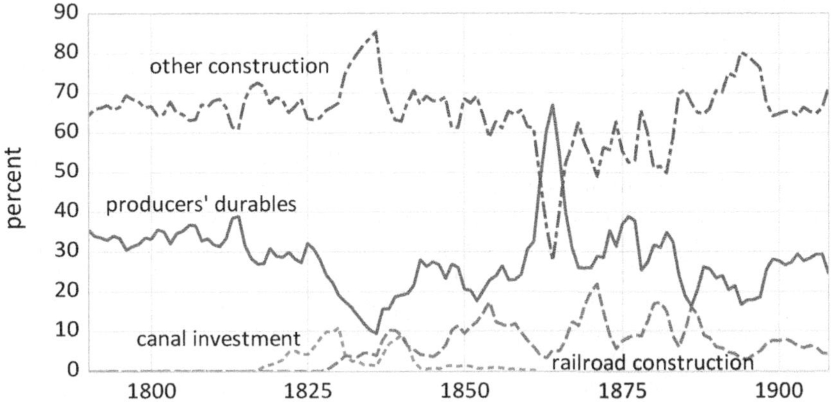

Fig. 8 Gross domestic investment: components, 1790–1908. *Note* The series are the percentage shares of the components of gross domestic investment. After 1862, "other construction" incorporates "canal investment"

Notes

1. Throughout the study, I adopt the Johnston-Williamson series (measuringworth.com) as the GDP measure.
2. See Lipsey (2000, pp. 685, 690–692) and Edelstein (2006, p. 5-441).
3. Real GDP is the Johnston-Williamson constant-dollar series converted to 1919 dollars. The series of real goods and services (in constant-1919 dollars) are constructed in Appendix 1.
4. The series "gross domestic investment" is developed in Appendix 2.

5. Of course, gross domestic investment cannot be negative; but that is not true for capital movements.
6. For a consistent figure for 1912, I extrapolate via the 1900 overlap of the data in his two writings.
7. The series, in current dollars, is developed from data in Gallman (1986, p. 204; 1992, pp. 82, 87, 94). The benchmark figure is for 1805. For other years, the proportion of structures and equipment in the domestic capital stock adjusts the stock. The 1912 figure is obtained via year-1900 overlap with the Goldsmith (1962, p. 117) sum of structures and producer-durables.
8. The years are 1799, 1805, 1815, 1840, 1850, 1860, 1870, 1880, 1890, 1900, 1912.
9. The merchandise TT series of *Historical Statistics* (2006, series Ee433, Ee436, Ee439, Ee442) have data sources identical to mine, but do not adjust the underlying price series for the gold dollar, fiscal year, or change in base. See the Appendix to Chapter 7.
10. The TT series are constructed in five steps. (1) Current-dollar series of six aggregates—exports and imports of goods, services, goods-and-services combined (the last by summation)—are assembled (Chapter 18, Sects. 1.1, 1.2). (2) Real (constant [1919]-dollar) series for the same six aggregates are generated (Appendix 1). (3) Implicit deflators for the six aggregates (goods, services, goods-and-services; exports, imports of each) are calculated as current-dollar/constant-dollar ratios. (4) For the three series—goods, services, goods-and-services combined: TT, base 1919 = 1, are computed as the export/import deflator ratio. (5) Division by the 1790 figure and multiplication by 100 converts the three TT series to base 1790 = 100.
11. Exports of goods and services divided by imports of goods and services, alternatively in current dollars and in constant dollars.
12. The extrapolator is inadequate statistically, but little else can be done to denominate slave imports in 1919 dollars—a century after slave imports ended! The base 1807 is logical, because that is the highest-activity slave-import year, whether in numbers or value. More fundamentally, though the technique is a logical way to adjust the data from a balance-of-payments standpoint, what results is an inadequate measure of the cruelty associated with enslavement and sale of human beings.
13. The number of imported slaves is the sum of columns (2)–(4) in Table 1 (Chapter 4).
14. The U.K. wholesale price index has components Board of Trade total index, Sauerbeck-*Statist* overall index, and Gayer-Rostow-Schwartz domestic-and-imported commodities index, linked via overlap years 1846 and 1871. Source is Mitchell (1988, pp. 721, 725, 728–729). The index

is converted to dollar denomination via multiplication by the dollar-pound exchange rate.

15. For 1869, 1879, 1889, 1899, weekly wage is the product of hourly wage and hours per week.
16. The Margo and Zabler data are controversial—for discussion and references, see Officer (2009, pp. 144–146, 150–151)—but, regarding the white-collar wage, their series are the best available for the purpose at hand. For lack of white-collar wage data in the eighteenth century, the David-Solar unskilled wage is used.
17. Routh's wage data are for 1911–1913, 1924. Feinstein's series interpolates 1914–1919. Routh's numbers of male clerks and of female clerks are linearly interpolated 1912–1919 between 1911 and 1921.
18. The Williamson years are 1781, 1797, 1805, 1810, 1815, 1819, 1827, 1835, 1851, 1861, 1871, 1881, 1891, 1901, 1911.
19. The number is: slaves embarked in Africa less those disembarked revenue-earning in the United States (column (1) *minus* column (2), Table 1, Chapter 4) *plus* creole slaves landed in Havana (column (5) *plus* column (6), Table 2, Chapter 4).
20. The Gallman-Rhode figures for 1869–1909 are revisions of Kuznets, who relies heavily on the work of William H. Shaw (1947). Shaw's data are excellent for the postbellum Census years (1869, 1879, 1889, 1899, 1904, 1909); but his interpolator series are satisfactory only for 1899–1919 (see Shaw 1947, pp. 98, 100–101; Richard Sutch 2006, p. 3-58). The *adopted* figures spanning 1839–1899 are reliable, because Gallman constructs them by working with, and carefully improving the federal Census data ("major benchmark years") and state censuses ("minor benchmark years").

    Gallman (1966, p. 34) and Gallman and Rhode (2019, p. 104) are correct that Census years (ending in "9") over 1869–1909 are calendar years. I also adopt that the Census years ending May 31 in 1840, 1850, 1860, correspond to the calendar years 1839, 1849, 1859 (see *Historical Statistics* 2006, pp. 3–13, and Officer 2009, pp. 35–36).
21. Series (1) is taken from Davis (2004), with years 1790–1826 extrapolated via total industrial production on the basis of the 1827 overlap. Series (2) begins with figures for the benchmark years spanning 1839–1899, the ratio of current-dollar figures per above to constant [1860]-dollar figures in Gallman and Rhode (2019, pp. 107–108). A secondary price series is obtained from the producer-durable price index in Shaw (1947, p. 294) for 1869, 1879, 1889–1899, with the Warren and Pearson (1933, pp. 25–26) wholesale price index of "metals and metal products" interpolating Shaw 1870–1878 and 1880–1888, and extrapolating 1790–1868 via the 1869 overlap. (For 1792 Warren and Pearson, the common figure for

1791 and 1793 is taken.) The extended Shaw index interpolates the inter-benchmark years of the implicit price deflator and extrapolates the deflator to 1790 (via the 1839 overlap).

22. Segal (1961, p. 209) states that investment in 1815 is "less than $10,000," which I take to be $5000. The figure for 1861 is for New York alone; there is no evidence of construction activity outside that state.
23. For any given year, the larger figure in the two sources is adopted. There is zero construction 1790–1793, 1795–1801, 1806, 1809, 1813–1814.
24. For 1840–1860, investment is the sum of "current dollar outlay on road" and "current dollar outlay on ties & iron." Equipment is excluded, to avoid double-counting with producers' durables. Investment is zero prior to 1828.
25. Wholesale price index of building materials from Warren and Pearson (1933, pp. 26–27); price of rails from *Historical Statistics* (2006, series Cc243, Cc244—linked via 1867 overlap); unskilled wage from Margo (2000, Table 5B.4) 1859–1860, extended to 1909 via 1860 overlap with the David-Solar wage.
26. The mileage series may be an underestimate (*Historical Statistics* 2006, p. 4-918), but is used only for interpolation.
27. Following Gallman (1966, p. 41), the price index is an unweighted average of the indexes "houses, churches, schools" and "factories, office buildings." The 1859 figure for "factories, office buildings" is estimated as the 1859/1854 ratio of "houses, churches, schools" *times* the 1854 figure for "factories, office buildings."

References

Adams, Donald R., Jr. 1975. Residential Construction Industry in the Early Nineteenth Century. *Journal of Economic History* 35 (December): 794–816.

Baer, Christopher T. 1981. *Canals and Railroads of the Mid-Atlantic States, 1800–1860*. Regional Economic History Research Center. Eleutherian Mills-Hagley Foundation.

Barger, Harold. 1960. Income Originating in Trade, 1869–1929. In *Output, Employment, and Productivity in the United States*, ed. Dorothy S. Brady, 327–361. New York: Columbia University Press.

Brady, Dorothy S. 1966. Price Deflators for Final Product Estimates. In *Output, Employment, and Productivity in the United States*, ed. Dorothy S. Brady, 91–115. New York: Columbia University Press.

Bullock, Charles J., John H. Williams, and Rufus S. Tucker [BWT]. 1919. The History of Our Foreign Trade Balance During the Great War. *Review of Economics and Statistics* 1 (July): 234–254.

Colean, Miles L., and Robinson Newcomb. 1952. *Stabilizing Construction: The Record and Potential*. New York: McGraw-Hill.

David, Paul A., and Peter Solar. 1977. A Bicentenary Contribution to the History of the Cost of Living in America. *Research in Economic History* 2: 1–80.

Davis, Joseph H. 2004. An Annual Index of U.S. Industrial Production, 1790–1915. *Quarterly Journal of Economics* 119 (November): 1177–1215, data appendix http://www.nber.org/data/industrial-production-index/.

Davis, Lance E., and Robert J. Cull. 2000. International Capital Movements, Domestic Capital Markets, and American Economic Growth, 1820–1914. In *The Cambridge Economic History of the United States*, vol. 2, ed. Stanley L. Engerman and Robert E. Gallman, 733–812. Cambridge: Cambridge University Press.

Douglas, Paul H. 1930. *Real Wages in the United States, 1890–1926*. Boston: Houghton Mifflin.

Edelstein, Michael. 2006. International Transactions and Foreign Commerce. In *Historical Statistics*, 5-441 to 444.

Feinstein, Charles H. 1995. Changes in Nominal Wages, the Cost of Living and Real Wages in the United Kingdom over Two Centuries, 1780–1990. In *Labour's Reward*, ed. Peter Scholliers and Vera Zamagni, 3–36, 258–266. Aldershot: Edward Elgar.

———. 1998. Pessimism Perpetuated: Real Wages and the Standard of Living in Great Britain During and After the Industrial Revolution. *Journal of Economic History* 58 (September): 625–658.

Fishlow, Albert. 1965. *American Railroads and the Transformation of the Ante-Bellum Economy*. Cambridge, MA: Harvard University Press.

Gallman, Robert E. 1966. Gross National Product in the United States, 1834–1909. In *Output, Employment, and Productivity in the United States*, ed. Dorothy S. Brady, 3–90. New York: Columbia University Press.

———. 1986. The United States Capital Stock in the Nineteenth Century. In *Long-Term Factors in American Economic Growth*, ed. Stanley L. Engerman and Robert E. Gallman, 165–214. Chicago: University of Chicago Press.

———. 1992. American Economic Growth Before the Civil War: The Testimony of the Capital Stock Estimates. In *American Economic Growth and Standards of Living Before the Civil War*, ed. Robert E. Gallman and John H. Wallis, pp. 79–120. Chicago: University of Chicago Press.

———, and Paul W. Rhode. 2019. *Capital in the Nineteenth Century*. Chicago: University of Chicago Press.

Goldsmith, Raymond W. 1962. *The National Wealth of the United States in the Postwar Period*. Princeton: Princeton University Press.

Gottlieb, Manuel. 1965. New Measures of Value of Nonfarm Building for the United States, Annually 1850–1939. *Review of Economics and Statistics* 47 (November): 412–419.

[*Historical Statistics*]. 1975. Bureau of the Census. *Historical Statistics of the United States, Colonial Times to 1970, Bicentennial Edition*. Washington: Government Printing Office.

———. 2006. *Historical Statistics of the United States, Millennial Edition*, ed. Susan B. Carter, Scott Sigmund Gartner, Michael R. Haines, Alan L. Olmstead, Richard Sutch, Gavin Wright. Cambridge: Cambridge University Press.

Isard, Walter. 1942. A Neglected Cycle: The Transport-Building Cycle. *Review of Economics and Statistics* 24 (November): 149–158.

Lebergott, Stanley. 1964. *Manpower in Economic Growth*. New York: McGraw-Hill.

———. 1996. *Consumer Expenditures*. Princeton: Princeton University Press.

Lipsey, Robert E. 2000. U.S. Foreign Trade and the Balance of Payments, 1800–1913. In *The Cambridge Economic History of the United States*, vol. 2, ed. Stanley L. Engerman and Robert E. Gallman, 685–732. Cambridge: Cambridge University Press.

———. 2008. Changing Patterns of International Investment in and by the United States. In *United States in the World Economy*, ed. Martin Feldstein, 475–517. Chicago: University of Chicago Press.

Margo, Robert A. 2000. *Wages and Labor Markets in the United States, 1820–1860*. Chicago: University of Chicago Press.

Mitchell, Brian R. 1988. *British Historical Statistics*. Cambridge: Cambridge University Press.

Officer, Lawrence H. 1996. *Between the Dollar-Sterling Gold Points*. Cambridge: Cambridge University Press.

———. 2009. *Two Centuries of Compensation for U.S. Production Workers in Manufacturing*. New York: Palgrave Macmillan.

Platt, Desmond C.M. 1984. *Foreign Finance in Continental Europe and the United States, 1815–1870*. London: Allen & Unwin.

Routh, Guy. 1980. *Occupation and Pay in Great Britain, 1906–79*. London: Macmillan.

Segal, Harvey H. 1956. Canal Cycles, 1834–1861. Ph.D. diss., Columbia University.

———. 1961. Cycles of Canal Construction. In *Canals and American Economic Development*, ed. Carter Goodrich, 169–215. New York: Columbia University Press.

Shaw, William H. 1947. *Value of Commodity Output Since 1869*. New York: National Bureau of Economic Research.

Smith, Walter B. 1963. Wage Rates on the Erie Canal, 1828–1881. *Journal of Economic History* 23 (September): 298–311.

Sutch, Richard. 2006. Value of Finished Commodity Output: 1869–1919. In *Historical Statistics*, pp. 3–57 to 58.

Ulmer, Melville J. 1960. *Capital in Transportation, Communications, and Public Utilities*. Princeton: Princeton University Press.
Warren, George F., and Frank A. Pearson. 1933. *Prices*. New York: Wiley.
Williamson, Jeffrey G. 1982. The Structure of Pay in Britain, 1710–1911. *Research in Economic History* 7: 1–54.
Zabler, Jeffrey F. 1972. Further Evidence on American Wage Differentials, 1800–1830. *Explorations in Economic History* 10 (Fall): 109–117.

CHAPTER 20

Sectors

In the historical literature, specific sectors of the U.S. economy have been emphasized. Utilizing the new balance-of-payments table and other data, this chapter measures the significance of three such sectors: slavery, shipping, and manufacturing. Oceanic travel by Americans has also received attention by scholars, and its importance is assessed as well.

1 Slavery

1.1 Ship Sales

Following Officer and Williamson (2020, p. 212), I compute the value of U.S.-built ships sold to foreign slavers as the product of slave-ship tonnage sold and general price per ton.[1] The Officer–Williamson tonnage series is accepted. However, in this book the price of ships is constructed differently, with richer data (Chapter 9, Sect 1.3). Hence the slave-ship sales series here varies from the series of Officer and Williamson (2020, Table 4, column [6]). The share of slave ships in total ship sales is shown in column (1) of Table 1.[2] On average, slave ships were never a substantial component of ship sales. However, for five isolated years spanning 1836–1851, the share of slave ships exceeds ten percent, ranging from 12 to 21%. The last year of any slave-ship sales is 1858—with only 1/2 of one percent of total ship sales.

L. H. Officer, *A New Balance of Payments for the United States, 1790–1919*, Palgrave Studies in American Economic History,
https://doi.org/10.1007/978-3-030-66099-4_20

Table 1 Shares of slave-related components (percent—average over period)

Period	*Share of slave ships in ship sales* (1)	*Share of slave trade in ocean revenue* (2)	*Share of slaves in immigration* (3)	*Share of items produced by enslaved persons in goods-and-services*	
				Exports (4)	*Imports* (5)
1790–1799	2.82	9.60	9.83	12.28	18.10
1800–1809	0.13	7.24	31.97	14.25	20.33
1810–1819	0	1.21	6.27	24.59	14.97
1820–1829	1.18	0.23	0.21	34.96	10.29
1830–1839	4.87	0	0.01	44.38	11.81
1840–1849	5.75	0	0	40.77	11.85
1850–1860	2.91	0	0.02	44.03	11.27

1.2 Ocean Revenue

Slave revenue accruing to U.S. ships includes both domestic and international transactions. The former consists of U.S. ship revenue from imports of African slaves, whether transatlantic-transported or Caribbean-transported, computed as the U.S. price of newly arrived African slaves *times* the number of slaves disembarked from Africa and from the Caribbean.[3] The latter transactions are carrying-trade credits (Chapter 13, Sect. 3.2), from transporting slaves from Africa to the non-U.S. Americas and from conveying creole slaves within the Caribbean.

U.S.-ship non-slave revenue again is both domestic and international, and from freight and passengers. Domestic freight revenue is composed of merchandise and gold-and-silver import earnings, while international freight revenue consists of direct trade (exports of merchandise *plus* gold-and-silver) and carrying trade.[4] Passenger revenue consists of sailing-ship and steamship earnings from both U.S. and foreign residents.[5]

Total U.S.-ship oceanic revenue ("shipping gross product") is the sum of all revenues from (1) the transport and sale of enslaved persons, (2) the transport of free-people passengers, and (3) the transport of freight. The slave proportion of this revenue is summarized in column (2) of Table 1. For no period does the average slave share exceed ten percent, and the share falls substantially after 1809. Except for four years, the slave share is below ten percent annually. The exceptional cases are 1790–1792 and 1807, for which years the share still does not reach 20%. Conclusion: revenue derived from enslaved persons was never dominant in U.S. shipping.

1.3 Immigration

Total immigration is the sum of free-people admittances and total (revenue-earning plus nonrevenue-earning) enslaved-people disembarkations ("involuntary immigrants"). The former is column (4) of Table 1 (Chapter 3); the latter is in Officer and Williamson (2020, Table 1, column [1]).[6] The share of enslaved persons in total immigration is exhibited in column (3) of Table 1. The averages conceal individual years of slave dominance in immigration (over 50% share 1804–1807), of other significant slave share (over 25% in 1796 and 1813), and of still-substantial share (over 15% in 1795, 1797–1798, 1803, 1808, and 1814).

1.4 Goods-and-Services Trade

For a complete assessment of the importance of slave-related items in goods-and-services trade, I include the slave-produced components of merchandise trade: plantation crops—cotton and tobacco in exports of goods and services, coffee and sugar in imports. Thus slavery items in exports of goods and services are slave carrying-trade credits, outfitting, and provisioning foreign slave ships, ships sold to foreign slavers, exports of cotton, and exports of tobacco.[7] Slavery items in imports of goods and services are imports of slaves, outfitting, and provisioning U.S. slave ships, purchase cost of non-imported slaves, imports of coffee, and imports of sugar.[8] Of course, the contributions of enslaved persons to exports and imports were built on the dehumanization and economic exploitation of these people.

The shares of slave items in goods-and-services trade are exhibited in columns (4) and (5) of Table 1. For exports, the high share of slave items after 1809 reflects the tremendous role of cotton in U.S. merchandise exports. That more than counteracts the decline in the slave trade in goods-and-services exports—but nothing plays that role in imports.

After the Civil War, slave-trade items ended, along with U.S. slavery itself; but trade in plantation crops remained. Both in 1860 and 1870,

Fig. 1 Importance of ships and shipping, 1790–1919. *Note* "Ship sales" are sales (exports) of ships as a percent of total goods exports. "Shipping gross product" is oceanic-shipping gross product as a percent of GDP

cotton *plus* tobacco constituted almost two-thirds of domestic merchandise exports, then shrank, but was still almost 30% in 1910.[9] In contrast, the share of coffee *plus* sugar, 15% of imports in 1860, increased in the postbellum period to 22% in 1890, falling to about ten percent in 1910.[10]

2 Shipping

2.1 *Ship Sales*

Exports of ships ("ship sales") as a proportion of goods exports are graphed in Fig. 1. The proportion exceeds two percent only during war years: 1794–1814 and 1862–1864. In the postbellum period, ship sales constitute less than half of one percent of goods exports in all years except 1873–1874, when the proportion is only slightly above that level. Clearly, ship sales never rivaled merchandise exports in quantitative importance.

2.2 *Gross Product*

The literature states that shipping earnings were a key credit item in the antebellum period but with the Civil War it lost this importance, never to regain it during our period of interest.[11] That finding is mirrored in the ratio of oceanic-shipping gross product to Johnston-Williamson GDP, shown ("shipping gross product") in Fig. 1. That ratio is in the 4 1/2-to-nine percent range throughout 1793–1807, and is above one percent in all but four years of the antebellum period. From 1861 on, the ratio is below one percent. The level of the ratio is overestimated because gross product exceeds value-added (the relevant concept corresponding to GDP); but the ratio understates "oceanic income" (a broader concept than "oceanic-shipping gross product"), which could include not only this gross product but also ship sales, whaling, oceanic fishing, and possibly coastal trade and transportation.

2.3 *Passenger Revenue*

Passenger revenue of U.S. ships (sailing-ships *plus* steamships) compared to foreign ships tells a similar story.[12] As shown in Figs. 2 and 3, U.S.-ship passenger revenue generally exceeds foreign-ship passenger revenue in the antebellum period (doing so in all but ten years over 1790–1857); but, from 1858 onward, it is uniformly below the foreign-ship revenue.[13] The shift from sailing-ship to steamship dominance, and British lead in the latter, is certainly a principal cause of the phenomenon.

Fig. 2 U.S. and foreign ship passenger revenue, 1790–1857. *Note* "U.S." and "foreign" are passenger revenues of U.S. ships and foreign ships, respectively. For each series, revenues of sailing ships and steamships are combined

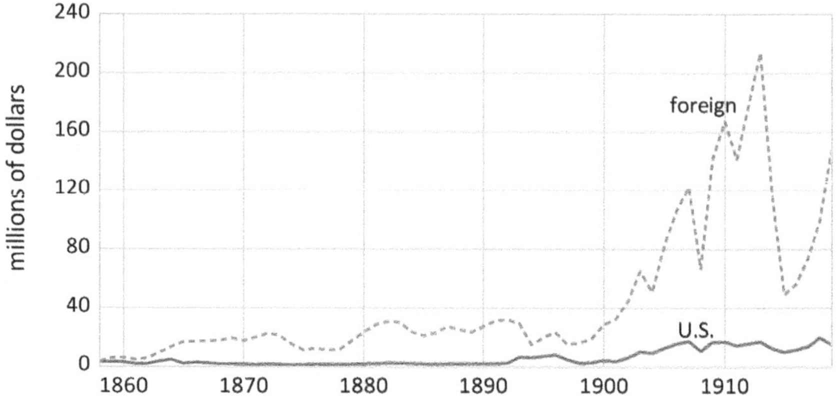

Fig. 3 U.S. and foreign ship passenger revenue, 1858–1919. *Note* "U.S." and "foreign" are passenger revenues of U.S. ships and foreign ships, respectively. For each series, revenues of sailing ships and steamships are combined

3 Manufacturing

Though the new balance-of-payments table is not utilized in assessing the importance of manufacturing, the sector is so important that I discuss it and bring new data and a new perspective to the issue. Figure 4 graphs the manufacturing shares of merchandise exports and imports. It is important to note that I define manufactured exports as solely *finished* manufactured goods—in contrast to the existing literature, which includes semi-manufactures. This definition enables a sharper distinction between manufacturing versus other sectors (agriculture, mining). Observe also that the basic source is continuous only for 1850–1919, including just three isolated years (1821, 1830, 1840) prior to 1850; but that the manufactured share of exports is carried back to 1790 via other data.[14]

An upward trend in the manufactured-export share and downward trend in the manufactured-import share are notable in the figure. The series cross in 1903–1904. Yet, except for World War I, manufactured exports remain less than one-third domestic exports. This is much lower than the standard statistics.[15] Admittedly, a full analysis would include sectoral analysis of imports and exports within manufacturing, which I leave to the existing literature.[16]

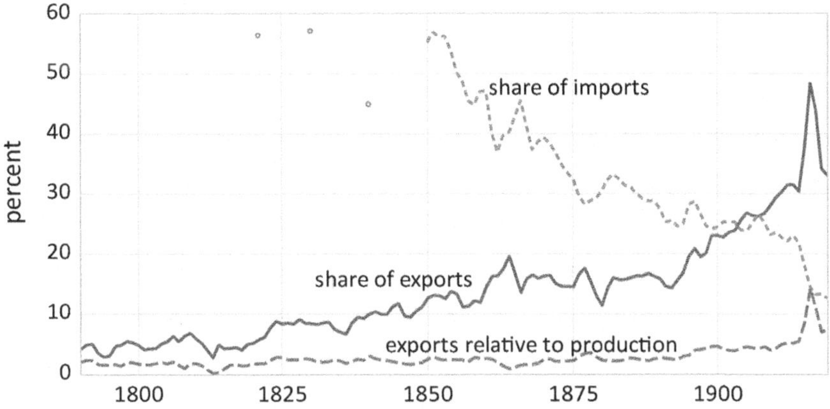

Fig. 4 Importance of manufacturing, 1790–1919. *Note* "Share of exports" and "share of imports" are the manufactured-goods percent share of merchandise exports and imports, respectively. "Exports relative to production" are manufactured-goods exports expressed as percent of manufacturing production

While the United States was becoming an industrial power, what percent of *aggregate* manufactured production took the form of finished manufactured exports? This question is not answered in the existing literature.[17] The foundation series for manufactured production is Shaw data on the manufacturing output of all finished commodities (*Historical Statistics* 2006, series Dd309), available for 1869, 1879, 1899–1919. Making use of other information, I complete the series for the full 1790–1919 period.[18]

The export/production ratio is shown in Fig. 4. Until World War I, the share of exports in the output of manufactures is amazingly low—never reaching five percent until 1912, and jumping from five to nine percent in 1915.[19] The implication is that manufacturing growth took the form mainly of import substitution rather than export expansion, though the issue is controversial.[20]

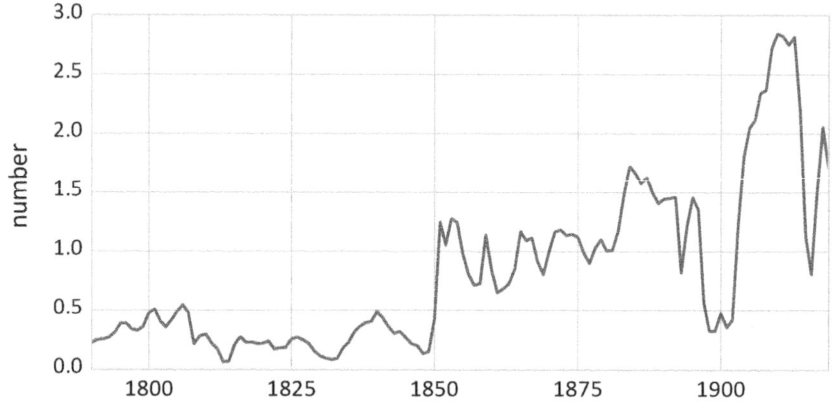

Fig. 5 Oceanic tourists per 1000 population, 1790–1919. *Note* The series is the number of U.S.-citizen oceanic round-trips per 1000 population

4 Travel

4.1 Travel-Population Ratio

The number of U.S.-citizen oceanic round-trips per 1000 population is graphed in Fig. 5.[21] There are profound jumps in 1851 (probably due to the steamship) and 1903 (possibly reflecting, in part, travel opportunities following the Spanish-American War) and a decline associated with World War I. DGW (2012, p. 156) and Dupont and Weiss (2013, p. 330) compute the same ratio (using data that presumably are superseded in this study), and provide summary statistics for 1852–1914. For that time period, the coefficient of variation (ratio of standard-deviation to mean) of their travel/population series is 0.38, whereas ours is 0.49. DGW and Dupont and Weiss also compute statistics for the logarithm of their series. Then the contrast is even greater: coefficient of variation 1.56 for their series, 3.70 for the new series. The implication is that U.S.-citizen travel was more variable than measured by these previous authors.[22]

4.2 Average Fare

The average fare paid by U.S. citizens for all oceanic travel, in both current and constant dollars, is presented annually over 1790–1919 in Fig. 6. These series are offered as an aggregate complement to the

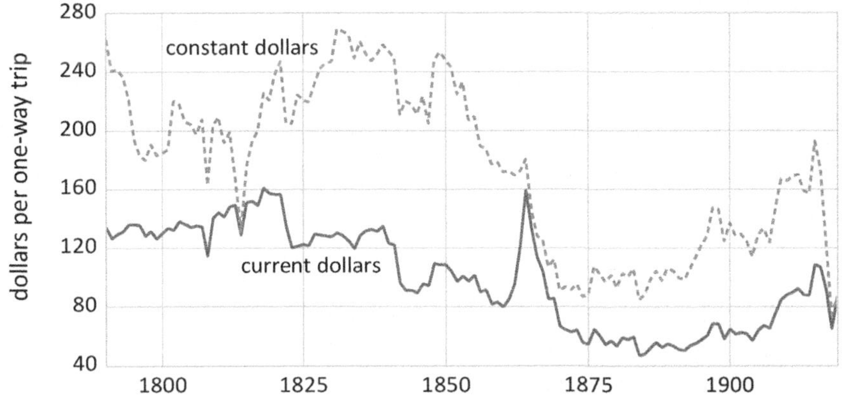

Fig. 6 Average fare paid by U.S. oceanic travelers, 1790–1919. *Note* "Current dollars" is the U.S.-citizen average fare, the ratio of passenger-fare expenditures to number of one-way trips. "Constant dollars" is the current-dollar series re-expressed in constant (1919) dollars, via division by the consumer price index

fare series in Chapter 15 and to the fare series constructed by previous authors.[23] The average fare is the ratio of passenger fares paid by U.S. citizens to the number of one-way trips of these travelers.[24] Thus the series is the average fare per one-way trip, allowing for annual variations in accommodation-class proportions and geographic-destination proportions. The constant-dollar series is obtained by division by the U.S. consumer price index (Officer 2007, pp. 142–145) and expression in 1919 dollars. The spike during the Civil War is far more noticeable in current than constant dollars. In effect, the new series is current-weighted in several dimensions; so its behavior does not lend itself to obvious explanation.

4.3 Fare Share of Expenditures

Total oceanic travel expenditures of U.S. citizens are the sum of passenger fares (per note 24) and overseas expenditures (Table 1, column (4), Chapter 14). The proportion of fares in these total expenditures is shown in Fig. 7. The share of fares is above 25% until 1869, followed by a downward movement to the early 1890s—and then generally upward, into the beginning years of World War I. The proportion of fares in expenditures

Fig. 7 Ratio of fares to U.S. oceanic travel expenditures, 1790–1919. *Note* The series is the percent share of U.S.-citizen passenger fares in these fares *plus* overseas travel expenditures

is perhaps generally higher than one's a priori. On reflection, a high share should be expected in the sailing-ship era, given long oceanic voyages. For steamships, there may be a paradoxical explanation: fast steamships meant one could take more voyages in a given year, while spending less time on the foreign land per voyage. From 1790 to the mid-1900s, the trend in fares/expenditures is flat or downward, while the travel/population ratio experienced jumps (Fig. 5).

Notes

1. There are no data to construct a slave-ship-specific price series.
2. Total ship sales are column (7), Table 1 (Chapter 6).
3. For price, see Chapter 9, Sect. 2. The disembarkations are listed in columns (2) and (3) of Table 1 (Chapter 4).
4. See Chapter 13, Sects. 2 and 3.
5. Sum of columns (1)–(4), Table 1 (Chapter 15).
6. The corresponding concept of the latter in this study is the sum of columns (2)–(4) of Table 1 (Chapter 4) *plus* disembarked slaves not earning revenue for the ship-owner.
7. For sale of ships, carrying trade, outfitting, and provisioning, see Sect. 1.1 and Chapter 13 (Sects. 3.2 and 5.2). Exports of cotton are from Fred J. Guetter and Albert E. McKinley (1924, p. 25) 1790–1791, MSCF

(August 1895, pp. 290–291) 1802–1861, and is the product of price per pound and pounds exported (MSCF, August 1895, pp. 290–291; Matthew B. Hammond 1897, p. 358) 1792–1801. Exports of leaf tobacco are from MSCF (June 1895, pp. 1418–1419) 1790–1791, 1802–1861; other years are interpolated via the product of the price index of leaf tobacco (annual average) and the volume of exports (BGH 1936, p. 366; MSCF, June 1895, p. 1418). Fiscal-year series are converted to calendar year as appropriate.

8. Imports and non-imported purchases are columns (1)–(3) and (4) of Table 1 (Chapter 9); "outfitting and provisioning" are in Chapter 13 (Sect. 5.3). Imports of coffee are in *Historical Statistics* (2006, series Ee592) 1821–1861, the product of the unit price of coffee—constructed as the value/volume ratio for 1821 and extrapolated by the price index of coffee (annual average)—and the volume of imports (*Historical Statistics* 2006, series Ee592, Ee591; BGH 1937, p. 47) 1790–1820. A similar construction is used for imports of sugar, with the wholesale price of sugar serving as the price index. Data sources are *Historical Statistics* (2006, series Ee595, Ee596, Cc218). Volumes for 1820 are linearly interpolated. Conversion to calendar year is performed as needed.
9. I am not doing justice to the immense—and, to some extent, controversial—literature on the role of cotton in the U.S. economy.
10. Data for this paragraph are in *Historical Statistics* (2006, series Ee366, Ee571, Ee573, Ee368, Ee592, Ee596).
11. "The Civil War marked the passing of our merchant fleet. From that time on, the profits of shipping, which…had been the chief factor in maintaining the equilibrium of our foreign exchanges, ceased to be a credit item, and became gradually an important feature of our debit account" (BWT 1919, p. 222). "Until the Civil War, the deficit on merchandise trade was roughly offset by a surplus on shipping earnings…That source of income dwindled during and after the Civil War…" (Lipsey 2000, p. 692).
12. Passenger-revenue data are in Chapter 15, Table 1: U.S. ships, columns (1)–(4); foreign ships, columns (5)–(8).
13. Looked at another way, U.S.-ship share falls below one-third in only one year (1790) of the antebellum period, but never even reaches that level after 1860.
14. Total domestic exports, finished manufactured exports, total imports, and finished manufactured imports are from *Historical Statistics* (2006, series Ee446, Ee451, Ee452, Ee457). The "other data" used for interpolating and extrapolating missing years of the manufactures export share are a series of the share of manufacturing in domestic merchandise exports in MSCF (April 1903, p. 3242). Conversion to calendar year is performed.
15. For example, Irwin (2003, p. 365).
16. See Lipsey (2000, pp. 699–711) and Irwin (2003).

17. However, *sectoral* export/output ratios within manufacturing for some years are presented in Lipsey (2000, p. 710).
18. Value-added for manufacturing in 1809, 1839, 1844, 1849, 1854, 1859, 1869, 1874, 1879, 1884, 1889 is in Barry W. Poulson (1965, p. 139) [year 1809] and Gallman (1960, p. 56) [other years]. I develop a synthetic value-added series: the (Warren and Pearson 1933) wholesale price index *times* (Davis 2004) industrial production, resulting in a continuous value-added series for 1790–1889. I use this series to interpolate and extrapolate the Gallman-Poulson figures to cover that same time period, and then employ the extended Gallman-Poulson series to complete the Shaw series—interpolating 1870–1878 and 1880–1888, extrapolating to 1790 via the 1869 overlap.
19. Correcting manufacturing value-added to include "hand trades" (especially blacksmithing) would increase the denominator of the ratio, and thereby make the export share even lower. The bias is slight, though likely greater as one goes deeper into the antebellum period. See Jeremy Atack and Robert A. Margo (2019, especially Appendix 2).
20. For a good discussion, with reference to important studies, see Lipsey (2000, pp. 725–727). Lipsey observes a declining aggregate manufacturing import/consumption ratio, which is consequential evidence.
21. The numerator consists of the number of U.S.-citizen cabin and steerage round-trips to Europe, "West Indies and Central America," and "South America and Far East" (column [1], Table 1, Chapter 3). The denominator is the revised U.S.-population series (Appendix, Chapter 5) *minus* the deviation of *Historical Statistics* net immigration from the new net immigration (Sect. 7 of Chapter 3).
22. For related discussion, see Sects. 1.2 and 1.3.3 of Chapter 3.
23. DGW (2012), Dupont and Weiss (2013), DKW (2017).
24. The numerator is constructed as passenger revenues of U.S. and foreign ships from U.S. residents *minus* revenue of these ships from U.S. emigrants (Chapter 15, Sect. 4). The denominator is *double* column (1) in Table 1 (Chapter 3). Alternatively, it is double the sum of the six U.S.-citizen travel series: destination Europe, West Indies and Central America, South America and Far East; each cabin, steerage (Chapter 15, Sect. 2.1). (Recall that, for one-way trips, the number of round-trips is doubled—Chapter 19, Appendix 1, Sect. B.3.)

References

Atack, Jeremy, and Robert A. Margo. 2019. Gallman Revisited: Blacksmithing and American Manufacturing, 1850–1870. *Cliometrica* 13 (January): 1–23.

Bezanson, Anne, Robert D. Gray, and Miriam Hussey [BGH]. 1936, 1937. *Wholesale Prices in Philadelphia, 1784–1861.* Philadelphia: University of Pennsylvania Press.

Bullock, Charles J., John H. Williams, and Rufus S. Tucker [BWT]. 1919. The History of Our Foreign Trade Balance from 1789 to 1914. *Review of Economics and Statistics* 1 (July): 215–233.

Davis, Joseph H. 2004. An Annual Index of U.S. Industrial Production, 1790–1915. *Quarterly Journal of Economics* 119 (November): 1177–1215, data appendix http://www.nber.org/data/industrial-production-index/.

Dupont, Brandon, Alka Gandhi, and Thomas Weiss [DGW]. 2012. The Long-Term Rise in Overseas Travel by Americans, 1820–2000. *Economic History Review* 65 (February): 144–167.

Dupont, Brandon, and Thomas Weiss. 2013. Variability in Overseas Travel by Americans, 1820–2000. *Cliometrica* 7 (September): 319–339.

Dupont, Brandon, Drew Keeling, and Thomas Weiss [DKW]. 2017. First Cabin Fares from New York to the British Isles, 1826–1914. *Research in Economic History* 33: 19–63.

Gallman, Robert E. 1960. Commodity Output, 1839–1899. In *Trends in the American Economy in the Nineteenth Century*, ed. William N. Parker, 13–67. Princeton: Princeton University Press.

Guetter, Fred J., and Albert E. McKinley. 1924. *The Economic Growth of the United States*. Philadelphia: McKinley.

Hammond, Matthew B. 1897. *The Cotton Industry*. New York: Macmillan.

[*Historical Statistics*]. 2006. *Historical Statistics of the United States, Millennial Edition*, ed. Susan B. Carter, Scott Sigmund Gartner, Michael R. Haines, Alan L. Olmstead, Richard Sutch, Gavin Wright. Cambridge: Cambridge University Press.

Irwin, Douglas A. 2003. Explaining America's Surge in Manufactured Exports, 1880–1913. *Review of Economics and Statistics* 85 (May): 364–376.

Lipsey, Robert E. 2000. U.S. Foreign Trade and the Balance of Payments, 1800–1913. In *The Cambridge Economic History of the United States*, vol. 2, ed. Stanley L. Engerman and Robert E. Gallman, 685–732. Cambridge: Cambridge University Press.

Monthly Summary of Commerce and Finance [MSCF].

Officer, Lawrence H. 2007. An Improved Long-Run Consumer Price Index for the United States. *Historical Methods* 40 (Summer): 135–147.

Officer, Lawrence H., and Samuel H. Williamson. 2020. The Antebellum Slave Trade: Numbers and Impact on the Balance of Payments. *Research in Economic History* 36: 181–212.

Poulson, Barry W. 1965. Value Added in Manufacturing, Mining, and Agriculture in the American Economy from 1809 to 1839. Ph.D. diss., Ohio State University.

Warren, George F., and Frank A. Pearson. 1933. *Prices*. New York: Wiley.

PART VII

Conclusions

CHAPTER 21

Concluding Comments

It is amazing that the standard U.S. historical balance-of-payments table has not changed since *Historical Statistics* (1960). And this in the face of (1) existing data neglected by underpinning authors (North, Simon, Goldsmith, OBE) and (2) newly published and unpublished data of relevance to individual items in the table. This book brings our understanding of the U.S. historical balance-of-payments sixty-years' forward!

The standard table is ***updated*** in various ways. First, varying year-definition is replaced with a consistent, calendar-year protocol. Second, assumed offsetting items are substituted with measured gross flows. Third, imposed zero amounts of items are similarly substituted.

More fundamentally, the standard table is ***upgraded***. Conceptual and statistical discontinuities in constructing an item over time are rejected in favor of definitions and techniques that are uniform for the entire time period 1790–1919. For comprehensiveness, previously neglected items are measured and included in the table. To enhance reliability, many items are constructed from disaggregate components. Important for several reasons is abandonment of (1) equating of capital flow to the measured residual of the balance of payments and (2) use of the residual (statistical discrepancy) in estimating items.

Comparisons show that, for many items, the new table substantially differs from the standard table. The divergence would be even greater

L. H. Officer, *A New Balance of Payments for the United States, 1790–1919*, Palgrave Studies in American Economic History,
https://doi.org/10.1007/978-3-030-66099-4_21

were allowance not made for the currency-dollar denomination of the new table in contrast to the standard gold-dollar dimension.

Given the truly independent residual in this study, statistical discrepancy is a meaningful indicator of the reliability (net error) of the new table throughout the period. The table does have conspicuous omissions: in particular, international-mail and commercial-banking flows. And it is a matter of judgment whether the overall table and individual component series, though superior to the standard table, are "good enough." I believe that, for most purposes, the new table and series possess sufficient reliability. The reader is invited to pick and choose as desired.

Regarding the historical structure of the economy, the new series indicate that the United States was a more-open economy than previous authors have shown. The switch from comparative advantage in services to that in goods is vividly presented in various ways, and is consistent with the newly measured terms-of-trade movement.

The study also has implications for sectors of the U.S. economy that are highlighted in the historical literature: slavery, shipping, manufacturing, and travel.

The importance of *slavery* is mixed. Slave ships were not a substantial part of ship sales, and slave-derived revenue never dominant in shipping. In contrast, the share of enslaved persons in total immigration was substantial—even dominant—in the early years. Allowing for slave-produced merchandise items, the importance of slavery is enhanced, especially for exports (led by cotton) in the later antebellum years.

The literature emphasizes *shipping* as an important source of foreign exchange in the antebellum period. The numbers for ship sales, gross shipping product, and passenger revenue indicate that the importance might be overstated. However, consistent with the literature, the numbers fall off in the postbellum period.

The findings of an upward trend in the share of *manufactures* in merchandise exports and a downward trend in manufactures' share of merchandise imports are supportive of the literature. But the shares are less than the findings of other authors. There is also evidence that manufacturing growth took the form mainly of import substitution rather than export expansion.

International *travel* has been studied by other authors. The contribution here is that U.S. travel was more variable than these authors measured. A novel average-fare series is constructed. The declining or flat trend of the fare/expenditures ratio in association with the jumps in U.S. travel is noticeable.

In sum, the new balance-of-payments table is presented with its own series and with related series as usable input for historical research and as interesting phenomena to the general reader.

Reference

[*Historical Statistics*]. 1960. Bureau of the Census. *Historical Statistics of the United States, Colonial Times to 1957*. Washington: Government Printing Office.

References

Abbott, Edith. 1926. *Historical Aspects of the Immigration Problem.* Chicago: University of Chicago Press.

Adams, Donald R., Jr. 1975. Residential Construction Industry in the Early Nineteenth Century. *Journal of Economic History* 35 (December): 794–816.

———. 1980. American Neutrality and Prosperity, 1793–1808: A Reconsideration. *Journal of Economic History* 40 (December): 713–737.

Adams, Henry C. 1895. Statistics of Steam Railroad Transportation. In *Report on Transportation Business in the United States at the Eleventh Census*, 591–620. Washington: Government Printing Office.

Adams, Thurston M. 1944. *Prices Paid by Vermont Farmers for Goods and Services and Received by Them for Farm Products, 1790–1940.* Burlington: Vermont Agricultural Experiment Station.

Adams, William F. 1932. *Ireland and Irish Emigration to the New World.* New Haven: Yale University Press.

Albion, Robert G. 1938. *Square-Riggers on Schedule.* Princeton: Princeton University Press.

———. 1939. *The Rise of New York Port.* New York: Scribner's.

———, and Jennie B. Pope. 1942. *Sea Lanes in Wartime.* New York: Norton.

Allen, W.H. 1904. What Becomes of Our Trade Balances? *Sewanee Review* 12 (July): 268–296.

American State Papers: Commerce and Navigation [ASPCN].

Angier, E.A.V. 1920. *Fifty Years' Freights.* London: Fairplay.

Annual Report of the Chamber of Commerce of the State of New York [ARCC].

Annual Report of the Chief of Bureau of Foreign and Domestic Commerce. 1916.

L. H. Officer, *A New Balance of Payments for the United States, 1790–1919*, Palgrave Studies in American Economic History,
https://doi.org/10.1007/978-3-030-66099-4

Annual Report of the Commissioner-General of Immigration [ARCGI].
Annual Report of the Commissioners of Emigration of the State of New York [ARCENY].
Annual Report of the Director of the Mint [ARDM].
Annual Report of the Secretary of the Treasury [ARSTR].
Appleton's European Guide Book. 1870. London: Longmans, Green.
Arnold, Bion J. 1910. *Report on the Pittsburgh Transportation Problem*. City of Pittsburgh.
Atack, Jeremy, and Robert A. Margo. 2019. Gallman Revisited: Blacksmithing and American Manufacturing, 1850–1870. *Cliometrica* 13 (January): 1–23.
Bacon, Nathaniel T. 1900. American International Indebtedness. *Yale Review* 9 (November): 265–285.
———. 1902. Why the United States Is Not Yet a Creditor Nation. *New York Times*, January 5, p. 7.
Baer, Christopher T. 1981. *Canals and Railroads of the Mid-Atlantic States, 1800–1860*. Regional Economic History Research Center. Eleutherian Mills-Hagley Foundation.
Bailey, Thomas A. 1980. *A Diplomatic History of the American People*. Englewood Cliffs: Prentice-Hall.
Baker, Anni P. 2004. *American Soldiers Overseas*. Westport: Praeger.
Baldwin, Leland D. 1937. *Pittsburgh: The Story of a City, 1750–1865*. Pittsburgh: University of Pittsburgh Press.
Bandiera, Oriana, Imran Rasul, and Martina Viarengo [BRV]. 2013. The Making of Modern America: Migratory Flows in the Age of Mass Migration. *Journal of Development Economics* 102 (May): 23–47.
Barger, Harold. 1951. *The Transportation Industries, 1889–1946*. New York: National Bureau of Economic Research.
———. 1960. Income Originating in Trade, 1869–1929. In *Output, Employment, and Productivity in the United States*, ed. Dorothy S. Brady, 327–361. New York: Columbia University Press.
Barker, Charles R. 1931. *Philadelphia in the Late 'Forties*. Philadelphia: City History Society of Philadelphia.
Baskerville, Peter. 1981. Americans in Britain's Backyard: The Railway Era in Upper Canada, 1850–1880. *Business History Review* 55 (Autumn): 314–336.
Beck, John. 2009. *A History of the Falmouth Packet Service*. Exton: South West Maritime History Society.
Berry, Thomas Senior. 1943. *Western Prices Before 1861*. Cambridge, MA: Harvard University Press.
Bezanson, Anne, Robert D. Gray, and Miriam Hussey [BGH]. 1936, 1937. *Wholesale Prices in Philadelphia, 1784–1861*. Philadelphia: University of Pennsylvania Press.
Blodget, Samuel. 1806. *Economica: A Statistical Manual*. Washington.

Board of Governors of the Federal Reserve System. 1943. *Banking and Monetary Statistics, 1914–1941.* Washington.

Bonsor, N.R.P. 1975, 1978, 1979. *North Atlantic Seaway*. New York: Arco.

Bowen, Frank C. 1930. *A Century of Atlantic Travel*. Boston: Little, Brown.

Brady, Dorothy S. 1966. Price Deflators for Final Product Estimates. In *Output, Employment, and Productivity in the United States*, ed. Dorothy S. Brady, 91–115. New York: Columbia University Press.

Bromwell, William J. 1856. *History of Immigration to the United States*. New York: Redfield.

Buck, Norman S. 1925. *Anglo-American Trade, 1800–1850*. New Haven: Yale University Press.

Bullock, Charles J. 1901. The Theory of the Balance of Trade. *North American Review* 173 (July): 111–133.

———, John H. Williams, and Rufus S. Tucker [BWT]. 1919a. The History of Our Foreign Trade Balance from 1789 to 1914. *Review of Economics and Statistics* 1 (July): 215–233.

———, John H. Williams, and Rufus S. Tucker [BWT]. 1919b. The History of Our Foreign Trade Balance During the Great War. *Review of Economics and Statistics* 1 (July): 234–254.

Bureau of the Census. 1920. *Electric Railways*. Washington: Government Printing Office.

Bureau of Statistics. 1893. *Arrivals of Alien Passengers and Immigrants in the United States from 1820 to 1892*. Treasury Department. Washington: Government Printing Office.

———. 1896. *Commerce of the United States and Europe with American Countries, 1851–1895*. Washington: Government Printing Office.

———. 1903. *Immigration into the United States… from 1820 to 1903*. [Reprinted from *Summary of Commerce and Finance* for June 1903.] Treasury Department. Washington: Government Printing Office.

Cairncross, Alexander K. 1953. *Home and Foreign Investment, 1870–1913*. Cambridge: Cambridge University Press.

Carman, Harry J. 1919. The Street Surface Railway Franchises of New York City. Ph.D. diss., Columbia University.

Carter, Susan B., and Richard Sutch. 1998. Historical Background to Current Immigration Issues. In *The Immigration Debate*, ed. James P. Smith and Barry Edmonston, 289–366. Washington: National Academy Press.

Cheape, Charles W. 1980. *Moving the Masses*. Cambridge, MA: Harvard University Press.

Clews, Henry. 1888. *Twenty-Eight Years in Wall Street*. New York: Irving.

Cohen, Andrew W. 2010. Smuggling, Globalization, and America's Outward State, 1870–1909. *Journal of American History* 97 (September): 371–398.

Cohn, Raymond L. 1984. Mortality on Immigrant Voyages to New York, 1836–1853. *Journal of Economic History* 44 (June): 289–300.

———. 1992. Transatlantic U.S. Passenger Travel at the Dawn of the Steamship Era. *International Journal of Maritime History* 4 (June): 43–64.

———. 2003. Passenger Mortality on Antebellum Immigrant Ships: Further Evidence. *International Journal of Maritime History* 15 (December): 1–19.

———. 2009. *Mass Migration Under Sail*. Cambridge: Cambridge University Press.

Colean, Miles L., and Robinson Newcomb. 1952. *Stabilizing Construction: The Record and Potential*. New York: McGraw-Hill.

Coleman, Terry. 1972. *Passage to America*. London: Hutchinson.

Colton, Calvin. 1832. *Manual for Emigrants to America*. London: Westley & Davis.

Commerce and Navigation [CN].

Commercial Year Book. 1896. Our International Balance Sheet, 225–231.

Cooley, Charles H. 1895. Statistics of Street Railway Transportation. In *Report on Transportation Business in the United States at the Eleventh Census*, 681–839. Washington: Government Printing Office.

Coxe, Tench. 1794. *A View of the United States of America*. Philadelphia: William Hall.

Crawford, Mark. 1999. *Encyclopedia of the Mexican-American War*. Santa Barbara: ABC-CLIO.

Crocker, George G. 1900. *From the Stage Coach to the Railroad Train and the Street Car*. Boston: W. B. Clarke.

Cuda, Brian J. 1990. *Cash, Tokens, and Transfers*. New York: Fordham University Press.

Cunard Steamship Company. 1877. *Official Guide*. London: Sutton Sharpe.

Cutler, Carl C. 1961. *Queens of the Western Ocean*. Annapolis: United States Naval Institute.

Dalzell, George W. 1940. *The Flight from the Flag*. Chapel Hill: University of North Carolina Press.

Dana, William B. 1895a. Why Do We Export Gold? *Commercial and Financial Chronicle* 60 (March 30): 542–544.

———. 1895b. Why Do We Export Gold? *Commercial and Financial Chronicle* 60 (April 13): 630–633.

Daniels, Roger. 2004. *Guarding the Golden Door*. New York: Hill & Wang.

David, Paul A., and Peter Solar. 1977. A Bicentenary Contribution to the History of the Cost of Living in America. *Research in Economic History* 2: 1–80.

Davis, Joseph H. 2004. An Annual Index of U.S. Industrial Production, 1790–1915. *Quarterly Journal of Economics* 119 (November): 1177–1215, data appendix http://www.nber.org/data/industrial-production-index/.

Davis, Lance E., and Robert J. Cull. 1994. *International Capital Markets and American Economic Growth, 1820–1914*. Cambridge: Cambridge University Press.

———. 2000. International Capital Movements, Domestic Capital Markets, and American Economic Growth, 1820–1914. In *The Cambridge Economic History of the United States*, vol. 2, ed. Stanley L. Engerman and Robert E. Gallman, 733–812. Cambridge: Cambridge University Press.

Davis, Marian R. 1931. Critique of Official United States Immigration Statistics. In *International Migrations*, vol. 2, ed. Walter F. Wilcox, 645–658. New York: National Bureau of Economic Research.

Dearborn, Nathaniel. 1848. *Boston Notions*. Boston: Nathaniel Dearborn.

Denzel, Markus A. 2010. *Handbook of World Exchange Rates, 1590–1914*. Surrey: Ashgate.

Department of Commerce. 1948. *International Transactions of the United States During the War, 1940–1945*. Washington: Government Printing Office.

Department of Trade and Commerce. 1898. *Special Report on Trade Between Canada and the United States*. Ottawa: S. E. Dawson.

———. 1908. *Report, Canadian Trade*. Ottawa: S. E. Dawson.

Derbyshire, Leland C. 1919. *Railroads of South and Central America*. Bloomington: Indiana University.

Dickens, Paul B. 1933. The Transition Period in American International Financing: 1897 to 1914. Ph.D., diss., George Washington University.

Disturnell, John. 1876. *New York As It Was and As It Is*. New York: Van Nostrand.

Dominion Bureau of Statistics. 1949. *The Canadian Balance of International Payments 1926 to 1948*. Ottawa: Edmond Cloutier.

Douglas, Edward M. 1932. *Boundaries, Areas, Geographic Centers and Altitudes*. Washington: Government Printing Office.

Douglas, Paul H. 1930. *Real Wages in the United States, 1890–1926*. Boston: Houghton Mifflin.

Dunbar, Seymour. 1937. *A History of Travel in America*. New York: Tudor.

Dunning, William A. 1912. Paying for Alaska. *Political Science Quarterly* 27 (September): 385–398.

Dupont, Brandon, Alka Gandhi, and Thomas Weiss [DGW]. 2008. The American Invasion of Europe: The Long Term Rise in Overseas Travel, 1820–2000. Working Paper 13977, National Bureau of Economic Research, Cambridge, MA.

———. 2012. The Long-Term Rise in Overseas Travel by Americans, 1820–2000. *Economic History Review* 65 (February): 144–167.

Dupont, Brandon, and Thomas Weiss. 2013. Variability in Overseas Travel by Americans, 1820–2000. *Cliometrica* 7 (September): 319–339.

Dupont, Brandon, Drew Keeling, and Thomas Weiss [DKW]. 2017. First Cabin Fares from New York to the British Isles, 1826–1914. *Research in Economic History* 33: 19–63.

Durand, Edward D. 1905. Street and Electric Railways. In Bureau of the Census, *Street and Electric Railways 1902*, 3–235. Washington: Government Printing Office.

Easton, Alexander. 1859. *A Practical Treatise on Street or Horse-Power Railways*. Philadelphia: Crissy & Markley.

Edelstein, Michael. 2006a. International Investment Position of the United States: 1843–1977. In *Historical Statistics*, pp. 5–467 to 469.

———. 2006b. International Transactions and Foreign Commerce. In *Historical Statistics*, 5–441 to 444.

Eichengreen, Barry. 2000. U.S. Foreign Financial Relations in the Twentieth Century. In *The Cambridge Economic History of the United States*, vol. 3, ed. Stanley L. Engerman and Robert E. Gallman, 463–504. Cambridge: Cambridge University Press.

Eltis, David. 1987. *Economic Growth and the Ending of the Transatlantic Slave Trade*. New York: Oxford University Press.

———, and David Richardson. 2004. Prices of African Slaves Newly Arrived in the Americas, 1673–1865: New Evidence on Long-Run Trends and Regional Differentials. In *Slavery in the Development of the Americas*, ed. David Eltis, Frank D. Lewis, and Kenneth L. Sokoloff, 181–218. Cambridge: Cambridge University Press.

Emmons, Frederick E. 1985. *American Passenger Ships*. Newark: University of Delaware Press.

Engelsing, Rolf. 1961. *Veröffentlichungen aus dem Staatsarchiv der Freien Hansestadt Bremen*. Bremen: Schunemann.

Esteves, Rui, and David Khoudour-Castéras. 2011. Remittances, Capital Flows, and Financial Development During the Mass Migration Period, 1870–1913. *European Review of Economic History* 15 (December): 443–474.

Evans, Charles H. 1884. *Exports, Domestic, from the United States to All Countries*. Washington: Government Printing Office.

Feinstein, Charles H. 1972. *National Income, Expenditure and Output of the United Kingdom, 1855–1965*. Cambridge: Cambridge University Press.

———. 1991. A New Look at the Cost of Living 1870–1914. In *New Perspectives on the Late Victorian Economy*, 151–179. Cambridge: Cambridge University Press.

———. 1995. Changes in Nominal Wages, the Cost of Living and Real Wages in the United Kingdom over Two Centuries, 1780–1990. In *Labour's Reward*, ed. Peter Scholliers and Vera Zamagni, 3–36, 258–266. Aldershot: Edward Elgar.

———. 1998. Pessimism Perpetuated: Real Wages and the Standard of Living in Great Britain During and After the Industrial Revolution. *Journal of Economic History* 58 (September): 625–658.

Ferenczi, Imre. 1929. *International Migrations*, vol. 1. New York: National Bureau of Economic Research.

Fishlow, Albert. 1965. *American Railroads and the Transformation of the Ante-Bellum Economy*. Cambridge, MA: Harvard University Press.

———. 1966. Productivity and Technological Change in the Railroad Sector, 1840–1910. In *Output, Employment, and Productivity in the United States*, ed. Dorothy S. Brady, 583–646. New York: Columbia University Press.

Foreign Commerce and Navigation [FCN].

Foster, George C. 1849. *New York in Slices*. New York: W. F. Burgess.

Friedman, Milton, and Anna Jacobson Schwartz. 1963. *A Monetary History of the United States 1867–1960*. Princeton: Princeton University Press.

———. 1970. *Monetary Statistics of the United States*. New York: Columbia University Press.

Gallatin, Albert. 1831. *Considerations on the Currency and Banking System of the United States*. Philadelphia: Carey & Lea.

———. 1832. *Memorial of the Committee of the Free Trade Convention*. 22nd Cong., 1st sess.

Gallman, Robert E. 1960. Commodity Output, 1839–1899. In *Trends in the American Economy in the Nineteenth Century*, ed. William N. Parker, 13–67. Princeton: Princeton University Press.

———. 1966. Gross National Product in the United States, 1834–1909. In *Output, Employment, and Productivity in the United States*, ed. Dorothy S. Brady, 3–90. New York: Columbia University Press.

———. 1986. The United States Capital Stock in the Nineteenth Century. In *Long-Term Factors in American Economic Growth*, ed. Stanley L. Engerman and Robert E. Gallman, 165–214. Chicago: University of Chicago Press.

———. 1992. American Economic Growth Before the Civil War: The Testimony of the Capital Stock Estimates. In *American Economic Growth and Standards of Living Before the Civil War*, ed. Robert E. Gallman and John H. Wallis, pp. 79–120. Chicago: University of Chicago Press.

———, and Paul W. Rhode. 2019. *Capital in the Nineteenth Century*. Chicago: University of Chicago Press.

———, and Thomas J. Weiss. 1969. The Service Industries in the Nineteenth Century. In *Production and Productivity in the Service Industries*, ed. Victor R. Fuchs, 287–352. New York: Columbia University Press.

Garber, Paul N. 1959. *The Gadsden Treaty*. Gloucester: Peter Smith.

Garber, Peter M. 1986. Interwar Movements of Dollars to Europe and the US Currency Supply. *Journal of International Money and Finance* 5 (March): S135–S156.

Gibbs, C.R.Vernon. 1957. *Passenger Liners of the Western Ocean*. New York: De Graff.

Glazebrook, George P. de T. 1938. *A History of Transportation in Canada*. Toronto: Ryerson.

Glance at New York. 1837. New York: A. Greene.

Goldsmith, Raymond W. 1955. *A Study of Saving in the United States*, vol. 1. Princeton: Princeton University Press.

———. 1962. *The National Wealth of the United States in the Postwar Period*. Princeton: Princeton University Press.

Gottlieb, Manuel. 1965. New Measures of Value of Nonfarm Building for the United States, Annually 1850–1939. *Review of Economics and Statistics* 47 (November): 412–419.

Gould, John D. 1979. European Inter-Continental Emigration 1815–1914: Patterns and Causes. *Journal of European Economic History* 8 (Winter): 593–679.

Grabbe, Hans-Jürgen. 1989. European Immigration to the United States in the Early National Period, 1783–1820. *Proceedings of the American Philosophical Society* 133 (June): 190–214.

———. 2001. *Vor der großen Flut*. Stuttgart: Franz Steiner.

Graham, Frank D. 1922. International Trade Under Depreciated Paper: The United States, 1862–79. *Quarterly Journal of Economics* 36 (February): 220–273.

Greer, Darroch. 2005. *Counting Civil War Casualties Week-By-Week for the Abraham Lincoln Presidential Library and Museum*. BRC Imagination Arts.

Grubb, Farley. 1990. The Reliability of U.S. Immigration Statistics: The Case of Philadelphia, 1815–1830. *International Journal of Maritime History* 1 (June): 29–54.

———. 2011. *German Immigration and Servitude in America, 1709–1920*. London: Routledge.

Guetter, Fred J., and Albert E. McKinley. 1924. *The Economic Growth of the United States*. Philadelphia: McKinley.

Hacker, J.David. 2011. A Census-Based Count of the Civil War Dead. *Civil War History* 57 (December): 307–348.

Haines, Michael R. 2000. The White Population of the United States, 1790–1920. In *A Population History of North America*, ed. Michael R. Haines and Richard H. Steckel, 305–369. Cambridge: Cambridge University Press.

Halsey, Frederic M. 1914. *The Railways of South and Central America*. New York: Fitch.

———. 1916. *Railway Expansion in Latin America*. New York: Moody.

Hammond, Matthew B. 1897. *The Cotton Industry*. New York: Macmillan.

Hanes, Christopher. 1998. Consistent Wholesale Price Series for the United States, 1860–1900. In *Business Cycles Since 1820*, ed. Trevor, J.O. Dick, 176–209. Cheltenham: Edward Elgar.

Hansen, Marcus Lee. 1945. *The Atlantic Migration, 1607–1860*. Cambridge, MA: Harvard University Press.

Harley, C. Knick. 1988. Ocean Freight Rates and Productivity, 1740–1913: The Primacy of Mechanical Invention Reaffirmed. *Journal of Economic History* 48 (December): 851–876.

Hatton, Timothy J., and Jeffrey G. Williamson. 1998. *The Age of Mass Migration*. New York: Oxford University Press.

———. 2005. *Global Migration and the World Economy*. Cambridge, MA: MIT Press.

Heidelbach, Alfred S. 1895a. Why Gold Is Exported. *Forum* XVIII (February): 647–651.

———. 1895b. Why Do We Export Gold? *Commercial and Financial Chronicle* 60 (March 30): 585.

Hennick, Louis C., and E. Harper Charlton. 1975. *The Streetcars of New Orleans*. Gretna: Pelican.

Herfindahl, Orris C. 1966. Development of the Major Metal Mining Industries in the United States from 1839 to 1909. In *Output, Employment, and Productivity in the United States*, ed. Dorothy S. Brady, 293–348. New York: Columbia University Press.

Hickey, Donald R. 2006. *Don't Give Up the Ship*. Urbana: University of Illinois Press.

Hind, Henry Y., et al. 1864. *Eighty Years' Progress of British North America*. Toronto: Stebbins.

[*Historical Statistics*]. 1949. Bureau of the Census. *Historical Statistics of the United States, 1789–1945*. Washington: Government Printing Office.

———. 1960. Bureau of the Census. *Historical Statistics of the United States, Colonial Times to 1957*. Washington: Government Printing Office.

———. 1975. Bureau of the Census. *Historical Statistics of the United States, Colonial Times to 1970, Bicentennial Edition*. Washington: Government Printing Office.

———. 2006. *Historical Statistics of the United States, Millennial Edition*, ed. Susan B. Carter, Scott Sigmund Gartner, Michael R. Haines, Alan L. Olmstead, Richard Sutch, Gavin Wright. Cambridge: Cambridge University Press.

Holley, Orville L. 1847. *A Description of the City of New York*. New York: J. Disturnell.

Holmes, Oliver W., and Peter T. Rohrbach. 1983. *Stagecoach East*. Washington: Smithsonian Institution Press.

Holt, Glen E. 1972. The Changing Perception of Urban Pathology. In *Cities in American History*, ed. Kenneth T. Jackson and Stanley K. Schultz, 324–343. New York: Alfred A. Knopf.

Huebner, Solomon. 1905. The Development and Present Status of Marine Insurance in the United States. *Annals of the American Academy of Political and Social Science* 26 (September): 241–272.

Hutchins, John G.B. 1941. *The American Maritime Industries and Public Policy, 1789–1914*. Cambridge, MA: Harvard University Press.

Hutchinson, Edward P. 1958. Notes on Immigration Statistics of the United States. *Journal of the American Statistical Association* 53 (December): 963–1025.

———. 1981. *Legislative History of American Immigration Policy, 1798–1965*. Philadelphia: University of Pennsylvania Press.

Hyde, Francis E. 1975. *Cunard and the North Atlantic*. London: Macmillan.

Immigration Commission. 1911. *Immigrant Banks*. Washington: Government Printing Office.

Irwin, Douglas A. 1998. Changes in U.S. Tariffs: The Role of Import Prices and Commercial Policies. *American Economic Review* 88 (September): 1015–1026.

———. 2003a. Explaining America's Surge in Manufactured Exports, 1880–1913. *Review of Economics and Statistics* 85 (May): 364–376.

———. 2003b. New Estimates of the Average Tariff of the United States, 1790–1820. *Journal of Economic History* 63 (June): 506–513.

———. 2005. The Welfare Cost of Autarky: Evidence from the Jeffersonian Trade Embargo, 1807–09. *Review of International Economics* 13 (September): 631–645.

Isard, Walter. 1942. A Neglected Cycle: The Transport-Building Cycle. *Review of Economics and Statistics* 24 (November): 149–158.

Jackson, Kenneth T. 1985. *Crabgrass Frontier*. New York: Oxford University Press.

Jarvis, Edward. 1872. Immigration. *Atlantic Monthly* 29 (April): 454–468.

Jobst, Clemens, and Thomas Scheiber. 2014. In *South-Eastern European Monetary and Economic Statistics from the Nineteenth Century to World War II*, 55–100. Bank of Greece, Bulgarian National Bank, National Bank of Romania, Osterreichische Nationalbank.

Johnson, Emory R., and Grover G. Huebner. 1920. *Principles of Ocean Transportation*. New York: Appleton.

Jones, Maldwyn A. 1973. The Background to Emigration from Great Britain in the Nineteenth Century. *Perspectives in American History* 7: 3–92.

———. 1980. Scotch-Irish. In *Harvard Encyclopedia of American Ethnic Groups*, ed. Stephan Thernstrom, 895–908. Cambridge, MA: Harvard University Press.

Kamphoefner, Walter D. 1991. The Volume and Composition of German-American Return Migration. In *A Century of European Migrations, 1830–1930*, ed. Rudolph J. Vecoli and Suzanne M. Sinke, 293–311. Urbana: University of Illinois Press.

Kapp, Friedrich. 1870. *Immigration and the Commissioners of Emigration*. New York: Douglas Taylor.

Keeling, Drew. 1999. The Transportation Revolution and Transatlantic Migration, 1850–1914. *Research in Economic History* 19: 39–74.

———. 2007. Costs, Risks and Migration Networks Between Europe and the United States, 1900–1914. In *Maritime Transport and Migration: The Connections Between Maritime and Migration Networks*, ed. Torsten Feys and others, 113–173. St. John's: International Maritime Economic History Association.

———. 2008. The Voyage Abstracts of the Cunard Line as a Source of Transatlantic Passenger Fares, 1883–1914. *Business Archives Sources and History* 96 (November): 15–36.

———. 2012. *The Business of Transatlantic Migration Between Europe and the United States, 1900–1914*. Zurich: Chronos.

Kennedy, Charles J. 1962. Commuter Services in the Boston Area, 1835–1860. *Business History Review* 36 (Summer): 153–170.

Killick, John. 2000. An Early Nineteenth-Century Shipping Line: The Cope Line of Philadelphia and Liverpool Packets, 1822–1872. *International Journal of Maritime History* 12 (June): 61–87.

———. 2014. Transatlantic Steerage Fares. British and Irish Migration, and Return Migration. *Economic History Review* 67 (1): 170–191.

Kingston, Christopher. 2011. Marine Insurance in Philadelphia During the Quasi-War with France, 1795–1801. *Journal of Economic History* 71 (March): 162–184.

Klebaner, Benjamin J. 1958. State and Local Immigration Regulation in the United States Before 1882. *International Review of Social History* 3: 269–295.

Kloft, Leonard J. 1995. Problems and Issues in Constructing National and Regional Price Indices for the United States: 1851–1880. Ph.D. diss., University of Iowa.

Knox, Frank A. 1939. *Dominion Monetary Policy, 1929–1934*. Ottawa: Royal Commission on Dominion-Provincial Relations.

Krim, Arthur J. 1967. The Innovation and Diffusion of the Street Railway in North America. Ph.D. diss., University of Chicago.

Kuznets, Simon. n.d.. *Annual Estimates, 1869–1853*. New York: National Bureau of Economic Research.

———, and Ernest Rubin. 1954. *Immigration and the Foreign Born*. New York: National Bureau of Economic Research.

Lambert, Frank. 2005. *The Barbary Wars*. New York: Hill & Wang.

Lary, Hal B. 1943. *The United States in the World Economy*. Washington: Government Printing Office.

Laughlin, J.Laurence. 1918. *Credit of the Nations*. New York: Scribner's.

Lebergott, Stanley. 1964. *Manpower in Economic Growth*. New York: McGraw-Hill.

———. 1971. Changes in Unemployment, 1800–1960. In *The Reinterpretation of American Economic History*, ed. Robert W. Fogel and Stanley L. Engerman, 73–83. New York: Harper & Row.

———. 1996. *Consumer Expenditures*. Princeton: Princeton University Press.

Leland, Anne, and Mari-Jana Oboroceanu. 2010. *American War and Military Operations Casualties: Lists and Statistics*. Washington: Congressional Research Service.

LeVeen, E.Phillip. 1977. *British Slave Trade Suppression Policies*. New York: Arno.

Lewis, Cleona. 1938. *America's Stake in International Investments*. Washington: Brookings.

Lindert, Peter H. 2000. U.S. Foreign Trade and Trade Policy in the Twentieth Century. In *The Cambridge Economic History of the United States*, vol. 3, ed. Stanley L. Engerman and Robert E. Gallman, 407–462. Cambridge: Cambridge University Press.

Lipsey, Robert E. 1963a. Foreign Trade. In *American Economic Growth*, ed. Lance E. Davis, and others, 548–581. New York: Harper & Row.

———. 1963b. *Price and Quantity Trends in the Foreign Trade of the United States*. Princeton: Princeton University Press.

———. 2000. U.S. Foreign Trade and the Balance of Payments, 1800–1913. In *The Cambridge Economic History of the United States*, vol. 2, ed. Stanley L. Engerman and Robert E. Gallman, 685–732. Cambridge: Cambridge University Press.

———. 2008. Changing Patterns of International Investment in and by the United States. In *United States in the World Economy*, ed. Martin Feldstein, 475–517. Chicago: University of Chicago Press.

Long, Clarence D. 1960. *Wages and Earnings in the United States, 1860–1890*. Princeton: Princeton University Press.

Madden, John J. 1985. *British Investment in the United States, 1860–1880*. New York: Garland.

Maffry, August. 1939. *Overseas Travel and Travel Expenditures in the Balance of International Payments of the United States, 1919–1938*. Washington: Government Printing Office.

Magee, Gary B., and Andrew S. Thompson. 2006. 'Lines of Credit, Debts of Obligation': Migrant Remittances to Britain c.1875–1913. *Economic History Review* 59 (August): 539–577.

Malloy, William M. 1910. *Treaties, Conventions, International Acts, Protocols and Agreements*. Washington: Government Printing Office.

Margo, Robert A. 1996. The Rental Price of Housing in New York City, 1830–1860. *Journal of Economic History* 56 (September): 605–625.

———. 2000. *Wages and Labor Markets in the United States, 1820–1860*. Chicago: University of Chicago Press.

Martin, David A. 1973. 1853: The End of Bimetallism in the United States. *Journal of Economic History* 33 (December): 825–844.

———. 1976. U.S. Gold Production Prior to the California Gold Rush. *Explorations in Economic History* 13 (October): 437–449.

McClelland, Peter D., and Richard J. Zeckhauser. 1982. *Demographic Dimensions of the New Republic*. Cambridge: Cambridge University Press.

McCullough, Alan B. 1984. *Money and Exchange in Canada to 1900*. Toronto: Dundurn.

McGuire, Robert A. 1990. Deflation-Induced Increases in Post-Civil War US Tariffs. *Economic History Review* 43 (November): 633–645.

McShane, Clay. 2001. Gelded Age Boston. *New England Quarterly* 74 (June): 274–302.

———. 2008. 1872: Great Epizootic. In *Disasters, Accidents, and Crises in American History*, ed. Ballard C. Campbell, 131–132. New York: Facts on File.

———, and Joel A. Tarr. 1997. The Centrality of the Horse in the Nineteenth-Century American City. In *The Making of Urban America*, ed. Raymond A. Mohl, 105–130. Wilmington: Scholarly Resources.

Mears, Eliot G. 1935. The Foreign Trade Statistics of the United States. *Journal of the American Statistical Association* 30 (September): 501–516.

Meinhard, Robert W. 1998. War Statistics. In *The Civil War Battlefield Guide*, ed. Frances H. Kennedy, 465. Boston: Houghton Mifflin.

Melish, John. 1815. *Travels Through the United States of America*. Philadelphia.

Middleton, William D. 1967. *The Time of the Trolley*. Milwaukee: Kalmbach.

Miles, Pliny. 1857. History of the Post Office. *Bankers' Magazine and Statistical Register* 7 (November): 337–365.

Miller, John A. 1941. *Fares, Please!*. New York: D. Appleton-Century.

Mitchell, Brian R. 1988. *British Historical Statistics*. Cambridge: Cambridge University Press.

Mitchell, C.Bradford. 1970. *A Premium on Progress*. New York: Newcomen Society.

Mitchell, Wesley C. 1908. *Gold, Prices, and Wages Under the Greenback Standard*. Berkeley: Berkeley University Press.

Mohammed, Saif I. Shah, and Jeffrey G. Williamson. 2004. Freight Rates and Productivity Gains in British Tramp Shipping 1869–1950. *Explorations in Economic History* 41 (April): 172–203.

Montgomery, Thomas H. 1885. *A History of the Insurance Company of North America*. Philadelphia: Review.

Monthly Summary of Commerce and Finance [MSCF].

Moore, John B. 1898. *History and Digest of the International Arbitrations*. Washington: Government Printing Office.

Morrison, John H. 1903. *History of American Steam Navigation*. New York: Sametz.

Morys, Matthias. 2005. The Classical Gold Standard in the European Periphery: A Case Study of Austria-Hungary and Italy, 1870–1913. Ph.D. diss., London School of Economics and Political Science.

Moulton, Harold G., and Leo Pasvolsky. 1932. *War Debts and World Prosperity*. New York: Appleton-Century.

National Foreign Trade Council. 1917. *Ocean Shipping*. Washington.

Nettels, Curtis P. 1962. *The Emergence of a National Economy, 1775–1815*. New York: Holt, Reinhart and Winston.

Neuman, Gerald L. 1996. *Strangers to the Constitution*. Princeton: Princeton University Press.

New York Annual Register [NYAR].

New York State Register [NYSR].

Noble, John. 1819. *Noble's Instructions to Emigrants*. Boston.

North, Douglass C. 1960. The United States Balance of Payments, 1790–1860. In *Trends in the American Economy in the Nineteenth Century*, ed. William N. Parker, 573–628. Princeton: Princeton University Press.

———. 1961a. *The Economic Growth of the United States, 1790–1860*. Englewood Cliffs: Prentice-Hall.

———. 1961b. The United States in the International Economy, 1790–1850. In *American Economic History*, ed. Seymour E. Harris, 181–206. New York: McGraw-Hill.

———. 1965. The Role of Transportation in the Economic Development of North America. In *Les Grandes Voies Maritimes dans le Monde*, 209–246. Paris: S.E.V.P.E.N.

———, and Alan Heston. 1960. The Estimation of Shipping Earnings in Historical Studies of the Balance of Payments. *Canadian Journal of Economics and Political Science* 26 (May): 265–276.

Observer. 1820. *A Review of the Trade and Commerce of New York*. New York: Van Winkle.

Officer, Lawrence H. 1996. *Between the Dollar-Sterling Gold Points*. Cambridge: Cambridge University Press.

———. 2002. The U.S. Specie Standard, 1792–1932: Some Monetarist Arithmetic. *Explorations in Economic History* 39 (April): 113–153.

———. 2007. An Improved Long-Run Consumer Price Index for the United States. *Historical Methods* 40 (Summer): 135–147.

———. 2009. *Two Centuries of Compensation for U.S. Production Workers in Manufacturing*. New York: Palgrave Macmillan.

———, and Samuel H. Williamson. 2020. The Antebellum Slave Trade: Numbers and Impact on the Balance of Payments. *Research in Economic History* 36: 181–212.

Olenkiewicz, John S. 2013. *British Packet Sailings, Falmouth–North America: 1755–1826*. Internet, accessed March 8, 2018.

Otis, Fessenden N. 1867. *History of the Panama Railroad*. New York: Harper.

Page, Thomas W. 1913. Some Economic Aspects of Immigration Before 1870. *Journal of Political Economy* 21 (January): 34–55.

Paish, George. 1910. *The Trade Balance of the United States*. Washington: Government Printing Office.

Parliamentary Papers. 1882. *Tables Showing the Progress of British Merchant Shipping*, vol. 62.

Pawlyn, Tony. 2003. *The Falmouth Packets*. Cornwall: Truran.

Pelzer, Lewis. 1936. Pioneer Stage-Coach Travel. *Mississippi Valley Historical Review* 23 (June): 3–26.

Platt, Desmond C.M. 1984. *Foreign Finance in Continental Europe and the United States, 1815–1870*. London: Allen & Unwin.

Pons, Frank M. 1998. *The Dominican Republic*. Princeton: Markus Wiener.

Poulson, Barry W. 1965. Value Added in Manufacturing, Mining, and Agriculture in the American Economy from 1809 to 1839. Ph.D. diss., Ohio State University.

Powell, James. 2005. *A History of the Canadian Dollar*. Ottawa: Bank of Canada.

Province of Canada. 1851. *Tables of the Trade and Navigation of the Province of Canada for the Year 1850*. Toronto: Derbishire.

Pushkarev, Boris S., Jeffrey M. Zupan, and Robert S. Cumella. 1982. *Urban Rail in America*. Bloomington: Indiana University Press.

Rates of Duty on Imports into the United States. 1891.

Rees, Albert. 1961. *Real Wages in Manufacturing, 1890–1914*. Princeton: Princeton University Press.

Rens, Jean-Guy. 2001. *The Invisible Empire*. Montreal: McGill-Queen's University Press.

Robinson, Howard. 1964. *Carrying British Mails Overseas*. London: Allen & Unwin.

Rockoff, Hugh. 2012. *America's Economic Way of War*. Cambridge: Cambridge University Press.

Rojas, Martha E. 2003. 'Insults Unpunished': Barbary Captives, American Slaves, and the Negotiation of Liberty. *Early American Studies* 1 (Fall): 159–186.

Routh, Guy. 1980. *Occupation and Pay in Great Britain, 1906–79*. London: Macmillan.

Rowsome, Frank, Jr. 1956. *Trolley Car Treasury*. New York: McGraw-Hill.

Rubin, Ernest. 1959. Immigration and the Economic Growth of the U.S.: 1790–1914. *R.E.M.P. Bulletin* 7 (October/December): 87–95.

Schaefer, Donald. 1994. U.S. Migration, 1850–59. In *American Economic Development in Historical Perspective*, ed. Thomas Weiss and Donald Schaefer, 53–69. Stanford: Stanford University Press.

Scharf, J. Thomas. 1874. *The Chronicles of Baltimore*. Baltimore: Turnbull.

Schneider, Jürgen, Oskar Schwarzer, and Friedrich Zellfelder. 1991. *Währungen der Welt I*, vol. 1. Stuttgart: Franz Steiner.

Schouler, James. 1910. *History of the United States of America*. New York: Dodd, Mead.

Seaman, Ezra C. 1846. *Essays on the Progress of Nations*. New York: Baker & Scribner.

———. 1852. *Essays on the Progress of Nations*. New York: Scribner.

———. 1857. The Panic and Financial Crisis of 1857. *Hunt's Merchants' Magazine*, December: 661–668.

Secretary of the Interior. 1866. *Statistics of the United States in 1860*. Washington: Government Printing Office.

Secretary of the Treasury. 1830. *Report Respecting the Relative Value of Gold and Silver*.

———. 1854. *Public Money*.

Segal, Harvey H. 1956. Canal Cycles, 1834–1861. Ph.D. diss., Columbia University.

———. 1961. Cycles of Canal Construction. In *Canals and American Economic Development*, ed. Carter Goodrich, 169–215. New York: Columbia University Press.

Seybert, Adam. 1818. *Statistical Annals*. Philadelphia: Thomas Dobson.

Shaw, William H. 1947. *Value of Commodity Output Since 1869*. New York: National Bureau of Economic Research.

Shay, Frank. 1876. *Chinese Immigration*. Sacramento: State Printing.

Shepherd, James F., and Gary M. Walton. 1972. *Shipping, Maritime Trade, and the Economic Development of Colonial North America*. Cambridge: Cambridge University Press.

Shuman, Armin E. 1883. *Statistical Report of the Railroads in the United States*. 1880 Census, vol. 4. Washington: Government Printing Office.

Simon, Matthew. 1960. The United States Balance of Payments, 1861–1900. In *Trends in the American Economy in the Nineteenth Century*, ed. William N. Parker, 629–716. Princeton: Princeton University Press.

Sloan, Edward W. 1992. Collins versus Cunard: The Realities of a North Atlantic Steamship Rivalry, 1850–1858. *International Journal of Maritime History* 1 (June): 83–100.

———. 1998.The First (and Very Secret) International Steamship Cartel, 1850–1856. In *Global Markets: The Internationalization of the Sea Transport*

Industries Since 1850, ed. David J. Starkey and Gelina Harlaftis, 29–52. St. John's, Newfoundland: International Maritime Economic History Association.
Smith, R.Elberton. 1948. *Customs Valuation in the United States*. Chicago: University of Chicago Press.
Smith, Walter B. 1953. *Economic Aspects of the Second Bank of the United States*. Cambridge, MA: Harvard University Press.
———. 1963. Wage Rates on the Erie Canal, 1828–1881. *Journal of Economic History* 23 (September): 298–311.
Soley, James R. 1894. The Maritime Industries of America. In *The United States of America*, ed. Nathaniel S. Shaler, 518–624. New York: D. Appleton.
Speare, Charles F. 1908. What America Pays Europe for Immigrant Labor. *North American Review* 187 (January): 106–116.
Speirs, Frederic W. 1897. *The Street Railway System of Philadelphia: Its History and Present Condition*. Baltimore: Johns Hopkins Press.
Staff, Frank. 1956. *The Transatlantic Mail*. London: Adlard Coles.
Statistical Abstract of the United States [SAUS].
Statistical Tables Relating to Emigration and Immigration [*Statistical Tables*]. 1880. Reprinted in British Parliamentary Papers, vol. 25, 1971. Shannon: Ireland.
Statistics on the Mexican Economy. 1966. Mexico: National Financiera.
Sterns, Worthy P. 1898. The Beginnings of American Financial Independence. *Journal of Political Economy* 6 (March): 187–208.
———. 1899. The Foreign Trade of the United States from 1820 to 1840. *Journal of Political Economy* 8 (December): 34–57.
Stevens, Walter B. 1909. *St Louis: The Fourth City, 1764–1909*. St. Louis: S. J. Clarke.
Stover, John F. 1987. *History of the Baltimore and Ohio Railroad*. West Lafayette: Purdue University Press.
Sutch, Richard. 2006. Value of Finished Commodity Output: 1869–1919. In *Historical Statistics*, pp. 3–57 to 58.
Talbot, John. 1820. *History of North America*. Leeds: Davies.
Tarr, Joel A. 1978. *Transportation Innovation and Changing Spatial Patterns in Pittsburgh, 1850–1934*. Chicago: Public Works Historical Society.
Tate, E. Mowbray. 1986. *Transpacific Steam*. New York: Cornwall.
Taussig, Frank W. 1923. *The Tariff History of the United States*. New York: Putnam.
———. 1928. *International Trade*. New York: Macmillan.
Taylor, George Rogers. 1951. *The Transportation Revolution*. New York: Holt, Rinehart, and Winston.
———. 1966a. The Beginnings of Mass Transportation in Urban America: Part I. *Smithsonian Journal of History* 1 (Summer): 35–50.

Taylor, George Rogers. 1966. The Beginnings of Mass Transportation in Urban America: Part II. *Smithsonian Journal of History* 1 (fall): 31–54.

Taylor, Philip. 1971. *The Distant Magnet*. London: Eyre & Spottiswoode.

The Balance of International Payments of the United States [BIPUS]. 1930. Annual.

Thomas, Brinley. 1973. *Migration and Economic Growth*. Cambridge: Cambridge University Press.

Thompson, Norman, and Major J.H. Edgar. 1933. *Canadian Railway Development*. Toronto: Macmillan.

Torreon, Barbara S., and Sofia Plagakis. 2018. *Instances of Use of United States Armed Forces Abroad, 1798–2018*. Congressional Research Service.

Treasury Department. 1915. *Information Respecting United States Bonds, Paper Currency and Coin*. Washington: Government Printing Office.

Tucker, George. 1843. *Progress of the United States in Population and Wealth*. New York: Hunt's Merchants' Magazine.

Turk, S. 1962. *Some Notes on Foreign Exchange in Canada Before 1919*. Bank of Canada Memorandum, 27 June. Ottawa: Bank of Canada Archives 4B-200, vol. 5.

Tyler, David B. 1939. *Steam Conquers the Atlantic*. New York: Appleton-Century.

Ulmer, Melville J. 1960. *Capital in Transportation, Communications, and Public Utilities*. Princeton: Princeton University Press.

United States Tariff Commission. 1924. *Dictionary of Tariff Information*. Washington: Government Printing Office.

Urquhart, Malcolm C., and Kenneth A.H. Buckley (eds.). 1965. *Historical Statistics of Canada*. Cambridge: Cambridge University Press.

Vanderlip, Frank A., and John H. Williams. 1920. The Future of Our Foreign Trade: A Study of Our International Balance in 1919. *Review of Economics and Statistics* 2 (April): 5–28.

Vangermeersch, Richard. 2013. The Correspondence Between Irving Fisher and Nathaniel Terry Bacon at the James P. Adams Library Rhode Island College. *Faculty Publications* 323.

Van Pelt, Henry W. 1921. American Shipping Earnings and the Balance of Trade. *Federal Reserve Bulletin*, April, pp. 400–410.

Vernon, J.R. 1994.Unemployment Rates in Postbellum America: 1869–1899. *Journal of Macroeconomics* 16 (Fall): 701–714.

Viner, Jacob. 1924. *Canada's Balance of International Indebtedness, 1900–1913*. Cambridge, MA: Harvard University Press.

Wallich, Henry C. 1950. *Monetary Problems of an Export Economy*. Cambridge, MA: Harvard University Press.

Warner, Adoniram J. 1879. Resumption and Regulation of Currency. *Bankers' Magazine and Statistical Register*, January: 522–527.

Warren, George F., and Frank A. Pearson. 1933. *Prices*. New York: Wiley.

Wasserman, Max J., and Ray M. Ware. 1965. *The Balance of Payments*. New York: Simmons-Boardman.

Wegge, Simone A. 1998. Chain Migration and Information Networks: Evidence from Nineteenth-Century Hesse-Cassel. *Journal of Economic History* 58 (December): 957–986.

Weir, David R. 1992. A Century of U.S. Unemployment, 1890–1900: Revised Estimates and Evidence for Stabilization. *Research in Economic History* 14: 301–346.

Wells, David A. 1869. *Report of the Special Commissioner of the Revenue*, House of Representatives Ex. Doc., 41st Cong., 2d sess.

Whitehurst, Clinton H., Jr. 1986. *The U.S. Shipbuilding Industry: Past, Present, and Future*. Annapolis: Naval Institute Press.

Wilkins, Mira. 1970. *The Emergence of Multinational Enterprise*. Cambridge, MA: Harvard University Press.

———. 1989. *The History of Foreign Investment in the United States to 1914*. Cambridge, MA: Harvard University Press.

———. 2004. *The History of Foreign Investment in the United States, 1914–1945*. Cambridge, MA: Harvard University Press.

———. n.d. *Flows Do Not Stock Make*. Miami: Florida International University.

Williams, Edwin. 1833, 1834. *New York As It Is*. New York: J. Disturnell.

Williams, John H. 1921. The Balance of International Payments of the United States for the Year 1920. *Review of Economics and Statistics* 3 (June): 169–212.

Williamson, Jeffrey G. 1964. *American Growth and the Balance of Payments, 1820–1913*. Chapel Hill: University of North Carolina Press.

———. 1982. The Structure of Pay in Britain, 1710–1911. *Research in Economic History* 7: 1–54.

Wright, Gavin. 2020. Slavery and Anglo-American Capitalism Revisited. *Economic History Review* 73 (May): 353–383.

Young, Edward. 1871. *Special Report on Immigration*. Washington: Government Printing Office.

———. 1874. Foreign Indebtedness of the United States. *Monthly Report of the Chief of the Bureau of Statistics*, February: 351–352.

———. 1877. *Special Report on the Customs-Tariff Legislation of the United States*. Washington: Government Printing Office.

Zabler, Jeffrey F. 1972. Further Evidence on American Wage Differentials, 1800–1830. *Explorations in Economic History* 10 (Fall): 109–117.

Index of Names

L. H. Officer, *A New Balance of Payments for the United States, 1790–1919*, Palgrave Studies in American Economic History,
https://doi.org/10.1007/978-3-030-66099-4

Index of Subjects

L. H. Officer, *A New Balance of Payments for the United States, 1790–1919*, Palgrave Studies in American Economic History,
https://doi.org/10.1007/978-3-030-66099-4

Y

Z

The manufacturer's authorised representative in the EU is Springer Nature Customer Service Centre GmbH, Europaplatz 3, 69115 Heidelberg, Germany. If you have any concerns regarding our products, please contact ProductSafety@springernature.com

Printed and bound by CPI Group (UK) Ltd, Croydon, CR0 4YY
30/09/2026
02225327-0016